M. HIPWELL

Cisco IOS WAN Solutions

Cisco Systems, Inc.

Macmillan Technical Publishing
201 West 103rd Street
Indianapolis, IN 46290 USA

Cisco IOS WAN Solutions

Cisco Systems, Inc.

Copyright© 1998 Cisco Systems, Inc.

Cisco Press logo is a trademark of Cisco Systems, Inc.

Published by:
Macmillan Technical Publishing
201 West 103rd Street
Indianapolis, IN 46290 USA

Printed in the United States of America 1 2 3 4 5 6 7 8 9 0

Library of Congress Cataloging-in-Publication: 97-80681

ISBN: 1-57870-054-x

Warning and Disclaimer

This book is designed to provide information about **Cisco IOS WAN Solutions**. Every effort has been made to make this book as complete and as accurate as possible, but no warranty or fitness is implied.

The information is provided on an "as is" basis. The author, Macmillan Technical Publishing, and Cisco Systems, Inc. shall have neither liability nor responsibility to any person or entity with respect to any loss or damages arising from the information contained in this book or from the use of the discs or programs that may accompany it.

The opinions expressed in this book belong to the author and are not necessarily those of Cisco Systems, Inc.

Associate Publisher	Jim LeValley
Executive Editor	Julie Fairweather
Cisco Systems Program Manager	H. Kim Lew
Managing Editor	Caroline Roop
Acquisitions Editor	Tracy Hughes
Development Editor	Brad Miser
Project Editor	Brian Sweany
Team Coordinator	Amy Lewis
Book Designer	Louisa Klucznik
Cover Designer	Jean Bisesi
Production Manager	Laurie Casey
Production Team Supervisor	Vic Peterson
Production Team	Kim Cofer Trina Wurst
Indexer	Kevin Fulcher
Director of Alliance Co-Marketing	Kourtnaye Sturgeon
Vice President of Brand Management	Jim Price
Brand Associate	Kim Spilker
Brand Coordinator	Linda Beckwith

Trademark Acknowledgments

All terms mentioned in this book that are known to be trademarks or service marks have been appropriately capitalized. Macmillan Technical Publishing or Cisco Systems, Inc. cannot attest to the accuracy of this information. Use of a term in this book should not be regarded as affecting the validity of any trademark or service mark.

Acknowledgments

The Cisco IOS Reference Library is the result of collaborative efforts of many Cisco technical writers and editors over the years. This bookset represents the continuing development and integration of user documentation for the ever-increasing set of Cisco IOS networking features and functionality.

The current team of Cisco IOS technical writers and editors includes Katherine Anderson, Jennifer Bridges, Joelle Chapman, Christy Choate, Meredith Fisher, Tina Fox, Marie Godfrey, Dianna Johansen, Sheryl Kelly, Yvonne Kucher, Doug MacBeth, Lavanya Mandavilli, Mary Mangone, Spank McCoy, Greg McMillan, Madhu Mitra, Oralee Murillo, Vicki Payne, Jane Phillips, George Powers, Teresa Oliver Schick, Wink Schuetz, Karen Shell, Grace Tai, and Bethann Watson.

The writing team wants to acknowledge the many engineering, customer support, and marketing subject-matter experts for their participation in reviewing draft documents and, in many cases, providing source material from which this bookset is developed.

Contents at a Glance

Table of Contents

About the Cisco IOS Reference Library

The Cisco IOS Reference Library is a series of books that describe the tasks and commands necessary to configure and maintain your Cisco IOS network.

This bookset is intended primarily for users who configure and maintain access servers and routers, but who are not necessarily familiar with individual tasks, the relationship between tasks, or the commands necessary to perform those tasks.

CISCO IOS REFERENCE LIBRARY ORGANIZATION

Each book in the Cisco IOS Reference Library contains technology-specific configuration chapters with corresponding command reference chapters. Each configuration chapter describes Cisco's implementation of protocols and technologies, explains related configuration tasks, and contains comprehensive configuration examples. Each command reference chapter complements the organization of its corresponding configuration chapter and provides complete command syntax information.

OTHER BOOKS AVAILABLE IN THE CISCO IOS REFERENCE LIBRARY

- *Cisco IOS Dial Solutions*, 1-57870-055-8; Available March 1998

  This book provides readers with real-world solutions and explains how to implement them on a network. Customers interested in implementing dial-up solutions across their network environment include remote sites dialing in to a central office, Internet Service Providers (ISPs), ISP customers at home offices, and enterprise Wide Area Network (WAN) system administrators implementing dial-on-demand routing (DDR).

- *Cisco IOS Switching Services*, 1-57870-053-1; Available March 1998

  This book is a comprehensive guide detailing available Cisco IOS switching alternatives; Cisco's switching services range from fast switching and Netflow switching to LAN Emulation.

- *Cisco IOS IP Network Protocols, Vol 1*, 1-57870-049-3; Available April 1998

1

This book is a comprehensive guide that explains available IP and IP routing alternatives. It describes how to implement IP addressing and IP services and how to configure support for a wide range of IP routing protocols, including BGP for ISP networks as well as basic and advanced IP Multicast functionality.

- *Cisco IOS Network Protocols, Vol II*, 1-57870-050-7, Available April 1998

  This book explains available network-protocol alternatives, and describes how to implement various protocols in your network. This book includes documentation of the latest functionality for the IPX and AppleTalk desktop protocols as well as other network protocols including Apollo Domain, Banyan VINES, DECNet, ISO CLNS, and XNS.

- *Cisco IOS Bridging and IBM Networking Solutions*, 1-57870-051-5, Available April 1998

  This book describes Cisco's support for networks in IBM and bridging environments. Cisco's support includes transparent and source-route transparent bridging, source-route bridging (SRB), remote source-route bridging (RSRB), data-link switching plus (DLS+), serial tunnel and block serial tunnel, SDLC and LLC2 parameter, IBM network media translation, downstream physical unit and SNA service point, SNA Frame Relay access support, Advanced Peer-to-Peer Networking, and native client interface architecture (NCIA).

- *Cisco IOS Router Security*, 1-57870-057-4, Available May 1998

  This book documents security configuration from a remote site as well as for a central enterprise or service provider network. It describes AAA, Radius, TACACS+, and Kerberos network security features. It also explains how to encrypt data across enterprise networks. The book includes many illustrations that show configurations and functionality, along with a discussion of network security policy choices and some decision-making guidelines.

LIBRARY CONVENTIONS

The Cisco IOS Reference library books use the following conventions:

- The caret character (^) represents the Control key.

  For example, the key combinations ^D and Ctrl-D are equivalent: Both mean hold down the Control key while you press the D key. While keys are indicated in capitals, they are not case sensitive.

- A string is defined as an italicized, nonquoted set of characters.

  For example, when setting an SNMP community string to *public*, do not use quotation marks around the string; otherwise, the string will include the quotation marks.

Command descriptions use these conventions:

- Vertical bars (|) separate alternative, mutually exclusive, elements.
- Square brackets ([ ]) indicate optional elements.
- Braces ({ }) indicate a required choice.

- Braces within square brackets ([{ }]) indicate a required choice within an optional element.
- **Boldface** indicates commands and keywords that are entered literally as shown by the boldface.
- *Italics* indicate arguments for which you supply values; in contexts that do not allow italics, arguments are enclosed in angle brackets (< >).

Examples use these conventions:

- Examples that contain system prompts denote interactive sessions, indicating that the user enters commands at the prompt. The system prompt indicates the current command mode. For example, the prompt Router(config)# indicates global configuration mode.
- Terminal sessions and information the system displays are in screen font.
- Information you enter is in **boldface screen** font.
- Nonprinting characters, such as passwords, are in angle brackets (< >).
- Default responses to system prompts are in square brackets ([ ]).
- Exclamation points (!) at the beginning of a line indicate a comment line. They are also displayed by the Cisco IOS software for certain processes.

CAUTION

Means *reader be careful.* In this situation, you might do something that could result in equipment damage or loss of data.

NOTES

Means *reader take note.* Notes contain helpful suggestions or references to materials not contained in this book.

TIMESAVER

Means *the described action saves time.* You can save time by performing the action described in the paragraph.

Within the Cisco IOS Reference Library, the term *router* is used to refer to both access servers and routers. When a feature is supported on the access server only, the term *access server* is used. When a feature is supported on one or more specific router platforms (such as the Cisco 4500), but not on other platforms (such as the Cisco 2500), the text specifies the supported platforms.

Within examples, routers and access servers are alternately shown. These products are used only for example purposes—an example that shows one product does not indicate that the other product is not supported.

CHAPTER 1

Wide-Area Networking Overview

Cisco IOS software provides a range of wide-area networking capabilities to fit almost every network environment. Cisco offers cell relay via the Switched Multimegabit Data Service (SMDS), circuit switching via Integrated Services Digital Network (ISDN), packet switching via Frame Relay, and the benefits of both circuit and packet switching via Asynchronous Transfer Mode (ATM). LAN emulation (LANE) provides connectivity between ATM and other LAN types.

OBJECTIVES OF THIS BOOK

This book presents a set of general guidelines for configuring the following software components:

- ATM
- Implementing Frame Relay
- Implementing SMDS
- Using X.25 and LAPB

This overview chapter provides a high-level description of each technology. Later in the book, there is a chapter containing specific configuration information as well as commands for each technology.

ORGANIZATION OF THIS BOOK

This book has 12 chapters and one appendix.

This chapter provides an introduction to the book and to Cisco wide-area networking.

Chapters 2 through 6 describe how to configure ATM for the different platform configurations. The ATM configuration chapters are the following:

- Chapter 2, "Configuring ATM Access over a Serial Interface"
- Chapter 3, "Configuring ATM on the AIP for Cisco 7500 Series Routers"

- Chapter 4, "Configuring ATM on the ATM Port Adapter for Cisco 7200 and 7500 Series Routers"
- Chapter 5, "Configuring ATM with the NPM for Cisco 4500 and 4700 Routers"

Chapter 6, "ATM Commands" provides a listing of ATM commands.

Chapter 7, "Configuring Frame Relay," and Chapter 8, "Frame Relay Commands," describe how to configure and use Frame Relay.

Chapter 9, "Configuring SMDS, " and Chapter 10, "SMDS Commands," provide coverage of SMDS.

Chapter 11, "Configuring X.25 and LAPB," and Chapter 12, "X.25 and LAPB Commands," provide complete coverage of X.25 and LAPB. Appendix A, "X.25 Facility Handling," provides information on x.25 facility handling.

UNDERSTANDING ATM

ATM is a cell-switching and multiplexing technology designed to combine the benefits of circuit switching (constant transmission delay and guaranteed capacity) with those of packet switching (flexibility and efficiency for intermittent traffic).

Depending on the hardware available in the router, Cisco provides ATM access in the following ways:

- Serial interface, in devices that lack an ATM Interface Processor (AIP), ATM port adapter, or network processor module (NPM)
- AIP, in supported routers
- ATM port adapters, in supported routers
- NPM, in supported routers

In routers outside the Cisco 4500, Cisco 4700, Cisco 7200 series, and Cisco 7500 series, a serial interface can be configured for multiprotocol encapsulation over the Asynchronous Transfer Mode-Data Exchange Interface (ATM-DXI), as specified by RFC 1483. This standard describes two methods for transporting multiprotocol connectionless network interconnect traffic over an ATM network. One method allows multiplexing of multiple protocols over a single permanent virtual circuit (PVC). The other method uses different virtual circuits to carry different protocols. Cisco implementation supports transport of AppleTalk, Banyan VINES, Internet Protocol (IP), and Novell Internetwork Packet Exchange protocol (IPX) traffic.

NOTES

In Cisco IOS Release 11.3, all commands supported on the Cisco 7500 series routers are also supported on Cisco 7000 series routers equipped with RSP7000.

If you configure ATM access over a serial interface, an ATM data service unit (ADSU) is required to do the following:

- Provide the ATM interface to the network.
- Compute the DXI Frame Address (DFA) from the virtual path identifier (VPI) and virtual channel identifier (VCI) values defined for the protocol or protocols carried on the PVC.
- Convert outgoing packets into ATM cells.
- Reassemble incoming ATM cells into packets.

On the Cisco 7500 series routers, network interfaces reside on modular interface processors, which provide a direct connection between the high-speed Cisco Extended Bus (CxBus) and the external networks. Each AIP provides a single ATM network interface; the maximum number of AIPs that the Cisco 7500 series supports depends on the bandwidth configured. The total bandwidth through all the AIPs in the system should be limited to 200 Mbps full duplex (two TAXI interfaces, or one SONET and one E3, or one SONET and one lightly used SONET, five E3s, or four T3s).

ATM port adapters are available on Cisco 7200 series routers and on the second-generation Versatile Interface Processor (VIP2) in Cisco 7500 series routers.

Cisco 4500 and Cisco 4700 routers support one OC-3c NPM or up to two slower E3/DS3 NPMs. Physical Layer Interface Modules (PLIMs) that support Synchronous Optical Network/Synchronous Digital Hierarchy (SONET/SDH) 155 Mbps are available for both single-mode and multimode fiber.

Cisco IOS ATM software supports a subset of the specification in *AToM MIB* (RFC 1695) for Cisco IOS Release 11.2 software or later. Cisco IOS Release 11.3 software or later supports the proprietary *Cisco AAL5 MIB* that is an extension to RFC 1695.

Understanding the ATM Environment

ATM is a connection-oriented environment. All traffic to or from an ATM network is prefaced with a virtual path identifier (VPI) and virtual channel identifier (VCI). A VPI-VCI pair is considered a single virtual circuit. Each virtual circuit is a private connection to another node on the ATM network. Each virtual circuit is treated as a point-to-point mechanism to another router or host and is capable of supporting bidirectional traffic.

Each ATM node is required to establish a separate connection to every other node in the ATM network with which it needs to communicate. All such connections are established by means of a PVC or a switched virtual circuit (SVC) with an ATM signaling mechanism. This signaling is based on the ATM Forum User-Network Interface (UNI) Specification V3.0.

Each virtual circuit is considered a complete and separate link to a destination node. Users can encapsulate data as needed across the connection. The ATM network disregards the contents of the data. The only requirement is that data be sent to the router's ATM processor card in a manner that follows the specific ATM adaptation layer (AAL) format.

An AAL defines the conversion of user information into cells. An AAL segments upper-layer information into cells at the transmitter and reassembles the cells at the receiver. AAL1 and AAL2 handle isochronous traffic, such as voice and video, and are not relevant to the router. AAL3/4 and AAL5 support data communications; that is, they segment and reassemble packets. Cisco supports both AAL3/4 and AAL5 on the AIP for Cisco 7500 series routers. On the ATM port adapter for Cisco 7200 series routers and Cisco 7500 series routers, only AAL5 is supported. On the NPM for Cisco 4500 and Cisco 4700 routers, AAL3/4 and AAL5 are supported, but AAL3/4 is not supported at OC-3 rates; if AAL3/4 is configured on an OC-3c interface, you must limit the interface to E3 or DS3 rates by configuring a rate queue. See the "Configuring the Rate Queue" section in Chapter 5 for more information.

An ATM connection is used simply to transfer raw bits of information to a destination router or host. The ATM router takes the common part convergence sublayer (CPCS) frame, carves it up into 53-byte cells, and sends these cells to the destination router or host for reassembly. In AAL5 format, 48 bytes of each cell are used for the CPCS data; the remaining five bytes are used for cell routing. The five-byte cell header contains the destination VPI-VCI pair, payload type, cell loss priority (CLP), and header error control.

The ATM network is considered a LAN with high bandwidth availability. Each end node in the ATM network is a host on a specific subnet. All end nodes needing to communicate with one another must be within the same subnet in the network.

Unlike a LAN, which is connectionless, ATM requires certain features to provide a LAN environment to the users. One such feature is broadcast capability. Protocols wishing to broadcast packets to all stations in a subnet must be allowed to do so with a single call to Layer 2. To support broadcasting, the router allows the user to specify particular virtual circuits as broadcast virtual circuits. When the protocol passes a packet with a broadcast address to the drivers, the packet is duplicated and sent to each virtual circuit marked as a broadcast virtual circuit. This method is known as *pseudobroadcasting*.

Effective with Cisco IOS Release 11.0, point-to-multipoint signaling allows pseudobroadcasting to be eliminated. On routers with point-to-multipoint signaling, the router can set up calls between itself and multiple destinations; drivers no longer need to duplicate broadcast packets. A single packet can be sent to the ATM switch, which replicates it to multiple ATM hosts.

Understanding Classical IP and ARP

Cisco implements classical IP and Address Resolution Protocol (ARP) over ATM as described in RFC 1577. RFC 1577 defines an application of classical IP and ARP in an ATM environment configured as a logical IP subnetwork (LIS). It also describes the functions of an ATM ARP server and ATM ARP clients in requesting and providing destination IP addresses and ATM addresses in situations when one or both are unknown. Cisco routers can be configured to act as an ARP client, or to act as a combined ARP client and ARP server.

The ATM ARP server functionality allows classical IP networks to be constructed with ATM as the connection medium. Without this functionality, you must configure both the IP network address and the ATM address of each end device with which the router needs to communicate. This static configuration task takes administrative time and makes moves and changes more difficult.

Cisco's implementation of the ATM ARP server functionality provides a robust environment in which network changes can be made more easily and more quickly than in a pure ATM environment. Cisco's ATM ARP client works with any ARP server that is fully compliant with RFC 1577.

Using Cisco AIP

This section provides an overview of the ATM features, interfaces, microcode, and virtual circuits available on the AIP, and currently supported on the Cisco 7500 series routers.

Understanding AIP Features

The AIP supports the following features:

- Multiple rate queues

- Reassembly of up to 512 buffers simultaneously where each buffer represents a packet

- Per-virtual-circuit counters, which improve the accuracy of the statistics shown in the output of **show** commands by ensuring that autonomously switched packets are counted as well as fast-switched and process-switched packets

- Support for up to 2048 virtual circuits

- Support for both AAL3/4 and AAL5

- Support for both process-switched transparent bridging and fast-switched transparent bridging over ATM

  Process-switched bridging over ATM supports AAL3/4-SMDS encapsulated packets only. All frames that originate at, or are forwarded by, the Cisco IOS software are sent as 802.3 bridge frames without frame check sequence (FCS)—that is, in RFC 1483 bridge frame formats with 0x0007 in the Protocol Identification (PID) field of the Subnetwork Access Protocol (SNAP) header. You can enable process-switched bridging for SMDS as described later in this chapter.

  Fast-switched transparent bridging over ATM supports AAL5-SNAP encapsulated packets only. All bridged AAL5-SNAP encapsulated packets are fast switched. Fast-switched transparent bridging supports Ethernet, Fiber Distributed Data Interface (FDDI), and Token Ring packets sent in AAL5-SNAP encapsulation over ATM. You can enable fast-switched bridging for AAL5-SNAP as described later in this chapter. Fast-switched bridging includes the following:

- Exception queue, which is used for event reporting. Events such as cyclic redundancy check (CRC) errors are reported to the exception queue.

- Support for transmitting Operation, Administration, and Maintenance (OAM) F5 loopback cells. OAM F5 cells must be echoed back on receipt by the remote host, thus demonstrating connectivity on the PVC between the router and the remote host.

- Raw queue, which is used for all raw traffic over the ATM network. Raw traffic includes OAM cells and Interim Local Management Interface (ILMI) cells. (ATM signaling cells are not considered raw.)

Setting AIP Interface Types

All ATM interfaces are full duplex. You must use the appropriate ATM interface cable to connect the AIP with an external ATM network.

The AIP provides an interface to ATM switching fabrics for transmitting and receiving data at rates of up to 155 Mbps bidirectionally; the actual rate is determined by the physical layer interface module (PLIM). The PLIM contains the interface to the ATM cable. The AIP can support PLIMs that connect to the following physical layers:

- Transparent Asynchronous Transmitter/Receiver Interface (TAXI) 4B/5B 100-Mbps multimode fiber optic cable
- SONET/SDH 155-Mbps multimode fiber optic cable—STS-3C or STM-1
- SONET/SDH 155-Mbps single-mode fiber optic cable—STS-3C or STM-1
- E3 34-Mbps coaxial cable

For wide-area networking, ATM is currently being standardized for use in Broadband Integrated Services Digital Networks (BISDNs) by the International Telecommunication Union Telecommunication Standardization Sector (ITU-T) and the American National Standards Institute (ANSI). BISDN supports rates from E3 (34 Mbps) to multiple gigabits per second (Gbps).

NOTES

The ITU-T carries out the functions of the former Consultative Committee for International Telegraph and Telephone (CCITT).

Using AIP Microcode

The AIP microcode is a software image that provides card-specific software instructions. An onboard read-only memory (ROM) component contains the default AIP microcode. The Cisco 7500 series supports downloadable microcode, which enables you to upgrade microcode versions by loading new microcode images onto the Route Processor (RP), storing them in Flash memory, and instructing the AIP to load an image from Flash memory instead of the default ROM image. You can store multiple images for an interface type and instruct the system to load any one of them or the default ROM image with a configuration command. All processor modules of the same type will load the same microcode image from either the default ROM image or a single image stored in Flash memory.

Although multiple microcode versions for a specific interface type can be stored concurrently in Flash memory, only one image can load at startup. The **show controller cxbus** command displays the currently loaded and running microcode version for the Switch Processor (SP) and for each IP.

The **show running-config** command shows the current system instructions for loading microcode at startup.

Understanding AIP Virtual Circuits

A virtual circuit is a connection between remote hosts and routers. A virtual circuit is established for each ATM end node with which the router communicates. The characteristics of the virtual circuit that are established for the AIP when the virtual circuit is created include the following:

- Quality of service (QoS)
- AAL mode—AAL3/4 and AAL5
- Encapsulation type—Logical Link Control (LLC)/SNAP, MUX (one protocol per PVC), NLPID (multiprotocol encapsulation consistent with RFC 1294 and RFC 1490), QSAAL (encapsulation used on a signaling PVC that is used for setting up or tearing down SVCs), SMDS, and PPP over ATM
- Protocol traffic to be carried—multiprotocol or single-protocol traffic
- Peak and average transmission rates
- Point-to-point or point-to-multipoint

Each virtual circuit supports the following router functions:

- Multiprotocol—AppleTalk, Connectionless Network Service (CLNS), DECnet, IP, IPX, Banyan VINES, and Xerox Network Systems (XNS)
- On routers with a serial interface configured for ATM, fast switching of IP, IPX, AppleTalk, and VINES packets; on the Cisco 7500 series routers, fast switching of AppleTalk, CLNS, IP, IPX, and VINES
- Autonomous switching of IP packets
- Pseudobroadcast support for multicast packets

By default, fast switching is enabled on all AIP interfaces. These switching features can be turned off with interface configuration commands. Autonomous switching must be explicitly enabled per interface.

Using the Cisco ATM Port Adapter

This section provides an overview of the ATM features, interfaces, and virtual circuits available on the ATM port adapter, currently supported on the Cisco 7200 series and Cisco 7500 series routers.

Understanding ATM Port Adapter Features

The ATM port adapter supports the following features:

- Segmentation and Reassembly (SAR) of up to 512 buffers simultaneously, where each buffer represents a packet
- Up to 256 transmit buffers for simultaneous fragmentation

- Per-virtual-circuit counters, which improve the accuracy of the statistics shown in the output of **show** commands by ensuring that autonomously switched packets are counted, as well as fast-switched and process-switched packets
- Support for up to 2048 SAR virtual circuits
- Support for AAL5
- Support for transmitting Operation, Administration, and Maintenance (OAM) F5 loopback cells; OAM F5 cells must be echoed back on receipt by the remote host, thus demonstrating connectivity on the PVC between the router and the remote host
- Support for both process-switched transparent bridging and fast-switched transparent bridging over ATM

  Process-switched bridging over ATM supports AAL3/4-SMDS encapsulated packets only. All frames that originate at, or are forwarded by, the Cisco IOS software are sent as 802.3 bridge frames without frame check sequence (FCS)—that is, in RFC 1483 bridge frame formats with 0x0007 in the Protocol Identification (PID) field of the Subnetwork Access Protocol (SNAP) header. You can enable process-switched bridging for SMDS as described later in this chapter.

  Fast-switched transparent bridging over ATM supports AAL5-SNAP encapsulated packets only. All bridged AAL5-SNAP encapsulated packets are fast-switched. Fast-switched transparent bridging supports Ethernet, Fiber Distributed Data Interface (FDDI), and Token Ring packets sent in AAL5-SNAP encapsulation over ATM. You can enable fast-switched bridging for AAL5-SNAP as described later in this chapter.

Understanding the ATM Port Adapter Interface Types

The ATM port adapter provides a single SONET/SDH OC-3 full-duplex interface (either multimode or single-mode intermediate reach) and supports data rates of up to 155 Mbps bidirectionally. The ATM port adapter connects to a SONET/SDH multimode or SONET/STC-3C single-mode optical fiber cable (STS-3C or STM-1 physical layer) to connect the router to an external DSU (an ATM network).

Establishing ATM Port Adapter Virtual Circuits

A virtual circuit is a connection between remote hosts and routers. A virtual circuit is established for each ATM end node with which the router communicates. The characteristics of the virtual circuit that are established for the AIP when the virtual circuit is created include the following:

- AAL mode—AAL5
- Encapsulation type—Logical Link Control (LLC)/SNAP and QSAAL (encapsulation used on a signaling PVC that is used for setting up or tearing down SVCs)
- Protocol traffic to be carried—multiprotocol or single-protocol traffic
- Point-to-multipoint

Each virtual circuit supports the following router functions:

- Multiprotocol—AppleTalk, Connectionless Network Service (CLNS), DECnet, IP, IPX, Banyan VINES, and Xerox Network Systems (XNS)

- On routers with a serial interface configured for ATM, fast switching of IP, IPX, AppleTalk, and VINES packets; on the Cisco 7500 series routers, fast switching of AppleTalk, CLNS, IP, IPX and VINES

- Autonomous switching of IP packets

- Pseudobroadcast support for multicast packets

By default, optimum switching is enabled on all ATM port adapter interfaces.

Using the Cisco NPM

This section provides an overview of the ATM features, interfaces, and virtual circuits available on the NPM, currently supported on the Cisco 4500 and 4700 routers.

Understanding NPM Features

The NPM supports the following features:

- Up to four rate queues

- Reassembly of up to 192 buffers simultaneously, where each buffer represents a packet

- Support for up to 1023 virtual circuits

- Fast switching of IP and IPX

- Support for AAL3/4 and AAL5

  An ATM adaptation layer (AAL) defines the conversion of user information into cells by segmenting upper-layer information into cells at the transmitter and reassembling them at the receiver. AAL1 and AAL2 handle isochronous traffic, such as voice and video, and are not relevant to the router. AAL3/4 and AAL5 support data communications by segmenting and reassembling packets. On the Cisco 4500 and 4700 routers, Cisco supports both AAL3/4 (except at OC-3 rates) and AAL5.

Using NPM Interface Types

All ATM interfaces are full duplex. You must use the appropriate ATM interface cable to connect the NPM with an external ATM network.

The NPM provides an interface to ATM switching fabrics for transmitting and receiving data at rates of up to 155 Mbps bidirectionally; the actual rate is determined by the physical layer interface module (PLIM). The PLIM contains the interface to the ATM cable. The NPM can support PLIMs that connect to the following physical layers:

- SDH/SONET 155-Mbps multimode fiber optic cable—STS-3C or STM-1

- SDH/SONET 155-Mbps single-mode fiber optic cable—STS-3C or STM-1

Understanding NPM Virtual Circuits

A virtual circuit is a point-to-point connection between remote hosts and routers. A virtual circuit is established for each ATM end node with which the router communicates. The characteristics of the virtual circuit that are established for the NPM when the virtual circuit is created include the following:

- Quality of service—QoS
- AAL mode—AAL5 or AAL3/4
- Encapsulation type—LLC/SNAP, MUX, NLPID, NLPID/SNAP, RFC 1483, and PPP over ATM
- Protocol traffic to be carried—multiprotocol or single-protocol traffic
- Peak and average transmission rates

Each virtual circuit supports the following router functions:

- Multiprotocol—AppleTalk, CLNS, DECnet, IP, IPX, Banyan VINES, and XNS
- Fast switching of IP, IPX, AppleTalk, and CLNS

IMPLEMENTING FRAME RELAY

Cisco's Frame Relay implementation currently supports routing on IP, DECnet, AppleTalk, Xerox Network Service (XNS), Novell IPX, International Organization for Standards (ISO) Connectionless Network Service (CLNS), Banyan VINES, and transparent bridging.

Although Frame Relay access was originally restricted to leased lines, dial-up access is now supported.

The Frame Relay software provides the following capabilities:

- Support for the three generally implemented specifications of Frame Relay Local Management Interfaces (LMIs):
  - The *Frame Relay Interface* joint specification produced by Northern Telecom, Digital Equipment Corporation, StrataCom, and Cisco Systems
  - The ANSI-adopted Frame Relay signal specification, T1.617 Annex D
  - The International Telecommunication Union Telecommunication Standardization Sector (ITU-T)-adopted Frame Relay signal specification, Q.933 Annex A
- Conformity to ITU-T I-series (ISDN) recommendation as I122, "Framework for Additional Packet Mode Bearer Services:"
  - The ANSI-adopted Frame Relay encapsulation specification, T1.618
  - The ITU-T-adopted Frame Relay encapsulation specification, Q.922 Annex A
- Conformity to Internet Engineering Task Force (IETF) encapsulation in accordance with RFC 1294, except bridging

- Support for a keepalive mechanism, a multicast group, and a status message, as follows:
  - The keepalive mechanism provides an exchange of information between the network server and the switch to verify that data is flowing.
  - The multicast mechanism provides the network server with a local data link connection identifier (DLCI) and a multicast DLCI; this feature is specific to Cisco's implementation of the Frame Relay joint specification.
  - The status mechanism provides an ongoing status report on the DLCIs known by the switch.
- Support for both PVCs and SVCs in the same sites and routers: Switched virtual circuits (SVCs) allow access through a Frame Relay network by setting up a path to the destination endpoints only when the need arises and tearing down the path when it is no longer needed.
- Support for Frame Relay traffic shaping beginning with Cisco IOS Release 11.2; traffic shaping provides the following:
  - Rate enforcement on a per-virtual circuit basis—The peak rate for outbound traffic can be set to the committed information rate (CIR) or some other user-configurable rate.
  - Dynamic traffic throttling on a per-virtual circuit basis—When Backward Explicit Congestion Notification (BECN) packets indicate congestion on the network, the outbound traffic rate is automatically stepped down; when congestion eases, the outbound traffic rate is stepped up again.
  - Enhanced queuing support on a per-virtual circuit basis—Custom queuing, priority queuing, and weighted fair queuing can be configured for individual virtual circuits.
- Transmission of congestion information from Frame Relay to DECnet Phase IV and CLNS. This mechanism promotes Forward Explicit Congestion Notification (FECN) bits from the Frame Relay layer to upper-layer protocols after checking for the FECN bit on the incoming DLCI; use this Frame Relay congestion information to adjust the sending rates of end hosts; FECN-bit promotion is enabled by default on any interface using Frame Relay encapsulation; no configuration is required.
- Support for Frame Relay Inverse Address Resolution Protocol (Inverse ARP) as described in RFC 1293 for the AppleTalk, Banyan VINES, DECnet, IP, and IPX protocols, as well as native hello packets for DECnet, CLNP, and Banyan VINES; it allows a router running Frame Relay to discover the protocol address of a device associated with the virtual circuit.
- Support for Frame Relay switching, whereby packets are switched based on the DLCI—a Frame Relay equivalent of a media access control (MAC)-level address; routers are configured as a hybrid DTE switch or pure Frame Relay DCE access node in the Frame Relay network. Cisco's implementation of Frame Relay switching allows the following configurations:
  - Switching over an IP tunnel
  - Network-to-Network Interface (NNI) to other Frame Relay switches

○ Local serial-to-serial switching

Frame Relay switching is used when all traffic arriving on one DLCI can be sent out on another DLCI to the same next hop address. In such cases, the Cisco IOS software does not have to examine the frames individually to discover the destination address, and as a result, the processing load on the router decreases.

- Support for *subinterfaces* associated with a physical interface; the software groups one or more permanent virtual circuits (PVCs) under separate subinterfaces, which in turn are located under a single physical interface (see the "Configuring Frame Relay Subinterfaces" and the "Subinterface Examples" sections of Chapter 7).

- Support for fast-path transparent bridging, as described in RFC 1490, for Frame Relay encapsulated serial and High-Speed Serial Interfaces) (HSSI) on all platforms.

- Support of the Frame Relay DTE Management Information Base (MIB) specified in RFC 1315—however, the error table is not implemented; to use the Frame Relay MIB, refer to your MIB publications.

IMPLEMENTING SMDS

Cisco's implementation of the SMDS protocol is based on cell-relay technology as defined in the Bellcore Technical advisories, which are based on the IEEE 802.6 standard. Cisco provides an interface to an SMDS network using DS-1 or DS-3 high-speed transmission facilities. Connection to the network is made through a device called an *SDSU*—an SMDS channel service unit/digital service unit (CSU/DSU) developed jointly by Cisco Systems and Kentrox. The SDSU attaches to a Cisco router or access server through a serial port. On the other side, the SDSU terminates the line.

Cisco's implementation of SMDS supports the IP, DECnet, AppleTalk, XNS, Novell IPX, Banyan VINES, OSI internetworking protocols, and transparent bridging.

Cisco's implementation of SMDS also supports SMDS encapsulation over an Asynchronous Transfer Mode (ATM) interface.

Routing of AppleTalk, DECnet, IP, IPX, and ISO CLNS is fully dynamic—that is, the routing tables are determined and updated dynamically. Routing of the other supported protocols requires that you establish a static routing table of SMDS neighbors in a user group. Once this table is set up, all interconnected routers and access servers provide dynamic routing.

─── **NOTES** ──

When configuring IP routing over SMDS, you may need to make adjustments to accommodate split-horizon effects. By default, split horizon is *disabled* for SMDS networks.

──

Cisco's SMDS implementation includes multiple logical IP subnetworks support as defined by RFC 1209. This RFC describes routing IP over an SMDS cloud in which each connection is considered a host on one specific private network, and points to cases in which traffic must transit from network to network. Cisco's implementation of SMDS also provides the Data Exchange Interface (DXI) Version 3.2 with *heartbeat*. The heartbeat mechanism periodically generates a heartbeat poll frame. When a multicast address is not available to a destination, *pseudobroadcasting* can be enabled to broadcast packets to those destinations using a unicast address.

USING X.25 AND LAPB

X.25 is one of a group of specifications published by the International Telecommunication Union Telecommunication Standardization Sector (ITU-T); these specifications are international standards that are formally called *Recommendations*. The ITU-T Recommendation X.25 defines how connections between data terminal equipment (DTE) and data communications equipment (DCE) are maintained for remote terminal access and computer communications. The X.25 specification defines protocols for two layers of the Open Systems Interconnection (OSI) reference model. The data link layer protocol defined is Link Access Procedure, Balanced (LAPB). The network layer is sometimes called the *packet level protocol* (PLP), but is commonly (although less correctly) referred to as *the X.25 protocol*.

The ITU-T updates its Recommendations periodically. The specifications dated 1980 and 1984 are the most common versions currently in use. Additionally, the International Standards Organization (ISO) has published ISO 7776:1986 as an equivalent to the LAPB standard, and ISO 8208:1989 as an equivalent to the ITU-T 1984 X.25 Recommendation packet layer. Cisco's X.25 software follows the ITU-T 1984 X.25 Recommendation, except for its Defense Data Network (DDN) and Blacker Front End (BFE) operation, which follow the ITU-T 1980 X.25 Recommendation.

NOTES

The ITU-T carries out the functions of the former Consultative Committee for International Telegraph and Telephone (CCITT). The 1988 X.25 standard was the last published as a CCITT Recommendation. The first ITU-T Recommendation is the 1993 revision.

In addition to providing remote terminal access, Cisco's X.25 software provides transport for LAN protocols—IP, DECnet, XNS, ISO CLNS, AppleTalk, Novell IPX, Banyan VINES, and Apollo Domain—and bridging.

Cisco IOS X.25 software provides the following capabilities:

- LAPB datagram transport—LAPB is a protocol that operates at Level 2 (the data link layer) of the OSI reference model. It offers a reliable connection service for exchanging data (in units called *frames*) with one other host. The LAPB connection is configured to carry a single protocol or multiple protocols. Protocol datagrams (IP, DECnet, AppleTalk, and so forth) are carried over a reliable LAPB connection, or datagrams of several of these protocols are encapsulated in a proprietary protocol and carried over a LAPB connection. Cisco also implements transparent bridging over multiprotocol LAPB encapsulations on serial interfaces.

- X.25 datagram transport—X.25 can establish connections with multiple hosts; these connections are called *virtual circuits*. Protocol datagrams (IP, DECnet, AppleTalk, and so forth) are encapsulated inside packets on an X.25 virtual circuit. Mappings between a host's X.25 address and its datagram protocol addresses allow these datagrams to be routed through an X.25 network, thereby allowing an X.25 public data network (PDN) to transport LAN protocols.

- X.25 switch—X.25 calls can be routed based on their X.25 addresses either between serial interfaces on the same router (local switching) or across an IP network to another router (*X.25-over-TCP* or *XOT*, previously called *remote switching* or *tunneling*). XOT encapsulates the X.25 packet level inside a TCP connection, allowing X.25 equipment to be connected via a TCP/IP-based network. Cisco's X.25 switching features provide a convenient way to connect X.25 equipment, but does not provide the specialized features and capabilities of an X.25 public data network (PDN).

- ISDN D Channel—X.25 traffic over the D channel (up to a speed of 9.6 Kbps) can be used to support many applications. For example, it may be required as a primary interface in which low-volume sporadic interactive traffic is the normal mode of operation.

- PAD—User sessions can be carried across an X.25 network using the packet assembler/disassembler (PAD) protocols defined by the ITU-T Recommendations X.3 and X.29.

- QLLC—The Cisco IOS software can use the Qualified Logical Link Control (QLLC) protocol to carry SNA traffic through an X.25 network.

- Connection-Mode Network Service (CMNS)—CMNS is a mechanism that uses OSI-based network service access point (NSAP) addresses to extend local X.25 switching to nonserial media (for example, Ethernet, FDDI, and Token Ring). This implementation provides the X.25 PLP over Logical Link Control, type 2 (LLC2) to allow connections over nonserial interfaces. Cisco's CMNS implementation supports services defined in ISO Standards 8208 (packet level) and 8802-2 (frame level).

- DDN and BFE X.25—The DDN-specified Standard Service is supported. The DDN X.25 Standard Service is the required protocol for use with DDN Packet-Switched Nodes (PSNs). The Defense Communications Agency (DCA) has certified Cisco Systems' DDN X.25 Standard Service implementation for attachment to the Defense Data Network. Cisco's DDN implementation also includes Blacker Front End (BFE) and Blacker Emergency Mode operation.

- X.25 MIB—Subsets of the specifications in *SNMP MIB Extension for X.25 LAPB* (RFC 1381) and *SNMP MIB Extension for the X.25 Packet Layer* (RFC 1382) are supported. The LAPB XID Table, X.25 Cleared Circuit Table, and X.25 Call Parameter Table are not implemented. All values are read-only. To use the X.25 MIB, refer to the RFCs.

Cisco's X.25 implementation does not support fast switching.

CHAPTER 2

Configuring ATM Access over a Serial Interface

This chapter describes how to configure routers that use a serial interface for ATM access through an ATM data service unit (ADSU). The configuration tasks include the steps necessary to enable Asynchronous Transfer Mode-Data Exchange Interface (ATM-DXI) encapsulation, select a multi-protocol encapsulation method using ATM-DXI, and set up a permanent virtual circuit (PVC) for the selected encapsulation.

For a complete description of the ATM commands in this chapter, refer to Chapter 6, "ATM Commands."

CONFIGURING ATM ACCESS OVER A SERIAL INTERFACE

In routers with a serial interface, an ADSU is required to provide the ATM interface to the network, convert outgoing packets into ATM cells, and reassemble incoming ATM cells into packets.

Any serial interface can be configured for multiprotocol encapsulation over ATM-DXI, as specified by RFC 1483. At the ADSU, the DXI header is stripped off, and the protocol data is segmented into cells for transport over the ATM network.

RFC 1483 describes two methods of transporting multiprotocol connectionless network interconnect traffic over an ATM network. One method allows multiplexing of multiple protocols over a single PVC. The other method uses different virtual circuits to carry different protocols. Cisco's implementation of RFC 1483 supports both methods and supports transport of Apollo Domain, AppleTalk, Banyan VINES, DECnet, IP, Novell IPX, ISO CLNS, and XNS traffic.

ATM SERIAL ACCESS CONFIGURATION TASK LIST

To configure ATM access over a serial interface, complete the tasks in the following sections. The first four tasks in the following list are required; the last task is optional:

- Enabling the Serial Interface
- Enabling ATM-DXI Encapsulation

- Setting Up the ATM-DXI PVC
- Mapping Protocol Addresses to the ATM-DXI PVC
- Monitoring and Maintaining the ATM-DXI Serial Interface (optional)

For an example of configuring ATM access over a serial interface, see the section "ATM Access over a Serial Interface Example," at the end of this chapter.

ENABLING THE SERIAL INTERFACE

To begin configuring the serial interface for ATM access, enable the serial interface by performing the following steps beginning in global configuration mode:

Task	Command
Enable the serial interface.	**interface serial** *number*
For each protocol to be carried, assign a protocol address to the interface. (The commands shown are a partial list for the supported protocols.)	**appletalk address** *network.node* **ip address** *address mask* **ipx network** *number*

The supported protocols are Apollo Domain, AppleTalk, Banyan VINES, DECnet, IP, Novell IPX, ISO CLNS, and XNS.

ENABLING ATM-DXI ENCAPSULATION

To enable ATM-DXI encapsulation on a serial or High-Speed Serial Interface (HSSI), perform the following task in interface configuration mode:

Task	Command
Enable ATM-DXI encapsulation.	**encapsulation atm-dxi**

SETTING UP THE ATM-DXI PVC

An ATM-DXI PVC can be defined to carry one or more protocols as described by RFC 1483, or multiple protocols as described by RFC 1490.

To set up the ATM-DXI PVC and select an encapsulation method, perform the following task in interface configuration mode:

Task	Command
Define the ATM-DXI PVC and the encapsulation method.	**dxi pvc** *vpi vci* [**snap** | **nlpid** | **mux**]

The MUX (multiplex) option defines the PVC to carry one protocol only; each protocol must be carried over a different PVC. The SNAP (Subnetwork Access Protocol) option is LLC/SNAP multiprotocol encapsulation, compatible with RFC 1483; SNAP is the current default option. The network layer protocol identification (NLPID) option is multiprotocol encapsulation, compatible with RFC 1490. This option is provided for backward compatibility with the default setting in earlier versions in the Cisco IOS software.

─ **NOTES** ──

The default encapsulation was NLPID in software earlier than Release 10.3. Starting with that release, the default encapsulation is SNAP. Select the **nlpid** keyword if you had previously selected the default.

MAPPING PROTOCOL ADDRESSES TO THE ATM-DXI PVC

This section describes how to map protocol addresses to the virtual channel identifier (VCI) and the virtual path identifier (VPI) of a PVC that can carry multiprotocol traffic. The protocol addresses belong to the host at the other end of the link. To map a protocol address to an ATM-DXI PVC, complete the following task in interface configuration mode:

Task	Command
Map a protocol address to the ATM-DXI PVC's VPI and VCI.	**dxi map** *protocol protocol-address vpi vci* [**broadcast**]

Repeat this task for each protocol to be carried on the PVC.

The supported protocols are Apollo Domain, AppleTalk, Banyan VINES, DECnet, IP, Novell IPX, ISO CLNS, and XNS. For an example of configuring a serial interface for ATM, see the "ATM Access over a Serial Interface Example" section at the end of this chapter.

MONITORING AND MAINTAINING THE ATM-DXI SERIAL INTERFACE

After configuring the serial interface for ATM, you can display the status of the interface, the ATM-DXI PVC, or the ATM-DXI map. To display interface, PVC, or map information, complete the following tasks in EXEC mode:

Task	Command
Display the serial ATM interface status.	**show interfaces atm** [*slot/port*]
Display the ATM-DXI PVC information.	**show dxi pvc**
Display the ATM-DXI map information.	**show dxi map**

ATM ACCESS OVER A SERIAL INTERFACE EXAMPLE

The example in this section illustrates how to configure a serial interface for ATM access.

In the following example, serial interface 0 is configured for ATM-DXI with MUX encapsulation. Because MUX encapsulation is used, only one protocol is carried on the PVC. This protocol is explicitly identified by a **dxi map** command, which also identifies the protocol address of the remote node. This PVC can carry IP broadcast traffic.

```
interface serial 0
 ip address 172.21.178.48
 encapsulation atm-dxi
 dxi pvc 10 10 mux
 dxi map ip 172.21.178.4 10 10 broadcast
```

CHAPTER 3

Configuring ATM on the AIP for Cisco 7500 Series Routers

This chapter describes how to configure ATM on the ATM Interface Processor (AIP) card in the Cisco 7500 series routers.

NOTES

In Cisco IOS Release 11.3, all commands supported on the Cisco 7500 series routers are also supported on Cisco 7000 series routers equipped with RSP7000.

For a complete description of the ATM commands in this chapter, refer to Chapter 6, "ATM Commands." For information about Switched Multimegabit Data Service (SMDS) support using AIP, refer to Chapter 9, "Configuring SMDS."

ATM CONFIGURATION TASK LIST

To configure ATM on the AIP for a Cisco 7500 series router, complete the tasks in the following sections.

The first task of the following list is required, and then you must configure at least one PVC or SVC. The virtual circuit options you configure must match in three places: on the router, on the ATM switch, and at the remote end of the PVC or SVC connection. The remaining tasks are optional. The configuration tasks are the following:

- Enabling the AIP
- Configuring PVCs
- Configuring SVCs
- Configuring Classical IP and ARP over ATM (optional)
- Configuring Traffic Shaping for ATM SVCs (optional)

- Customizing the AIP (optional)
- Configuring ATM Subinterfaces for SMDS Networks (optional)
- Configuring Transparent Bridging for the AIP (optional)
- Configuring PPP over ATM (optional)
- Monitoring and Maintaining the ATM Interface (optional)

See the "ATM Configuration Examples" section near the end of this chapter for configuration examples.

ENABLING THE AIP

This section describes how to begin configuring the AIP on the Cisco 7500 series routers. These routers identify an ATM interface address by its slot number (slots 0 to 4) and port number in the format *slot/port*. Because each AIP contains a single ATM interface, the port number is always 0. For example, the *slot/port* address of an ATM interface on an AIP installed in slot 1 is *1/0*.

To begin to configure the AIP, start the following task in privileged EXEC mode:

Task	Command
Step 1 At the privileged EXEC prompt, enter configuration mode from the terminal.	**configure terminal**
Step 2 Specify an AIP interface.	**interface atm** *slot*/0
Step 3 If IP routing is enabled on the system, optionally assign a source IP address and subnet mask to the interface.	**ip address** *ip-address mask*

To enable the AIP, perform the following task in interface configuration mode:

Task	Command
Change the shutdown state to up and enable the ATM interface, thereby starting the segmentation and reassembly (SAR) operation on the interface.	**no shutdown**

The **no shutdown** command passes an **enable** command to the AIP, which then begins segmentation and reassembly (SAR) operations. It also causes the AIP to configure itself based on the previously sent configuration commands.

CONFIGURING PVCS

To use a permanent virtual circuit (PVC), you must configure the PVC into both the router and the ATM switch. PVCs remain active until the circuit is removed from either configuration.

All virtual circuit characteristics listed in the section "Understanding AIP Virtual Circuits" in Chapter 1, "Wide-Area Networking Overview," apply to these PVCs. When a PVC is configured, all the configuration options are passed on to the AIP. These PVCs are writable into the nonvolatile RAM (NVRAM) as part of the Route Processor (RP) configuration and are used when the RP image is reloaded.

Some ATM switches might have point-to-multipoint PVCs that do the equivalent of broadcasting. If a point-to-multipoint PVC exists, then that PVC can be used as the sole broadcast PVC for all multicast requests.

To configure a PVC, perform the tasks in the following sections. The first three tasks in the following list are required; the last two are optional:

- Creating a PVC
- Mapping a Protocol Address to a PVC
- Configuring Communication with the ILMI
- Configuring ATM UNI Version Override (optional)
- Configuring Transmission of Loopback Cells to Verify Connectivity (optional)

Creating a PVC

To create a PVC on the AIP interface, perform the following task in interface configuration mode:

Task	Command
Create a PVC.	**atm pvc** *vcd vpi vci aal-encap* [[*midlow midhigh*] [*peak average burst*]] [**oam** *seconds*]

When you create a PVC, you create a virtual circuit descriptor (VCD) and attach it to the VPI and VCI. A VCD is an AIP-specific mechanism that identifies to the AIP which VPI-VCI pair to use for a particular packet. The ATM interface requires this feature to manage the packets for transmission. The number chosen for the VCD is independent of the VPI-VCI pair used.

When you create a PVC, you also specify the ATM adaptation layer (AAL) and encapsulation. If you specify AAL3/4-SMDS encapsulation, you have the option of setting the starting message identifier (MID) number and ending MID number using the *midlow* and *midhigh* arguments. A rate queue is used that matches the *peak* and *average* rate selections, which are specified in kilobits per second. Omitting a *peak* and *average* value causes the PVC to be connected to the highest bandwidth rate queue available. In this case, the *peak* and *average* values are equal.

You can also configure the PVC for communication with the Interim Local Management Interface (ILMI) so the router can receive Simple Network Management Protocol (SNMP) traps and new network prefixes. Refer to the "Configuring Communication with the ILMI" section of this chapter for details.

You can also optionally configure the PVC to send Operation, Administration, and Maintenance (OAM) F5 loopback cells to verify connectivity on the virtual circuit. The remote end must respond by echoing back such cells.

See examples of PVC configurations in the section "ATM Configuration Examples" at the end of this chapter.

Mapping a Protocol Address to a PVC

The ATM interface supports a static mapping scheme that identifies the ATM address of remote hosts or routers. This address is specified as a virtual circuit descriptor (VCD) for a PVC (or an NSAP address for SVC operation). This section describes how to map a PVC to an address, which is a required task if you are configuring a PVC.

You enter mapping commands as groups. You first create a map list and then associate it with an interface. Begin the following tasks in global configuration mode:

Task	Command
Step 1 Create a map list by naming it, and enter map-list configuration mode.	**map-list** *name*
Step 2 Associate a protocol and address with a specific virtual circuit.	*protocol protocol-address* **atm-vc** *vcd* [**broadcast**]
Step 3 Associate a protocol and address to a different virtual circuit.	*protocol protocol-address* **atm-vc** *vcd* [**broadcast**]
Step 4 Specify an AIP interface and enter interface configuration mode.	**interface atm** *slot*/0
Step 5 Associate a map list to an interface.	**map-group** *name*

A map list can contain multiple map entries, as Steps 2 and 3 in the preceding task table illustrate. The **broadcast** keyword specifies that this map entry is to be used when the corresponding protocol sends broadcast packets to the interface (for example, any network routing protocol updates). If you do not specify **broadcast**, the ATM software is prevented from sending routing protocol updates to the remote hosts.

If you do specify **broadcast**, but do *not* set up point-to-multipoint signaling, pseudobroadcasting is enabled. To eliminate pseudobroadcasting and set up point-to-multipoint signaling on virtual circuits configured for broadcasting, see the "Configuring Point-to-Multipoint Signaling" section in this chapter. In Step 5, associate the map list with the ATM interface you specified in Step 4. Use the same *name* argument you used in the **map-list** command

You can create multiple map lists, but only one map list can be associated with an interface. Different map lists can be associated with different interfaces. See the examples at the end of this chapter.

Configuring Communication with the ILMI

You can configure a PVC for communication with the Interim Local Management Interface (ILMI) so the router can receive SNMP traps and new network prefixes. The recommended *vpi* and *vci* values for the ILMI PVC are 0 and 16, respectively. To configure ILMI communication, complete the following task in interface configuration mode:

Task	Command
Create an ILMI PVC on a major interface.	**atm pvc** *vcd vpi vci* **ilmi**

NOTES

This ILMI PVC can be set up only on a major interface, not on the subinterfaces.

Once you have configured an ILMI PVC, you can optionally enable the **ILMI-keepalive** function by completing the following task in interface configuration mode:

Task	Command
Optionally, enable ILMI keepalives and set the interval between keepalives.	**atm ilmi-keepalive** [*seconds*]

No other configuration steps are required.

ILMI address registration for receipt of SNMP traps and new network prefixes is enabled by default. The ILMI keepalive function is disabled by default; when enabled, the default interval between keepalives is 3 seconds.

Configuring ATM UNI Version Override

Normally, when ILMI link autodetermination is enabled on the interface and is successful, the router takes the user-network interface (UNI) version returned by ILMI. If the ILMI link autodetermination process is unsuccessful or ILMI is disabled, the UNI version defaults to 3.0. You can override this default by using the **atm uni-version** command. The **no** form of the command sets the UNI version to the one returned by ILMI if ILMI is enabled and the link autodetermination is successful. Otherwise, the UNI version will revert to 3.0.

Task	Command
Override UNI version used by router.	**atm uni-version** *version number*

No other configuration steps are required.

Configuring Transmission of Loopback Cells to Verify Connectivity

You can optionally configure the PVC to send OAM F5 loopback cells to verify connectivity on the virtual circuit. The remote end must respond by echoing back such cells. If OAM response cells are missed (indicating the lack of connectivity), the system console displays a debug message indicating the failure of the PVC, provided the **debug atm errors** command is enabled. If you suspect that a PVC is faulty, enabling OAM cell generation and the **debug atm errors** command allows you to monitor the status of the PVC.

To configure the transmission of OAM F5 loopback cells, add the **oam** keyword to the **atm pvc** command, as shown in the following task:

Task	Command
Configure transmission of OAM F5 cells on the PVC, specifying how often OAM F5 cells should be sent.	**atm pvc** *vcd vpi vci aal-encap* [[*midlow midhigh*] [*peak average burst*]] [**oam** *seconds*] [**inarp** *minutes*]

CONFIGURING SVCS

ATM switched virtual circuit (SVC) service operates much like X.25 SVC service, although ATM allows much higher throughput. Virtual circuits are created and released dynamically, providing user bandwidth on demand. This service requires a signaling protocol between the router and the switch.

The ATM signaling software provides a method of dynamically establishing, maintaining, and clearing ATM connections at the User-Network Interface (UNI). The ATM signaling software conforms to ATM Forum UNI 3.0 or ATM Forum UNI 3.1 depending on what version is selected by ILMI or configuration.

In UNI mode, the user is the router and the network is an ATM switch. This is an important distinction. The Cisco router does not perform ATM-level call routing. Instead, the ATM switch does the ATM call routing, and the router routes packets through the resulting circuit. The router is viewed as the user and the LAN interconnection device at the end of the circuit, and the ATM switch is viewed as the network.

Figure 3–1 illustrates the router position in a basic ATM environment. The router is used primarily to interconnect LANs via an ATM network. The workstation connected directly to the destination ATM switch illustrates that you can connect not only routers to ATM switches, but also any computer with an ATM interface that conforms to the ATM Forum UNI specification.

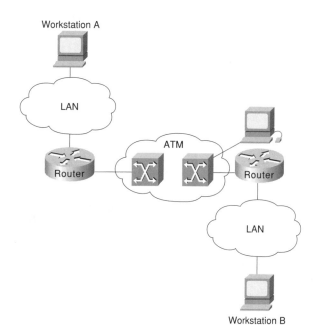

Figure 3–1
Basic ATM environment.

You must complete the following tasks to use SVCs:

- Configuring the PVC that Performs SVC Call Setup
- Configuring the NSAP Address

The following tasks are optional SVC tasks to customize your network. These tasks are considered advanced; the default values are almost always adequate. You should not have to perform these tasks unless you need to customize your particular SVC connection:

- Configuring the Idle Timeout Interval
- Configuring Point-to-Multipoint Signaling
- Changing Traffic Values
- Configuring SSCOP
- Closing an SVC

Configuring the PVC that Performs SVC Call Setup

Unlike X.25 service, which uses in-band signaling (connection establishment done on the same circuit as data transfer), ATM uses out-of-band signaling. One dedicated PVC exists between the router and the ATM switch, over which all SVC call establishment and call termination requests flow. After the call is established, data transfer occurs over the SVC, from router to router. The signaling that accomplishes the call setup and teardown is called *Layer 3 signaling* or the *Q.2931 protocol*.

For out-of-band signaling, a signaling PVC must be configured before any SVCs can be set up. Figure 3–2 illustrates that a signaling PVC from the source router to the ATM switch is used to set up two SVCs. This is a fully meshed network; workstations A, B, and C all can communicate with each other.

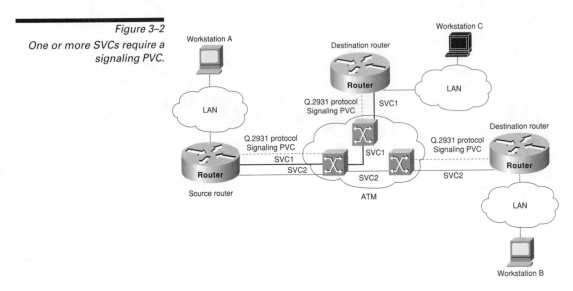

Figure 3–2

One or more SVCs require a signaling PVC.

To configure the signaling PVC for all SVC connections, perform the following task in interface configuration mode:

Task	Command
Configure the signaling PVC for a major interface that uses SVCs.	**atm pvc** *vcd vpi vci* **qsaal**

This signaling PVC can be set up only on a major interface, not on the subinterfaces.

The VPI and VCI values must be configured consistently with the local switch. The standard value of VPI is 0; the standard value of VCI is 5. See the section "SVCs in a Fully Meshed Network Example" at the end of this chapter for a sample ATM signaling configuration.

Configuring the NSAP Address

Every ATM interface involved with signaling must be configured with a network service access point (NSAP) address. The NSAP address is the ATM address of the interface and must be unique across the network.

To configure an NSAP address, complete one of the following tasks:

- Configuring the Complete NSAP Address Manually
- Configuring the ESI and Selector Fields

Configuring the Complete NSAP Address Manually

When you configure the ATM NSAP address manually, you must enter the entire address in hexadecimal format since each digit entered represents a hexadecimal digit. To represent the complete NSAP address, you must enter 40 hexadecimal digits in the following format:

```
XX.XXXX.XX.XXXXXX.XXXX.XXXX.XXXX.XXXX.XXXX.XXXX.XX
```

— **NOTES** ————————————————————————————————————

All ATM NSAP addresses may be entered in the dotted hexadecimal format shown, which conforms to the UNI specification. The dotted method provides some validation that the address is a legal value. If you know your address format is correct, the dots may be omitted.

Because the interface has no default NSAP address, you must configure the NSAP address for SVCs. To set the ATM interface's source NSAP address, perform the following task in interface configuration mode:

Task	Command
Configure the ATM NSAP address for an interface.	**atm nsap-address** *nsap-address*

An example of assigning an NSAP address to an ATM interface is shown in the section "ATM NSAP Address Example" at the end of this chapter.

Configuring the ESI and Selector Fields

To configure the end station ID (ESI) and selector fields, the switch must be capable of delivering the NSAP address prefix to the router via ILMI and the router must be configured with a PVC for communication with the switch via ILMI.

To configure the router to get the NSAP prefix from the switch and use locally entered values for the remaining fields of the address, complete the following tasks in interface configuration mode:

Task	Command
Step 1 Configure a PVC for communicating with the switch via ILMI.	**atm pvc** *vcd* **0 16 ilmi**
Step 2 Enter the ESI and selector fields of the NSAP address.	**atm esi-address** *esi.selector*

The **atm esi-address** command allows you to configure the ATM address by entering the ESI (12 hexadecimal characters) and the selector byte (2 hexadecimal characters). The ATM prefix (26 hexadecimal characters) is provided by the ATM switch. To get the prefix from the ATM switch, the ILMI PVC must be configured on the router and the ATM switch must be able to supply a prefix via ILMI.

The **atm esi-address** and **atm nsap-address** commands are mutually exclusive. Configuring the router with the **atm esi-address** command negates the **atm nsap-address** setting, and vice versa.

You can also specify a keepalive interval for the ILMI PVC. See the "Configuring Communication with the ILMI," section earlier in this chapter for more information. To see an example of setting up the ILMI PVC and assigning the ESI and selector fields of an NSAP address, go to the section "ATM ESI Address Example," near the end of this chapter.

Configuring the Idle Timeout Interval

You can specify an interval of inactivity after which any idle SVC on an interface is disconnected. This timeout interval might help control costs and free router memory and other resources for other uses.

To change the idle timeout interval, perform the following task in interface configuration mode:

Task	Command
Configure the interval of inactivity after which an idle SVC will be disconnected.	**atm idle-timeout** *seconds*

The default idle timeout interval is 300 seconds (5 minutes).

Configuring Point-to-Multipoint Signaling

Point-to-multipoint signaling (or multicasting) allows the router to send one packet to the ATM switch and have the switch replicate the packet to the destinations. It replaces pseudobroadcasting on specified virtual circuits for protocols configured for broadcasting.

You configure multipoint signaling on an ATM interface after you have mapped protocol addresses to NSAPs and configured one or more protocols for broadcasting.

After multipoint signaling is set, the router uses existing static map entries that have the **broadcast** keyword set to establish multipoint calls. The call is established to the first destination with a Setup message. Additional parties are added to the call with AddParty messages each time a multicast packet is sent. One multipoint call will be established for each logical subnet of each protocol that has the **broadcast** keyword set.

To configure multipoint signaling on an ATM interface, complete the following tasks beginning in global configuration mode. The first task is required to configure this feature; the others are optional.

Task	Command
Step 1 Specify an AIP interface.	**interface atm** *slot*/0

Task	Command
Step 2 Provide a protocol address for the interface.	*protocol protocol-address mask*
Step 3 Associate a map list to the interface.	**map-group** *name*
Step 4 Provide an ATM NSAP address for the interface.	**atm nsap-address** *nsap-address*
Step 5 Configure the signaling PVC for the interface that uses SVCs.	**atm pvc** *vcd vpi vci* **qsaal**
Step 6 Associate a map list with the map group.	**map-list** *name*
Step 7 Configure a broadcast protocol for the remote NSAP address on the SVC. Repeat this step for other NSAP addresses, as needed.	*protocol protocol-address* **atm-nsap** *atm-nsap-address* **broadcast**
Step 8 Enable multipoint signaling to the ATM switch.	**atm multipoint-signalling**
Step 9 Limit the frequency of sending AddParty messages (optional).	**atm multipoint-interval interval**

If multipoint virtual circuits are closed, they are reopened with the next multicast packet. Once the call is established, additional parties are added to the call when additional multicast packets are sent. If a destination never comes up, the router constantly attempts to add it to the call by means of multipoint signaling.

For an example of configuring multipoint signaling on an interface that is configured for SVCs, see the "SVCs with Multipoint Signaling Example" section later in this chapter.

Changing Traffic Values

The tasks in this section are optional and advanced. The ATM signaling software can specify to the AIP card and the ATM switch a limit on how much traffic the source router will be sending. It provides this information in the form of traffic parameters. (These parameters have default values.) The ATM switch in turn sends these parameters as requested by the source to the ATM destination node. If the destination cannot provide such capacity levels, the call may fail (for Cisco 7500 series behavior, see the per-interface **atm sig-traffic-shaping strict** command in Chapter 6). There is a single attempt to match traffic parameters.

This section describes how to change traffic values to customize your SVC connection. The individual tasks that separately specify **peak**, **sustainable**, or **burst** values for an SVC are analogous to the *peak*, *average*, and *burst* values defined when you create a PVC. Valid values for the peak rate on the AIP are between 130 Kbps and the PLIM rate. The valid values for the average rate are fractions of the peak rate—the peak rate divided by a number between 1 and 64. When the average rate is below one-half the peak rate, the average rate defaults to the next available fraction. The valid range for the maximum burst size is between 32 cells and 2016 cells. Values between 32 and 2016 will round up to the next multiple of 32 cells.

Forward commands apply to the flow of cells from the source router to the destination router. Backward commands apply to the flow of cells from the destination router to the source router.

Most of the SVC traffic parameters include the concept of cell loss priority (CLP). CLP defines the following two levels of cell importance:

- A cell that has a CLP of 0 is a high-priority cell, indicating to the ATM switch that the switch should not readily discard the cell.

- A cell that has a CLP of 1 is a low-priority cell, indicating to the ATM switch that the switch can discard the cell if necessary, due to congestion. For example, a cell with a CLP of 1 should be dropped before a cell with a CLP of 0.

Figure 3–3 illustrates a source and destination router implementing traffic settings that correspond end-to-end. The value for the forward command at the source router corresponds to the value for the backward command at the destination router.

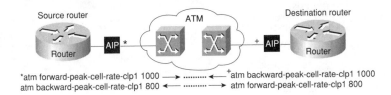

Figure 3–3
Source and destination routers have corresponding traffic settings.

You can define map lists and map groups to tie specified SVCs to the protocol addresses of remote hosts and to specify whether broadcast protocols are supported. Then you can define map classes and specify the traffic parameters needed for the specified protocol traffic on those SVCs.

You must enter map-class configuration mode before you can change the traffic values from their default values. To enter map-class configuration mode, perform the following task in global configuration mode:

Task	Command
Enter map-class configuration mode, specifying a map-class name.	**map-class atm** *class-name*

If a map class with the specified name does not exist, the router creates a new one. All the following commands apply to the named map class. See the "Traffic Parameters Example" section near the end of this chapter for an example defining map classes, map groups, map lists, and traffic parameters.

To change traffic parameters, perform one or more of the following tasks in map-class configuration mode:

Task	Command
Set the source-to-destination peak cell rate for high-priority cells.	**atm forward-peak-cell-rate-clp0** *rate*
Set the destination-to-source peak cell rate for high-priority cells.	**atm backward-peak-cell-rate-clp0** *rate*
Set the source-to-destination peak cell rate for the aggregate of low-priority and high-priority cells.	**atm forward-peak-cell-rate-clp1** *rate*
Set the destination-to-source peak cell rate for the aggregate of low-priority and high-priority cells.	**atm backward-peak-cell-rate-clp1** *rate*
Set the source-to-destination sustainable cell rate for high-priority cells.	**atm forward-sustainable-cell-rate-clp0** *rate*
Set the destination-to-source sustainable cell rate for high-priority cells.	**atm backward-sustainable-cell-rate-clp0** *rate*
Set the source-to-destination sustainable cell rate for the aggregate of low-priority and high-priority cells.	**atm forward-sustainable-cell-rate-clp1** *rate*
Set the destination-to-source sustainable cell rate for the aggregate of low-priority and high-priority cells.	**atm backward-sustainable-cell-rate-clp1** *rate*
Set the source-to-destination burst size for high-priority cells.	**atm forward-max-burst-size-clp0** *cell-count*
Set the destination-to-source burst size for high-priority cells.	**atm backward-max-burst-size-clp0** *cell-count*
Set the source-to-destination burst size for the aggregate of low-priority and high-priority cells.	**atm forward-max-burst-size-clp1** *cell-count*
Set the destination-to-source burst size for the aggregate of low-priority and high-priority cells.	**atm backward-max-burst-size-clp1** *cell-count*

Configuring SSCOP

The Service-Specific Connection-Oriented Protocol (SSCOP) resides in the service-specific convergence sublayer (SSCS) of the ATM adaptation layer (AAL). SSCOP is used to transfer variable-length service data units (SDUs) between users of SSCOP. SSCOP provides for the recovery of lost or corrupted SDUs.

NOTES

The tasks in this section customize the SSCOP feature to a particular network or environment and are optional. The features have default values and are valid in most installations. Before customizing these features, you should have a good understanding of SSCOP and the network involved.

Setting the Poll Timer

The poll timer controls the maximum time between transmission of a POLL PDU when sequential data (SD) or SDP PDUs are queued for transmission or are outstanding pending acknowledgments. To change the poll timer from the default value of 10 seconds, perform the following task in interface configuration mode:

Task	Command
Set the poll timer.	sscop poll-timer *seconds*

Setting the Keepalive Timer

The keepalive timer controls the maximum time between transmission of a POLL PDU when no SD or SDP PDUs are queued for transmission or are outstanding pending acknowledgments. To change the keepalive timer from the default value of 30 seconds, perform the following task in interface configuration mode:

Task	Command
Set the keepalive timer.	sscop keepalive-timer *seconds*

Setting the Connection Control Timer

The connection control timer determines the time between transmission of BGN, END, or RS (resynchronization) PDUs as long as an acknowledgment has not been received. Connection control performs the establishment, release, and resynchronization of an SSCOP connection.

To change the connection control timer from the default value of 10 seconds, perform the following task in interface configuration mode:

Task	Command
Set the connection control timer.	sscop cc-timer *seconds*

To change the retry count of the connection control timer from the default value of 10, perform the following task in interface configuration mode:

Task	Command
Set the number of times that SSCOP will retry to transmit BGN, END, or RS PDUs when they have not been acknowledged.	sscop max-cc *retries*

Setting the Transmitter and Receiver Windows

A transmitter window controls how many packets can be transmitted before an acknowledgment is required. To change the transmitter's window from the default value of 7, perform the following task in interface configuration mode:

Task	Command
Set the transmitter's window.	sscop send-window *packets*

A receiver window controls how many packets can be received before an acknowledgment is required. To change the receiver's window from the default value of 7, perform the following task in interface configuration mode:

Task	Command
Set the receiver's window.	sscop rcv-window *packets*

Closing an SVC

You can disconnect an idle SVC by completing the following task in EXEC mode:

Task	Command
Close the signaling PVC for an SVC.	atmsig close atm *slot*/0 *vcd*

CONFIGURING CLASSICAL IP AND ARP OVER ATM

Cisco implements both the ATM Address Resolution Protocol (ARP) server and ATM ARP client functions described in RFC 1577. RFC 1577 models an ATM network as a logical IP subnetwork on a LAN.

The tasks required to configure classical IP and ARP over ATM depend on whether the environment uses SVCs or PVCs.

Configuring Classical IP and ARP in an SVC Environment

The ATM ARP mechanism is applicable to networks that use SVCs. It requires a network administrator to configure only the device's own ATM address and that of a single ATM ARP server into each client device. When the client makes a connection to the ATM ARP server, the server sends ATM Inverse ARP requests to learn the IP network address and ATM address of the client on the network. It uses the addresses to resolve future ATM ARP requests from clients. Static configuration of the server is not required or needed.

In Cisco's implementation, the ATM ARP client tries to maintain a connection to the ATM ARP server. The ATM ARP server can tear down the connection, but the client attempts once each minute to bring the connection back up. No error messages are generated for a failed connection, but the client will not route packets until the ATM ARP server is connected and translates IP network addresses.

For each packet with an unknown IP address, the client sends an ATM ARP request to the server. Until that address is resolved, any IP packet routed to the ATM interface will cause the client to send another ATM ARP request. When the ARP server responds, the client opens a connection to the new destination so that any additional packets can be routed to it.

Cisco routers may be configured as ATM ARP clients to work with any ATM ARP server conforming to RFC 1577. Alternatively, one of the Cisco routers in a logical IP subnet (LIS) may be configured to act as the ATM ARP server itself. In this case, it automatically acts as a client as well. To configure classical IP and ARP in an SVC environment, perform one of following tasks:

- Configuring the Router as an ATM ARP Client
- Configuring the Router as an ATM ARP Server

Configuring the Router as an ATM ARP Client

In an SVC environment, configure the ATM ARP mechanism on the interface by performing the following tasks beginning in global configuration mode:

Task	Command
Step 1 Specify an AIP interface.	**interface atm** *slot*/0
Step 2 Specify the ATM address of the interface.	**atm nsap-address** *nsap-address*
Step 3 Specify the IP address of the interface.	**ip address** *address mask*
Step 4 Specify the ATM address of the ATM ARP server.	**atm arp-server nsap** *nsap-address*
Step 5 Enable the ATM interface.	**no shutdown**

NOTES

You can designate the current router interface as the ATM ARP server in Step 4 by typing **self** instead the NSAP address.

For an example of configuring the ATM ARP client, see the "ATM ARP Client Configuration in an SVC Environment Example" section later in this chapter.

Configuring the Router as an ATM ARP Server

Cisco's implementation of the ATM ARP server supports a single, nonredundant server per logical IP subnetwork (LIS) and supports one ATM ARP server per subinterface. Thus, a single AIP card can support multiple ARP servers by using multiple subinterfaces.

To configure the ATM ARP server, complete the following tasks beginning in global configuration mode:

Task	Command
Step 1 Specify an AIP interface.	**interface atm** *slot*/0
Step 2 Specify the ATM address of the interface.	**atm nsap-address** *nsap-address*
Step 3 Specify the IP address of the interface.	**ip address** *address mask*
Step 4 Identify the ATM ARP server for the IP subnetwork network and set the idle timer.	**atm arp-server time-out** *minutes*[*]
Step 5 Enable the ATM interface.	**no shutdown**

[*] When you use this form of the **atm arp-server** command, it indicates that this interface will perform the ATM ARP server functions. When you configure the ATM ARP client (as described earlier), the **atm arp-server** command is used—with a different keyword and argument—to identify a different ATM ARP server to the client.

NOTES

You can designate the current router interface as the ATM ARP server in Step 4 by typing **self** instead of the NSAP address.

The idle timer interval is the number of minutes a destination entry listed in the ATM ARP server's ARP table can be idle before the server takes any action to time out the entry.

For an example of configuring the ATM ARP server, see the "ATM ARP Server Configuration in an SVC Environment Example" section later in this chapter.

Configuring Classical IP and Inverse ARP in a PVC Environment

The ATM Inverse ARP mechanism is applicable to networks that use PVCs, where connections are established but the network addresses of the remote ends are not known. A server function is *not* used in this mode of operation.

In a PVC environment, configure the ATM Inverse ARP mechanism by performing the following tasks, beginning in global configuration mode:

Task	Command
Step 1 Specify an AIP interface and enter interface configuration mode.	**interface atm** *slot*/0
Step 2 Create a PVC and enable Inverse ARP on it.	**atm pvc** *vcd vci* **aal5snap** [**inarp** *minutes*][*]
Step 3 Enable the ATM interface.	**no shutdown**

[*] Additional options are permitted in the command in Step 2, but the order of options is important.

Repeat Step 2 for each PVC you want to create.

The **inarp** *minutes* interval specifies how often Inverse ARP datagrams will be sent on this virtual circuit. The default value is 15 minutes.

NOTES ——————————————————————————————————————

The ATM ARP and Inverse ATM ARP mechanisms work with IP only. All other protocols require **map-list** command entries to operate.

For an example of configuring the ATM Inverse ARP mechanism, see the "ATM Inverse ARP Configuration in a PVC Environment Example" section later in this chapter.

CONFIGURING TRAFFIC SHAPING FOR ATM SVCS

When you configure SVCs, you can define an ATM class to add support for traffic shaping on ATM SVCs. This applies a map class to an ATM interface. When an outgoing call is made by a static map client, or by a classical IP over ATM client, a map class will be determined for the call.

You must enter map-class configuration mode before you can define an ATM class. To enter map-class configuration mode and specify the ATM class for an ATM interface, perform the following tasks in global configuration mode:

Task	Command
Enter map-class configuration mode, specifying a map-class name.	**map-class atm** *class-name*
Specify an ATM class for an ATM interface.	**atm class** *class-name*

You can specify that an SVC be established on an ATM interface using only signaled traffic parameters. When you configure strict traffic-shaping on the router ATM interface, an SVC is established only if traffic shaping can be provided for the transmit cell flow per the signaled traffic parameters. If such shaping cannot be provided, the SVC is released.

If you do not configure strict traffic-shaping on the router ATM interface, an attempt is made to establish an SVC with traffic shaping for the transmit cell flow per the signaled traffic parameters. If such shaping cannot be provided, the SVC is installed with default shaping parameters; that is, it behaves as though a PVC were created without specifying traffic parameters.

To specify that an SVC be established on an ATM interface using only signaled traffic parameters, perform the following task in interface configuration mode:

Task	Command
Specify that an SVC be established on an ATM interface using only signaled traffic parameters.	**atm sig-traffic-shaping strict**

CUSTOMIZING THE AIP

You can customize the AIP. The features you can customize have default values that will most likely suit your environment and probably need not be changed. However, you might need to enter configuration commands, depending upon the requirements for your system configuration and the protocols you plan to route on the interface. Perform the following tasks if you need to customize the AIP:

- Configuring the Rate Queue
- Configuring MTU Size
- Setting the SONET PLIM
- Setting Loopback Mode
- Setting the Exception-Queue Length
- Limiting the Number of Virtual Circuits
- Setting the Raw-Queue Size
- Configuring Buffer Size
- Setting the VCI-to-VPI Ratio
- Setting the Source of the Transmit Clock

Configuring the Rate Queue

A rate queue defines the speed at which individual virtual circuits will transmit data to the remote end. You can configure permanent rate queues, allow the software to set up dynamic rate queues, or perform some combination of the two. The software dynamically creates rate queues when an **atm pvc** command specifies a peak/average rate that does not match any user-configured rate queue. The software dynamically creates all rate queues if you have not configured any.

Using Dynamic Rate Queues

The Cisco IOS software automatically creates rate queues as necessary to satisfy the requests of **atm pvc** commands. The peak rate for a virtual circuit descriptor (VCD) is set to the maximum that the physical layer interface module (PLIM) will allow, and the average rate is set equal to the peak rate. Then a rate queue is dynamically created for the peak rate of the VCD.

If dynamic rate queues do not satisfy your traffic shaping needs, you can configure permanent rate queues. See the "Dynamic Rate Queue Examples" section for examples of different rate queues created in response to **atm pvc** commands.

Configuring a Permanent Rate Queue

The AIP supports up to eight different peak rates. The peak rate is the maximum rate, in kilobits per second, at which a virtual circuit can transmit. Once attached to this rate queue, the virtual circuit is assumed to have its peak rate set to that of the rate queue. The rate queues are broken into a high-priority (0 through 3) and low-priority (4 through 7) bank.

You can configure each permanent rate queue independently to a portion of the overall bandwidth available on the ATM link. The combined bandwidths of all rate queues should not exceed the total bandwidth available. A warning message is displayed if you attempt to configure the combined rate queues beyond what is available to the AIP. The total bandwidth depends on the PLIM (see the "Setting AIP Interface Types" section in Chapter 1).

To set a permanent rate queue, perform the following task in interface configuration mode:

Task	Command
Configure a permanent rate queue, which defines the maximum speed at which an individual virtual circuit transmits data to a remote ATM host.	atm rate-queue *queue-number speed*

NOTES

In Cisco IOS Release 11.3, a permanent rate queue is automatically configured when you configure the peak rate using the **atm pvc** command. Therefore, you are not required to use the **atm rate-queue** command to configure the permanent rate queue.

Configuring MTU Size

Each interface has a default maximum packet size or maximum transmission unit (MTU) size. On the AIP, this number defaults to 4470 bytes; the maximum is 9188 bytes. The MTU can be set on a per-sub-interface basis as long as the interface MTU is as large or larger than the largest subinterface MTU. To set the maximum MTU size, perform the following task in interface configuration mode:

Task	Command
Set the maximum MTU size.	mtu *bytes*

Setting the SONET PLIM

The default SONET PLIM is STS-3C. To set the SONET PLIM to STM-1, perform the following task in interface configuration mode:

Task	Command
Set the SONET PLIM to STM-1.	atm sonet stm-1

Setting Loopback Mode

To loop all packets back to the AIP instead of the network, perform the following task in interface configuration mode:

Task	Command
Set loopback mode.	loopback diagnostic

To loop the incoming network packets back to the ATM network, perform the following task in interface configuration mode:

Task	Command
Set line loopback mode.	loopback line

Setting the Exception-Queue Length

The exception queue is used to report ATM events, such as CRC errors. By default, it holds 32 entries; the range is 8 to 256. It is unlikely you will need to configure the exception queue length; if you do, perform the following task in interface configuration mode:

Task	Command
Set the exception queue length.	atm exception-queue *number*

Limiting the Number of Virtual Circuits

By default, the ATM interface allows the maximum of 2048 virtual circuits. However, you can configure a lower number, thereby limiting the number of virtual circuits on which the AIP allows segmentation and reassembly to occur. Limiting the number of virtual circuits does not affect the VPI-VCI pair of each virtual circuit.

To set the maximum number of virtual circuits supported (including PVCs and SVCs), perform the following task in interface configuration mode:

Task	Command
Limit the number of virtual circuits.	atm maxvc *number*

Setting the Raw-Queue Size

The raw queue is used for raw ATM cells, which include Operation, Administration, and Maintenance (OAM) and Interim Local Management Interface (ILMI) cells. ILMI is a means of passing information to the router, including information about virtual connections and addresses.

The raw-queue size is in the range of 8 to 256 cells; the default is 32 cells. To set the raw-queue size, perform the following task in interface configuration mode:

Task	Command
Set the raw-queue size.	atm rawq-size *number*

Configuring Buffer Size

The number of receive buffers determines the maximum number of reassemblies that the AIP can perform simultaneously. The number of buffers defaults to 256, although it can be in the range from 0 to 512. To set the number of receive buffers, perform the following task in interface configuration mode:

Task	Command
Set the number of receive buffers.	atm rxbuff *number*

The number of transmit buffers determines the maximum number of fragmentations that the AIP can perform simultaneously. The number of buffers defaults to 256, although it can be in the range from 0 to 512. To set the number of transmit buffers, perform the following task in interface configuration mode:

Task	Command
Set the number of transmit buffers.	atm txbuff *number*

Setting the VCI-to-VPI Ratio

By default, the AIP supports 1024 VCIs per VPI. This value can be any power of 2 in the range from 16 to 1024. This value controls the memory allocation on the AIP to deal with the VCI table. It defines only the maximum number of VCIs to support per VPI.

To set the maximum number of VCIs to support per VPI and limit the highest VCI accordingly, perform the following task in interface configuration mode:

Task	Command
Set the number of VCIs per VPI.	atm vc-per-vp *number*

Setting the Source of the Transmit Clock

By default, the AIP expects the ATM switch to provide transmit clocking. To specify that the AIP generate the transmit clock internally for SONET and E3 PLIM operation, perform the following task in interface configuration mode:

Task	Command
Specify that the AIP generate the transmit clock internally.	atm clock internal

CONFIGURING ATM SUBINTERFACES FOR SMDS NETWORKS

An ATM adaption layer (AAL) defines the conversion of user information into cells by segmenting upper-layer information into cells at the transmitter and reassembling them at the receiver. AAL1 and AAL2 handle isochronous traffic, such as voice and video, and are not relevant to the router. AAL3/4 and AAL5 support data communications by segmenting and reassembling packets. Starting with Cisco IOS Release 10.2, both AAL3/4 and AAL5 are supported.

Our implementation of the AAL3/4 encapsulates each AAL3/4 packet in a Switched Multimegabit Data Service (SMDS) header and trailer. This feature supports both unicast and multicast addressing, and provides subinterfaces for multiple AAL3/4 connections over the same physical interface.

─── **NOTES** ──

Each subinterface configured to support AAL3/4 is allowed only one SMDS E.164 unicast address and one E.164 multicast address. The multicast address is used for all broadcast operations. In addition, only one virtual circuit is allowed on each subinterface that is being used for AAL3/4 processing, and it must be an AAL3/4 virtual circuit.

Support for AAL3/4 on an ATM interface requires static mapping of all protocols except IP. However, dynamic routing of IP can coexist with static mapping of other protocols on the same ATM interface.

To configure an ATM interface for SMDS networks, perform the following tasks in interface configuration mode:

Task		Command
Step 1	Enable AAL3/4 support on the affected ATM subinterface.	atm aal aal3/4
Step 2	Provide an SMDS E.164 unicast address for the subinterface.	atm smds-address *address*
Step 3	Provide an SMDS E.164 multicast address.	atm multicast *address*
Step 4	Configure a virtual path filter for the affected ATM subinterface.	atm vp-filter *hexvalue*
Step 5	Create an AAL3/4 PVC.	atm pvc *vcd vpi vci* aal34smds

The virtual path filter provides a mechanism for specifying which VPIs (or a range of VPIs) will be used for AAL3/4 processing during datagram reassembly. All other VPIs are mapped to AAL5 processing.

After configuring the ATM interface for SMDS networks, configure the interface for standard protocol configurations as needed.

For examples of configuring an ATM interface for AAL3/4 support, see the "PVC with AAL3/4 and SMDS Encapsulation Examples" section later in this chapter.

Limiting the Message Identifiers Allowed on Virtual Circuits

Message identifier (MID) numbers are used by receiving devices to reassemble cells from multiple sources into packets.

To ensure that the message identifiers are unique at the receiving end and, therefore, that messages can be reassembled correctly, you can limit the number of message identifiers allowed on a virtual circuit and assign different ranges of message identifiers to different PVCs.

To limit the number of message identifier numbers allowed on each virtual circuit and to assign different ranges of message identifiers to different PVCs, complete the following tasks in interface configuration mode:

Task	Command
Limit the number of message identifiers allowed per virtual circuit.	**atm mid-per-vc** *maximum*
Limit the range of message identifier values used on a PVC.	**atm pvc** *vcd vpi vci aal-encap midlow midhigh*

The maximum number of message identifiers per virtual circuit is set at 16 by default; valid values are 16, 32, 64, 128, 256, 512, or 1024. The default value for both *midlow* and *midhigh* is zero.

Setting the Virtual Path Filter Register

The virtual path filter allows you to specify which VPI or range of VPIs will be used for AAL3/4 processing. The default value of the AIP's virtual path filter register is 0x7B. To set the AIP virtual path filter register, perform the following task in interface configuration mode:

Task	Command
Set the virtual path filter register.	**atm vp-filter** *hexvalue*

CONFIGURING TRANSPARENT BRIDGING FOR THE AIP

Cisco's implementation of transparent bridging over ATM allows the spanning tree for an interface to support two different types of MAC addresses: E.164 addresses for AAL3/4-SMDS encapsulations and virtual circuit descriptors (VCDs) for AAL5-LLC Subnetwork Access Protocol (SNAP) encapsulations.

If the relevant interface or subinterface is explicitly put into a bridge group, as described in the "Enabling Fast-Switched Transparent Bridging for SNAP PVCs" section, AAL5-SNAP encapsulated bridge packets on a PVC are fast-switched.

If the relevant interface or subinterface is explicitly put into a bridge group, as described in the "Enabling Process-Switched Transparent Bridging for SMDS Subinterfaces" section, AAL3/4-SMDS encapsulated bridge packets are process-switched.

Cisco's bridging implementation supports IEEE 802.3 frame formats and IEEE 802.10 frame formats. The router can accept IEEE 802.3 frames with or without frame check sequence (FCS). When the router receives frames with FCS (RFC 1483 bridge frame formats with 0x0001 in the PID field of the SNAP header), it strips off the FCS and forwards the frame as necessary. All IEEE 802.3 frames that originate at or are forwarded by the router are sent as 802.3 bridge frames without FCS (bridge frame formats with 0x0007 in the PID field of the SNAP header).

NOTES

Transparent bridging for the AIP on Cisco 7500 series routers works only on AAL3/4-SMDS encapsulations (process-switched) and AAL5-LLC/SNAP PVCs (fast-switched). AAL5-MUX and AAL5-NLPID bridging are not yet supported on the Cisco 7500 series routers. Transparent bridging for ATM also does not operate in a switched virtual circuit (SVC) environment.

Enabling Process-Switched Transparent Bridging for SMDS Subinterfaces

To configure transparent bridging for AAL3/4 SMDS subinterfaces, complete the following steps beginning in global configuration mode:

Task		Command
Step 1	Specify an AIP interface and, optionally, a subinterface.	interface atm *slot*/0[.*subinterface*]
Step 2	Assign a source IP address and subnet mask to the interface, if needed.	ip address *ip-address mask*
Step 3	Enable an AAL3/4 (SMDS) subinterface.	atm aal aal3/4
Step 4	Configure a virtual path filter for the affected ATM subinterface.	atm vp-filter *hexvalue*
Step 5	Provide an SMDS E.164 unicast address for the subinterface.	atm smds-address *address*
Step 6	Provide an SMDS E.164 multicast address.	atm multicast *address*
Step 7	Create an AAL3/4 PVC.	atm pvc *vcd vpi vci* aal34smds
Step 8	Assign the interface to a bridge group.	bridge-group *group*

Task	Command
Step 9 Return to global configuration mode.	**exit**
Step 10 Define the type of spanning tree protocol as DEC.	**bridge** *group* **protocol dec**

No other configuration steps are required. All spanning tree updates are sent to the multicast E.164 address specified in Step 6. Routers on the remote end learn the unicast address of this router from the packets this router sends to them.

For an example of transparent bridging for an SMDS interface, see the "Transparent Bridging on an SMDS Subinterface Example" section at the end of this chapter. Process-switched transparent bridging is not supported on the ATM port adapter.

Enabling Fast-Switched Transparent Bridging for SNAP PVCs

To configure transparent bridging for LLC/SNAP PVCs, complete the following steps beginning in global configuration mode:

Task	Command
Step 1 Specify an AIP interface and, optionally, a subinterface.	**interface atm** *slot*/0[.*subinterface-number*]
Step 2 Assign a source IP address and subnet mask to the interface, if needed.	**ip address** *ip-address mask*
Step 3 Create one or more PVCs using AAL5-SNAP encapsulation.	**atm pvc** *vcd vpi vci* **aal5snap** **atm pvc** *vcd vpi vci* **aal5snap** **atm pvc** *vcd vpi vci* **aal5snap**
Step 4 Assign the interface to a bridge group.	**bridge-group** *group*
Step 5 Return to global configuration mode.	**exit**
Step 6 Define the type of spanning tree protocol as DEC.	**bridge** *group* **protocol dec**

No other configuration is required. Spanning tree updates are broadcast to all AAL5-SNAP virtual circuits that exist on the ATM interface. Only the AAL5-SNAP virtual circuits on the specific subinterface receive the updates. The router does not send spanning tree updates to AAL5-MUX and AAL5-NLPID virtual circuits.

For an example of transparent bridging for an AAL5-SNAP PVC, see the "Transparent Bridging on an AAL5-SNAP PVC Example" section at the end of this chapter.

CONFIGURING PPP OVER ATM

This section describes how to configure the AIP on the Cisco 7500 series routers to terminate multiple remote Point-to-Point Protocol (PPP) connections.

Before configuring PPP over ATM, the Cisco 7500 series routers must be equipped with Cisco IOS Release 11.2(4)F or later software. Remote branch offices must have PPP configured on PPP-compatible devices interconnecting directly to Cisco StrataCom's ATM Switch Interface Shelf (AXIS) equipment through a leased-line connection. The shelves provide frame forwarding encapsulation and are terminated on BPX cores prior to connecting to a Cisco 7500 series router. Figure 3–4 shows a typical scenario for using PPP over ATM.

Figure 3–4
A typical scenario for using PPP-over-ATM network environment.

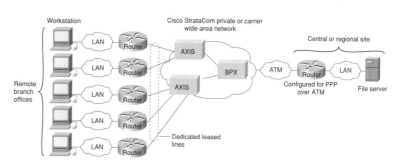

NOTES

If you need to configure the Cisco StrataCom AXIS shelf for frame forwarding at the remote sites, refer to the *AXIS 4 Command Supplement* for command line instructions or the *StrataView Plus Operations Guide* for StrataView Plus instructions. If you configure the AXIS using the command line interface, use the **addport** and **addchan** commands and select frame forwarding for the *port_type* and *chan_type* arguments, respectively.

When you configure PPP over ATM, a logical interface known as a virtual access interface associates each PPP connection to an ATM permanent virtual circuit (PVC). You can create this logical interface by configuring an ATM PVC as described in the "Creating a PPP-over-ATM PVC" section. This configuration encapsulates each PPP connection in a separate PVC, allowing each PPP connection to terminate at the router ATM interface as if received from a typical PPP serial interface.

The virtual access interface for each PVC obtains its configuration from a virtual interface template (virtual template) when the PVC is created. Before creating the ATM PVC, it is recommended that you create and configure a virtual template as described in the following "Creating and Configuring a Virtual Template" section.

To configure PPP over ATM, complete the following tasks. The first task in the following list is optional, but recommended; the remaining tasks are required:

- Creating and Configuring a Virtual Template

- Specifying an ATM Point-to-Point Subinterface
- Creating a PPP-over-ATM PVC

See an example of configuring PPP over ATM in the section "PPP-over-ATM Example" at the end of this chapter.

Creating and Configuring a Virtual Template

Prior to configuring the ATM PVC for PPP over ATM, you typically create and configure a virtual template. To create and configure a virtual template, complete the following tasks beginning in global configuration mode:

Task	Command
Step 1 Create a virtual template, and enter interface configuration mode.	**interface virtual-template** *number*
Step 2 Enable PPP encapsulation on the virtual template.	**encapsulation ppp**
Step 3 Optionally, enable IP without assigning a specific IP address on the LAN.	**ip unnumbered ethernet** *number*

Other optional configuration commands can be added to the virtual template configuration. For example, you can enable the PPP authentication on the virtual template using the **ppp authentication chap** command.

All PPP parameters are managed within the virtual template configuration. Configuration changes made to the virtual template are automatically propagated to the individual virtual access interfaces. Multiple virtual access interfaces can spawn from a single virtual template; hence, multiple PVCs can use a single virtual template. Cisco IOS software supports up to 25 virtual template configurations. If greater numbers of tailored configurations are required, an authentication, authorization, and accounting (AAA) server may be employed.

If the parameters of the virtual template are not explicitly defined before configuring the ATM PVC, the PPP interface is brought up using default values from the virtual template identified. Some parameters (such as an IP address) take effect only if specified before the PPP interface comes up. Therefore, it is recommended that you explicitly create and configure the virtual template before configuring the ATM PVC to ensure such parameters take effect. Alternatively, if parameters are specified after the ATM PVC has already been configured, you should issue a **shutdown** command followed by a **no shutdown** command on the ATM subinterface to restart the interface; this restart will cause the newly configured parameters (such as an IP address) to take effect.

Network addresses for the PPP-over-ATM connections are not configured on the main ATM interface or subinterface. Instead, these are configured on the appropriate virtual template or obtained via AAA.

The virtual templates support all standard PPP configuration commands; however, not all configurations are supported by the PPP-over-ATM virtual access interfaces. These restrictions are enforced at the time the virtual template configuration is applied (cloned) to the virtual access interface. These restrictions are described in the following paragraphs.

Only standard first-in, first-out (FIFO) queuing is supported when applied to PPP-over-ATM virtual access interfaces. Other types of queuing which are typically configured on the main interface are not (for example, fair-queuing). If configured, these configuration lines are ignored when applied to a PPP-over-ATM interface.

While fast switching is supported, flow and optimum switching are not; these configurations are ignored on the PPP-over-ATM virtual access interface. Fast switching is enabled by default for the virtual template configuration. If fast switching is not desired, use the **no ip route-cache** command to disable it.

The PPP reliable link that uses Link Access Procedure, Balanced (LAPB) is not supported.

Because an ATM PVC is configured for this feature, the following standard PPP features are not applicable and should not be configured:

- Asynchronous interfaces
- Dialup connections
- Callback on PPP

Specifying an ATM Point-to-Point Subinterface

After you create a virtual template for PPP over ATM, you must specify a point-to-point subinterface per PVC connection. To specify an ATM point-to-point subinterface, complete the following task in global configuration mode:

Task	Command
Specify an ATM point-to-point subinterface.	**interface atm** *slot/port.subinterface-number* **point-to-point**

Creating a PPP-over-ATM PVC

After you create a virtual template and point-to-point subinterfaces for PPP over ATM, you must create a PPP-over-ATM PVC. To create a PPP-over-ATM PVC, perform the following task in subinterface configuration mode:

Task	Command
Create a PPP-over-ATM PVC.	**atm pvc** *vcd vpi vci* **aal5ciscoppp** [*peak average* [*burst*]] [**oam** [*seconds*]] **virtual-template** *number*

The *peak* rate value is typically identical to the *average* rate or some suitable multiple thereof (up to 64 times for the Cisco 7500 series routers).

The *average* rate value should be set to the line rate available at the remote site, because the remote line rate will typically have the lowest speed of the connection. For example, if the remote site has a T1 link, set the line rate to 1.536 Mbps. Because the average rate calculation on the ATM PVC includes the cell headers, a line rate value plus 10 or 15 percent may result in better remote line utilization.

The *burst* size depends on the number of cells that can be buffered by receiving ATM switches and is coordinated with the ATM network connection provider. If this value is not specified, the default, which is the equivalent to one maximum length frame on the interface, is used.

Operations, Administration, and Maintenance (OAM) F5 cell loopback is provided by the remote AXIS shelf so OAM may be enabled. However, PPP over ATM is not typically an end-to-end ATM connection, and therefore enabling OAM is not recommended.

Once you configure the router for PPP over ATM, the PPP subsystem starts and the router attempts to send a PPP configure request to the remote peer. If the peer does not respond, the router periodically goes into a "listen" state and waits for a configuration request from the peer. After a timeout (typically 45 seconds), the router again attempts to reach the remote router by sending configuration requests.

The virtual access interface remains associated with a PVC as long as the PVC is configured. If you deconfigure the PVC, the virtual access interface is marked as deleted. If you shut down the associated ATM interface, you will also cause the virtual access interface to be marked as down (within 10 seconds), and you will bring the PPP connection down. If you set a keepalive timer of the virtual template on the interface, the virtual access interface uses the PPP echo mechanism to verify the existence of the remote peer. If an interface failure is detected and the PPP connection is brought down, the virtual access interface remains up.

MONITORING AND MAINTAINING THE ATM INTERFACE

After configuring the new interface, you can display its status. You can also display the current state of the ATM network and connected virtual circuits. To show current virtual circuits and traffic information, perform the following tasks in EXEC mode:

Task	Command
Display ATM-specific information about the ATM interface on the AIP.	**show atm interface atm** *slot*/0
Display the configured list of ATM static maps to remote hosts on an ATM network.	**show atm map**

Task	Command
Display global traffic information to and from all ATM networks connected to the router. Display a list of counters of all ATM traffic on this router.	show atm traffic
Display ATM virtual circuit information about all PVCs and SVCs (or a specific virtual circuit).	show atm vc [*vcd*]
Display statistics for the ATM interface.	show interfaces atm *slot*/0
Display SSCOP details for the ATM interface.	show sscop

ATM CONFIGURATION EXAMPLES

The examples in the following sections illustrate how to configure an ATM interface on the AIP for Cisco 7500 series routers. The following examples are provided:

- PVC with AAL5 and LLC/SNAP Encapsulation Examples
- PVCs in a Fully Meshed Network Example
- SVCs in a Fully Meshed Network Example
- ATM NSAP Address Example
- ATM ESI Address Example
- SVCs with Multipoint Signaling Example
- Traffic Parameters Example
- Classical IP and ARP Examples
- Dynamic Rate Queue Examples
- PVC with AAL3/4 and SMDS Encapsulation Examples
- Transparent Bridging on an SMDS Subinterface Example
- Transparent Bridging on an AAL5-SNAP PVC Example
- PPP-over-ATM Example

PVC with AAL5 and LLC/SNAP Encapsulation Examples

The following example creates PVC 5 on ATM interface 3/0. It uses LLC/SNAP encapsulation over AAL5. The interface is at IP address 1.1.1.1 with 1.1.1.5 at the other end of the connection. The static map list named *atm* declares that the next node is a broadcast point for multicast packets from IP. For further information, refer to the related task section "Creating a PVC," earlier in this chapter.

```
interface atm 3/0
 ip address 1.1.1.1 255.255.255.0
 atm rate-queue 1 100
 atm pvc 5 0 10 aal5snap
```

```
 ip route-cache cbus
 map-group atm
!
map-list atm
 ip 1.1.1.5 atm-vc 5 broadcast
```

The following example is of a typical ATM configuration for a PVC:

```
interface atm 4/0
 ip address 172.21.168.112 255.255.255.0
 map-group atm
 atm rate-queue 1 100
 atm maxvc 512
 atm pvc 1 1 1 aal5snap
 atm pvc 2 2 2 aal5snap
 atm pvc 6 6 6 aal5snap
 atm pvc 7 7 7 aal5snap
 decnet cost 1
 clns router iso-igrp comet
!
router iso-igrp comet
 net 47.0004.0001.0000.0c00.6666.00
!
router igrp 109
 network 172.21.0.0
!
ip domain-name CISCO.COM
!
map-list atm
 ip 172.21.168.110 atm-vc 1 broadcast
 clns 47.0004.0001.0000.0c00.6e26.00 atm-vc 6 broadcast
 decnet 10.1 atm-vc 2 broadcast
```

PVCs in a Fully Meshed Network Example

Figure 3–5 illustrates a fully meshed network. The configurations for Routers A, B, and C follow the figure. In this example, the routers are configured to use PVCs. *Fully meshed* indicates that any workstation can communicate with any other workstation. Note that the two **map-list** statements configured in Router A identify the ATM addresses of Routers B and C. The two **map-list** statements in Router B identify the ATM addresses of Routers A and C. The two **map-list** statements in Router C identify the ATM addresses of Routers A and B. For further information, refer to the related task section "Creating a PVC," earlier in this chapter.

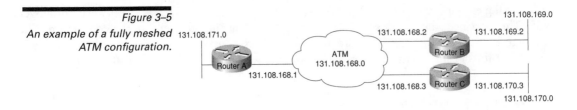

Figure 3–5
An example of a fully meshed ATM configuration.

Router A

```
ip routing
!
interface atm 4/0
 ip address 131.108.168.1 255.255.255.0
 atm rate-queue 1 100
 atm pvc 1 0 10 aal5snap
 atm pvc 2 0 20 aal5snap
 map-group test-a
!
map-list test-a
 ip 131.108.168.2 atm-vc 1 broadcast
 ip 131.108.168.3 atm-vc 2 broadcast
```

Router B

```
ip routing
!
interface atm 2/0
 ip address 131.108.168.2 255.255.255.0
 atm rate-queue 1 100
 atm pvc 1 0 20 aal5snap
 atm pvc 2 0 21 aal5snap
 map-group test-b
!
map-list test-b
 ip 131.108.168.1 atm-vc 1 broadcast
 ip 131.108.168.3 atm-vc 2 broadcast
```

Router C

```
ip routing
!
interface atm 4/0
 ip address 131.108.168.3 255.255.255.0
 atm rate-queue 1 100
 atm pvc 2 0 21 aal5snap
 atm pvc 4 0 22 aal5snap
 map-group test-c
!
map-list test-c
 ip 131.108.168.1 atm-vc 2 broadcast
 ip 131.108.168.2 atm-vc 4 broadcast
```

SVCs in a Fully Meshed Network Example

The following example is also a configuration for the fully meshed network shown in Figure 3–5, but this example uses SVCs. PVC 1 is the signaling PVC. For further information, refer to the related task section "Configuring the PVC that Performs SVC Call Setup," earlier in this chapter.

Router A

```
interface atm 4/0
 ip address 131.108.168.1 255.255.255.0
```

```
    map-group atm
    atm nsap-address AB.CDEF.01.234567.890A.BCDE.F012.3456.7890.1234.12
    atm rate-queue 1 100
    atm maxvc 1024
    atm pvc 1 0 5 qsaal
    !
    map-list atm
     ip 131.108.168.2 atm-nsap BC.CDEF.01.234567.890A.BCDE.F012.3456.7890.1334.13
     ip 131.108.168.3 atm-nsap BC.CDEF.01.234567.890A.BCDE.F012.3456.7890.1224.12
```

Router B

```
    interface atm 2/0
     ip address 131.108.168.2 255.255.255.0
    map-group atm
    atm nsap-address BC.CDEF.01.234567.890A.BCDE.F012.3456.7890.1334.13
    atm rate-queue 1 100
    atm maxvc 1024
    atm pvc 1 0 5 qsaal
    !
    map-list atm
     ip 131.108.168.1 atm-nsap AB.CDEF.01.234567.890A.BCDE.F012.3456.7890.1234.12
     ip 131.108.168.3 atm-nsap BC.CDEF.01.234567.890A.BCDE.F012.3456.7890.1224.12
```

Router C

```
    interface atm 4/0
     ip address 131.108.168.3 255.255.255.0
    map-group atm
    atm nsap-address BC.CDEF.01.234567.890A.BCDE.F012.3456.7890.1224.12
    atm rate-queue 1 100
    atm maxvc 1024
    atm pvc 1 0 5 qsaal
    !
    map-list atm
     ip 131.108.168.1 atm-nsap AB.CDEF.01.234567.890A.BCDE.F012.3456.7890.1234.12
     ip 131.108.168.2 atm-nsap BC.CDEF.01.234567.890A.BCDE.F012.3456.7890.1334.13
```

ATM NSAP Address Example

The following example assigns NSAP address AB.CDEF.01.234567.890A.BCDE.F012.3456.7890.
1234.12 to ATM interface 4/0. For further information, refer to the related task section "Configuring the Complete NSAP Address Manually," earlier in this chapter.

```
    interface atm 4/0
     atm nsap-address AB.CDEF.01.234567.890A.BCDE.F012.3456.7890.1234.12
```

You can display the ATM address for the interface by executing the **show interface atm** command.

ATM ESI Address Example

The following example on a Cisco 7500 series router assigns the ESI and selector field values and
sets up the ILMI PVC. For further information, refer to the related task section "Configuring the
ESI and Selector Fields," earlier in this chapter.

```
interface atm 4/0
 atm pvc 2 0 16 ilmi
 atm esi-address 345678901234.12
```

SVCs with Multipoint Signaling Example

The following example configures an ATM interface for SVCs using multipoint signaling. For further information, refer to the related task section "Configuring Point-to-Multipoint Signaling," earlier in this chapter.

```
interface atm 2/0
 ip address 4.4.4.6
 map-group atm_pri
 atm nsap-address de.cdef.01.234567.890a.bcde.f012.3456.7890.1234.12
 atm multipoint-signalling
 atm rate-queue 1 100
 atm maxvc 1024
 atm pvc 1 0 5 qsaal
!
map-list atm_pri
 ip 4.4.4.4 atm-nsap cd.cdef.01.234566.890a.bcde.f012.3456.7890.1234.12 broadcast
 ip 4.4.4.7 atm-nsap 31.3233.34.353637.3839.3031.3233.3435.3637.3839.30 broadcast
```

Traffic Parameters Example

The following example defines a map list to tie specified SVCs to protocol addresses of remote hosts and to specified map classes. Then it defines the map classes and sets traffic parameters for certain protocol traffic. For further information, refer to the related task section "Changing Traffic Values," earlier in this chapter.

```
map-list atmlist
 ip 131.108.170.21 atm-vc 12
 ip 131.108.180.121 atm-nsap 47.0091.81.000000.0041.0B0A.1581.0040.0B0A.1585.00 class
atmclass1
 ip 131.108.190.221 atm-nsap 47.0091.81.000000.0041.0B0A.1581.0040.0B0B.1585.00 class
atmclass2
map-class atm atmclass1
 atm forward-peak-cell-rate-clp1 8000
 atm backward-peak-cell-rate-clp1 8000
map-class atm atmclass2
 atm forward-peak-cell-rate-clp1 7000
 atm backward-peak-cell-rate-clp1 7000
interface atm 2/0
 map-group atmlist
```

Classical IP and ARP Examples

This section provides three examples of classical IP and ARP configuration, one each for a client and a server in an SVC environment, and one for ATM Inverse ARP in a PVC environment.

ATM ARP Client Configuration in an SVC Environment Example

This example configures an ATM ARP client in an SVC environment. Note that the client in this example and the ATM ARP server in the next example are configured to be on the same IP network. For further information, refer to the related task section "Configuring the Router as an ATM ARP Client," earlier in this chapter.

```
interface atm 2/0.5
 atm nsap-address ac.2456.78.040000.0000.0000.0000.0000.0000.0000.00
 ip address 10.0.0.2 255.0.0.0
 atm pvc 1 0 5 qsaal
 atm arp-server nsap ac.1533.66.020000.0000.0000.0000.0000.0000.0000.00
```

ATM ARP Server Configuration in an SVC Environment Example

The following example configures ATM on an interface and configures the interface to function as the ATM ARP server for the IP subnetwork. For further information, refer to the related task section "Configuring the Router as an ATM ARP Server," earlier in this chapter.

```
interface atm 0/0
 ip address 10.0.0.1 255.0.0.0
 atm nsap-address ac.1533.66.020000.0000.0000.0000.0000.0000.0000.00
 atm rate-queue 1 100
 atm maxvc 1024
 atm pvc 1 0 5 qsaal
 atm arp-server self
```

ATM Inverse ARP Configuration in a PVC Environment Example

The following example configures ATM on an interface and then configures the ATM Inverse ARP mechanism on the PVCs on the interface, with Inverse ARP datagrams sent every 5 minutes on three of the PVCs. The fourth PVC will not send Inverse ATM ARP datagrams, but will receive and respond to Inverse ATM ARP requests. For further information, refer to the related task section "Configuring Classical IP and Inverse ARP in a PVC Environment," earlier in this chapter.

```
interface atm 4/0
 ip address 172.21.1.111 255.255.255.0
 atm pvc 1 1 1 aal5snap inarp 5
 atm pvc 2 2 2 aal5snap inarp 5
 atm pvc 3 3 3 aal5snap inarp 5
 atm pvc 4 4 4 aal5snap inarp
```

No **map-group** and **map-list** commands are needed for IP.

Dynamic Rate Queue Examples

Both of the following examples assume that no permanent rate queues have been configured. The software dynamically creates rate queues when an **atm pvc** command specifies a peak or average rate that does not match any user-configured rate queue. For further information, refer to the related task section "Using Dynamic Rate Queues," earlier in this chapter.

In the following example, the software sets the peak rate for VCD 1 to the maximum that the PLIM will allow and sets the average rate to the peak rate. Then it creates a rate queue for the peak rate of this VCD.

```
atm pvc 1 1 1 aal5snap
```

In the following example, the software creates a 100-Mbps rate queue and assigns VCD 2 to that rate queue with an average rate of 50 Mbps and a burst size of 64 cells:

```
atm pvc 2 2 2 aal5snap 100000 50000 2
```

PVC with AAL3/4 and SMDS Encapsulation Examples

The following example provides a minimal configuration of an ATM interface to support AAL3/4 and SMDS encapsulation; no protocol configuration is shown. For further information, refer to the related task section "Configuring ATM Subinterfaces for SMDS Networks," earlier in this chapter.

```
interface atm 3/0
atm aal aal3/4
atm smds-address c140.888.9999
atm vp-filter 0
atm multicast e180.0999.9999
atm pvc 30 0 30 aal34smds
```

The following example shows how IP dynamic routing might coexist with static routing of another protocol:

```
interface atm 3/0
ip address 172.21.168.112 255.255.255.0
atm aal aal3/4
atm smds-address c140.888.9999
atm multicast e180.0999.9999
atm vp-filter 0
atm pvc 30 0 30 aal34smds
map-group atm
appletalk address 10.1
appletalk zone atm
!
map-group atm
atalk 10.2 smds c140.8111.1111 broadcast
```

This example shows that IP configured is dynamically routed, but that AppleTalk is statically routed. An AppleTalk remote host is configured at address 10.2 and is associated with SMDS address c140.8111.1111.

AAL3/4 associates a protocol address with an SMDS address, as shown in the last line of this example. In contrast, AAL5 static maps associate a protocol address with a PVC number.

Transparent Bridging on an SMDS Subinterface Example

In the following example, the router will send all spanning tree updates to the multicast address e111.1111.1111.1111. Routers receiving packets from this router will learn its unicast SMDS address, c111.1111.1111.1111, by examining the packets. For further information, refer to the related task section "Enabling Process-Switched Transparent Bridging for SMDS Subinterfaces," earlier in this chapter.

```
interface atm 4/0
 ip address 1.1.1.1 255.0.0.0
 atm aal aal3/4
 atm vp-filter 0
 atm smds-address c111.1111.1111.1111
 atm multicast e111.1111.1111.1111
 atm pvc 1 0 1 aal34smds
 bridge-group 1
!
bridge 1 protocol dec
```

Transparent Bridging on an AAL5-SNAP PVC Example

In the following example, three AAL5-SNAP PVCs are created on the same ATM interface. The router will broadcast all spanning tree updates to these AAL5-SNAP PVCs. No other virtual circuits will receive spanning tree updates. For further information, refer to the related task section "Enabling Fast-Switched Transparent Bridging for SNAP PVCs," earlier in this chapter.

```
interface atm 4/0
 ip address 1.1.1.1 255.0.0.0
 atm pvc 1 1 1 aal5snap
 atm pvc 2 2 2 aal5snap
 atm pvc 3 3 3 aal5snap
 bridge-group 1
!
bridge 1 protocol dec
```

PPP-over-ATM Example

The following example configures PPP over ATM to use PPP unnumbered link and Challenge Handshake Authentication Protocol (CHAP) authentication. For further information, refer to the related task section "Configuring PPP over ATM," earlier in this chapter.

```
configure terminal
!
interface virtual-template 2
 encapsulation ppp
 ip unnumbered ethernet 0/0
 ppp authentication chap
!
interface atm 2/0.2 point-to-point
!
 atm pvc 2 0 34 aal5ciscoppp 1536 1536 2 virtual-template 2
end
```

CHAPTER 4.

Configuring ATM on the ATM Port Adapter for Cisco 7200 and 7500 Series Routers

This chapter describes how to configure ATM on the ATM port adapter in the Cisco 7200 series routers and on the second generation Versatile Interface Processor (VIP2) in Cisco 7500 series routers.

NOTES

In Cisco IOS Release 11.3, all commands supported on the Cisco 7500 series routers are also supported on Cisco 7000 series routers equipped with RSP7000.

For a complete description of the ATM commands in this chapter, refer to Chapter 6, "ATM Commands."

ATM CONFIGURATION TASKS

To configure ATM on the ATM port adapter for a Cisco 7200 series router or Cisco 7500 series router, complete the tasks in the following list (they are described in the following sections). The first task is required, and you must configure at least one PVC or SVC. The virtual circuit options you configure must match in three places: on the router, on the ATM switch, and at the remote end of the PVC or SVC connection. The remaining tasks in the list are optional. The configuration tasks are as follows:

- Enabling the ATM Port Adapter Interface
- Configuring PVCs
- Configuring SVCs
- Configuring Classical IP and ARP over ATM (optional)
- Customizing the ATM Port Adapter Interface (optional)
- Configuring Transparent Bridging for the ATM Port Adapter (optional)
- Monitoring and Maintaining the ATM Interface (optional)

See the "ATM Configuration Examples" section of this chapter for examples.

ENABLING THE ATM PORT ADAPTER INTERFACE

This section describes how to begin configuring the ATM port adapter interface. The Cisco 7500 series routers identify an ATM port adapter interface address by its slot number (0 to the maximum number of available slots), port adapter number (0 or 1), and port number in the format *slot/port-adapter/port*. The Cisco 7200 series routers identify an ATM port adapter interface address by its slot number and port number in the format *slot/port*. Because each ATM port adapter contains a single ATM interface, the port number is always 0. For example, the *slot/port-adapter/port* address of an ATM port adapter interface on a Cisco 7500 series router installed in slot 1, port adapter 1, is 1/1/0.

To begin to configure the ATM port adapter interface, start the following task in privileged EXEC mode:

Task	Command
Step 1 At the privileged EXEC prompt, enter configuration mode from the terminal.	**configure terminal**
Step 2 Specify an ATM port adapter interface:	
• Cisco 7200 series router	**interface atm** *slot*/0
• Cisco 7500 series router	**interface atm** *slot/port-adapter*/0
Step 3 If IP routing is enabled on the system, optionally assign a source IP address and subnet mask to the interface.	**ip address** *ip-address mask*

To enable the ATM port adapter interface, perform the following task in interface configuration mode:

Task	Command
Change the shutdown state to up and enable the ATM interface, thereby starting the segmentation and reassembly (SAR) operation on the interface.	**no shutdown**

The **no shutdown** command passes an **enable** command to the ATM port adapter interface, which then begins segmentation and reassembly (SAR) operations. It also causes the ATM port adapter interface to configure itself based on the previous configuration commands sent.

CONFIGURING PVCS

To use a permanent virtual circuit (PVC), you must configure the PVC into both the router and the ATM switch. PVCs remain active until the circuit is removed from either configuration.

All virtual circuit characteristics listed in the section "Establishing ATM Port Adapter Virtual Circuits" in Chapter 1, "Wide-Area Networking Overview," apply to these PVCs. When a PVC is configured, all the configuration options are passed on to the ATM port adapter interface. These PVCs are writable into the nonvolatile RAM (NVRAM) as part of the Route Switch Processor (RSP) and Network Processing Engine (NPE) configuration and are used when the images are reloaded.

Some ATM switches might have point-to-multipoint PVCs that do the equivalent of broadcasting. If a point-to-multipoint PVC exists, then that PVC can be used as the sole broadcast PVC for all multicast requests.

To configure a PVC, perform the tasks in the following list. The first three tasks are required; the last two are optional:

- Creating a PVC
- Mapping a Protocol Address to a PVC
- Configuring Communication with the ILMI
- Configuring ATM UNI Version Override (optional)
- Configuring Transmission of Loopback Cells to Verify Connectivity (optional)

Creating a PVC

To create a PVC on the ATM port adapter interface, perform the following task in interface configuration mode:

Task	Command
Create a PVC.	**atm pvc** *vcd vpi vci aal-encap* [**oam** *seconds*]

When you implement a PVC, you create a virtual circuit descriptor (VCD) and attach it to the VPI and VCI. A VCD is an ATM interface-specific mechanism that identifies to the ATM interface which VPI-VCI pair to use for a particular packet. The ATM interface requires this feature to manage the packets for transmission. The number chosen for the VCD is independent of the VPI-VCI pair used.

When you create a PVC, you also specify the ATM adaptation layer (AAL) and encapsulation. If you specify AAL3/4-SMDS encapsulation, you have the option of setting the starting message identifier (MID) number and ending MID number using the *midlow* and *midhigh* arguments.

You can also configure the PVC for communication with the Interim Local Management Interface (ILMI) so the router can receive Simple Network Management Protocol (SNMP) traps and new network prefixes. Refer to the "Configuring Communication with the ILMI" section of this chapter for details.

You can also optionally configure the PVC to send Operation, Administration, and Maintenance (OAM) F5 loopback cells to verify connectivity on the virtual circuit. The remote end must respond by echoing back such cells.

See examples of PVC configurations in the section "ATM Configuration Examples," later in this chapter.

Mapping a Protocol Address to a PVC

The ATM interface supports a static mapping scheme that identifies the ATM address of remote hosts or routers. This address is specified as a virtual circuit descriptor (VCD) for a PVC (or an NSAP address for SVC operation). This section describes how to map a PVC to an address, which is a required task if you are configuring a PVC.

You enter mapping commands as groups. You first create a map list and then associate it with an interface. Begin the following tasks in global configuration mode:

Task		Command
Step 1	Create a map list by naming it, and enter map-list configuration mode.	**map-list** *name*
Step 2	Associate a protocol and address to a specific virtual circuit.	*protocol protocol-address* **atm-vc** *vcd* [**broadcast**]
Step 3	Associate a protocol and address to a different virtual circuit.	*protocol protocol-address* **atm-vc** *vcd* [**broadcast**]
Step 4	Specify an ATM port adapter interface and enter interface configuration mode:	
	• Cisco 7200 series router	**interface atm** *slot*/0
	• Cisco 7500 series router	**interface atm** *slot*/*port-adapter*/0
Step 5	Associate a map list to an interface.	**map-group** *name*

A map list can contain multiple map entries, as Steps 2 and 3 in the preceding task table illustrate. The **broadcast** keyword specifies that this map entry is to be used when the corresponding protocol sends broadcast packets to the interface (for example, any network routing protocol updates). If you do not specify **broadcast**, the ATM software is prevented from sending routing protocol updates to the remote hosts.

If you do specify **broadcast**, but do *not* set up point-to-multipoint signaling, pseudobroadcasting is enabled. To eliminate pseudobroadcasting and set up point-to-multipoint signaling on virtual circuits configured for broadcasting, see the "Configuring Point-to-Multipoint Signaling" section in this chapter.

In Step 5, associate the map list with the ATM interface you specified in Step 4. Use the same *name* argument you used in the **map-list** command.

You can create multiple map lists, but only one map list can be associated with an interface. Different map lists can be associated with different interfaces.

Configuring Communication with the ILMI

You can configure a PVC for communication with the Interim Local Management Interface (ILMI) so the router can receive SNMP traps and new network prefixes. The recommended vpi/vci for ILMI is 0 16. To configure ILMI communication, complete the following task in interface configuration mode:

Task	Command
Create an ILMI PVC on a major interface.	**atm pvc** *vcd vpi vci* **ilmi**

--- **NOTES** ---

This ILMI PVC can be set up only on a major interface, not on the subinterfaces.

After you have configured an ILMI PVC, you can optionally enable the ILMI keepalive function by completing the following task in interface configuration mode:

Task	Command
Optionally, enable ILMI keepalives and set the interval between keepalives.	**atm ilmi-keepalive** [*seconds*]

No other configuration steps are required.

ILMI address registration for receipt of SNMP traps and new network prefixes is enabled by default. The ILMI keepalive function is disabled by default; when enabled, the default interval between keepalives is 3 seconds.

Configuring ATM UNI Version Override

Normally, when ILMI link autodetermination is enabled on the interface and is successful, the router takes the user-network interface (UNI) version returned by ILMI. If the ILMI link autodetermination process is unsuccessful or ILMI is disabled, the UNI version defaults to 3.0. You can override this default by using the **atm uni-version** command. The **no** form of the command sets the UNI version to the one returned by ILMI if ILMI is enabled and the link autodetermination is successful. Otherwise, the UNI version will revert to 3.0.

Task	Command
Override UNI version used by router.	**atm uni-version** *version number*

No other configuration steps are required.

Configuring Transmission of Loopback Cells to Verify Connectivity

You can optionally configure the PVC to send OAM F5 loopback cells to verify connectivity on the virtual circuit. The remote end must respond by echoing back such cells. If OAM response cells are missed (indicating the lack of connectivity), the system console displays a debug message indicating the failure of the PVC, provided the **debug atm errors** command is enabled. If you suspect that a PVC is faulty, enabling OAM cell generation and the **debug atm errors** command allows you to monitor the status of the PVC.

To configure the transmission of OAM F5 loopback cells, add the **oam** keyword to the **atm pvc** command, as shown in the following task:

Task	Command
Configure transmission of OAM F5 cells on the PVC.	**atm pvc** *vcd vpi vci aal-encap* [**oam** *seconds*]

CONFIGURING SVCS

ATM switched virtual circuit (SVC) service operates much like X.25 SVC service, although ATM allows much higher throughput. Virtual circuits are created and released dynamically, providing user bandwidth on demand. This service requires a signaling protocol between the router and the switch.

The ATM signaling software provides a method of dynamically establishing, maintaining, and clearing ATM connections at the User-Network Interface (UNI). The ATM signaling software conforms to ATM Forum UNI 3.0 or ATM Forum UNI 3.1, depending on what version is selected by ILMI or configuration.

In UNI mode, the user is the router and the network is an ATM switch. This is an important distinction. The Cisco router does not perform ATM-level call routing. Instead, the ATM switch does the ATM call routing, and the router routes packets through the resulting circuit. The router is viewed as the user and the LAN interconnection device at the end of the circuit, and the ATM switch is viewed as the network.

Figure 4–1 illustrates the router position in a basic ATM environment. The router is used primarily to interconnect LANs via an ATM network. The workstation connected directly to the destination ATM switch illustrates that you can connect not only routers to ATM switches, but also any computer with an ATM interface that conforms to the ATM Forum UNI specification.

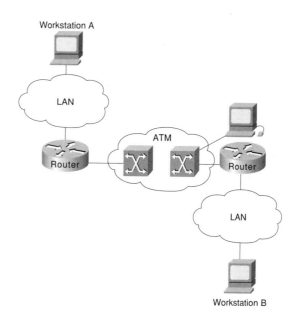

Figure 4–1
The router in a basic ATM environment.

You must complete the tasks in the following list to use SVCs:

- Configuring the PVC that Performs SVC Call Setup
- Configuring the NSAP Address

The tasks in the following list are optional SVC tasks for customizing your network. These tasks are considered advanced; the default values are almost always adequate. You should not have to perform these tasks unless you need to customize your particular SVC connection. The tasks are as follows:

- Configuring the Idle Timeout Interval
- Configuring Point-to-Multipoint Signaling
- Configuring IP Multicast over ATM Point-to-Multipoint Virtual Circuits
- Configuring SSCOP
- Closing an SVC

Configuring the PVC that Performs SVC Call Setup

Unlike X.25 service, which uses in-band signaling (connection establishment done on the same circuit as data transfer), ATM uses out-of-band signaling. One dedicated PVC exists between the router and the ATM switch, over which all SVC call establishment and call termination requests flow. After the call is established, data transfer occurs over the SVC, from router to router. The signaling that accomplishes the call setup and teardown is called *Layer 3 signaling* or the *Q.2931 protocol*.

For out-of-band signaling, a signaling PVC must be configured before any SVCs can be set up. Figure 4–2 illustrates that a signaling PVC from the source router to the ATM switch is used to set up two SVCs. This is a fully meshed network; workstations A, B, and C all can communicate with each other.

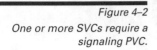

Figure 4–2

One or more SVCs require a signaling PVC.

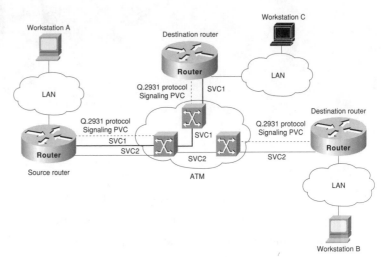

To configure the signaling PVC for all SVC connections, perform the following task in interface configuration mode:

Task	Command
Configure the signaling PVC for a major interface that uses SVCs.	**atm pvc** *vcd vpi vci* **qsaal**

— **NOTES** ————————————————————————————————

This signaling PVC can be set up only on a major interface, not on the subinterfaces.

The VPI and VCI values must be configured consistently with the local switch. The standard value of VPI is 0; the standard value of VCI is 5.

See the section "SVCs in a Fully Meshed Network Example," near the end of this chapter for a sample ATM signaling configuration.

Configuring the NSAP Address

Every ATM interface involved with signaling must be configured with a network service access point (NSAP) address. The NSAP address is the ATM address of the interface and must be unique across the network.

To configure an NSAP address, complete one of the following tasks:

- Configuring the Complete NSAP Address Manually
- Configuring the ESI and Selector Fields

Configuring the Complete NSAP Address Manually

When you configure the ATM NSAP address manually, you must enter the entire address in hexadecimal format because each digit entered represents a hexadecimal digit. To represent the complete NSAP address, you must enter 40 hexadecimal digits in the following format:

```
xx.xxxx.xx.xxxxxx.xxxx.xxxx.xxxx.xxxx.xxxx.xxxx.xx
```

— **NOTES** ——————————————————————————————————————

All ATM NSAP addresses may be entered in the dotted hexadecimal format shown, which conforms to the UNI specification. The dotted method provides some validation that the address is a legal value. If you know your address format is correct, the dots may be omitted.

Because the interface has no default NSAP address, you must configure the NSAP address for SVCs. To set the ATM interface's source NSAP address, perform the following task in interface configuration mode:

Task	Command
Configure the ATM NSAP address for an interface.	**atm nsap-address** *nsap-address*

See an example of assigning an NSAP address to an ATM interface in the section "ATM NSAP Address Example," near the end of this chapter.

Configuring the ESI and Selector Fields

To configure the end station ID (ESI) and selector fields, the switch must be capable of delivering the NSAP address prefix to the router via ILMI and the router must be configured with a PVC for communication with the switch via ILMI.

To configure the router to get the NSAP prefix from the switch and use locally entered values for the remaining fields of the address, complete the following tasks in interface configuration mode:

Task	Command
Step 1 Configure a PVC for communicating with the switch via ILMI.	**atm pvc** *vcd* **0 16 ilmi**
Step 2 Enter the ESI and selector fields of the NSAP address.	**atm esi-address** *esi.selector*

The **atm esi-address** command allows you to configure the ATM address by entering the ESI (12 hexadecimal characters) and the selector byte (2 hexadecimal characters). The ATM prefix (26 hexadecimal characters) is provided by the ATM switch. To get the prefix from the ATM switch, the ILMI PVC must be configured on the router and the ATM switch must be able to supply a prefix via ILMI.

The **atm esi-address** and **atm nsap-address** commands are mutually exclusive. Configuring the router with the **atm esi-address** command negates the **atm nsap-address** setting, and vice versa.

You can also specify a keepalive interval for the ILMI PVC. See the "Configuring Communication with the ILMI" section of this chapter for more information.

To see an example of setting up the ILMI PVC and assigning the ESI and selector fields of an NSAP address, go to the section "ATM ESI Address Example" near the end of this chapter.

Configuring the Idle Timeout Interval

You can specify an interval of inactivity after which any idle SVC on an interface is disconnected. This timeout interval might help control costs and free router memory and other resources for other uses.

To change the idle timeout interval, perform the following task in interface configuration mode:

Task	Command
Configure the interval of inactivity after which an idle SVC will be disconnected.	**atm idle-timeout** *seconds*

The default idle timeout interval is 300 seconds (5 minutes).

Configuring Point-to-Multipoint Signaling

Point-to-multipoint signaling (or multicasting) allows the router to send one packet to the ATM switch and have the switch replicate the packet to the destinations. It replaces pseudobroadcasting on specified virtual circuits for protocols configured for broadcasting.

You configure multipoint signaling on an ATM interface after you have mapped protocol addresses to NSAPs and configured one or more protocols for broadcasting.

After multipoint signaling is set, the router uses existing static map entries that have the **broadcast** keyword set to establish multipoint calls. The call is established to the first destination with a Setup message. Additional parties are added to the call with AddParty messages each time a multicast packet is sent. One multipoint call will be established for each logical subnet of each protocol that has the **broadcast** keyword set.

To configure multipoint signaling on an ATM port adapter interface, complete the following tasks beginning in global configuration mode. The first task is required to configure this feature; the others are optional:

Task		Command
Step 1	Specify an ATM port adapter interface:	
	• Cisco 7200 series router	**interface atm** *slot*/0
	• Cisco 7500 series router	**interface atm** *slot*/*port-adapter*/0
Step 2	Provide a protocol address for the interface.	*protocol protocol-address mask*
Step 3	Associate a map list to the interface.	**map-group** *name*
Step 4	Provide an ATM NSAP address for the interface.	**atm nsap-address** *nsap-address*
Step 5	Configure the signaling PVC for the interface that uses SVCs.	**atm pvc** *vcd vpi vci* **qsaal**
Step 6	Associate a map list with the map group.	**map-list** *name*
Step 7	Configure a broadcast protocol for the remote NSAP address on the SVC. Repeat this step for other NSAP addresses, as needed.	*protocol protocol-address* **atm-nsap** a*tm-nsap-address* **broadcast**
Step 8	Enable multipoint signaling to the ATM switch.	**atm multipoint-signalling**
Step 9	Limit the frequency of sending AddParty messages (optional).	**atm multipoint-interval interval**

If multipoint virtual circuits are closed, they are reopened with the next multicast packet. Once the call is established, additional parties are added to the call when additional multicast packets are sent. If a destination never comes up, the router constantly attempts to add it to the call by means of multipoint signaling.

For an example of configuring multipoint signaling on an interface that is configured for SVCs, see the "SVCs with Multipoint Signaling Example" section later in this chapter.

Configuring SSCOP

The Service-Specific Connection-Oriented Protocol (SSCOP) resides in the service-specific convergence sublayer (SSCS) of the ATM adaptation layer (AAL). SSCOP is used to transfer variable-length service data units (SDUs) between users of SSCOP. SSCOP provides for the recovery of lost or corrupted SDUs.

The tasks in this section customize the SSCOP feature to a particular network or environment and are optional. The features have default values and are valid in most installations. Before customizing these features, you should have a good understanding of SSCOP and the network involved.

Setting the Poll Timer

The poll timer controls the maximum time between transmission of a POLL PDU when sequential data (SD) or SDP PDUs are queued for transmission or are outstanding pending acknowledgments. To change the poll timer from the default value of 10 seconds, perform the following task in interface configuration mode:

Task	Command
Set the poll timer.	**sscop poll-timer** *seconds*

Setting the Keepalive Timer

The keepalive timer controls the maximum time between transmission of a POLL PDU when no SD or SDP PDUs are queued for transmission or are outstanding pending acknowledgments. To change the keepalive timer from the default value of 30 seconds, perform the following task in interface configuration mode:

Task	Command
Set the keepalive timer.	**sscop keepalive-timer** *seconds*

Setting the Connection Control Timer

The connection control timer determines the time between transmission of BGN, END, or RS (resynchronization) PDUs as long as an acknowledgment has not been received. Connection control performs the establishment, release, and resynchronization of an SSCOP connection.

To change the connection control timer from the default value of 10 seconds, perform the following task in interface configuration mode:

Task	Command
Set the connection control timer.	**sscop cc-timer** *seconds*

To change the retry count of the connection control timer from the default value of 10, perform the following task in interface configuration mode:

Task	Command
Set the number of times that SSCOP will retry to transmit BGN, END, or RS PDUs when they have not been acknowledged.	**sscop max-cc** *retries*

Setting the Transmitter and Receiver Windows

A transmitter window controls how many packets can be transmitted before an acknowledgment is required. To change the transmitter's window from the default value of 7, perform the following task in interface configuration mode:

Task	Command
Set the transmitter's window.	**sscop send-window** *packets*

A receiver window controls how many packets can be received before an acknowledgment is required. To change the receiver's window from the default value of 7, perform the following task in interface configuration mode:

Task	Command
Set the receiver's window.	**sscop rcv-window** *packets*

Closing an SVC

You can disconnect an idle SVC by completing the following task in EXEC mode:

Task	Command
Close the signaling PVC for an SVC:	
• Cisco 7200 series router	**atmsig close atm** *slot*/0 *vcd*
• Cisco 7500 series router	**atmsig close atm** *slot*/*port-adapter*/0 *vcd*

CONFIGURING CLASSICAL IP AND ARP OVER ATM

Cisco implements both the ATM Address Resolution Protocol (ARP) server and ATM ARP client functions described in RFC 1577. RFC 1577 models an ATM network as a logical IP subnetwork on a LAN.

The tasks required to configure classical IP and ARP over ATM depend on whether the environment uses SVCs or PVCs.

Configuring Classical IP and ARP in an SVC Environment

The ATM ARP mechanism is applicable to networks that use SVCs. It requires a network administrator to configure only the device's own ATM address and that of a single ATM ARP server into each client device. When the client makes a connection to the ATM ARP server, the server sends ATM Inverse ARP requests to learn the IP network address and ATM address of the client on the network. It uses the addresses to resolve future ATM ARP requests from clients. Static configuration of the server is not required or needed.

In Cisco's implementation, the ATM ARP client tries to maintain a connection to the ATM ARP server. The ATM ARP server can tear down the connection, but the client attempts once each minute to bring the connection back up. No error messages are generated for a failed connection, but the client will not route packets until the ATM ARP server is connected and translates IP network addresses.

For each packet with an unknown IP address, the client sends an ATM ARP request to the server. Until that address is resolved, any IP packet routed to the ATM interface will cause the client to send another ATM ARP request. When the ARP server responds, the client opens a connection to the new destination so that any additional packets can be routed to it.

Cisco routers may be configured as ATM ARP clients to work with any ATM ARP server conforming to RFC 1577. Alternatively, one of the Cisco routers in a logical IP subnet (LIS) may be configured to act as the ATM ARP server itself. In this case, it automatically acts as a client as well. To configure classical IP and ARP in an SVC environment, perform one of the following tasks:

- Configuring the Router as an ATM ARP Client
- Configuring the Router as an ATM ARP Server

Configuring the Router as an ATM ARP Client

In an SVC environment, configure the ATM ARP mechanism on the interface by performing the following tasks beginning in global configuration mode:

Task	Command
Step 1 Specify an ATM port adapter interface:	
• Cisco 7200 series router	**interface atm** *slot*/0
• Cisco 7500 series router	**interface atm** *slot*/*port-adapter*/0
Step 2 Specify the ATM address of the interface.	**atm nsap-address** *nsap-address*
Step 3 Specify the IP address of the interface.	**ip address** *address mask*
Step 4 Specify the ATM address of the ATM ARP server.	**atm arp-server nsap** *nsap-address*
Step 5 Enable the ATM interface.	**no shutdown**

You can designate the current router interface as the ATM ARP server in Step 4 by typing **self** instead of the NSAP address. For an example of configuring the ATM ARP client, see the "ATM ARP Client Configuration in an SVC Environment Example" section later in this chapter.

Configuring the Router as an ATM ARP Server

Cisco's implementation of the ATM ARP server supports a single, nonredundant server per logical IP subnetwork (LIS) and supports one ATM ARP server per subinterface. Thus, a single ATM port adapter interface can support multiple ARP servers by using multiple subinterfaces.

To configure the ATM ARP server, complete the following tasks beginning in global configuration mode:

Task		Command
Step 1	Specify an ATM port adapter interface:	
	• Cisco 7200 series router	**interface atm** *slot*/0
	• Cisco 7500 series router	**interface atm** *slot*/*port-adapter*/0
Step 2	Specify the ATM address of the interface.	**atm arp-server nsap** *nsap-address*
Step 3	Specify the IP address of the interface.	**ip address** *address mask*
Step 4	Identify the ATM ARP server for the IP subnetwork network and set the idle timer.	**atm arp-server time-out** *minutes*[*]
Step 5	Enable the ATM interface.	**no shutdown**

[*] When you use the form of the **atm arp-server** command in step 4, it indicates that this interface will perform the ATM ARP server functions. When you configure the ATM ARP client (as described earlier), the **atm arp-server** command is used—with a different keyword and argument—to identify a different ATM ARP server to the client.

You can designate the current router interface as the ATM ARP server in Step 2 by typing **self** instead of the NSAP address.

The idle timer interval is the number of minutes a destination entry listed in the ATM ARP server's ARP table can be idle before the server takes any action to timeout the entry.

For an example of configuring the ATM ARP server, see the "ATM ARP Server Configuration in an SVC Environment Example" section later in this chapter.

Configuring Classical IP and Inverse ARP in a PVC Environment

The ATM Inverse ARP mechanism is applicable to networks that use PVCs where connections are established, but the network addresses of the remote ends are not known. A server function is *not* used in this mode of operation.

In a PVC environment, configure the ATM Inverse ARP mechanism by performing the following tasks, beginning in global configuration mode:

Task	Command
Step 1 Specify an ATM port adapter interface and enter interface configuration mode:	
• Cisco 7200 series router	**interface atm** *slot*/0
• Cisco 7500 series router	**interface atm** *slot*/*port-adapter*/0
Step 2 Create a PVC and enable Inverse ARP on it.	**atm pvc** *vcd vci* **aal5snap** [**inarp** *minutes*]*
Step 3 Enable the ATM interface.	**no shutdown**

* Additional options are permitted in the **atm** command in Step 2, but the order of options is important.

Repeat Step 2 for each PVC you want to create.

The **inarp** *minutes* interval specifies how often Inverse ARP datagrams will be sent on this virtual circuit. The default value is 15 minutes.

NOTES

The ATM ARP and Inverse ATM ARP mechanisms work with IP only. All other protocols require **map-list** command entries to operate.

For an example of configuring the ATM Inverse ARP mechanism, see the "ATM Inverse ARP Configuration in a PVC Environment Example" section later in this chapter.

CUSTOMIZING THE ATM PORT ADAPTER INTERFACE

You can customize the ATM port adapter interface. The features you can customize have default values that will most likely suit your environment and probably do not need to be changed. However, you might need to enter configuration commands, depending upon the requirements for your system configuration and the protocols you plan to route on the interface. Perform the tasks in the following list if you need to customize the ATM port adapter interface:

- Configuring MTU Size
- Setting the SONET PLIM
- Setting Loopback Mode
- Limiting the Number of Virtual Circuits
- Configuring Buffer Sizes
- Setting the VCI-to-VPI Ratio
- Setting the Source of the Transmit Clock

Configuring MTU Size

Each interface has a default maximum packet size or maximum transmission unit (MTU) size. On the ATM port adapter interface, this number defaults to 4470 bytes; the maximum is 17966 bytes. The MTU can be set on a per-subinterface basis as long as the interface MTU is as large as or larger than the largest subinterface MTU. To set the maximum MTU size, perform the following task in interface configuration mode:

Task	Command
Set the maximum MTU size.	mtu *bytes*

Setting the SONET PLIM

The default SONET PLIM is STS-3C. To set the SONET PLIM to STM-1, perform the following task in interface configuration mode:

Task	Command
Set the SONET PLIM to STM-1.	atm sonet stm-1

Setting Loopback Mode

To loop all packets back to the ATM port adapter interface instead of the network, perform the following task in interface configuration mode:

Task	Command
Set loopback mode.	loopback [diagnostic	line]

Limiting the Number of Virtual Circuits

By default, the ATM interface allows the maximum of 2048 virtual circuits. However, you can configure a lower number, thereby limiting the number of virtual circuits on which the ATM port adapter interface allows segmentation and reassembly to occur. Limiting the number of virtual circuits does not affect the VPI-VCI pair of each virtual circuit.

To set the maximum number of virtual circuits supported (including PVCs and SVCs), perform the following task in interface configuration mode:

Task	Command
Limit the number of virtual circuits.	atm maxvc *number*

Configuring Buffer Sizes

The number of receive buffers determines the maximum number of reassemblies that the ATM port adapter interface can perform simultaneously. The number of buffers defaults to 256, although it can range from 0 to 512. To set the number of receive buffers, perform the following task in interface configuration mode:

Task	Command
Set the number of receive buffers.	**atm rxbuff** *number*

The number of transmit buffers determines the maximum number of fragmentations that the ATM port adapter interface can perform simultaneously. The number of buffers defaults to 256, although it can range from 0 to 512. To set the number of transmit buffers, perform the following task in interface configuration mode:

Task	Command
Set the number of transmit buffers.	**atm txbuff** *number*

Setting the VCI-to-VPI Ratio

By default, the ATM port adapter interface supports 1024 VCIs per VPI. This value can be any power of 2 ranging from 16 to 2048. This value controls the memory allocation on the ATM port adapter interface to deal with the VCI table. It defines only the maximum number of VCIs to support per VPI.

To set the maximum number of VCIs to support per VPI and limit the highest VCI accordingly, perform the following task in interface configuration mode:

Task	Command
Set the number of VCIs per VPI.	**atm vc-per-vp** *number*

Setting the Source of the Transmit Clock

By default, the ATM port adapter interface expects the ATM switch to provide transmit clocking. To specify that the ATM port adapter interface generate the transmit clock internally for SONET and E3 PLIM operation, perform the following task in interface configuration mode:

Task	Command
Specify that the ATM port adapter interface generate the transmit clock internally.	**atm clock internal**

CONFIGURING TRANSPARENT BRIDGING FOR THE ATM PORT ADAPTER

Cisco's implementation of transparent bridging over ATM on the ATM port adapter allows the spanning tree for an interface to support virtual circuit descriptors (VCDs) for AAL5-LLC Subnetwork Access Protocol (SNAP) encapsulations. If the relevant interface or subinterface is explicitly put into a bridge group, as described in the next task table, AAL5-SNAP encapsulated bridge packets on a PVC are fast-switched.

Cisco's bridging implementation supports IEEE 802.3 frame formats and IEEE 802.10 frame formats. The router can accept IEEE 802.3 frames with or without frame check sequence (FCS). When the router receives frames with FCS (RFC 1483 bridge frame formats with 0x0001 in the PID field of the SNAP header), it strips off the FCS and forwards the frame as necessary. All IEEE 802.3 frames that originate at, or are forwarded by, the router are sent as 802.3 bridge frames without FCS (bridge frame formats with 0x0007 in the PID field of the SNAP header).

NOTES

Transparent bridging for the ATM port adapter on Cisco 7500 series routers works only on AAL5-LLC/SNAP PVCs (fast-switched). AAL3/4-SMDS, AAL5-MUX, and AAL5-NLPID bridging are not yet supported on the Cisco 7500 series routers. Transparent bridging for ATM also does not operate in a switched virtual circuit (SVC) environment.

To configure transparent bridging for LLC/SNAP PVCs, complete the following steps beginning in global configuration mode:

Task		Command
Step 1	Specify an ATM port adapter interface and, optionally, a subinterface:	
	• Cisco 7200 series router	**interface atm** *slot*/0
	• Cisco 7500 series router	**interface atm** *slot*/*port-adapter*/0
Step 2	Assign a source IP address and subnet mask to the interface, if needed.	**ip address** *ip-address mask*
Step 3	Create one or more PVCs using AAL5-SNAP encapsulation.	**atm pvc** *vcd vpi vci* **aal5snap**
		atm pvc *vcd vpi vci* **aal5snap**
		atm pvc *vcd vpi vci* **aal5snap**
Step 4	Assign the interface to a bridge group.	**bridge-group** *group*
Step 5	Return to global configuration mode.	**exit**
Step 6	Define the type of spanning tree protocol as DEC.	**bridge** *group* **protocol dec**

No other configuration is required. Spanning tree updates are broadcast to all AAL5-SNAP virtual circuits that exist on the ATM interface. Only the AAL5-SNAP virtual circuits on the specific sub-interface receive the updates. The router does not send spanning tree updates to AAL5-MUX and AAL5-NLPID virtual circuits.

For an example of transparent bridging for an AAL5-SNAP PVC, see the "Transparent Bridging on an AAL5-SNAP PVC Example" section in this chapter.

MONITORING AND MAINTAINING THE ATM INTERFACE

After configuring the new interface, you can display its status. You can also display the current state of the ATM network and connected virtual circuits. To show current virtual circuits and traffic information, perform the following tasks in EXEC mode:

Task	Command
Display ATM-specific information about the ATM port adapter interface:	
• Cisco 7200 series router	**show atm interface atm** *slot*/0
• Cisco 7500 series router	**show atm interface atm** *slot*/*port-adapter*/0
Display the configured list of ATM static maps to remote hosts on an ATM network.	**show atm map**
Display global traffic information to and from all ATM networks connected to the router. Display a list of counters of all ATM traffic on this router.	**show atm traffic**
Display ATM virtual circuit information about all PVCs and SVCs (or a specific virtual circuit).	**show atm vc** [*vcd*]
Display statistics for the ATM port adapter interface:	
• Cisco 7200 series router	**show interfaces atm** *slot*/0
• Cisco 7500 series router	**show interfaces atm** *slot*/*port-adapter*/0
Display SSCOP details for the ATM interface.	**show sscop**

ATM CONFIGURATION EXAMPLES

The examples in the following sections illustrate how to configure an ATM port adapter interface on the Cisco 7200 and 7500 series routers:

- PVC with AAL5 and LLC/SNAP Encapsulation Examples
- PVCs in a Fully Meshed Network Example
- SVCs in a Fully Meshed Network Example

- ATM NSAP Address Example
- ATM ESI Address Example
- SVCs with Multipoint Signaling Example
- Classical IP and ARP Examples
- Transparent Bridging on an AAL5-SNAP PVC Example
- ATM Port Adapters Connected Back-to-Back Example

PVC with AAL5 and LLC/SNAP Encapsulation Examples

The following example creates PVC 5 on ATM interface 3/0. It uses LLC/SNAP encapsulation over AAL5. The interface is at IP address 1.1.1.1 with 1.1.1.5 at the other end of the connection. The static map list named *atm* declares that the next node is a broadcast point for multicast packets from IP. For further information, refer to the related task section "Creating a PVC," earlier in this chapter.

```
interface atm 3/0
 ip address 1.1.1.1 255.255.255.0
 atm pvc 5 0 10 aal5snap
 map-group atm
!
map-list atm
 ip 1.1.1.5 atm-vc 5 broadcast
```

The following example is of a typical ATM configuration for a PVC:

```
interface atm 4/0
 ip address 172.21.168.112 255.255.255.0
 map-group atm
 atm pvc 1 1 1 aal5snap
 atm pvc 2 2 2 aal5snap
 atm pvc 6 6 6 aal5snap
 atm pvc 7 7 7 aal5snap
 decnet cost 1
 clns router iso-igrp comet
!
router iso-igrp comet
 net 47.0004.0001.0000.0c00.6666.00
!
router igrp 109
 network 172.21.0.0
!
ip domain-name CISCO.COM
!
map-list atm
 ip 172.21.168.110 atm-vc 1 broadcast
 clns 47.0004.0001.0000.0c00.6e26.00 atm-vc 6 broadcast
 decnet 10.1 atm-vc 2 broadcast
```

PVCs in a Fully Meshed Network Example

Figure 4–3 illustrates a fully meshed network. The configurations for Routers A, B, and C follow the figure. In this example, the routers are configured to use PVCs. *Fully meshed* indicates that any workstation can communicate with any other workstation. Note that the two **map-list** statements configured in Router A identify the ATM addresses of Routers B and C. The two **map-list** statements in Router B identify the ATM addresses of Routers A and C. The two **map list** statements in Router C identify the ATM addresses of Routers A and B. For further information, refer to the related task section "Creating a PVC," earlier in this chapter.

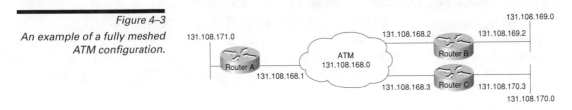

Figure 4–3

An example of a fully meshed ATM configuration.

Router A

```
ip routing
!
interface atm 4/0
 ip address 131.108.168.1 255.255.255.0
 atm rate-queue 1 100
 atm pvc 1 0 10 aal5snap
 atm pvc 2 0 20 aal5snap
 map-group test-a
!
map-list test-a
 ip 131.108.168.2 atm-vc 1 broadcast
 ip 131.108.168.3 atm-vc 2 broadcast
```

Router B

```
ip routing
!
interface atm 2/0
 ip address 131.108.168.2 255.255.255.0
 atm rate-queue 1 100
 atm pvc 1 0 20 aal5snap
 atm pvc 2 0 21 aal5snap
 map-group test-b
!
map-list test-b
 ip 131.108.168.1 atm-vc 1 broadcast
 ip 131.108.168.3 atm-vc 2 broadcast
```

Router C

```
ip routing
!
```

```
interface atm 4/0
 ip address 131.108.168.3 255.255.255.0
 atm rate-queue 1 100
 atm pvc 2 0 21 aal5snap
 atm pvc 4 0 22 aal5snap
 map-group test-c
!
map-list test-c
 ip 131.108.168.1 atm-vc 2 broadcast
 ip 131.108.168.2 atm-vc 4 broadcast
```

SVCs in a Fully Meshed Network Example

The following example is also a configuration for the fully meshed network shown in Figure 4–3, but this example uses SVCs. PVC 1 is the signaling PVC. For further information, refer to the related task section "Configuring the PVC that Performs SVC Call Setup," earlier in this chapter.

Router A

```
interface atm 4/0
 ip address 131.108.168.1 255.255.255.0
 map-group atm
 atm nsap-address AB.CDEF.01.234567.890A.BCDE.F012.3456.7890.1234.12
 atm rate-queue 1 100
 atm maxvc 1024
 atm pvc 1 0 5 qsaal
!
map-list atm
 ip 131.108.168.2 atm-nsap BC.CDEF.01.234567.890A.BCDE.F012.3456.7890.1334.13
 ip 131.108.168.3 atm-nsap BC.CDEF.01.234567.890A.BCDE.F012.3456.7890.1224.12
```

Router B

```
interface atm 2/0
 ip address 131.108.168.2 255.255.255.0
 map-group atm
 atm nsap-address BC.CDEF.01.234567.890A.BCDE.F012.3456.7890.1334.13
 atm rate-queue 1 100
 atm maxvc 1024
 atm pvc 1 0 5 qsaal
!
map-list atm
 ip 131.108.168.1 atm-nsap AB.CDEF.01.234567.890A.BCDE.F012.3456.7890.1234.12
 ip 131.108.168.3 atm-nsap BC.CDEF.01.234567.890A.BCDE.F012.3456.7890.1224.12
```

Router C

```
interface atm 4/0
 ip address 131.108.168.3 255.255.255.0
 map-group atm
 atm nsap-address BC.CDEF.01.234567.890A.BCDE.F012.3456.7890.1224.12
 atm rate-queue 1 100
 atm maxvc 1024
 atm pvc 1 0 5 qsaal
!
```

```
map-list atm
 ip 131.108.168.1 atm-nsap AB.CDEF.01.234567.890A.BCDE.F012.3456.7890.1234.12
 ip 131.108.168.2 atm-nsap BC.CDEF.01.234567.890A.BCDE.F012.3456.7890.1334.13
```

ATM NSAP Address Example

The following example assigns NSAP address AB.CDEF.01.234567.890A.BCDE.F012.3456.7890. 1234.12 to ATM interface 4/0. For further information, refer to the related task section "Configuring the Complete NSAP Address Manually," earlier in this chapter.

```
interface atm 4/0
 atm nsap-address AB.CDEF.01.234567.890A.BCDE.F012.3456.7890.1234.12
```

You can display the ATM address for the interface by executing the **show interface atm** command.

ATM ESI Address Example

The following example on a Cisco 7500 series router assigns the ESI and selector field values and sets up the ILMI PVC. For further information, refer to the related task section "Configuring the ESI and Selector Fields," earlier in this chapter.

```
interface atm 4/0
 atm pvc 2 0 16 ilmi
 atm esi-address 345678901234.12
```

SVCs with Multipoint Signaling Example

The following example configures an ATM interface for SVCs using multipoint signaling. For further information, refer to the related task section "Configuring Point-to-Multipoint Signaling," earlier in this chapter.

```
interface atm 2/0
 ip address 4.4.4.6
 map-group atm_pri
 atm nsap-address de.cdef.01.234567.890a.bcde.f012.3456.7890.1234.12
 atm multipoint-signalling
 atm rate-queue 1 100
 atm maxvc 1024
 atm pvc 1 0 5 qsaal
!
map-list atm_pri
 ip 4.4.4.4 atm-nsap cd.cdef.01.234566.890a.bcde.f012.3456.7890.1234.12 broadcast
 ip 4.4.4.7 atm-nsap 31.3233.34.353637.3839.3031.3233.3435.3637.3839.30 broadcast
```

Classical IP and ARP Examples

This section provides three examples of classical IP and ARP configuration, one each for a client and a server in an SVC environment, and one for ATM Inverse ARP in a PVC environment.

ATM ARP Client Configuration in an SVC Environment Example

This example configures an ATM ARP client in an SVC environment. Note that the client in this example and the ATM ARP server in the next example are configured to be on the same IP network.

For further information, refer to the related task section "Configuring the Router as an ATM ARP Client," earlier in this chapter.

```
interface atm 2/0.5
 atm nsap-address ac.2456.78.040000.0000.0000.0000.0000.0000.0000.00
 ip address 10.0.0.2 255.0.0.0
 atm pvc 1 0 5 qsaal
 atm arp-server nsap ac.1533.66.020000.0000.0000.0000.0000.0000.0000.00
```

ATM ARP Server Configuration in an SVC Environment Example

The following example configures ATM on an interface and configures the interface to function as the ATM ARP server for the IP subnetwork. For further information, refer to the related task section "Configuring the Router as an ATM ARP Server," earlier in this chapter.

```
interface atm 0/0
 ip address 10.0.0.1 255.0.0.0
 atm nsap-address ac.1533.66.020000.0000.0000.0000.0000.0000.0000.00
 atm rate-queue 1 100
 atm maxvc 1024
 atm pvc 1 0 5 qsaal
 atm arp-server self
```

ATM Inverse ARP Configuration in a PVC Environment Example

The following example configures ATM on an interface and then configures the ATM Inverse ARP mechanism on the PVCs on the interface, with Inverse ARP datagrams sent every 5 minutes on three of the PVCs. The fourth PVC will not send Inverse ATM ARP datagrams, but will receive and respond to Inverse ATM ARP requests. For further information, refer to the related task section "Configuring Classical IP and Inverse ARP in a PVC Environment," earlier in this chapter.

```
interface atm 4/0
 ip address 172.21.1.111 255.255.255.0
 atm pvc 1 1 1 aal5snap inarp 5
 atm pvc 2 2 2 aal5snap inarp 5
 atm pvc 3 3 3 aal5snap inarp 5
 atm pvc 4 4 4 aal5snap inarp
```

No **map-group** and **map-list** commands are needed for IP.

Transparent Bridging on an AAL5-SNAP PVC Example

In the following example, three AAL5-SNAP PVCs are created on the same ATM interface. The router will broadcast all spanning tree updates to these AAL5-SNAP PVCs. No other virtual circuits will receive spanning tree updates. For further information, refer to the related task section "Configuring Transparent Bridging for the ATM Port Adapter," earlier in this chapter.

```
interface atm4/0
 ip address 1.1.1.1 255.0.0.0
 atm pvc 1 1 1 aal5snap
 atm pvc 2 2 2 aal5snap
 atm pvc 3 3 3 aal5snap
 bridge-group 1
!
bridge 1 protocol dec
```

ATM Port Adapters Connected Back-to-Back Example

The following example shows the configuration needed to connect two ATM port adapters back to back. Two routers, each containing an ATM port adapter, are connected directly with a standard cable that allows you to verify the operation of the ATM port or to directly link the routers to build a larger node.

By default, the ATM port adapter expects a connected ATM switch to provide transmit clocking. To specify that the ATM port adapter generates the transmit clock internally for SONET PLIM operation, add the **atm clock internal** command to your configuration.

Router A

```
interface atm 3/0
 ip address 192.168.1.10 255.0.0.0
 no keepalive
 map-group atm-in
 atm clock internal
 atm pvc 1 1 5 aal5snap
 !
map-list atm-in
 ip 192.168.1.20 atm-vc 1 broadcast
```

Router B

```
interface atm 3/0
 ip address 192.168.1.20 255.0.0.0
 no keepalive
 map-group atm-in
 atm clock internal
 atm pvc 1 1 5 aal5snap
 !
map-list atm-in
 ip 192.168.1.10 atm-vc 1 broadcast
```

CHAPTER 5

Configuring ATM on the NPM for Cisco 4500 and 4700 Routers

This chapter describes how to configure ATM on the Cisco 4500 and 4700 routers that have the ATM Network Processor Module (NPM).

For a complete description of the ATM commands in this chapter, refer to Chapter 6, "ATM Commands."

ATM CONFIGURATION TASK LIST

To configure ATM in Cisco 4500 and Cisco 4700 routers, complete the tasks in the following list. The first task is required, and then you must configure at least one PVC or SVC. The virtual circuit options you configure must match in three places: on the router, on the ATM switch, and at the remote end of the PVC or SVC connection. The remaining tasks in the list are optional. The configuration tasks are as follows:

- Enabling the NPM
- Configuring PVCs
- Configuring SVCs
- Configuring Classical IP and ARP over ATM (optional)
- Configuring Traffic Shaping for ATM SVCs (optional)
- Customizing the NPM (optional)
- Configuring ATM Subinterfaces for SMDS Networks (optional)
- Configuring Transparent Bridging for the NPM (optional)
- Configuring PPP over ATM (optional)
- Monitoring and Maintaining the ATM Interface (optional)

See the "ATM Configuration Examples" section near the end of this chapter for configuration examples.

ENABLING THE NPM

This section describes how to begin configuring the network processor module (NPM). The Cisco 4500 and Cisco 4700 identify an interface address by its unit number. To begin to configure the NPM, start the following task in privileged EXEC mode:

Task	Command
Step 1 At the privileged EXEC prompt, enter configuration mode from the terminal.	**configure terminal**
Step 2 Specify the NPM interface number.	**interface atm** *number*
Step 3 If IP routing is enabled on the system, optionally assign a source IP address and subnet mask to the interface.	**ip address** *ip-address mask*

To enable the ATM interface, perform the following task in interface configuration mode:

Task	Command
Change the shutdown state to up and enable the ATM interface, thereby starting the segmentation and reassembly (SAR) operation on the interface.	**no shutdown**

The **no shutdown** command passes an **enable** command to the NPM, which then begins segmentation and reassembly (SAR) operations. It also causes the NPM to configure itself based on the previous configuration commands sent.

CONFIGURING PVCS

To use a permanent virtual circuit (PVC), you must configure the PVC into both the router and the ATM switch. PVCs remain active until the circuit is removed from either configuration.

All virtual circuit characteristics listed in the section "Understanding NPM Virtual Circuits" in Chapter 1, "Wide-Area Networking Overview," apply to these PVCs. When a PVC is configured, all the configuration options are passed on to the NPM. These PVCs are writable into the nonvolatile RAM (NVRAM) as part of the Route Processor (RP) configuration and are used when the RP image is reloaded.

Some ATM switches might have point-to-multipoint PVCs that do the equivalent of broadcasting. If a point-to-multipoint PVC exists, then that PVC can be used as the sole broadcast PVC for all multicast requests.

To configure a PVC, perform the tasks in the following list. The first three tasks are required; the last two are optional:

- Creating a PVC
- Mapping a Protocol Address to a PVC
- Configuring Communication with the ILMI
- Configuring ATM UNI Version Override (optional)
- Configuring Transmission of Loopback Cells to Verify Connectivity (optional)

Creating a PVC

To create a PVC on the NPM interface, perform the following task in interface configuration mode:

Task	Command
Create a PVC.	**atm pvc** *vcd vpi vci aal-encap* [[*midlow midhigh*] [*peak average burst*]] [**oam** *seconds*] [**inarp** *minutes*]

When you create a PVC, you create a virtual circuit descriptor (VCD) and attach it to the VPI and VCI. A VCD is an NPM-specific mechanism that identifies to the NPM which VPI-VCI pair to use for a particular packet. The NPM requires this feature to manage the packets for transmission. The number chosen for the VCD is independent of the VPI-VCI pair used.

When you create a PVC, you also specify the ATM adaptation layer (AAL) and encapsulation. If you specify AAL3/4-SMDS encapsulation, you have the option of setting the starting message identifier (MID) number and ending MID number using the *midlow* and *midhigh* arguments. A rate queue is used that matches the *peak* and *average* rate selections, which are specified in kilobits per second. Omitting a *peak* and *average* value causes the PVC to be connected to the highest bandwidth rate queue available. In this case, the *peak* and *average* values are equal.

You can also configure the PVC for communication with the Interim Local Management Interface (ILMI) so the router can receive Simple Network Management Protocol (SNMP) traps and new network prefixes. Refer to the "Configuring Communication with the ILMI" section in this chapter for details.

You can also optionally configure the PVC to send Operation, Administration, and Maintenance (OAM) F5 loopback cells to verify connectivity on the virtual circuit. The remote end must respond by echoing back such cells.

See examples of PVC configurations on the Cisco 4500 in the section "ATM Configuration Examples," near the end of this chapter.

Mapping a Protocol Address to a PVC

The ATM interface supports a static mapping scheme that identifies the ATM address of remote hosts or routers. This address is specified as a virtual circuit descriptor (VCD) for a PVC (or an

NSAP address for SVC operation). This section describes how to map a PVC to an address, which is a required task if you are configuring a PVC.

You enter mapping commands as groups. You first create a map list and then associate it with an interface. Begin the following tasks in global configuration mode:

Task		Command
Step 1	Create a map list by naming it, and enter map-list configuration mode.	**map-list** *name*
Step 2	Associate a protocol and address to a specific virtual circuit.	*protocol protocol-address* **atm-vc** *vcd* [**broadcast**]
Step 3	Associate a protocol and address to a different virtual circuit.	*protocol protocol-address* **atm-vc** *vcd* [**broadcast**]
Step 4	Specify the NPM interface number and enter interface configuration mode.	**interface atm** *number*
Step 5	Associate a map list to an interface.	**map-group** *name*

A map list can contain multiple map entries, as Steps 2 and 3 in the preceding task table illustrate. The **broadcast** keyword specifies that this map entry is to be used when the corresponding protocol sends broadcast packets to the interface (for example, any network routing protocol updates). If you do not specify **broadcast**, the ATM software is prevented from sending routing protocol updates to the remote host.

If you do specify **broadcast**, but do *not* set up point-to-multipoint signaling, pseudobroadcasting is enabled. To eliminate pseudobroadcasting and set up point-to-multipoint signaling on virtual circuits configured for broadcasting, see the "Configuring Point-to-Multipoint Signaling" section in this chapter.

In Step 5, associate the map list with the ATM interface you specified in Step 4. Use the same *name* argument you used in the **map-list** command. You can create multiple map lists, but you can associate only one map list with an interface. Different map lists can be associated with different interfaces. See the examples at the end of this chapter.

Configuring Communication with the ILMI

You can configure a PVC for communication with the Interim Local Management Interface (ILMI) so the router can receive SNMP traps and new network prefixes. The recommended *vpi* and *vci* values for the ILMI PVC are 0 and 16, respectively. To configure ILMI communication, complete the following task in interface configuration mode:

Task	Command
Create an ILMI PVC on a major interface.	**atm pvc** *vcd vpi vci* **ilmi**

NOTES

This ILMI PVC can be set up only on a major interface, not on the subinterfaces.

Once you have configured an ILMI PVC, you can optionally enable the ILMI keepalive function by completing the following task in interface configuration mode:

Task	Command
Optionally, enable ILMI keepalives and set the interval between keepalives.	**atm ilmi-keepalive** [*seconds*]

No other configuration steps are required.

ILMI address registration for receipt of SNMP traps and new network prefixes is enabled by default. The ILMI keepalive function is disabled by default; when enabled, the default interval between keepalives is 3 seconds.

Configuring ATM UNI Version Override

Normally, when ILMI link autodetermination is enabled on the interface and is successful, the router takes the user-network interface (UNI) version returned by ILMI. If the ILMI link autodetermination process is unsuccessful or if ILMI is disabled, the UNI version defaults to 3.0. You can override this default by using the **atm uni-version** command. The **no** form of the command sets the UNI version to the one returned by ILMI if ILMI is enabled and the link autodetermination is successful. Otherwise, the UNI version will revert to 3.0.

Task	Command
Override UNI version used by router.	**atm uni-version** *version number*

No other configuration steps are required.

Configuring Transmission of Loopback Cells to Verify Connectivity

You can optionally configure the PVC to send OAM F5 loopback cells to verify connectivity on the virtual circuit. The remote end must respond by echoing back such cells. If OAM response cells are missed (indicating the lack of connectivity), the system console displays a debug message indicating the failure of the PVC, provided the **debug atm errors** command is enabled. If you suspect that a

PVC is faulty, enabling OAM cell generation and the **debug atm errors** command allows you to monitor the status of the PVC.

To configure the transmission of OAM F5 loopback cells, add the **oam** keyword to the **atm pvc** command, as shown in the following task:

Task	Command
Configure transmission of OAM F5 cells on the PVC, specifying how often OAM F5 cells should be sent.	**atm pvc** *vcd vpi vci aal-encap* [[*midlow midhigh*] [*peak average burst*]] [**oam** *seconds*] [**inarp** *minutes*]

CONFIGURING SVCs

ATM switched virtual circuit (SVC) service operates much like X.25 SVC service, although ATM allows much higher throughput. Virtual circuits are created and released dynamically, providing user bandwidth on demand. This service requires a signaling protocol between the router and the switch.

The ATM signaling software provides a method of dynamically establishing, maintaining, and clearing ATM connections at the User-Network Interface (UNI). The ATM signaling software conforms to ATM Forum UNI 3.0 or ATM Forum UNI 3.1, depending on what version is selected by ILMI or configuration.

In UNI mode, the user is the router and the network is an ATM switch. This is an important distinction. The Cisco router does not perform ATM-level call routing; the ATM switch does the ATM call routing. The router routes packets through the resulting circuit. The router is viewed as the user and the LAN interconnection device at the end of the circuit, and the ATM switch is viewed as the network.

Figure 5–1 illustrates the router position in a basic ATM environment. The router is used primarily to interconnect LANs via an ATM network. The workstation connected directly to the destination ATM switch illustrates that you can connect not only routers to ATM switches, but also any computer with an ATM interface that conforms to the ATM Forum UNI specification.

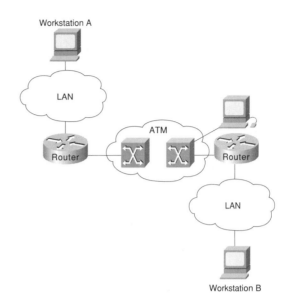

Figure 5–1
The router position in a basic
ATM environment.

You must complete the tasks in the following list to use SVCs:

- Configuring the PVC that Performs SVC Call Setup
- Configuring the NSAP Address

The tasks in the following list are optional SVC tasks for customizing your network. These tasks are considered advanced; the default values are almost always adequate. You should not have to perform these tasks unless you need to customize your particular SVC connection:

- Configuring the Idle Timeout Interval
- Configuring Point-to-Multipoint Signaling
- Configure IP Multicast over ATM Point-to-Multipoint Virtual Circuits
- Changing Traffic Values
- Configuring SSCOP
- Closing an SVC

Configuring the PVC that Performs SVC Call Setup

Unlike X.25 service, which uses in-band signaling (connection establishment done on the same circuit as data transfer), ATM uses out-of-band signaling. This means that one dedicated PVC exists between the router and the ATM switch, over which all SVC call establishment and call termination requests flow. After the call is established, data transfer occurs over the SVC, from router to router. The signaling that accomplishes the call setup and teardown is called *Layer 3 signaling* or the *Q.2931 protocol*.

For out-of-band signaling, a signaling PVC must be configured before any SVCs can be set up. Figure 5–2 illustrates a signaling PVC from the source router to the ATM switch used to set up two SVCs. This is a fully meshed network; workstations A, B, and C all can communicate with each other.

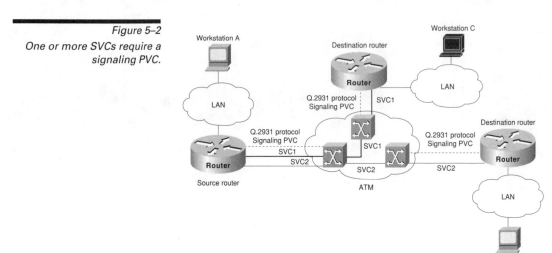

Figure 5–2
One or more SVCs require a signaling PVC.

To configure the signaling PVC for all SVC connections, perform the following task in interface configuration mode:

Task	Command
Configure the signaling PVC for a major interface that uses SVCs.	**atm pvc** *vcd vpi vci* **qsaal**

NOTES

This signaling PVC can be set up only on a major interface, not on the subinterfaces.

The VPI and VCI values must be configured consistently with the local switch. The standard value of VPI is 0; the standard value of VCI is 5. See the section "SVCs in a Fully Meshed Network Example" at the end of this chapter for a sample ATM signaling configuration.

Configuring the NSAP Address

Every ATM interface involved with signaling must be configured with a network service access point (NSAP) address. The NSAP address is the ATM address of the interface and must be unique across the network.

Complete one of the following tasks to configure an NSAP address:

- Configuring the Complete NSAP Address Manually
- Configuring the ESI and Selector Fields

   If you choose to configure the end station ID (ESI) and selector fields, you also must configure a PVC to communicate with the switch via ILMI. The switch then provides the prefix field of the NSAP address.

Configuring the Complete NSAP Address Manually

When you configure the ATM NSAP address manually, you must enter the entire address in hexadecimal format since each digit entered represents a hexadecimal digit. To represent the complete NSAP address, you must enter 40 hexadecimal digits in the following format:

```
xx.xxxx.xx.xxxxxx.xxxx.xxxx.xxxx.xxxx.xxxx.xxxx.xx
```

NOTES

All ATM NSAP addresses may be entered in the dotted hexadecimal format shown, which conforms to the UNI specification. The dotted method provides some validation that the address is a legal value. If you know your address format is correct, the dots may be omitted.

Because the interface has no default NSAP address, you must configure the NSAP address for SVCs. To set the ATM interface's source NSAP address, perform the following task in interface configuration mode:

Task	Command
Configure the ATM NSAP address for an interface.	**atm nsap-address** *nsap-address*

See an example of assigning an NSAP address to an ATM interface in the section "ATM NSAP Address Example," near the end of this chapter.

Configuring the ESI and Selector Fields

To use this method of entering the router's NSAP address, the switch must be capable of delivering the NSAP address prefix to the router via ILMI and the router must be configured with a PVC for communication with the switch via ILMI.

To configure the router to get the NSAP prefix from the switch and use locally entered values for the remaining fields of the address, complete the following tasks in interface configuration mode:

Task	Command
Step 1 Configure a PVC for communicating with the switch via ILMI.	**atm pvc** *vcd* **0 16 ilmi**
Step 2 Enter the ESI and selector fields of the NSAP address.	**atm esi-address** *esi.selector*

The **atm esi-address** command allows you to configure the ATM address by entering the ESI (12 hexadecimal characters) and the selector byte (2 hexadecimal characters). The ATM prefix (26 hexadecimal characters) is provided by the ATM switch. To get the prefix from the ATM switch, the ILMI PVC must be configured on the router and the ATM switch must be able to supply a prefix via ILMI.

The **atm esi-address** and **atm nsap-address** commands are mutually exclusive. Configuring the router with the **atm esi-address** command negates the **atm nsap-address** setting, and vice versa. You can also specify a keepalive interval for the ILMI PVC. See the "Configuring Communication with the ILMI" section earlier in this chapter for more information. To see an example of setting up the ILMI PVC and assigning the ESI and selector fields of an NSAP address, go to the section "ATM ESI Address Example," near the end of this chapter.

Configuring the Idle Timeout Interval

You can specify an interval of inactivity after which any idle SVC on an interface is disconnected. This timeout interval might help control costs and free router memory and other resources for other uses.

To change the idle timeout interval, perform the following task in interface configuration mode:

Task	Command
Configure the interval of inactivity after which an idle SVC will be disconnected.	**atm idle-timeout** *seconds*

The default idle timeout interval is 300 seconds (5 minutes).

Configuring Point-to-Multipoint Signaling

Point-to-multipoint signaling (or multicasting) allows the router to send one packet to the ATM switch and have the switch replicate the packet to the destinations. It replaces pseudobroadcasting on specified virtual circuits for protocols configured for broadcasting. You configure multipoint signaling on an ATM interface after you have mapped protocol addresses to NSAPs and configured one or more protocols for broadcasting.

After multipoint signaling is set, the router uses existing static map entries that have the **broadcast** keyword set to establish multipoint calls. The call is established to the first destination with a Setup message. Additional parties are added to the call with AddParty messages each time a multicast packet is sent. One multipoint call will be established for each logical subnet of each protocol that has the **broadcast** keyword set.

To configure multipoint signaling on an ATM interface, complete the following tasks beginning in global configuration mode. The first task is required to configure this feature; the others are optional.

Task		Command
Step 1	Specify the NPM interface number.	**interface atm** *number*
Step 2	Provide a protocol address for the interface.	*protocol protocol-address mask*
Step 3	Associate a map list to the interface.	**map-group** *name*
Step 4	Provide an ATM NSAP address for the interface.	**atm nsap-address** *nsap-address*
Step 5	Configure the signaling PVC for the interface that uses SVCs.	**atm pvc** *vcd vpi vci* **qsaal**
Step 6	Associate a map list with the map group.	**map-list** *name*
Step 7	Configure a broadcast protocol for the remote NSAP address on the SVC. Repeat this step for other NSAP addresses, as needed.	*protocol protocol-address* **atm-nsap** *atm-nsap-address* **broadcast**
Step 8	Enable multipoint signaling to the ATM switch.	**atm multipoint-signalling**
Step 9	Limit the frequency of sending AddParty messages (optional).	**atm multipoint-interval interval**

If multipoint virtual circuits are closed, they are reopened with the next multicast packet. Once the call is established, additional parties are added to the call when additional multicast packets are sent. If a destination never comes up, the router constantly attempts to add it to the call by means of multipoint signaling.

For an example of configuring multipoint signaling on an interface that is configured for SVCs, see the "SVCs with Multipoint Signaling Example" section later in this chapter.

Changing Traffic Values

The tasks in this section are optional and advanced. The ATM signaling software can specify to the NPM card and the ATM switch a limit on how much traffic the source router will be sending. It provides this information in the form of traffic parameters. (These parameters have default values.) The ATM switch in turn sends these parameters as requested by the source to the ATM destination node. If the destination cannot provide such capacity levels, the call may fail. There is a single attempt to match traffic parameters.

This section describes how to change traffic values to customize your SVC connection. The individual tasks that separately specify **peak, sustainable,** or **burst** values for an SVC are analogous to the *peak, average,* and *burst* values defined when you create a PVC. Valid values for the peak rate on the Cisco 4500 and Cisco 4700 routers are from 56 Kbps to the PLIM rate, valid values for the average rate are from 1 Kbps to the peak rate, and valid values for the maximum burst size are from 1 cell to 65,535 cells.

Forward commands apply to the flow of cells from the source router to the destination router. Backward commands apply to the flow of cells from the destination router to the source router.

Most of the SVC traffic parameters include the concept of cell loss priority (CLP). CLP defines the following two levels of cell importance:

- A cell that has a CLP of 0 is a high-priority cell, indicating to the ATM switch that the switch should not readily discard the cell.
- A cell that has a CLP of 1 is a low-priority cell, indicating to the ATM switch that the switch can discard the cell if necessary due to congestion. For example, a cell with a CLP of 1 should be dropped before a cell with a CLP of 0.

Figure 5–3 illustrates a source and destination router implementing traffic settings that correspond end-to-end. The value for the forward command at the source router corresponds to the value for the backward command at the destination router.

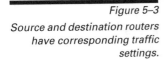
Figure 5–3
Source and destination routers have corresponding traffic settings.

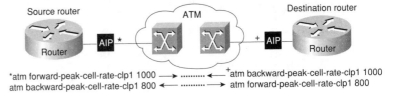

You can define map lists and map groups to tie specified SVCs to the protocol addresses of remote hosts and to specify whether broadcast protocols are supported. Then you can define map classes and specify the traffic parameters needed for the specified protocol traffic on those SVCs.

You must enter map-class configuration mode before you can change the traffic values from their default values. To enter map-class configuration mode, perform the following task in global configuration mode:

Task	Command
Enter map-class configuration mode, specifying a map-class name.	**map-class atm** *class-name*

If a map class with the specified name does not exist, the router creates a new one. All the following commands apply to the named map class. See the "Traffic Parameters Example" section near the end of this chapter for an example defining map classes, map groups, map lists, and traffic parameters.

To change the traffic values from their default values, perform one or more of the following tasks in map-class configuration mode:

Task	Command
Set the source-to-destination peak cell rate for high-priority cells.	**atm forward-peak-cell-rate-clp0** *rate*
Set the destination-to-source peak cell rate for high-priority cells.	**atm backward-peak-cell-rate-clp0** *rate*
Set the source-to-destination peak cell rate for the aggregate of low-priority and high-priority cells.	**atm forward-peak-cell-rate-clp1** *rate*
Set the destination-to-source peak cell rate for the aggregate of low-priority and high-priority cells.	**atm backward-peak-cell-rate-clp1** *rate*
Set the source-to-destination sustainable cell rate for high-priority cells.	**atm forward-sustainable-cell-rate-clp0** *rate*
Set the destination-to-source sustainable cell rate for high-priority cells.	**atm backward-sustainable-cell-rate-clp0** *rate*
Set the source-to-destination sustainable cell rate for the aggregate of low-priority and high-priority cells.	**atm forward-sustainable-cell-rate-clp1** *rate*
Set the destination-to-source sustainable cell rate for the aggregate of low-priority and high-priority cells.	**atm backward-sustainable-cell-rate-clp1** *rate*
Set the source-to-destination burst size for high-priority cells.	**atm forward-max-burst-size-clp0** *cell-count*
Set the destination-to-source burst size for high-priority cells.	**atm backward-max-burst-size-clp0** *cell-count*
Set the source-to-destination burst size for the aggregate of low-priority and high-priority cells.	**atm forward-max-burst-size-clp1** *cell-count*
Set the destination-to-source burst size for the aggregate of low-priority and high-priority cells.	**atm backward-max-burst-size-clp1** *cell-count*

Configuring SSCOP

The Service-Specific Connection-Oriented Protocol (SSCOP) resides in the service-specific convergence sublayer (SSCS) of the ATM adaptation layer (AAL). SSCOP is used to transfer variable-length service data units (SDUs) between users of SSCOP. SSCOP provides for the recovery of lost or corrupted SDUs.

NOTES

The tasks in this section customize the SSCOP feature to a particular network or environment and are optional. The features have default values that are valid in most installations. Before customizing these features, you should have a good understanding of SSCOP and the network involved.

Setting the Poll Timer

The poll timer controls the maximum time between transmission of a POLL PDU when SD or SDP PDUs are queued for transmission or are outstanding pending acknowledgments. To change the poll timer from the default value of 10 seconds, perform the following task in interface configuration mode:

Task	Command
Set the poll timer.	**sscop poll-timer** *seconds*

Setting the Keepalive Timer

The keepalive timer controls the maximum time between transmission of a POLL PDU when no SD or SDP PDUs are queued for transmission or are outstanding pending acknowledgments. To change the keepalive timer from the default value of 30 seconds, perform the following task in interface configuration mode:

Task	Command
Set the keepalive timer.	**sscop keepalive-timer** *seconds*

Setting the Connection Control Timer

The connection control timer determines the time between transmission of BGN, END, or RS (resynchronization) PDUs as long as an acknowledgment has not been received. Connection control performs the establishment, release, and resynchronization of an SSCOP connection.

To change the connection control timer from the default value of 10 seconds, perform the following task in interface configuration mode:

Task	Command
Set the connection control timer.	**sscop cc-timer** *seconds*

To change the retry count of the connection control timer from the default value of 10, perform the following task in interface configuration mode:

Task	Command
Set the number of times that SSCOP will retry to transmit BGN, END, or RS PDUs when they have not been acknowledged.	sscop max-cc *retries*

Setting the Transmitter and Receiver Windows

A transmitter window controls how many packets can be transmitted before an acknowledgment is required. To change the transmitter's window from the default value of 7, perform the following task in interface configuration mode:

Task	Command
Set the transmitter's window.	sscop send-window *packets*

A receiver window controls how many packets can be received before an acknowledgment is required. To change the receiver's window from the default value of 7, perform the following task in interface configuration mode:

Task	Command
Set the receiver's window.	sscop rcv-window *packets*

Closing an SVC

You can disconnect an idle SVC by completing the following task in EXEC mode:

Task	Command
Close the signaling PVC for an SVC.	atmsig close atm *number vcd*

CONFIGURING CLASSICAL IP AND ARP OVER ATM

Cisco implements both the ATM Address Resolution Protocol (ARP) server and ATM ARP client functions described in RFC 1577. RFC 1577 and models an ATM network as a logical IP subnetwork on a LAN.

The tasks required to configure classical IP and ARP over ATM depend on whether the environment uses SVCs or PVCs.

Configuring Classical IP and ARP in an SVC Environment

The ATM ARP mechanism is applicable to networks that use SVCs. It requires a network administrator to configure only the device's own ATM address and that of a single ATM ARP server into each client device. When the client makes a connection to the ATM ARP server, the server sends ATM Inverse ARP requests to learn the IP network address and ATM address of the client on the network. It uses the addresses to resolve future ATM ARP requests from clients. Static configuration of the server is not required or needed.

In Cisco's implementation, the ATM ARP client tries to maintain a connection to the ATM ARP server. The ATM ARP server can tear down the connection, but the client attempts once each minute to bring the connection back up. No error messages are generated for a failed connection, but the client will not route packets until the ATM ARP server is connected and translates IP network addresses.

For each packet with an unknown IP address, the client sends an ATM ARP request to the server. Until that address is resolved, any IP packet routed to the ATM interface will cause the client to send another ATM ARP request. When the ARP server responds, the client opens a connection to the new destination so that any additional packets can be routed to it.

Cisco routers may be configured as ATM ARP clients to work with any ATM ARP server conforming to RFC 1577. Alternatively, one of the Cisco routers in a logical IP subnet (LIS) may be configured to act as the ATM ARP server itself. In this case, it automatically acts as a client as well. To configure classical IP and ARP in an SVC environment, perform one of the tasks in the following list:

- Configuring the Router as an ATM ARP Client
- Configuring the Router as an ATM ARP Server

Configuring the Router as an ATM ARP Client

In an SVC environment, configure the ATM ARP mechanism on the interface by performing the following tasks beginning in global configuration mode:

Task	Command
Step 1 Specify the NPM interface number.	interface atm *number*
Step 2 Specify the ATM address of the interface.	atm nsap-address *nsap-address*
Step 3 Specify the IP address of the interface.	ip address *address mask*
Step 4 Specify the ATM address of the ATM ARP server.	atm arp-server nsap *nsap-address*
Step 5 Enable the ATM interface.	no shutdown

You can designate the current router as the ATM ARP server in Step 4 by typing **self** instead of the NSAP address.

For an example of configuring the ATM ARP client, see the "ATM ARP Client Configuration in an SVC Environment Example" section later in this chapter.

Configuring the Router as an ATM ARP Server

Cisco's implementation of the ATM ARP server supports a single, nonredundant server per logical IP subnetwork (LIS) and supports one ATM ARP server per subinterface. Thus, a single NPM card can support multiple ARP servers by using multiple subinterfaces.

To configure the ATM ARP server, complete the following tasks beginning in global configuration mode:

Task	Command
Step 1 Specify the NPM interface number.	**interface atm** *number*
Step 2 Specify the ATM address of the interface.	**atm nsap-address** *nsap-address*
Step 3 Specify the IP address of the interface.	**ip address** *address mask*
Step 4 Identify the ATM ARP server for the IP subnetwork network and set the idle timer.	**atm arp-server time-out** *minutes*[*]
Step 5 Enable the ATM interface.	**no shutdown**

[*] When you use the form of the **atm arp-server** command shown in Step 4, it indicates that this interface will perform the ATM ARP server functions. When you configure the ATM ARP client (as described earlier), the **atm arp-server** command is used—with a different keyword and argument—to identify a different ATM ARP server to the client.

You can designate the current router as the ATM ARP server in Step 4 by typing **self** instead of the NSAP address.

The idle timer interval is the number of minutes a destination entry listed in the ATM ARP server's ARP table can be idle before the server takes any action to time out the entry.

For an example of configuring the ATM ARP server, see the "ATM ARP Server Configuration in an SVC Environment Example" section later in this chapter.

Configuring Classical IP and Inverse ARP in a PVC Environment

The ATM Inverse ARP mechanism is applicable to networks that use PVCs, where connections are established, but the network addresses of the remote ends are not known. A server function is *not* used in this mode of operation.

In a PVC environment, configure the ATM Inverse ARP mechanism by performing the following tasks, beginning in global configuration mode:

Task	Command
Step 1 Specify the NPM interface number and enter interface configuration mode.	**interface atm** *number*
Step 2 Create a PVC and enable Inverse ARP on it.	**atm pvc** *vcd vci* **aal5snap inarp** *minutes*[*]
Step 3 Enable the ATM interface.	**no shutdown**

[*] Additional options are permitted in the **atm pvc** command, but the order of options is important.

Repeat Step 2 for each PVC you want to create.

The **inarp** *minutes* interval specifies how often Inverse ARP datagrams will be sent on this virtual circuit. The default value is 15 minutes.

── **NOTES** ──

The ATM ARP and Inverse ATM ARP mechanisms work with IP only. All other protocols require **map-list** command entries to operate.

For an example of configuring the ATM Inverse ARP mechanism, see the "ATM Inverse ARP Configuration in a PVC Environment Example" section later in this chapter.

Configuring Traffic Shaping for ATM SVCs

When you configure SVCs, you can define an ATM class to add support for traffic shaping on ATM SVCs. This applies a map class to an ATM interface. When an outgoing call is made by a static map client, or by a classical IP over ATM client, a map class will be determined for the call.

You must enter map-class configuration mode before you can define an ATM class. To enter map-class configuration mode and specify the ATM class for an ATM interface, perform the following tasks in global configuration mode:

Task	Command
Enter map-class configuration mode, specifying a map-class name.	**map-class atm** *class-name*
Specify an ATM class for an ATM interface.	**atm class** *class-name*

You can specify that an SVC be established on an ATM interface using only signaled traffic parameters. When you configure strict traffic-shaping on the router ATM interface, an SVC is established only if traffic shaping can be provided for the transmit cell flow per the signaled traffic parameters. If such shaping cannot be provided, the SVC is released.

If you do not configure strict traffic-shaping on the router ATM interface, an attempt is made to establish an SVC with traffic shaping for the transmit cell flow per the signaled traffic parameters. If such shaping cannot be provided, the SVC is installed with default shaping parameters; that is, it behaves as though a PVC were created without specifying traffic parameters.

To specify that an SVC be established on an ATM interface using only signaled traffic parameters, perform the following task in interface configuration mode:

Task	Command
Specify that an SVC be established on an ATM interface using only signaled traffic parameters.	**atm sig-traffic-shaping strict**

CUSTOMIZING THE NPM

You can customize the NPM interface on the Cisco 4500 and Cisco 4700 routers. The features you can customize have default values that will most likely suit your environment, and they probably do not need to be changed. However, you might need to enter configuration commands, depending on the requirements for your system configuration and the protocols you plan to route on the interface. Perform the tasks in the following list if you need to customize the NPM:

- Configuring the Rate Queue
- Configuring MTU Size
- Setting the PLIM Framing
- Setting Loopback Mode
- Setting the VCI-to-VPI Ratio
- Setting the Source of the Transmit Clock

Configuring the Rate Queue

A rate queue defines the speed at which individual virtual circuits will transmit data to the remote end. You can configure permanent rate queues, allow the software to set up dynamic rate queues, or perform some combination of the two. The software dynamically creates rate queues when an **atm pvc** command specifies a peak/average rate that does not match any user-configured rate queue. The software dynamically creates all rate queues if you have not configured any.

Using Dynamic Rate Queues

The Cisco IOS software automatically creates rate queues as necessary to satisfy the requests of **atm pvc** commands. The peak rate for a virtual circuit descriptor (VCD) is set to the maximum that the physical layer interface module (PLIM) will allow, and the average rate is set equal to the peak rate; then a rate queue is dynamically created for the peak rate of the VCD.

If dynamic rate queues do not satisfy your traffic shaping needs, you can configure permanent rate queues.

See the "Dynamic Rate Queue Examples" section at the end of this chapter for examples of different rate queues created in response to **atm pvc** commands.

Configuring a Permanent Rate Queue

The NPM supports up to four different peak rates. The peak rate is the maximum rate, in kilobits per second, at which a virtual circuit can transmit. Once attached to this rate queue, the virtual circuit is assumed to have its peak rate set to that of the rate queue.

You can configure each permanent rate queue independently to a portion of the overall bandwidth available on the ATM link. The combined bandwidths of all rate queues should not exceed the total bandwidth available. A warning message is displayed if you attempt to configure the combined rate queues beyond what is available to the NPM. The total bandwidth depends on the PLIM (see the "Using NPM Interface Types" section in Chapter 1).

To set a permanent rate queue, perform the following task in interface configuration mode:

Task	Command
Configure a permanent rate queue, which defines the maximum speed at which an individual virtual circuit transmits data to a remote ATM host.	**atm rate-queue** *queue-number speed*

NOTES

In Cisco IOS Release 11.3, a permanent rate queue is automatically configured when you configure the peak rate using the **atm pvc** command. Therefore, you are not required to use the **atm rate-queue** command to configure the permanent rate queue.

Configuring MTU Size

Each interface has a default maximum packet size or maximum transmission unit (MTU) size. On the NPM, this number defaults to 4470 bytes; the maximum is 9188 bytes. The MTU can be set on a per sub-interface basis as long as the interface MTU is as large or larger than the largest sub-interface MTU. To set the maximum MTU size, perform the following task in interface configuration mode:

Task	Command
Set the maximum MTU size.	**mtu** *bytes*

Setting the PLIM Framing

The default SONET PLIM is STS-3C. To set the SONET PLIM to STM-1 or to set the PLIM framing for E3 or DS3, perform one of the following tasks in interface configuration mode:

Task	Command
Set the OC-3c SONET PLIM to STM-1.	atm sonet stm-1
or	
Set DS3 framing mode.	atm framing [m23adm | cbitplcp | m23plcp]
or	
Set E3 framing mode.	atm framing [g832adm | g751adm]

The default for DS3 is C-Bit ADM framing; the default for E3 is G.751 with PLCP framing.

Setting Loopback Mode

To loop all packets back to the NPM instead of the network, perform the following task in interface configuration mode:

Task	Command
Set loopback mode.	loopback diagnostic

To loop the incoming network packets back to the ATM network, perform the following task in interface configuration mode:

Task	Command
Set line loopback mode.	loopback line

Setting the VCI-to-VPI Ratio

By default, the NPM supports 1024 VCIs per VPI. This value can be any power of 2 in the range from 32 to 8192. This value controls the memory allocation in the NPM to deal with the VCI table. It defines only the maximum number of VCIs to support per VPI.

To set the maximum number of VCIs to support per VPI and limit the highest VCI accordingly, perform the following task in interface configuration mode:

Task	Command
Set the number of VCIs per VPI.	atm vc-per-vp *number*

The product of VC and VP is fixed at 8192; the number of virtual circuits supported per virtual path will decrease in proportion to an increase in the number of virtual paths.

Setting the Source of the Transmit Clock

By default, the NPM expects the ATM switch to provide transmit clocking. To specify that the NPM generate the transmit clock internally for SONET and E3 PLIM operation, perform the following task in interface configuration mode:

Task	Command
Specify that the NPM generate the transmit clock internally.	**atm clock internal**

CONFIGURING ATM SUBINTERFACES FOR SMDS NETWORKS

An ATM adaptation layer (AAL) defines the conversion of user information into cells by segmenting upper-layer information into cells at the transmitter and reassembling them at the receiver. AAL1 and AAL2 handle isochronous traffic, such as voice and video, and are not relevant to the router. AAL3/4 and AAL5 support data communications by segmenting and reassembling packets. Release 11.0(5) supports both AAL3/4 and AAL5 on Cisco 4500 series routers.

Cisco's implementation of the AAL3/4 encapsulates each AAL3/4 packet in a Switched Multimegabit Data Service (SMDS) header and trailer. This feature supports both unicast and multicast addressing, and provides subinterfaces for up to four AAL3/4 connections over the same physical interface.

NOTES

Each subinterface configured to support AAL3/4 is allowed only one SMDS E.164 unicast address and one E.164 multicast address. The multicast address is used for all broadcast operations. In addition, only one virtual circuit is allowed on each subinterface that is being used for AAL3/4 processing, and it must be an AAL3/4 virtual circuit.

Support for AAL3/4 on an ATM interface requires static mapping of all protocols except IP. However, dynamic routing of IP can coexist with static mapping of other protocols on the same ATM interface.

To configure an ATM interface for SMDS networks, perform the following tasks in interface configuration mode:

Task		Command
Step 1	Provide an SMDS E.164 unicast address for the subinterface.	**atm smds-address** *address*
Step 2	Provide an SMDS E.164 multicast address.	**atm multicast** *address*
Step 3	Create an AAL3/4 PVC.	**atm pvc** *vcd vpi vci* **aal34smds**

AAL3/4 is not supported at OC-3c rates on Cisco 4500 series routers. If AAL3/4 is configured on an OC-3c interface, it must be limited to E3 or DS3 rates by setting up a permanent rate queue for the interface. See the "Configuring the Rate Queue" section earlier in this chapter.

After configuring the ATM interface for SMDS networks, configure the interface for standard protocol configurations as needed.

For examples of configuring an ATM interface for AAL3/4 support, see the "PVC with AAL3/4 and SMDS Encapsulation Examples" section later in this chapter. Unlike the Cisco 7500 AAL3/4, the **aal** command to enable aal3/4, the **mid-per-vc** command, and the **vp-filter** command are not used on the Cisco 4500 or the Cisco 4700 routers.

CONFIGURING TRANSPARENT BRIDGING FOR THE NPM

Cisco's implementation of transparent bridging over ATM on the Cisco 4500 and Cisco 4700 routers allows the spanning tree for an interface to support virtual circuit descriptors (VCDs) for AAL5-LLC Subnetwork Access Protocol (SNAP) encapsulations.

If the relevant interface or subinterface is explicitly put into a bridge group, as described in the following task table, AAL5-SNAP encapsulated bridge packets on a PVC are fast-switched.

Cisco's bridging implementation supports IEEE 802.3 frame formats and IEEE 802.10 frame formats. The router can accept IEEE 802.3 frames with or without frame check sequence (FCS). When the router receives frames with FCS (RFC 1483 bridge frame formats with 0x0001 in the PID field of the SNAP header), it strips off the FCS and forwards the frame as necessary. All IEEE 802.3 frames that originate at or are forwarded by the router are sent as 802.3 bridge frames without FCS (bridge frame formats with 0x0007 in the PID field of the SNAP header).

Transparent bridging for ATM on the Cisco 4500 works only on AAL5-LLC/SNAP PVCs (fast-switched). AAL3/4-SMDS, AAL5-MUX, and AAL5-NLPID bridging are not yet supported on the Cisco 4500. Transparent bridging for ATM also does not operate in a switched virtual circuit (SVC) environment.

To configure transparent bridging for LLC/SNAP PVCs, complete the following steps beginning in global configuration mode:

Task	Command
Step 1 Specify the NPM interface number and, optionally, a subinterface.	**interface atm** *number*[*.subinterface*]
Step 2 Assign a source IP address and subnet mask to the interface, if needed.	**ip address** *ip-address mask*

Task		Command
Step 3	Create one or more PVCs using AAL5-SNAP encapsulation.	**atm pvc** *vcd vpi vci* **aal5snap** **atm pvc** *vcd vpi vci* **aal5snap** **atm pvc** *vcd vpi vci* **aal5snap**
Step 4	Assign the interface to a bridge group.	**bridge-group** *group*
Step 5	Return to global configuration mode.	**exit**
Step 6	Define the type of spanning tree protocol as DEC.	**bridge** *group* **protocol dec**

No other configuration is required. Spanning tree updates are broadcast to all AAL5-SNAP virtual circuits that exist on the ATM interface. Only the AAL5-SNAP virtual circuits on the specific sub-interface receive the updates. The router does not send spanning tree updates to AAL5-MUX and AAL5-NLPID virtual circuits.

For an example of transparent bridging for an AAL5-SNAP PVC, see the "Transparent Bridging on an AAL5-SNAP PVC Example" section at the end of this chapter.

CONFIGURING PPP OVER ATM

This section describes how to configure the NPM on the Cisco 4500 and 4700 routers to terminate multiple remote Point-to-Point Protocol (PPP) connections.

Before configuring PPP over ATM, the Cisco 4500 and 4700 routers must be equipped with Cisco IOS Release 11.2(4)F or later software. Remote branch offices must have PPP configured on PPP-compatible devices interconnecting directly to Cisco StrataCom's ATM Switch Interface Shelf (AXIS) equipment through a leased-line connection. The AXIS shelves provide frame forwarding encapsulation and are terminated on BPX cores prior to connecting to a Cisco 4500 or Cisco 4700 router. Figure 5–4 shows a typical scenario for using PPP over ATM.

Figure 5–4

Typical PPP-over-ATM network environment.

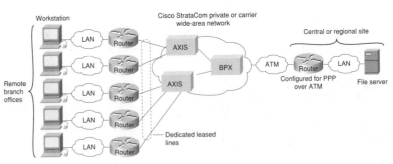

— NOTES ◗

If you need to configure the Cisco StrataCom AXIS shelf for frame forwarding at the remote sites, refer to the *AXIS 4 Command Supplement* for command line instructions or the *StrataView Plus Operations Guide* for StrataView Plus instructions. If you configure the AXIS using the command line interface, use the **addport** and **addchan** commands and select frame forwarding for the *port_type* and *chan_type* arguments, respectively.

When you configure PPP over ATM, a logical interface known as a virtual access interface associates each PPP connection to an ATM permanent virtual circuit (PVC). You can create this logical interface by configuring an ATM PVC as described in the "Creating a PPP-over-ATM PVC" section. This configuration encapsulates each PPP connection in a separate PVC, allowing each PPP connection to terminate at the router ATM interface as if received from a typical PPP serial interface.

The virtual access interface for each PVC obtains its configuration from a virtual interface template (virtual template) when the PVC is created. Before creating the ATM PVC, we suggest you create and configure a virtual template as described in the following section, "Creating and Configuring a Virtual Template."

To configure PPP over ATM, complete the tasks in the following list. The first task is optional, but it is recommended. The remaining tasks in the list are required:

- Creating and Configuring a Virtual Template
- Specifying an ATM Point-to-Point Subinterface
- Creating a PPP-over-ATM PVC

See an example of configuring PPP over ATM in the section "PPP-over-ATM Example" at the end of this chapter.

Creating and Configuring a Virtual Template

Prior to configuring the ATM PVC for PPP over ATM, you typically create and configure a virtual template. To create and configure a virtual template, complete the following tasks beginning in global configuration mode:

Task	Command
Step 1 Create a virtual template, and enter interface configuration mode.	**interface virtual-template** *number*
Step 2 Enable PPP encapsulation on the virtual template.	**encapsulation ppp**
Step 3 Optionally, enable PPP encapsulation on the virtual interface template.	**ip unnumbered ethernet** *number*

Other optional configuration commands can be added to the virtual template configuration. For example, you can enable the PPP authentication on the virtual template using the **ppp authentication chap** command.

All PPP parameters are managed within the virtual template configuration. Configuration changes made to the virtual template are automatically propagated to the individual virtual access interfaces. Multiple virtual access interfaces can spawn from a single virtual template; hence, multiple PVCs can use a single virtual template. Cisco IOS software supports up to 25 virtual template configurations. If greater numbers of tailored configurations are required, an authentication, authorization, and accounting (AAA) server may be employed.

If the parameters of the virtual template are not explicitly defined before configuring the ATM PVC, the PPP interface is brought up using default values from the virtual template identified. Some parameters (such as an IP address) take effect only if specified before the PPP interface comes up. Therefore, it is recommended that you explicitly create and configure the virtual template before configuring the ATM PVC to ensure such parameters take effect. Alternatively, if parameters are specified after the ATM PVC has already been configured, you should issue a **shutdown** command followed by a **no shutdown** command on the ATM subinterface to restart the interface; this restart will cause the newly configured parameters (such as an IP address) to take effect.

Network addresses for the PPP-over-ATM connections are not configured on the main ATM interface or subinterface. Instead, these are configured on the appropriate virtual template or obtained via AAA.

The virtual templates support all standard PPP configuration commands; however, not all configurations are supported by the PPP-over-ATM virtual access interfaces. These restrictions are enforced at the time the virtual template configuration is applied (cloned) to the virtual access interface. These restrictions are described in the following paragraphs.

Only standard first-in, first-out (FIFO) queuing is supported when applied to PPP-over-ATM virtual access interfaces. Other types of queuing which are typically configured on the main interface are not (for example, fair-queuing). If configured, these configuration lines are ignored when applied to a PPP-over-ATM interface.

While fast switching is supported, flow and optimum switching are not; these configurations are ignored on the PPP-over-ATM virtual access interface. Fast switching is enabled by default for the virtual template configuration. If fast switching is not desired, use the **no ip route-cache** command to disable it.

The PPP reliable link that uses Link Access Procedure, Balanced (LAPB) is not supported.

Because an ATM PVC is configured for this feature, the following standard PPP features are not applicable and should not be configured:

- Asynchronous interfaces
- Dialup connections
- Callback on PPP

Specifying an ATM Point-to-Point Subinterface

After you create a virtual template for PPP over ATM, you must specify a point-to-point subinterface per PVC connection. To specify an ATM point-to-point subinterface, complete the following task beginning in global configuration mode:

Task	Command
Specify an ATM point-to-point subinterface.	**interface atm** *number.subinterface-number* **point-to-point**

Creating a PPP-over-ATM PVC

After you create a virtual template and point-to-point subinterfaces for PPP over ATM, you must create a PPP-over-ATM PVC. To create a PPP-over-ATM PVC, perform the following task in sub-interface configuration mode:

Task	Command
Create a PPP-over-ATM PVC.	**atm pvc** *vcd vpi vci* **aal5ciscoppp** [*peak average* [*burst*]] [**oam** [*seconds*]] **virtual-template** *number*

The *peak* rate value is typically identical to the *average* rate or some suitable multiple thereof (the *peak* rate value is an unlimited multiple of the *average* rate value for the Cisco 4500 and 4700 routers).

The *average* rate value should be set to the line rate available at the remote site, because the remote line rate will have the lowest speed of the connection. For example, if the remote site has a T1 link, set the line rate to 1.536 Mbps. Because the average rate calculation on the ATM PVC includes the cell headers, a line rate value plus 10 or 15 percent may result in better remote line utilization.

The *burst* size depends on the number of cells that can be buffered by receiving ATM switches and is coordinated with the ATM network connection provider. If this value is not specified, the default, which is the equivalent to one maximum length frame on the interface, is used.

Operations, Administration and Maintenance (OAM) F5 cell loopback is provided by the remote AXIS shelf so OAM may be enabled. However, PPP over ATM is not typically an end-to-end ATM connection, and therefore enabling OAM is not recommended.

Once you configure the router for PPP over ATM, the PPP subsystem starts and the router attempts to send a PPP configure request to the remote peer. If the peer does not respond, the router periodically goes into a "listen" state and waits for a configuration request from the peer. After a timeout (typically 45 seconds), the router again attempts to reach the remote router by sending configuration requests.

The virtual access interface remains associated with a PVC as long as the PVC is configured. If you deconfigure the PVC, the virtual access interface is marked as deleted. If you shut down the associated

ATM interface, you will also cause the virtual access interface to be marked as down (within 10 seconds), and you will bring the PPP connection down. If you set a keepalive timer of the virtual template on the interface, the virtual access interface uses the PPP echo mechanism to verify the existence of the remote peer. If an interface failure is detected and the PPP connection is brought down, the virtual access interface remains up.

MONITORING AND MAINTAINING THE ATM INTERFACE

After configuring the new interface, you can display its status. You can also display the current state of the ATM network and connected virtual circuits. To show current virtual circuits and traffic information, perform the following tasks in EXEC mode:

Task	Command
Display ATM-specific information about an ATM interface.	show atm interface atm *number*
Display the configured list of ATM static maps to remote hosts on an ATM network.	show atm map
Display global traffic information to and from all ATM networks connected to the router. Display a list of counters of all ATM traffic on this router.	show atm traffic
Display ATM virtual circuit information about all PVCs and SVCs (or a specific virtual circuit).	show atm vc [*vcd*]
Display statistics for the ATM interface.	show interfaces atm *number*
Display SSCOP details for the ATM interface.	show sscop

ATM CONFIGURATION EXAMPLES

The examples in the following sections illustrate how to configure an ATM interface on the NPM for Cisco 4500 and Cisco 4700 routers. The examples provided are the following:

- PVC with AAL5 and LLC/SNAP Encapsulation Examples
- PVCs in a Fully Meshed Network Example
- SVCs in a Fully Meshed Network Example
- ATM NSAP Address Example
- ATM ESI Address Example
- SVCs with Multipoint Signaling Example
- Traffic Parameters Example
- Classical IP and ARP Examples
- Dynamic Rate Queue Examples

- Transparent Bridging on an AAL5-SNAP PVC Example
- PPP-over-ATM Example

PVC with AAL5 and LLC/SNAP Encapsulation Examples

The following example creates PVC 5 on ATM interface 0. It uses LLC/SNAP encapsulation over AAL5. The interface is at IP address 1.1.1.1 with 1.1.1.5 at the other end of the connection. The static map list named *atm* declares that the next node is a broadcast point for multicast packets from IP. For further information, refer to the related task section "Creating a PVC" presented earlier in this chapter.

```
interface atm 0
 ip address 1.1.1.1 255.255.255.0
 atm rate-queue 1 100
 atm pvc 5 0 10 aal5snap
 ip route-cache cbus
 map-group atm
!
map-list atm
 ip 1.1.1.5 atm-vc 5 broadcast
```

The following example is of a typical ATM configuration for a PVC:

```
interface atm 0
 ip address 172.21.168.112 255.255.255.0
 map-group atm
 atm rate-queue 1 100
 atm pvc 1 1 1 aal5snap
 atm pvc 2 2 2 aal5snap
 atm pvc 6 6 6 aal5snap
 atm pvc 7 7 7 aal5snap
 decnet cost 1
 clns router iso-igrp comet
!
router iso-igrp comet
 net 47.0004.0001.0000.0c00.6666.00
!
router igrp 109
 network 172.21.0.0
!
ip domain-name CISCO.COM
!
map-list atm
 ip 172.21.168.110 atm-vc 1 broadcast
 clns 47.0004.0001.0000.0c00.6e26.00 atm-vc 6 broadcast
 decnet 10.1 atm-vc 2 broadcast
```

PVCs in a Fully Meshed Network Example

Figure 5–5 illustrates a fully meshed network. The configurations for Routers A, B, and C follow the figure. In this example, the routers are configured to use PVCs. *Fully meshed* indicates that any workstation can communicate with any other workstation. Note that the two **map-list** statements configured in Router A identify the ATM addresses of Routers B and C. The two **map-list** statements in Router B identify the ATM addresses of Routers A and C. The two **map list** statements in Router C identify the ATM addresses of Routers A and B. For further information, refer to the related task section "Creating a PVC," earlier in this chapter.

Figure 5–5
An example of fully meshed
ATM configuration.

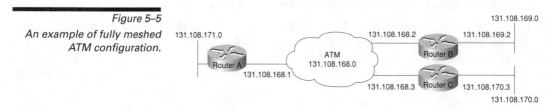

Router A

```
ip routing
!
interface atm 0
 ip address 131.108.168.1 255.255.255.0
 atm rate-queue 1 100
 atm pvc 1 0 10 aal5snap
 atm pvc 2 0 20 aal5snap
 map-group test-a
!
map-list test-a
 ip 131.108.168.2 atm-vc 1 broadcast
 ip 131.108.168.3 atm-vc 2 broadcast
```

Router B

```
ip routing
!
interface atm 0
 ip address 131.108.168.2 255.255.255.0
 atm rate-queue 1 100
 atm pvc 1 0 20 aal5snap
 atm pvc 2 0 21 aal5snap
 map-group test-b
!
map-list test-b
 ip 131.108.168.1 atm-vc 1 broadcast
 ip 131.108.168.3 atm-vc 2 broadcast
```

Router C

```
ip routing
!
interface atm 0
 ip address 131.108.168.3 255.255.255.0
 atm rate-queue 1 100
 atm pvc 2 0 21 aal5snap
 atm pvc 4 0 22 aal5snap
 map-group test-c
```

```
!
map-list test-c
 ip 131.108.168.1 atm-vc 2 broadcast
 ip 131.108.168.2 atm-vc 4 broadcast
```

SVCs in a Fully Meshed Network Example

The following example is also a configuration for the fully meshed network shown in Figure 5–5, but this example uses SVCs. PVC 1 is the signaling PVC. For further information, refer to the related task section "Configuring the PVC that Performs SVC Call Setup," earlier in this chapter.

Router A

```
interface atm 0
 ip address 131.108.168.1 255.255.255.0
 map-group atm
 atm nsap-address AB.CDEF.01.234567.890A.BCDE.F012.3456.7890.1234.12
 atm rate-queue 1 100
 atm maxvc 1024
 atm pvc 1 0 5 qsaal
!
map-list atm
 ip 131.108.168.2 atm-nsap BC.CDEF.01.234567.890A.BCDE.F012.3456.7890.1334.13
 ip 131.108.168.3 atm-nsap BC.CDEF.01.234567.890A.BCDE.F012.3456.7890.1224.12
```

Router B

```
interface atm 0
 ip address 131.108.168.2 255.255.255.0
 map-group atm
 atm nsap-address BC.CDEF.01.234567.890A.BCDE.F012.3456.7890.1334.13
 atm rate-queue 1 100
 atm pvc 1 0 5 qsaal
!
map-list atm
 ip 131.108.168.1 atm-nsap AB.CDEF.01.234567.890A.BCDE.F012.3456.7890.1234.12
 ip 131.108.168.3 atm-nsap BC.CDEF.01.234567.890A.BCDE.F012.3456.7890.1224.12
```

Router C

```
interface atm 0
 ip address 131.108.168.3 255.255.255.0
 map-group atm
 atm nsap-address BC.CDEF.01.234567.890A.BCDE.F012.3456.7890.1224.12
 atm rate-queue 1 100
 atm pvc 1 0 5 qsaal
!
map-list atm
 ip 131.108.168.1 atm-nsap AB.CDEF.01.234567.890A.BCDE.F012.3456.7890.1234.12
 ip 131.108.168.2 atm-nsap BC.CDEF.01.234567.890A.BCDE.F012.3456.7890.1334.13
```

ATM NSAP Address Example

The following example assigns NSAP address AB.CDEF.01.234567.890A.BCDE.F012.3456.7890.
1234.12 to ATM interface 0. For further information, refer to the related task section "Configuring
the Complete NSAP Address Manually," earlier in this chapter.

```
interface atm 0
 atm nsap-address AB.CDEF.01.234567.890A.BCDE.F012.3456.7890.1234.12
```

You can display the ATM address for the interface by executing the **show interface atm** command.

ATM ESI Address Example

The following example on a Cisco 4500 router assigns the ESI and selector field values and sets up
the ILMI PVC. For further information, refer to the related task section "Configuring the ESI and
Selector Fields," earlier in this chapter.

```
interface atm 0
 atm pvc 2 0 16 ilmi
 atm esi-address 345678901234.12
```

SVCs with Multipoint Signaling Example

The following example configures an ATM interface for SVCs using multipoint signaling. For further information, refer to the related task section "Configuring Point-to-Multipoint Signaling," earlier in this chapter.

```
interface atm 0
 ip address 4.4.4.6
 map-group atm_pri
 atm nsap-address de.cdef.01.234567.890a.bcde.f012.3456.7890.1234.12
 atm multipoint-signalling
 atm rate-queue 1 100
 atm pvc 1 0 5 qsaal
!
map-list atm_pri
 ip 4.4.4.4 atm-nsap cd.cdef.01.234566.890a.bcde.f012.3456.7890.1234.12 broadcast
 ip 4.4.4.7 atm-nsap 31.3233.34.353637.3839.3031.3233.3435.3637.3839.30 broadcast
```

Traffic Parameters Example

The following example defines a map list to tie specified SVCs to protocol addresses of remote hosts
and to specified map classes. Then it defines the map classes and sets traffic parameters for certain
protocol traffic. For further information, refer to the related task section "Changing Traffic Values," earlier in this chapter.

```
map-list atmlist
 ip 131.108.170.21 atm-vc 12
 ip 131.108.180.121 atm-nsap 47.0091.81.000000.0041.0B0A.1581.0040.0B0A.1585.00 class
atmclass1
 ip 131.108.190.221 atm-nsap 47.0091.81.000000.0041.0B0A.1581.0040.0B0B.1585.00 class
atmclass2
map-class atm atmclass1
 atm forward-peak-cell-rate-clp1 8000
 atm backward-peak-cell-rate-clp1 8000
```

```
map-class atm atmclass2
 atm forward-peak-cell-rate-clp1 7000
 atm backward-peak-cell-rate-clp1 7000
interface atm 0
 map-group atmlist
```

Classical IP and ARP Examples

This section provides three examples of classical IP and ARP configuration, one each for a client and a server in an SVC environment, and one for ATM Inverse ARP in a PVC environment.

ATM ARP Client Configuration in an SVC Environment Example

This example configures an ATM ARP client in an SVC environment. Note that the client in this example and the ATM ARP server in the next example are configured to be on the same IP network. For further information, refer to the related task section "Configuring the Router as an ATM ARP Client," earlier in this chapter.

```
interface atm 0.5
 atm nsap-address ac.2456.78.040000.0000.0000.0000.0000.0000.0000.00
 ip address 10.0.0.2 255.0.0.0
 atm pvc 1 0 5 qsaal
 atm arp-server nsap ac.1533.66.020000.0000.0000.0000.0000.0000.0000.00
```

ATM ARP Server Configuration in an SVC Environment Example

The following example configures ATM on an interface and configures the interface to function as the ATM ARP server for the IP subnetwork. For further information, refer to the related task section "Configuring the Router as an ATM ARP Server," earlier in this chapter.

```
interface atm 0
 ip address 10.0.0.1 255.0.0.0
 atm nsap-address ac.1533.66.020000.0000.0000.0000.0000.0000.0000.00
 atm rate-queue 1 100
 atm pvc 1 0 5 qsaal
 atm arp-server
```

ATM Inverse ARP Configuration in a PVC Environment Example

The following example configures ATM on an interface and then configures the ATM Inverse ARP mechanism on the PVCs on the interface, with Inverse ARP datagrams sent every 5 minutes on three of the PVCs. The fourth PVC will not send Inverse ATM ARP datagrams, but will receive and respond to Inverse ATM ARP requests. For further information, refer to the related task section "Configuring Classical IP and Inverse ARP in a PVC Environment," earlier in this chapter.

```
interface atm 0
 ip address 172.21.1.111 255.255.255.0
 atm pvc 1 1 1 aal5snap inarp 5
 atm pvc 2 2 2 aal5snap inarp 5
 atm pvc 3 3 3 aal5snap inarp 5
 atm pvc 4 4 4 aal5snap inarp
```

No **map-group** and **map-list** commands are needed for IP.

Dynamic Rate Queue Examples

Both of the following examples assume that no permanent rate queues have been configured. The software dynamically creates rate queues when an **atm pvc** command specifies a peak or average rate that does not match any user-configured rate queue. For further information, refer to the related task section "Using Dynamic Rate Queues," earlier in this chapter.

In the following example, the software sets the peak rate for VCD 1 to the maximum that the PLIM will allow and sets the average rate to the peak rate. Then it creates a rate queue for the peak rate of this VCD.

```
atm pvc 1 1 1 aal5snap
```

In the following example, the software creates a 100-Mbps rate queue and assigns VCD 2 to that rate queue with an average rate of 50 Mbps and a burst size of 64 cells:

```
atm pvc 2 2 2 aal5snap 100000 50000 2
```

PVC with AAL3/4 and SMDS Encapsulation Examples

The following example provides a minimal configuration of an ATM interface to support AAL3/4 and SMDS encapsulation; no protocol configuration is shown. For further information, refer to the related task section "Configuring ATM Subinterfaces for SMDS Networks," earlier in this chapter.

```
interface atm 0
 atm smds-address c140.888.9999
 atm multicast e180.0999.9999
 atm pvc 30 0 30 aal34smds
```

The following example shows how IP dynamic routing might coexist with static routing of another protocol:

```
interface atm 0
 ip address 172.21.168.112 255.255.255.0
 atm smds-address c140.888.9999
 atm multicast e180.0999.9999
 atm pvc 30 0 30 aal34smds
 map-group atm
 appletalk address 10.1
 appletalk zone atm
 !
 map-group atm
 atalk 10.2 smds c140.8111.1111 broadcast
```

This example shows that IP configured is dynamically routed, but that AppleTalk is statically routed. An AppleTalk remote host is configured at address 10.2 and is associated with SMDS address c140.8111.1111.

AAL3/4 associates a protocol address with an SMDS address, as shown in the last line of this example. In contrast, AAL5 static maps associate a protocol address with a PVC number.

Transparent Bridging on an AAL5-SNAP PVC Example

In the following example, three AAL5-SNAP PVCs are created on the same ATM interface. The router will broadcast all spanning tree updates to these AAL5-SNAP PVCs. No other virtual circuits will receive spanning tree updates. For further information, refer to the related task section "Configuring Transparent Bridging for the NPM," earlier in this chapter.

```
interface atm 0
 ip address 1.1.1.1 255.0.0.0
 atm pvc 1 1 1 aal5snap
 atm pvc 2 2 2 aal5snap
 atm pvc 3 3 3 aal5snap
 bridge-group 1
!
bridge 1 protocol dec
```

PPP-over-ATM Example

The following example configures PPP over ATM to use PPP unnumbered link and Challenge Handshake Authentication Protocol (CHAP) authentication. For further information, refer to the related task section "Configuring PPP over ATM," earlier in this chapter.

```
configure terminal
!
interface virtual-template 2
 encapsulation ppp
 ip unnumbered ethernet 0/0
 ppp authentication chap
!
interface atm 0.2 point-to-point
!
 atm pvc 2 0 34 aal5ciscoppp 1536 1536 2 virtual-template 2
end
```

CHAPTER 6

ATM Commands

This chapter describes how to use the commands available to configure Asynchronous Transfer Mode (ATM) interfaces on the following:

- Cisco 7200 series routers with ATM port adapter
- Cisco 7500 series routers with AIP or ATM port adapter
- Cisco 4500 and Cisco 4700 routers with Network Processor Module (NPM)

This chapter also describes the commands available to configure a serial interface for ATM access in other routers.

NOTES

ATM is currently not supported on Cisco 2500 series, Cisco AS5100, and Cisco AS5200 access servers. In Cisco IOS Release 11.3, all commands supported on the Cisco 7500 series routers are also supported on the Cisco 7000 series routers equipped with RSP7000.

For ATM configuration information and examples, refer to Chapter 2, "Configuring ATM Access over a Serial Interface;" Chapter 3, "Configuring ATM on the AIP for Cisco 7500 Series Routers;" Chapter 4, "Configuring ATM on the ATM Port Adapter for Cisco 7200 and 7500 Series Routers;" and Chapter 5, "Configuring ATM on the NPM for Cisco 4500 and 4700 Routers."

ATM AAL AAL3/4

To enable support for ATM adaptation layer 3/4 (AAL3/4) on an ATM interface, use the **atm aal aal3/4** interface configuration command. To disable support for ATM adaptation layer 3/4 (AAL3/4) on an ATM interface, use the **no** form of this command.

    atm aal aal3/4
    no atm aal aal3/4

123

Syntax Description

This command has no arguments or keywords.

Default

Support for AAL3/4 is disabled.

Command Mode

Interface configuration

Usage Guidelines

This command first appeared in Cisco IOS Release 10.3.

This command is supported on Cisco 7500 series routers with AIP. This command is not supported on the ATM port adapter. Because Cisco 4500 and Cisco 4700 routers always support both AAL3/4 and AAL5, this command is not required on Cisco 4500 and Cisco 4700 routers.

Only one virtual circuit can exist on a subinterface that is being used for AAL3/4 processing, and that virtual circuit must be an AAL3/4 virtual circuit.

The AAL3/4 support feature requires static mapping of all protocols except IP.

Example

The following example enables AAL3/4 on ATM interface 2/0:

```
interface atm2/0
 ip address 172.21.177.178 255.255.255.0
 atm aal aal3/4
```

Related Commands

atm mid-per-vc
atm multicast
atm pvc
atm smds-address

ATM ADDRESS-REGISTRATION

To enable the router to engage in address registration and callback functions with the Interim Local Management Interface (ILMI), use the **atm address-registration** interface configuration command. To disable ILMI address registration functions, use the **no** form of this command.

> **atm address-registration**
> **no atm address-registration**

Syntax Description

This command has no keywords or arguments.

Default

Enabled

Command Mode

Interface configuration

Usage Guidelines

This command first appeared in Cisco IOS Release 11.0.

This command enables a router to register its address with the ILMI for callback when specific events occur, such as incoming Simple Network Management Protocol (SNMP) traps or incoming new network prefixes.

Example

The following example enables ATM interface I/O to register its address:

```
interface atm 1/0
  atm address-registration
```

Related Commands

atm ilmi-keepalive

ATM ARP-SERVER

To identify an ATM Address Resolution Protocol (ARP) server for the IP network or set time-to-live (TTL) values for entries in the ATM ARP table, use the **atm arp-server** interface configuration command. To remove the definition of an ATM ARP server, use the **no** form of this command.

    atm arp-server [**self** [**time-out** *minutes*] | **nsap** *nsap-address*]]

    no atm arp-server [**self** [**time-out** *minutes*] | **nsap** *nsap-address*]]

Syntax	Description
self	(Optional) Specifies the current router as the ATM ARP server.
time-out *minutes*	(Optional) Number of minutes a destination entry listed in the ATM ARP server's ARP table will be kept before the server takes any action to verify or time out the entry. The default is 20 minutes.
nsap *nsap-address*	(Optional) Network service access point (NSAP) address of an ATM ARP server.

Defaults

The ARP server process is disabled. The default timeout value is 20 minutes.

Command Mode

Interface configuration

Usage Guidelines

This command first appeared in Cisco IOS Release 11.1.

If an NSAP address is specified, the ARP client on this interface uses the specified host as an ARP server. You can specify multiple ATM ARP servers by repeating the command. If **self** is specified, this interface acts as the ARP server for the logical IP network.

The ATM ARP server takes one of the following actions if a destination listed in the server's ARP table expires:

- If a virtual circuit still exists to that destination, the server sends an Inverse ARP request. If no response arrives, the entry times out.
- If a virtual circuit does not exist to the destination, the entry times out immediately.

This implementation follows RFC 1577, Classical IP over ATM.

Example

The following example configures ATM on an interface and configures the interface to function as the ATM ARP server for the IP subnetwork:

```
interface atm 0/0
 ip address 10.0.0.1.255.0.0.0
atm nsap-address ac.1533.66.020000.0000.0000.0000.0000.0000.0000.00
atm rate-queue 1 100
atm maxvc 1024
atm pvc 1 0 5 qsaal
atm arp-server self
```

ATM BACKWARD-MAX-BURST-SIZE-CLP0

To change the maximum number of high-priority cells coming from the destination router to the source router at the burst level on the switched virtual circuit (SVC), use the **atm backward-max-burst-size-clp0** map-class configuration command. The **no** form of this command restores the default.

> **atm backward-max-burst-size-clp0** *cell-count*
> **no atm backward-max-burst-size-clp0**

Syntax	Description
cell-count	Maximum number of high-priority cells coming from the destination router at the burst level.

Default

The default is –1. The router does not request this traffic parameter of the ATM switch. The switch drops cells if there is not enough buffer space.

Command Mode

Map-class configuration

Usage Guidelines

This command first appeared in Cisco IOS Release 10.0.

This command is supported on the following:

- Cisco 4500 and Cisco 4700 routers with NPM
- Cisco 7500 series routers with AIP

This command is not supported on the ATM port adapter. This command defines a traffic parameter for the SVC connection. The suffix clp0 indicates that this command affects only cells with a cell loss priority (CLP) of 0 (high-priority cells).

On the Cisco 7500 series, this parameter can be between 32 and 2016 cells, with values that are not multiples of 32 rounded to the nearest multiple of 32. On the Cisco 4500 and Cisco 4700 routers, this parameter can be between 1 and 65535 cells.

Example

The following example sets the maximum number of high-priority cells coming from the destination router at the burst level to 800 cells:

```
atm backward-max-burst-size-clp0 800
```

ATM BACKWARD-MAX-BURST-SIZE-CLP1

To request the maximum number of low-priority and high-priority cells coming from the destination router to the source router at the burst level on the SVC, use the **atm backward-max-burst-size-clp1** map-class configuration command. The **no** form of this command restores the default value.

atm backward-max-burst-size-clp1 *cell-count*
no atm backward-max-burst-size-clp1

Syntax   Description

cell-count   Maximum number of low-priority and high-priority cells coming from the destination router at the burst level.

Default

The default is –1. The router does not request this traffic parameter of the ATM switch. The switch drops cells if there is not enough buffer space.

Command Mode

Map-class configuration

Usage Guidelines

This command first appeared in Cisco IOS Release 10.0.

This command is supported on the following:

- Cisco 4500 and Cisco 4700 routers with NPM
- Cisco 7500 series routers with AIP

This command is not supported on the ATM port adapter. This command defines a traffic parameter for the SVC connection. The suffix **clp1** applies to the cumulative flow of CLP0 and CLP1 (high-priority and low-priority) cells.

On the Cisco 7500 series, this parameter can be between 32 and 2016 cells, with values that are not multiples of 32 rounded to the nearest multiple of 32. On the Cisco 4500 and 4700 series, this parameter can be between 1 and 65,535 cells.

Example

The following example requests the maximum number of low-priority and high-priority cells coming from the destination router at the burst level to 2016:

```
atm backward-max-burst-size-clp1 2016
```

ATM BACKWARD-PEAK-CELL-RATE-CLP0

To change the peak rate of high-priority cells coming from the destination router to the source router on the SVC, use the **atm backward-peak-cell-rate-clp0** map-class configuration command. The **no** form of this command restores the default.

> **atm backward-peak-cell-rate-clp0** *rate*
> **no atm backward-peak-cell-rate-clp0**

Syntax	*Description*
rate	Maximum rate in kilobits per second (Kbps) at which this SVC can receive high-priority cells from the destination router. Maximum upper range is 155,000 Kbps.

Default

The default is –1. The router does not request this traffic parameter of the ATM switch. The switch drops cells if there is not enough buffer space.

Command Mode

Map-class configuration

Usage Guidelines

This command first appeared in Cisco IOS Release 10.0.

This command is supported on the following:

- Cisco 4500 and Cisco 4700 routers with NPM
- Cisco 7500 series routers with AIP

This command is not supported on the ATM port adapter. This command defines a traffic parameter for the SVC connection. The suffix **clp0** indicates that this command affects only cells with a cell loss priority (CLP) of 0 (high-priority cells).

Example

The following example sets the peak rate for high-priority cells from the destination router to 8000 Kbps:

```
atm backward-peak-cell-rate-clp0 8000
```

ATM BACKWARD-PEAK-CELL-RATE-CLP1

To request the peak rate of low-priority and high-priority cells coming from the destination router to the source router on the SVC, use the **atm backward-peak-cell-rate-clp1** map-class configuration command. The **no** form of this command restores the default.

> **atm backward-peak-cell-rate-clp1** *rate*
> **no atm backward-peak-cell-rate-clp1**

Syntax	Description
rate	Maximum rate in kilobits per second (Kbps) at which this SVC can receive low-priority and high-priority cells from the destination router. Maximum upper range is 7,113,539 Kbps (limited by 0xffffff cells-per-second).

Default

The default is –1. The router does not request this traffic parameter of the ATM switch. The switch drops cells if there is not enough buffer space.

Command Mode

Map-class configuration

Usage Guidelines

This command first appeared in Cisco IOS Release 10.0.

This command is supported on the following:

- Cisco 4500 and Cisco 4700 routers with NPM
- Cisco 7500 series routers with AIP

This command is not supported on the ATM port adapter. This command defines a traffic parameter for the SVC connection. The suffix **clp1** applies to the cumulative flow of CLP0 and CLP1 (high-priority and low-priority) cells.

Example

The following example requests the peak rate for low-priority and high-priority cells from the destination router to 7000 Kbps:

```
atm backward-peak-cell-rate-clp1 7000
```

ATM BACKWARD-SUSTAINABLE-CELL-RATE-CLP0

To change the sustainable rate of high-priority cells coming from the destination router to the source router on the SVC, use the **atm backward-sustainable-cell-rate-clp0** map-class configuration command. The **no** form of this command restores the default.

    atm backward-sustainable-cell-rate-clp0 *rate*
    no atm backward-sustainable-cell-rate-clp0

Syntax	Description
rate	Sustainable rate in kilobits per second (Kbps) at which this SVC can receive high-priority cells from the destination router. Maximum upper range is 155,000 Kbps.

Default

The default is –1. The router does not request this traffic parameter of the ATM switch. The switch drops cells if there is not enough buffer space.

Command Mode

Map-class configuration

Usage Guidelines

This command first appeared in Cisco IOS Release 10.0.

This command is supported on the following:

- Cisco 4500 and Cisco 4700 routers with NPM
- Cisco 7500 series routers with AIP

This command is not supported on the ATM port adapter. This command defines a traffic parameter for the SVC connection. The suffix **clp0** indicates that this command affects only cells with a cell loss priority (CLP) of 0 (high-priority cells).

Example

The following example sets the sustainable rate for high-priority cells from the destination router to 800 Kbps:

```
atm backward-sustainable-cell-rate-clp0 800
```

ATM BACKWARD-SUSTAINABLE-CELL-RATE-CLP1

To request the sustainable rate of low-priority and high-priority cells coming from the destination router to the source router on the SVC, use the **atm backward-sustainable-cell-rate-clp1** map-class configuration command. The **no** form of this command restores the default value.

atm backward-sustainable-cell-rate-clp1 *rate*
no atm backward-sustainable-cell-rate-clp1

Syntax	Description
rate	Sustainable rate in kilobits per second (Kbps) at which this SVC can receive low-priority and high-priority cells from the destination router. Maximum upper range is 7,113,539 Kbps (limited by 0xffffff cells-per-second).

Default

The default is –1. The router does not request this traffic parameter of the ATM switch. The switch drops cells if there is not enough buffer space.

Command Mode

Map-class configuration

Usage Guidelines

This command first appeared in Cisco IOS Release 10.0.

This command is supported on the following:

- Cisco 4500 and Cisco 4700 routers with NPM
- Cisco 7500 series routers with AIP

This command is not supported on the ATM port adapter. This command defines a traffic parameter for the SVC connection. The suffix **clp1** applies to the cumulative flow of CLP0 and CLP1 (high-priority and low-priority) cells.

Example

The following example requests the sustainable rate for low-priority and high-priority cells from the destination router to 700 Kbps:

```
atm backward-sustainable-cell-rate-clp1 700
```

ATM CLASS

To specify a class for an ATM interface, use the **atm class** global configuration command. The **no** form of this command deletes this class from the interface.

    atm class *class-name*
    no atm class *class-name*

Syntax   *Description*

class-name   User-assigned name of the traffic parameters table.

Default

No class is defined.

Command Mode

Global configuration

Usage Guidelines

This command first appeared in Cisco IOS Release 11.2.

One command is permitted per interface. Entering a second **atm class** command on an interface results in the original entry being overwritten.

Example

The following example illustrates the configuration of an ATM ARP client in an SVC environment using the class *classicip* for traffic shaping:

```
interface atm 2/0
 atm pvc 1 0 5 qsaal
 atm pvc 2 0 16 ilmi
 atm esi-address 345678901234.12
 ip address 10.0.0.2 255.0.0.0
 atm arp-server nsap ac.1533.66.020000.0000.0000.0000.0000.0000.0000.00
 atm class classicip
 no shutdown

map-class classicip
 atm forward-peak-cell-rate-clp1 7000
 atm backward-peak-cell-rate-clp1 7000
 atm forward-sustainable-cell-rate-clp0 800
```

Related Commands

map-class atm

ATM CLOCK INTERNAL

To cause the ATM interface to generate the transmit clock internally, use the **atm clock internal** interface configuration command. The **no** form of this command restores the default value.

    atm clock internal
    no atm clock internal

Syntax Description

This command has no arguments or keywords.

Default

The ATM interface uses the transmit clock signal from the remote connection (the line). The switch provides the clocking.

Command Mode

Interface configuration

Usage Guidelines

This command first appeared in Cisco IOS Release 10.0. This command is meaningless on a 4B/5B physical layer interface module (PLIM). For SONET interfaces, use the **atm clock internal** command to configure an ATM port adapter to supply its internal clock to the line.

Example

The following example causes the ATM interface to generate the transmit clock internally:

```
atm clock internal
```

ATM DS3-SCRAMBLE

To enable scrambling of the ATM cell payload for the DS-3 PLIM, use the **atm ds3-scramble** interface configuration command. To disable this functionality, use the **no** form of this command.

    atm ds3-scramble
    no atm ds3-scramble

Syntax Description

This command has no arguments or keywords.

Default

Disabled

Command Mode

Interface configuration

Usage Guidelines

This command first appeared in Cisco IOS Release 11.0.

Example

The following example enables scrambling of the ATM cell payload for the DS-3 PLIM on the ATM interface 2/0:

```
interface atm 2/0
atm ds3-scramble
```

ATM ESI-ADDRESS

To enter the end station ID (ESI) and selector byte fields of the ATM NSAP address, use the **atm esi-address** interface configuration command. The NSAP address prefix is filled in via ILMI from the ATM switch. The **no** form deletes the end station address.

    atm esi-address *esi.selector*
    no atm esi-address *esi.selector*

Syntax	Description
esi	End station ID field value in hexadecimal; 6 bytes long.
selector	Selector field value in hexadecimal; 1 byte long.

Default

No end station is defined.

Command Mode

Interface configuration

Usage Guidelines

This command first appeared in Cisco IOS Release 11.1.

Before Cisco IOS Release 11.1, ATM addresses were configured on the router only by use of the **atm nsap-address** interface configuration command. The complete 20-byte NSAP (40 hexadecimal characters) had to be configured.

The **atm esi-address** command allows you to configure the ATM address by entering the ESI (12 hexadecimal characters) and the selector byte (2 hexadecimal characters). The ATM prefix (26 hexadecimal characters) will be provided by the ATM switch. To get the prefix from the ATM switch, the ILMI permanent virtual circuit (PVC) must be configured on the router and the ATM switch must be able to supply a prefix via ILMI.

> **NOTES**
>
> When ILMI is configured, use the **atm esi-address** command instead of the **atm nsap-address** command. The **atm esi-address** and **atm nsap-address** commands are mutually exclusive. Configuring the router with the **atm esi-address** command negates the **atm nsap-address** setting, and vice versa.

The ILMI PVC must be configured in order to get an NSAP address prefix from the switch.

Example

The following example sets up the ILMI PVC and assigns the ESI and selector field values on the ATM interface 4/0:

```
interface atm 4/0
 atm pvc 2 0 16 ilmi
 atm esi-address 345678901234.12
```

Related Commands

atm nsap-address
atm pvc ilmi

ATM EXCEPTION-QUEUE

To set the exception queue length, use the **atm exception-queue** interface configuration command. The **no** form of this command restores the default value.

    atm exception-queue *number*
    no atm exception-queue

Syntax	Description
number	Number of entries in the range of 8 to 256. The default is 32 entries.

Default

32 entries

Command Mode

Interface configuration

Usage Guidelines

This command first appeared in Cisco IOS Release 10.0.

This command is supported on AIP for Cisco 7500 series routers. This command is not supported on the ATM port adapter for Cisco 7200 and 7500 series routers, nor is it supported on Cisco 4500 and Cisco 4700 routers.

The exception queue is used for reporting ATM events, such as cycle redundancy check (CRC) errors.

Example

In the following example, the exception queue is set to 50 entries:
```
atm exception-queue 50
```

ATM FORWARD-MAX-BURST-SIZE-CLP0

To change the maximum number of high-priority cells going from the source router to the destination router at the burst level on the SVC, use the **atm forward-max-burst-size-clp0** map-class configuration command. The **no** form of this command restores the default value.

> **atm forward-max-burst-size-clp0** *cell-count*
> **no atm forward-max-burst-size-clp0**

Syntax	Description
cell-count	Maximum number of high-priority cells going from the source router at the burst level.

Default

The default is −1. The router does not request this traffic parameter of the ATM switch. The switch drops cells if there is not enough buffer space.

Command Mode

Map-class configuration

Usage Guidelines

This command first appeared in Cisco IOS Release 10.0.

This command is supported on the following:

- Cisco 4500 and Cisco 4700 routers with NPM
- Cisco 7500 series routers with AIP

This command is not supported on the ATM port adapter. This command defines a traffic parameter for the SVC connection. The suffix **clp0** indicates that this command affects only cells with a cell loss priority (CLP) of 0 (high-priority cells).

On the Cisco 7500 series, this parameter can be between 32 and 2016 cells, with values that are not multiples of 32 rounded to the nearest multiple of 32. On the Cisco 4500 and Cisco 4700 routers, this parameter can be between 1 and 65,535 cells.

Example

The following example sets the maximum number of high-priority cells going from the source router at the burst level to 2016:

```
atm forward-max-burst-size-clp0 2016
```

ATM FORWARD-MAX-BURST-SIZE-CLP**1**

To request the maximum number of low-priority and high-priority cells going from the source router to the destination router at the burst level on the SVC, use the **atm forward-max-burst-size-clp1** map-class configuration command. The **no** form of this command restores the default value.

> **atm forward-max-burst-size-clp1** *cell-count*
> **no atm forward-max-burst-size-clp1**

Syntax   *Description*

cell-count   Maximum number of low-priority and high-priority cells going from the source router at the burst level.

Default

The default is –1. The router does not request this traffic parameter of the ATM switch. The switch drops cells if there is not enough buffer space.

Command Mode

Map-class configuration

Usage Guidelines

This command first appeared in Cisco IOS Release 10.0.

This command is supported on the following:

- Cisco 4500 and Cisco 4700 routers with NPM
- Cisco 7500 series routers with AIP

This command is not supported on the ATM port adapter. This command defines a traffic parameter for the SVC connection. The suffix **clp1** applies to the cumulative flow of CLP0 and CLP1 (high-priority and low-priority) cells.

On the Cisco 7500 series, this parameter can be between 32 and 2016 cells, with values that are not multiples of 32 rounded to the nearest multiple of 32. On the Cisco 4500 and 4700 series, this parameter can be between 1 and 65,535 cells.

Example

The following example requests the maximum number of low-priority and high-priority cells going from the source router at the burst level to 2016:

```
atm forward-max-burst-size-clp1 2016
```

ATM FORWARD-PEAK-CELL-RATE-CLP0

To change the peak rate of high-priority cells going from the source router to the destination router on the SVC, use the **atm forward-peak-cell-rate-clp0** map-class configuration command. The **no** form of this command restores the default value.

> **atm forward-peak-cell-rate-clp0** *rate*
> **no atm forward-peak-cell-rate-clp0**

Syntax   *Description*

rate   Maximum rate in kilobits per second (Kbps) at which this SVC can send high-priority cells from the source router. Maximum upper range is 155,000 Kbps.

Default

The default is –1. The router does not request this traffic parameter of the ATM switch. The switch drops cells if there is not enough buffer space.

Command Mode

Map-class configuration

Usage Guidelines

This command first appeared in Cisco IOS Release 10.0.

This command is supported on the following:

- Cisco 4500 and Cisco 4700 routers with NPM
- Cisco 7500 series routers with AIP

This command is not supported on the ATM port adapter. This command defines a traffic parameter for the SVC connection. The suffix **clp0** indicates that this command affects only cells with a cell loss priority (CLP) of 0 (high-priority cells).

Example

The following example sets the peak high-priority cell rate from the source router to 1000 Kbps:

```
atm forward-peak-cell-rate-clp0 1000
```

ATM FORWARD-PEAK-CELL-RATE-CLP1

To request the peak rate of low-priority and high-priority cells coming from the source router to the destination router on the SVC, use the **atm forward-peak-cell-rate-clp1** map-class configuration command. The **no** form of this command restores the default value.

> **atm forward-peak-cell-rate-clp1** *rate*
> **no atm forward-peak-cell-rate-clp1**

Syntax	Description
rate	Maximum rate in kilobits per second (Kbps) at which this SVC can send low-priority and high-priority cells from the source router. Maximum upper range is 7,113,539 Kbps (limited by 0xffffff cells-per-second).

Default

The default is –1. The router does not request this traffic parameter of the ATM switch. The switch drops cells if there is not enough buffer space.

Command Mode

Map-class configuration

Usage Guidelines

This command first appeared in Cisco IOS Release 10.0.

This command is supported on the following:

Cisco 4500 and Cisco 4700 routers with NPM

Cisco 7500 series routers with AIP

This command is not supported on the ATM port adapter. This command defines a traffic parameter for the SVC connection. The suffix **clp1** applies to the cumulative flow of CLP0 and CLP1 (high-priority and low-priority) cells.

Example

The following example requests the peak rate for low-priority and high-priority cells from the source router to 100,000 Kbps:

```
atm forward-peak-cell-rate-clp1 100000
```

ATM FORWARD-SUSTAINABLE-CELL-RATE-CLP0

To change the sustainable rate of high-priority cells coming from the source router to the destination router on the SVC, use the **atm forward-sustainable-cell-rate-clp0** map-class configuration command. The **no** form of this command restores the default value.

> **atm forward-sustainable-cell-rate-clp0** *rate*
> **no atm forward-sustainable-cell-rate-clp0**

Syntax	Description
rate	Sustainable rate in kilobits per second (Kbps) at which this SVC can send high-priority cells from the source router. Maximum upper range is 155,000 Kbps.

Default

The default is –1. The router does not request this traffic parameter of the ATM switch. The switch drops cells if there is not enough buffer space.

Command Mode

Map-class configuration

Usage Guidelines

This command first appeared in Cisco IOS Release 10.0.

This command is supported on the following:

- Cisco 4500 and Cisco 4700 routers with NPM
- Cisco 7500 series routers with AIP

This command is not supported on the ATM port adapter. This command defines a traffic parameter for the SVC connection. The suffix **clp0** indicates that this command affects only cells with a cell loss priority (CLP) of 0 (high-priority cells).

Example

The following example sets the sustainable rate for high-priority cells from the source router to 100,000 Kbps:

```
atm forward-sustainable-cell-rate-clp0 100000
```

ATM FORWARD-SUSTAINABLE-CELL-RATE-CLP1

To request the sustainable rate of low-priority and high-priority cells coming from the source router to the destination router on the SVC, use the **atm forward-sustainable-cell-rate-clp1** map-class configuration command. The **no** form of this command restores the default value.

> **atm forward-sustainable-cell-rate-clp1** *rate*
> **no atm forward-sustainable-cell-rate-clp1**

Syntax	Description
rate	Sustainable rate in kilobits per second (Kbps) at which this SVC can send low-priority and high-priority cells from the source router. Maximum upper range is 7,113,539 Kbps (limited by 0xffffff cells-per-second).

Default

The default is –1. The router does not request this traffic parameter of the ATM switch. The switch drops cells if there is not enough buffer space.

Command Mode

Map-class configuration

Usage Guidelines

This command first appeared in Cisco IOS Release 10.0.

This command is supported on the following:

- Cisco 4500 and Cisco 4700 routers with NPM
- Cisco 7500 series routers with AIP

This command is not supported on the ATM port adapter. This command defines a traffic parameter for the SVC connection. The suffix **clp1** applies to the cumulative flow of CLP0 and CLP1 (high-priority and low-priority) cells.

Example

The following example requests the sustainable rate for low-priority and high-priority cells from the source router to 100,000 Kbps:

```
atm forward-sustainable-cell-rate-clp1 100000
```

ATM FRAMING (DS3)

To specify DS3 line framing on Cisco 4500 and Cisco 4700 routers, use the following form of the **atm framing** interface configuration command. To return to the default C-bit with Physical Layer Convergence Protocol (PLCP) framing, use the **no** form of this command.

    atm framing [m23adm | cbitplcp | m23plcp]
    no atm framing [m23adm | cbitplcp | m23plcp]

Syntax	Description
m23adm	(Optional) Specifies M-23 ATM direct mapping.
cbitplcp	(Optional) Specifies C-bit with PLCP framing.
m23plcp	(Optional) Specifies M-23 with PLCP framing.

Default

No framing

Command Mode

Interface configuration

Usage Guidelines

This command first appeared in Cisco IOS Release 11.2.

This command is available only on Cisco 4500 and Cisco 4700 routers with DS3 access speeds. This command is not available on the Cisco 7200 and 7500 series routers.

Framing on the interface must match that on the switch for this ATM link.

Example

The following example specifies M-23 ADM framing on a Cisco 4500 or Cisco 4700 router that has been set up with DS3 access to an ATM network:

```
atm framing m32adm
```

ATM FRAMING (E3)

To specify E3 line framing, use the **atm framing** interface configuration command. To return to the default G.751 Physical Layer Convergence Protocol (PLCP) framing, use the **no** form of this command.

> **atm framing g832adm** (Cisco 7200 and 7500 series routers)
> **no atm framing g832adm**
> **atm framing [g832adm | g751adm]** (Cisco 4500 and Cisco 4700 routers)
> **no atm framing [g832adm | g751adm]**

Syntax	Description
g832adm	Required for Cisco 7200 and 7500 series routers; optional for Cisco 4500 and Cisco 4700 routers. Specifies G.832 ATM Direct Mapping.
g751adm	(Optional) Specifies G.751 ATM Direct Mapping.

Default

No framing

Command Mode

Interface configuration

Usage Guidelines

This command first appeared in Cisco IOS Release 11.0.

This command is available on the Cisco 7200 and 7500 series routers, Cisco 4500 routers, and Cisco 4700 routers with E3 access speeds. This command is not available on the Cisco 7500 with DS3 access speeds; that combination supports only one type of line framing. The default framing is described in the ITU-T Recommendation G.751.

Command Reference

NOTES

The ITU-T carries out the functions of the former Consultative Committee for International Telegraph and Telephone (CCITT).

Framing on the interface must match that on the switch for this ATM link.

Example

The following example specifies G.832 ADM framing on a Cisco 7500 router that has been set up with E3 access to an ATM network:

```
atm framing g832adm
```

ATM IDLE-TIMEOUT

To change the idle timer for SVCs on an interface that will cause the SVCs to disconnect when inactive for a specified interval, use the **atm idle-timeout** interface configuration command. To return to the default setting, use the **no** form of this command.

> **atm idle-timeout** *seconds*
> **no atm idle-timeout**

Syntax	Description
seconds	Number of seconds the SVC can be inactive before disconnecting. Setting *seconds* to 0 disables idle timeouts.

Default

The default is 300 seconds (5 minutes).

Command Mode

Interface configuration

Usage Guidelines

This command first appeared in Cisco IOS Release 11.0.

To disable idle timeouts entirely, set the value of *seconds* to zero.

Prior to Cisco IOS Release 11.0, idle timeouts were not supported; that is, the prior configuration was equivalent to **atm idle-timeout 0**.

Example

The following example disconnects an SVC after 300 seconds for the ATM interface 1/0:

```
interface atm 1/0
 atm idle-timeout 300
```

ATM ILMI-KEEPALIVE

To enable Interim Local Management Interface (ILMI) keepalives, use the **atm ilmi-keepalive** interface configuration command. To disable ILMI keepalives, use the **no** form of this command.

> **atm ilmi-keepalive** [*seconds*]
> **no atm ilmi-keepalive** [*seconds*]

Syntax   *Description*

seconds   (Optional) Number of seconds between keepalives. The default is 3 seconds. Values less than 3 seconds are rounded to 3 seconds; there is no upper bound to the range of values.

Default

Disabled

Command Mode

Interface configuration

Usage Guidelines

This command first appeared in Cisco IOS Release 11.0.

Example

The following example enables ILMI keepalives for the ATM interface 1/0:

```
interface atm 1/0
 atm address-registration
 atm ilmi-keepalive
```

Related Commands

atm address-registration

ATM MAXVC

To set the ceiling value of the virtual circuit descriptor (VCD) on the ATM interface, use the **atm maxvc** interface configuration command. To restore the default value, use the **no** form of this command.

> **atm maxvc** *number*
> **no atm maxvc**

Syntax   *Description*

number   Maximum number of supported virtual circuits. Valid values are 256, 512, 1024, or 2048.

Default

2048 virtual circuits

Command Mode

Interface configuration

Usage Guidelines

This command first appeared in Cisco IOS Release 10.0.

This command is supported on Cisco 7500 series routers; it is not supported on the Cisco 4500 and Cisco 4700 routers, which have a fixed maximum of 1024.

This command sets the maximum value supported for the *vcd* argument in the **atm pvc** command. It also determines the maximum number of virtual circuits on which the AIP allows segmentation and reassembly (SAR) to occur. However, if you set a **maxvc** limit and then enter the **atm pvc** command with a larger value for the *vcd* argument, the software does not generate an error message.

This command does not affect the virtual path identifier (VPI)-virtual channel identifier (VCI) pair of each virtual circuit.

Example

The following example sets a ceiling VCD value of 1024 and restricts the AIP to supporting no more than 1024 virtual circuits:

```
atm maxvc 1024
```

Related Commands

atm pvc

ATM MID-PER-VC

To limit the number of message identifier (MID) numbers allowed on each virtual circuit, use the **atm mid-per-vc** interface configuration command.

    atm mid-per-vc *maximum*

Syntax	Description
maximum	Number of MIDs allowed per virtual circuit on this interface. The values allowed are 16, 32, 64, 128, 256, 512, and 1024.

Default

The default limit is 16 MIDs per virtual circuit.

Command Mode

Interface configuration

Usage Guidelines

This command first appeared in Cisco IOS Release 10.3.

This command is supported on Cisco 7200 and 7500 series routers.

Message identifier (MID) numbers are used by receiving devices to reassemble cells from multiple sources into packets. This command limits the number of discrete messages allowed on the PVC at the same time. It does not limit the number of cells associated with each message.

The *maximum* set by the **atm mid-per-vc** command overrides the range between the *midhigh* and *midlow* values set by the **atm pvc** command. If you set a *maximum* of 16 but a *midlow* of 0 and a *midhigh* of 255, only 16 MIDs (not 256) are allowed on the virtual circuit.

Example

The following example allows 64 MIDs per ATM virtual circuit:

```
atm mid-per-vc 64
```

Related Commands

atm pvc

ATM MULTICAST

To assign a Switched Multimegabit Data Service (SMDS) E.164 multicast address to the ATM sub-interface that supports AAL3/4 and SMDS encapsulation, use the **atm multicast** interface configuration command.

atm multicast *address*

Syntax	*Description*
address	Multicast E.164 address assigned to the subinterface.

Default

No multicast E.164 address is defined.

Command Mode

Interface configuration

Usage Guidelines

This command first appeared in Cisco IOS Release 10.3.

This command is supported on Cisco 7500 series, Cisco 4500, and Cisco 4700 routers. This command is not supported on the ATM port adapter.

Each AAL3/4 subinterface is allowed only one multicast E.164 address. This multicast address is used for all protocol broadcast operations.

Example

The following example assigns a multicast E.164 address to the ATM subinterface that is being configured:

```
atm multicast e180.0999.000
```

Related Commands

atm aal aal3/4
atm pvc
atm smds-address

ATM MULTIPOINT-INTERVAL

To specify how often new destinations can be added to multipoint calls to an ATM switch in the network, use the **atm multipoint-interval** interface configuration command. To return to the default interval, use the **no** form of this command.

> **atm multipoint-interval** *interval*
> **no atm multipoint-interval** *interval*

Syntax	Description
interval	Interval length in seconds, in the range between 0 and 4294967.

Default

30 seconds

Command Mode

Interface configuration

Usage Guidelines

This command first appeared in Cisco IOS Release 11.0.

This command applies to SVCs only, not to PVCs. This command has no effect unless ATM multipoint signaling is enabled on the interface.

Example

The following example enables point-to-multipoint signaling on the ATM interface 2/0. It also specifies that new destinations can be added to multipoint calls every 60 seconds:

```
interface atm 2/0
 atm multipoint-signalling
 atm multipoint-interval 60
```

Related Commands

atm multipoint-signalling

ATM MULTIPOINT-SIGNALLING

To enable point-to-multipoint signaling to the ATM switch, use the **atm multipoint-signalling** interface configuration command. To disable point-to-multipoint signaling to the ATM switch, use the **no** form of this command.

> **atm multipoint-signalling**
> **no atm multipoint-signalling**

Syntax Description

This command has no keywords or arguments.

Default

Disabled

Command Mode

Interface configuration

Usage Guidelines

This command first appeared in Cisco IOS Release 11.0.

If multipoint signaling is enabled, the router uses existing static map entries that have the **broadcast** keyword set to establish multipoint calls. One call is established for each logical subnet of each protocol.

All destinations are added to the call. One multicast packet is sent to the ATM switch for each multipoint call. The ATM switch replicates the packet to all destinations.

The **atm multipoint-interval** command determines how often new destinations can be added to a multipoint call.

Example

The following example enables point-to-multipoint signaling on the ATM interface 2/0:

```
interface atm 2/0
 atm multipoint-signalling
```

Related Commands

atm multipoint-interval

ATM-NSAP

To define an ATM map statement for an SVC, use the **atm-nsap** map-list configuration command in conjunction with the **map-list** global configuration command. The **no** form of this command removes the address.

protocol protocol-address **atm-nsap** *atm-nsap-address* [**class** *class-name*] [**broadcast**]

no *protocol protocol-address* **atm-nsap** *atm-nsap-address* [**class** *class-name*] [**broadcast**]

Syntax	Description
protocol	One of the following keywords: **appletalk, apollo, bridge, clns, decnet, ip, ipx, vines,** or **xns.**
protocol-address	Destination address that is being mapped to this SVC.
atm-nsap-address	Destination ATM NSAP address. Must be exactly 40 hexadecimal digits long and in the correct dotted format.
class *class-name*	(Optional) Name of a table that contains encapsulation-specific parameters. Such a table can be shared between maps that have the same encapsulation.
broadcast	(Optional) Indicates this map entry is to be used when the corresponding *protocol* sends broadcast packets to the interface—for example, Interior Gateway Routing Protocol (IGRP) updates.

Default

No map statements are defined.

Command Mode

Map-list configuration

Usage Guidelines

This command first appeared in Cisco IOS Release 11.1.

This command is required with the **map-list** command when you are configuring an SVC.

Example

In the following example, a map list named *atmsvc* includes one map statement for a destination address being mapped:

```
map-list atmsvc
   ip 172.21.97.17 atm-nsap AB.CDEF.01.234567.890A.BCDE.F012.3456.7890.1234.12 class qos
   broadcast
```

Related Commands

map-list

ATM NSAP-ADDRESS

To set the NSAP address for an ATM interface using SVC mode, use the **atm nsap-address** interface configuration command. The **no** form of this command removes any configured address for the interface.

> **atm nsap-address** *nsap-address*
> **no atm nsap-address**

Syntax	*Description*
nsap-address	The 40-digit hexadecimal NSAP address of this interface (the source address).

Default

No NSAP address is defined for this interface.

Command Mode

Interface configuration

Usage Guidelines

This command first appeared in Cisco IOS Release 10.0.

When you are configuring an SVC, you must use the **atm nsap-address** command to define the source NSAP address. It identifies a particular port on the ATM network and must be unique across the network.

─ **NOTES** ───

When ILMI is configured, use the **atm esi-address** command instead of the **atm nsap-address** command. The **atm esi-address** and **atm nsap-address** commands are mutually exclusive. Configuring the router with the **atm esi-address** command negates the **atm nsap-address** setting, and vice versa.

───

Configuring a new address on the interface overwrites the previous address. The router considers the address as a string of bytes and will not prefix or suffix the address with any other strings or digits. The complete NSAP address must be specified, because this value is used in the Calling Party Address Information Element in the SETUP message to establish a virtual circuit.

ATM NSAP addresses have a fixed length of 40 hexadecimal digits. You must configure the complete address in the following dotted format:

```
xx.xxxx.xx.xxxxxx.xxxx.xxxx.xxxx.xxxx.xxxx.xxxx.xx
```

NOTES

All ATM NSAP addresses should be entered in the dotted hexadecimal format shown in the preceding text, which conforms to the User-Network Interface (UNI) specification.The dotted method provides some validation that the address is a legal value. If you know that your address format is correct, the dots may be omitted.

Example

In the following example, the source NSAP address for the interface is
AB.CDEF.01.234567.890A.BCDE.F012.3456.7890.1234.12:

```
atm nsap-address AB.CDEF.01.234567.890A.BCDE.F012.3456.7890.1234.12
```

ATM PVC

To create a permanent virtual circuit (PVC) on an ATM interface and, optionally, to generate Operation, Administration, and Maintenance (OAM) F5 loopback cells or enable Inverse ATM ARP, use the **atm pvc** interface configuration command. The **no** form of this command removes the specified PVC.

atm pvc *vcd vpi vci aal-encap* [[*midlow midhigh*] [*peak average* [*burst*]]] [**inarp** [*minutes*]]
[**oam** [*seconds*]]

no atm pvc *vcd vpi vci aal-encap* [[*midlow midhigh*] [*peak average* [*burst*]]] [**inarp** [*minutes*]
[**oam** [*seconds*]]

atm pvc *vcd vpi vci* **aal5ciscoppp** [*peak average* [*burst*]] [**oam** [*seconds*]] **virtual-template**
number (used for PPP over ATM only)

no atm pvc *vcd vpi vci* aal5ciscoppp [*peak average* [*burst*]] [**oam** [*seconds*]]**virtual-template**
number (used for PPP over ATM only)

Syntax	Description
vcd	Virtual circuit descriptor. A unique number that identifies to the processor which VPI-VCI pair to use for a particular packet. Valid values range from 1 to the value set with the **atm maxvc** command. The AIP or ATM port adapter requires this feature to manage packet transmission. The *vcd* value is not associated with the VPI-VCI pair used for the ATM network cells. The NPM has a hard coded max *vcd* value of 1023.
vpi	ATM network virtual path identifier (VPI) of this PVC. On the Cisco 7200 and 7500 series routers, this value ranges from 0 to 255; on the Cisco 4500 and Cisco 4700 series, this value ranges from 0 to 1 less than the quotient of 8192 divided by the value set by the **atm vc-per-vp** command.
	The VPI is an 8-bit field in the header of the ATM cell. The VPI value is unique only on a single link, not throughout the ATM network, because it has local significance only. The VPI value must match that of the switch.
	The arguments vpi and vci cannot both be set to 0; if one is 0, the other cannot be 0.

Syntax	Description
vci	ATM network virtual channel identifier (VCI) of this PVC, in the range of 0 to 1 less than the maximum value set for this interface by the **atm vc-per-vp** command. Typically, lower values 0 to 31 are reserved for specific traffic (for example, F4 OAM, SVC signaling, ILMI, and so on) and should not be used.
	The VCI is a 16-bit field in the header of the ATM cell. The VCI value is unique only on a single link, not throughout the ATM network, because it has local significance only.
	The arguments *vpi* and *vci* cannot both be set to 0; if one is 0, the other cannot be 0.
aal-encap	ATM adaptation layer (AAL) and encapsulation type. When the **aal5mux** keyword is specified, a protocol is required. Possible values are as follows:
	• **aal34smds**—Encapsulation for SMDS networks. This option is supported on the AIP and is not available for the ATM port adapter.
	• **aal5nlpid**—Encapsulation that allows ATM interfaces to interoperate with High-Speed Serial Interfaces (HSSIs) that are using an ATM data service unit (ADSU) and running ATM-Data Exchange Interface (DXI).
	• **aal5mux apollo**—A multiplex (MUX)-type virtual circuit.
	• **aal5mux appletalk**—A MUX-type virtual circuit.
	• **aal5mux decnet**—A MUX-type virtual circuit.
	• **aal5mux ip**—A MUX-type virtual circuit.
	• **aal5mux ipx**—A MUX-type virtual circuit.
	• **aal5mux vines**—A MUX-type virtual circuit.
	• **aal5mux xns**—A MUX-type virtual circuit.
	• **aal5ciscoppp**—Encapsulation for PPP over ATM.
	• **aal5snap**—Logical Link Control/Subnetwork Access Protocol (LLC/SNAP) precedes the protocol datagram. *This is the only encapsulation supported for Inverse ARP.*
	• **ilmi**—Used to set up communication with the ILMI; the associated *vpi* and *vci* values are ordinarily 0 and 16, respectively.
	• **qsaal**—A signaling-type PVC used for setting up or tearing down SVCs; the associated *vpi* and *vci* values are ordinarily 0 and 5, respectively.
midlow	(Set for the **aal34smds** encapsulation only.) (Optional) Starting message identifier (MID) number for this PVC. The default is 0. If you set the *peak* and *average* (*burst* is optional) values for **aal34smds** encapsulation, you must also set the *midlow* and *midhigh* values.
	This option is not available for the ATM port adapter.

Syntax	Description
midhigh	(Set for the **aal34smds** encapsulation only.) (Optional) Ending MID number for this PVC. The default is 0. If you set the *peak* and *average* (*burst* is optional) values for **aal34smds** encapsulation, you must also set the *midlow* and *midhigh* values.
	This option is not available for the ATM port adapter.
peak	(Optional) Maximum rate (in Kbps) at which this virtual circuit can transmit. Valid values are in the range from 1 to the maximum rate set for a rate queue. If you set this value, you must also specify the *average* (*burst* is optional) value. If you set the *peak* and *average* values for **aal34smds** encapsulation, you must also set the *midlow* and *midhigh* values.
	This option is not available for the ATM port adapter.
average	(Optional) Average rate (in Kbps) at which this virtual circuit transmits. Valid values are platform dependent. If you set this value, you must also specify the *peak* (*burst* is optional) value. If you set the *peak* and *average* values for **aal34smds** encapsulation, you must also set the *midlow* and *midhigh* values.
	This option is not available for the ATM port adapter.
burst	(Optional) Value that relates to the maximum number of ATM cells the virtual circuit can transmit to the network at the *peak* rate of the PVC. On the AIP, the actual burst cells equals *burst* * 32 cells, thereby allowing for a burst size of 32 cells to 2016 cells. On the ATMZR, the value is not multiplied. If you set this value, you must also specify a value for the *peak* and *average* values.
	On the AIP, *burst* can range from 1 to 63.
	On the ATMZR, *burst* can range from 1 to 65535.
	This option is not available for the ATM port adapter.
inarp *minutes*	(Set for the **aal5snap** encapsulation only.) (Optional) Specifies how often Inverse ARP datagrams are sent on this virtual circuit. The default value is 15 minutes.
oam *seconds*	(Optional) Specifies how often to generate an OAM F5 loopback cell from this virtual circuit. The default value is 10 seconds.
virtual-template *number*	(Required for **aal5ciscoppp** encapsulation only.) Specifies the number used to identify the virtual template.

Defaults

If *peak* and *average* rate values are omitted, the PVC defaults to peak and average rates equal to the link rate. The peak and average rates are then equal. By default, the virtual circuit is configured to run as fast as possible.

The default of both the *midlow* and *midhigh* values is 0.

If the **oam** keyword is omitted, OAM cells are not generated. If the **oam** keyword is present but the *seconds* value is omitted, the default value of **oam** *seconds* is 10 seconds.

If the **inarp** keyword is omitted, Inverse ARPs are not generated. If the **inarp** keyword is present, but the timeout value is not given, then Inverse ARPs are generated every 15 minutes.

Command Mode

Interface configuration

Subinterface configuration for **aal5ciscoppp** encapsulation

Usage Guidelines

This command first appeared in Cisco IOS Release 10.0. The *midlow* and *midhigh* arguments first appeared in Cisco IOS Release 10.3. The **oam** *seconds* and **inarp** *minutes* commands first appeared in Cisco IOS Release 11.0.

Because the ATM port adapters do not support traffic shaping, the *peak*, *average*, and *burst* rate options are not available.

The order of command options is important. The **inarp** keyword can be specified either separately or before the **oam** keyword has been enabled. The *peak*, *average*, and *burst* arguments, if specified, cannot be specified after either the **inarp** or the **oam** keywords.

The Cisco IOS software dynamically creates rate queues as necessary to satisfy the requests of **atm pvc** commands. The software dynamically creates a rate queue when an **atm pvc** command specifies a peak or average rate that does not match any user-configured rate queue.

The **atm pvc** command creates a PVC and attaches it to the VPI and VCI specified. Both *vpi* and *vci* cannot be specified as 0; if one is 0, the other cannot be 0. The *aal-encap* argument determines the AAL mode and the encapsulation method used. The *peak* and *average* arguments determine the rate queue used.

Use one of the **aal5mux** encapsulation options to dedicate the specified virtual circuit to a single protocol; use the **aal5snap** encapsulation option to multiplex two or more protocols over the same virtual circuit. Whether you select **aal5mux** or **aal5snap** encapsulation might depend on practical considerations, such as the type of network and the pricing offered by the network. If the network's pricing depends on the number of virtual circuits set up, **aal5snap** might be the appropriate choice. If pricing depends on the number of bytes transmitted, **aal5mux** might be the appropriate choice because it has slightly less overhead.

If you choose to specify *peak* or *average* values, you must specify both. If you set the *peak* and *average* values for **aal34smds** encapsulation, you must also specify the *midlow* and *midhigh* values; **aal34smds** encapsulation is not available for the ATM port adapter.

Message identifier (MID) numbers, which are available only with **aal34smds** encapsulation, are used by receiving devices to reassemble cells from multiple packets. You can assign different *midlow* to *midhigh* ranges to different PVCs to ensure that the message identifiers are unique at the receiving end and, therefore, that messages can be reassembled correctly.

When configuring an SVC, use the **atm pvc** command to configure the PVC that handles the SVC call setup and termination. In this case, specify the **qsaal** encapsulation for the *aal-encap* keyword. See the third example that follows.

The router generates and echoes OAM F5 loopback cells, which verify connectivity. Once OAM cell generation is enabled, a cell is transmitted periodically. The remote end must respond by echoing back the cells.

The router does not generate alarm indication signal (AIS) cells, which are used for alarm surveillance functions. However, if it receives an AIS cell, it responds by sending an OAM far-end remote failure (FERF) cell.

When configuring PPP over ATM, specify the **aal5ciscoppp** encapsulation for the *aal-encap* keyword and specify the virtual template using the **virtual-template** argument. It is possible to implicitly create a virtual template when configuring PPP over ATM. In other words, if the parameters of the virtual template are not explicitly defined before configuring the ATM PVC, the PPP interface will be brought up using default values from the virtual template identified. However, some parameters (such as an IP address) take effect only if they are specified before the PPP interface comes up. Therefore, it is recommended that you explicitly create and configure the virtual template before configuring the ATM PVC to ensure such parameters take effect. Alternatively, if parameters are specified after the ATM PVC has already been configured, you should issue a **shutdown** command followed by a **no shutdown** command on the ATM subinterface to restart the interface, thereby causing the newly configured parameters (such as an IP address) to take effect.

For PPP over ATM, the *average* rate value should be set to the line rate available at the remote site, because the remote line rate will have the lowest speed of the connection. For example, if the remote site has a T1 link, set the line rate to 1.536 Mbps. Because the average rate calculation on the ATM PVC includes the cell headers, a line rate value plus 10 or 15 percent may result in better remote line utilization. The *peak* rate value is typically identical to the *average* rate or some suitable multiple thereof (up to 64 times for the Cisco 7500 series and unlimited for the Cisco 4500 and 4700 routers). The *burst* size value depends on the number of cells that can be buffered by receiving ATM switches and is coordinated with the ATM network connection provider. If this value is not specified, the default, which is the equivalent to one maximum length frame on the interface, is used.

Examples

The following example creates a PVC with VPI 0 and VCI 6. The PVC uses AAL AAL5-MUX with IP protocol:

```
atm pvc 1 0 6 aal5mux ip
```

The following example creates a PVC with VPI 0 and VCI 6. The PVC uses AAL AAL3/4-SMDS protocol:

```
atm pvc 1 0 6 aal34smds 0 15 150000 70000 10
```

The following example creates a PVC to be used for ATM signaling for an SVC. It specifies VPI 0 and VCI 5:

```
atm pvc 1 0 5 qsaal
```

Assuming that no static rate queue has been defined, the following example creates the PVC and also creates a dynamic rate queue with the peak rate set to the maximum allowed by the physical layer interface module (PLIM) and the average set to equal the peak rate:

```
atm pvc 1 1 1 aal5snap
```

Assuming that no static rate queue has been defined, the following example creates the PVC and also creates a dynamic rate queue with the peak rate set to 100 Mbps (100,000 Kbps), the average rate set to 50 Mbps (50,000 Kbps), and a burst size of 64 cells (2 * 32 cells):

```
atm pvc 1 1 1 aal5snap 100000 50000 2
```

The following example creates a PVC to be used for PPP over ATM. It specifies VPI 0 and VCI 32. The PVC uses AAL AAL5-CISCOPPP and specifies a virtual template. If the remote site is using a T1 link, the peak and average rates are typically set equal to each other at 1.536 Mbps (1536 Kbps) and a burst size of 64 cells is chosen (2 * 32 cells).

```
atm pvc 1 0 32 aalciscoppp 1536 1536 2 virtual-template 2
```

Related Commands

atm aal aal3/4
atm maxvc
atm multicast
atm rate-queue
atm smds-address
mtu

ATM RATE-QUEUE

To create a permanent rate queue for the AIP or NPM, use the **atm rate-queue** interface configuration command. The **no** form of this command removes the rate queue.

> **atm rate-queue** *queue-number speed*
> **no atm rate-queue**

Syntax	Description
queue-number	Queue number in the range 0 through 7 for the Cisco 7500 series, and in the range 0 through 3 for the Cisco 4500 and Cisco 4700.
	Queues 0 through 3 are in the high-priority bank, and queues 4 through 7 are in the low-priority bank. Queues in the same priority bank have the same priority; for example, queues 0 and 3 have the same priority.

Syntax	Description
speed	Speed in megabits per second (Mbps) in the range from 1 through 155. The maximum speed is determined by the detected PLIM type on the AIP or NPM:
	34 Mbps for E3.
	45 Mbps for DS-3.
	100 Mbps for Transparent Asynchronous Transmitter/Receiver Interface (TAXI).
	155 Mbps for Synchronous Optical Network (SONET).

Default

No rate queue is defined.

Command Mode

Interface configuration

Usage Guidelines

This command first appeared in Cisco IOS Release 10.0.

If you do not create permanent rate queues or if you create PVCs with peak or average rates that are not matched by the rate queues you configure, the software dynamically creates rate queues as necessary to satisfy the requests of the **atm pvc** commands.

You can create multiple rate queues. A warning message appears if all rate queues are deconfigured or if the combined rate queues exceed the PLIM rate.

Example

In the following example, rate queue 1 is configured for 100 Mbps:

```
atm rate-queue 1 100
```

Related Commands

atm pvc

ATM RAWQ-SIZE

To define the AIP raw-queue size, use the **atm rawq-size** interface configuration command. The **no** form of this command restores the default value.

    atm rawq-size *number*
    no atm rawq-size

Syntax	Description
number	Maximum number of cells in the raw queue simultaneously, in the range 8 through 256.

Default

32 cells

Command Mode

Interface configuration

Usage Guidelines

This command first appeared in Cisco IOS Release 10.0.

This command is supported on the Cisco 7200 and 7500 series routers, but not on the Cisco 4500 and Cisco 4700 routers.

The raw queue is used for raw ATM cells, which include OAM (F4 and F5) and Interim Local Management Interface (ILMI) cells.

Example

In the following example, a maximum of 48 cells are allowed in the raw queue:

```
atm rawq-size 48
```

ATM RXBUFF

To set the maximum number of receive buffers for simultaneous packet reassembly, use the **atm rxbuff** interface configuration command. The **no** form of this command restores the default value.

> **atm rxbuff** *number*
> **no atm rxbuff**

Syntax	Description
number	Maximum number of packet reassemblies that the AIP can perform simultaneously, in the range 0 through 512.

Default

256 packet reassemblies

Command Mode

Interface configuration

Usage Guidelines

This command first appeared in Cisco IOS Release 10.0.

This command is supported on AIP for Cisco 7500 series routers. This command is not supported on the ATM port adapter for Cisco 7200 and 7500 series routers, nor is it supported on Cisco 4500 or Cisco 4700 routers.

Example

In the following example, the AIP can perform a maximum of 300 packet reassemblies simultaneously:

```
atm rxbuff 300
```

ATMSIG CLOSE ATM

To disconnect an SVC, use the **atmsig close** EXEC command.

> **atmsig close atm** *slot*/0 *vcd* (for the AIP on Cisco 7500 series routers, for the ATM port adapter on Cisco 7200 series routers)
>
> **atmsig close atm** *slot/port-adapter*/0 *vcd* (for the ATM port adapter on Cisco 7500 series routers)
>
> **atmsig close atm** *number vcd* (for the NPM on Cisco 4500 and Cisco 4700 routers)

Syntax	Description
number	ATM network processor module number for the NPM on Cisco 4500 and Cisco 4700 routers.
port-adapter	ATM port adapter number for the ATM port adapter on the Cisco 7500 series routers.
slot	ATM slot number for the following:
	AIP on Cisco 7500 series routers.
	ATM port adapter on Cisco 7200 series routers and Cisco 7500 series routers.
vcd	Virtual circuit descriptor of the signaling SVC to close.

Command Mode

EXEC

Usage Guidelines

The **atmsig close atm** *slot*/0 *vcd* command first appeared in Cisco IOS Release 10.3.
The **atmsig close atm** *number vcd* command first appeared in Cisco IOS Release 11.1

Execute this command if you want to close a particular SVC. Because virtual circuits are numbered per interface, you must specify the ATM interface by its slot number.

Example

The following example closes SVC 2 on ATM interface 4/0:

```
atmsig close atm4/0 2
```

ATM SIG-TRAFFIC-SHAPING STRICT

To specify that an SVC should be established on an ATM interface only if shaping can be done per the signaled traffic parameters, use the **atm sig-traffic-shaping strict** `interface` configuration command. To disable strict traffic shaping, use the **no** form of this command.

> **atm sig-traffic-shaping strict**
> **no atm sig-traffic-shaping**

Syntax Description

This command has no arguments or keywords.

Default

The default value is lenient (not strict) traffic shaping for SVCs.

Command Mode

Interface configuration

Usage Guidelines

This command first appeared in Cisco IOS Release 10.3.

This command is supported on the Cisco 7500 series routers, Cisco 4500 routers, and Cisco 4700 routers. This command is not supported on the ATM port adapter.

If strict traffic-shaping is configured on the router ATM interface, then an SVC is established only if traffic shaping can be provided for the transmit cell flow per the signaled traffic parameters. If such shaping cannot be provided, the SVC is released.

If strict traffic-shaping is not configured on the router ATM interface, an attempt is made to establish an SVC with traffic shaping for the transmit cell flow per the signaled traffic parameters. If such shaping cannot be provided, the SVC is installed with default shaping parameters (behaves as though a PVC were created without specifying traffic parameters).

The signaling SETUP message carries the forward and backward traffic parameters. For connections initiated by the source router, traffic is shaped to the SETUP message forward parameters. For connections initiated by another router/host, traffic is shaped to the backward parameters.

Example

The following example allows an SVC to be established on an ATM interface using only signaled traffic parameters:

```
atm sig-traffic-shaping strict
```

ATM SMDS-ADDRESS

To assign a unicast E.164 address to the ATM subinterface that supports AAL3/4 and SMDS encapsulation, use the **atm smds-address** interface configuration command.

> **atm smds-address** *address*

Syntax	Description
address	Unicast E.164 address assigned to the subinterface.

Default

No E.164 address is assigned.

Command Mode

Interface configuration

Usage Guidelines

This command first appeared in Cisco IOS Release 10.3.

This command is supported on Cisco 7500 series routers, Cisco 4500 routers, and Cisco 4700 routers. This command is not supported on the ATM port adapter.

Each AAL3/4 subinterface is allowed only one unicast E.164 address.

Example

The following example assigns a unicast E.164 address to the ATM subinterface that is being configured:

```
atm smds-address c141.555.1212
```

Related Commands

atm aal aal3/4
atm multicast
atm pvc

ATM SONET STM-1

To set the mode of operation, and thus control type, of ATM cell used for cell-rate decoupling on the SONET PLIM, use the **atm sonet** interface configuration command. The **no** form of this command restores the default Synchronous Transport Signal level 3, concatenated (STS-3c) operation.

    atm sonet stm-1
    no atm sonet stm-1

Syntax	Description
stm-1	Synchronous Digital Hierarchy/Synchronous Transport Signal level 1 (SDH/STM-1) operation (ITU-T specification).

Default

STS-3c

Command Mode

Interface configuration

Usage Guidelines

This command first appeared in Cisco IOS Release 10.0.

Use STM-1 in applications where the ATM switch requires "idle cells" for rate adaptation. An idle cell contains 31 zeros followed by a one.

Use the default (STS-3c) in applications where the ATM switch requires "unassigned cells" for rate adaptation. An unassigned cell contains 32 zeros.

Example

The following example specifies ATM SONET STM-1:

```
atm sonet stm-1
```

ATM TXBUFF

To set the maximum number of transmit buffers for simultaneous packet fragmentation, use the **atm txbuff** interface configuration command. The **no** form of this command restores the default value.

> **atm txbuff** *number*
> **no atm txbuff**

Syntax	Description
number	Maximum number of packet fragmentations that the AIP can perform simultaneously, in the range 0 through 512.

Default

256 packet fragmentations

Command Mode

Interface configuration

Usage Guidelines

This command first appeared in Cisco IOS Release 10.0.

This command is supported on AIP for Cisco 7500 series routers. This command is not supported on the ATM port adapter for Cisco 7200 and 7500 series routers, nor is it supported on Cisco 4500 and Cisco 4700 routers.

Example

In the following example, the AIP is configured to perform up to 300 packet fragmentations simultaneously:

```
atm txbuff 300
```

ATM UNI-VERSION

To specify the User-Network Interface (UNI) version (3.0 or 3.1) the router should use when ILMI link autodetermination is unsuccessful or ILMI is disabled, use the **atm uni-version** interface configuration command. To restore the default value to 3.0, use the **no** form of this command.

    atm uni-version *version-number*
    no atm uni-version *version-number*

Syntax	*Description*
version-number	UNI version selected on an interface. Valid values are 3.0 and 3.1.

Default

Version 3.0

Command Mode

Interface configuration

Usage Guidelines

This command first appeared in Cisco IOS Release 11.2.

Normally, when the ILMI link autodetermination is enabled on the interface and is successful, the router accepts the UNI version returned by ILMI. If the ILMI link autodetermination is unsuccessful or ILMI is disabled, the UNI version defaults to 3.0. You can override the default UNI version by using this command to enable UNI 3.1 signaling support. The **no** form of the command sets the UNI version to one returned by ILMI if ILMI is enabled and the link autodetermination process is successful. Otherwise, the UNI version reverts to 3.0.

Example

The following example specifies UNI version 3.1 signaling port on the ATM interface 2/0:

```
interface atm 2/0
 atm uni-version 3.1
```

ATM-VC

To define an ATM map statement for a PVC, use the **atm-vc** map-list configuration command in conjunction with the **map-list** global configuration command. To remove the address, use the **no** form of this command.

protocol protocol-address **atm-vc** *vcd* [**broadcast**]
no *protocol protocol-address* **atm-vc** *vcd* [**broadcast**]

Syntax	Description
protocol	One of the following keywords: **appletalk, apollo, bridge, clns, decnet, ip, ipx, vines,** or **xns.**
protocol-address	Destination address that is being mapped to this PVC.
vcd	Virtual circuit descriptor of the PVC.
broadcast	(Optional) Indicates that this map entry is to be used when the corresponding *protocol* sends broadcast packets to the interface—for example, IGRP updates. Provides pseudobroadcasting support.

Default

No map statements are defined.

Command Mode

Map-list configuration

Usage Guidelines

This command first appeared in Cisco IOS Release 10.0.

When operating in PVC mode, the ATM switch might not have multicast capabilities. For this reason, all static maps for a specific protocol should be marked as **broadcast** for multicasting. When a protocol sends a packet to its multicast address, all static maps marked as **broadcast** get a copy of that packet. This procedure simulates the multicast environment of a LAN.

Some switches might have point-to-multipoint PVCs that perform the equivalent process. If one exists, then that PVC might be used as the sole **broadcast** PVC for all multicast requests.

Example

In the following example, a map list named *atm* includes two map statements for protocol addresses being mapped:

```
map-list atm
  ip 172.21.168.112 atm-vc 1 broadcast
  decnet 10.2 atm-vc 2 broadcast
```

Related Commands

map-list

ATM VC-PER-VP

To set the maximum number of VCIs to support per VPI, use the **atm vc-per-vp** interface configuration command. The **no** form of this command restores the default value.

> **atm vc-per-vp** *number*
> **no atm vc-per-vp**

Syntax   *Description*

number   Maximum number of VCIs to support per VPI. On the AIP for Cisco 7500 series routers, valid values are: 16, 32, 64, 128, 256, 512, or 1024. On the ATM port adapter for Cisco 7200 series and Cisco 7500 series routers, valid values are: 16, 32, 64, 128, 256, 512, 1024, or 2048. On the NPM for Cisco 4500 and Cisco 4700 routers, valid values are: 32, 64, 128, 256, 512, 1024, 2048, 4096, or 8192.

Default

1024

Command Mode

Interface configuration

Usage Guidelines

This command first appeared in Cisco IOS Release 10.0.

This command controls the memory allocation in the AIP, ATM port adapter, or NPM to deal with the VCI table. It defines the maximum number of VCIs to support per VPI; it does not bound the VCI numbers.

An invalid VCI causes a warning message to be displayed.

Example

In the following example, the maximum number of VCIs to support per VPI is set to 512:

```
atm vc-per-vp 512
```

Related Commands

atm pvc

ATM VP-FILTER

To set the AIP filter register, use the **atm vp-filter** interface configuration command. The **no** form of this command restores the default value.

> **atm vp-filter** *hexvalue*
> **no atm vp-filter**

Syntax	Description
hexvalue	Value in hexadecimal format.

Default

0x7B

Command Mode

Interface configuration

Usage Guidelines

This command first appeared in Cisco IOS Release 10.0.

This command is supported on Cisco 7500 series routers, but not on Cisco 4500 and Cisco 4700 routers. This command is not supported on ATM port adapters.

This command allows you to specify a VPI or range of VPIs to be used for AAL3/4 processing. All other VPIs map to AAL5 processing. If only AAL5 processing is required, you can either let the virtual path filter default or set it to an arbitrary VPI so that AAL5 processing is performed on all VPIs.

This command configures the hexadecimal value used in the virtual path filter register in the reassembly operation. The virtual path filter comprises 16 bits. The virtual path filter register uses the most significant bits (bits 15 through 8, the left half of the filter) as mask bits, and uses bits 7 through 0 (the right half of the filter) as compare bits.

When a cell is received, the right half of the filter is exclusively NORed with the binary value of the incoming VPI. The result is then ORed with the left half of the filter (the mask). If the result is all 1s, then reassembly is done using the VCI/MID table (AAL3/4 processing). Otherwise, reassembly is done using the VPI-VCI pair table (AAL5 processing).

Examples

In the following example, all incoming cells are reassembled using AAL3/4 processing:

```
atm vp-filter ff00
```

In the following example, all incoming cells with the virtual path equal to 0 are reassembled using AAL3/4 processing; all other cells are reassembled using AAL5 processing:

```
atm vp-filter 0
```

In the following example, all incoming cells with the most significant bit of the virtual path set are reassembled using AAL3/4 processing; all other cells are reassembled using AAL5 processing:

```
atm vp-filter 7f80
```

DXI MAP

To map a protocol address to a given VPI and VCI, use the **dxi map** interface configuration command. Use the **no** form of this command to remove the mapping for that protocol and protocol address.

> **dxi map** *protocol protocol-address vpi vci* [**broadcast**]
> **no dxi map** *protocol protocol-address*

Syntax	Description
protocol	One of the following bridging or protocol keywords: **apollo**, **appletalk**, **bridge**, **clns**, **decnet**, **ip**, **novell**, **vines**, or **xns**.
protocol-address	Protocol-specific address.
vpi	Virtual path identifier in the range 0 to 15.
vci	Virtual circuit identifier in the range 0 to 63.
broadcast	(Optional) Broadcasts should be forwarded to this address.

Default

No map definition is established.

Command Mode

Interface configuration

Usage Guidelines

This command first appeared in Cisco IOS Release 10.3.

This command is used in configurations where the router is intended to communicate with an ATM network through an ATM data service unit (ADSU). Given the circuit identifier parameters (VPI and VCI) for the ATM permanent virtual circuit (PVC), the router computes and uses the DXI frame address (DFA) that is used for communication between the router and the ADSU.

The **dxi map** command can be used only on a serial interface or HSSI configured for ATM-DXI encapsulation.

Example

In the following example, all IP packets intended for the host with IP address 172.21.170.49 are converted into ATM cells identified with a VPI of 2 (binary 0000 0010) and a VCI of 46 (binary 0000 0000 0010 1110) by the ADSU:

```
interface serial 0
dxi map ip 172.21.170.49 2 46 broadcast
```

Using the mapping defined in Annex A of the ATM DXI Specification, the router uses the VPI and VCI information in this example to compute a DFA of 558 (binary 1000101110). The ADSU will use the DFA of the incoming frame to extract the VPI and VCI information when formulating ATM cells.

Related Commands

dxi pvc
encapsulation atm-dxi

DXI PVC

To configure multiprotocol or single protocol ATM-DXI encapsulation, use the **dxi pvc** interface configuration command. The **no** form of this command disables multiprotocol ATM-DXI encapsulation.

> **dxi pvc** *vpi vci* [**snap** | **nlpid** | **mux**]
> **no dxi pvc** *vpi vci* [**snap** | **nlpid** | **mux**]

Syntax	Description
vpi	ATM network virtual path identifier (VPI) of this PVC, in the range from 0 through 255. The VPI is an 8-bit field in the header of the ATM cell. The VPI value is unique only on a single interface, not throughout the ATM network, because it has local significance only.
	Both *vpi* and *vci* cannot be specified as 0; if one is 0, the other cannot be 0.
vci	ATM network virtual channel identifier (VCI) of this PVC, in the range of 0 through 65535. The VCI is a 16-bit field in the header of the ATM cell. The VCI value is unique only on a single interface, not throughout the ATM network, because it has local significance only.
	Both *vpi* and *vci* cannot be specified as 0; if one is 0, the other cannot be 0.
snap	(Optional) LLC/SNAP encapsulation based on the protocol used in the packet. This keyword defines a PVC that can carry multiple network protocols. This is the default.
nlpid	(Optional) RFC 1294/1490 encapsulation. This option is provided for backward compatibility with the default encapsulation in earlier versions of the Cisco IOS software.
mux	(Optional) MUX encapsulation; the carried protocol is defined by the **dxi map** command when the PVC is set up. This keyword defines a PVC that carries only one network protocol.

Default

LLC/SNAP encapsulation

Command Mode
Interface configuration

Usage Guidelines
This command first appeared in Cisco IOS Release 10.3.

This command can be used only on a serial interface or HSSI that is configured with ATM-DXI encapsulation.

Select the **nlpid** option if software earlier than Cisco IOS Release 10.3 was loaded on this router, and the router was configured for the default encapsulation, which was **nlpid** before Release 10.3.

Examples
The following example configures ATM-DXI MUX encapsulation on serial interface 1. The PVC identified by a VPI of 10 and a VCI of 10 can carry a single protocol. Then the protocol to be carried on this PVC is defined by the **dxi map** command.

```
interface serial 1
  dxi pvc 10 10 mux
  dxi map ip 172.21.176.45 10 10 broadcast
```

The following example configures ATM-DXI NLPID encapsulation on serial interface 1. The PVC identified by a VPI of 11 and a VCI of 12 can carry multiprotocol traffic that is encapsulated with a header described in RFC 1294/1490.

```
interface serial 1
  dxi pvc 11 12 nlpid
```

Related Commands
dxi map
encapsulation atm-dxi
show dxi pvc

ENCAPSULATION ATM-DXI

Use the **encapsulation atm-dxi** interface configuration command to enable ATM-DXI encapsulation. The **no** form of this command disables ATM-DXI.

    encapsulation atm-dxi
    no encapsulation atm-dxi

Syntax Description
This command has no arguments or keywords.

Default
HDLC

Command Mode

Interface configuration

Usage Guidelines

This command first appeared in Cisco IOS Release 10.0.

Example

The following example configures ATM-DXI encapsulation on serial interface 1:

```
interface serial 1
encapsulation atm-dxi
```

Related Commands

dxi map

INTERFACE ATM

To configure an ATM interface type and enter interface configuration mode, use the **interface atm** global configuration command.

       interface atm *number* (for the NPM on Cisco 4500 and 4700 routers)

       interface atm *slot*/**0**   (for the AIP on Cisco 7500 series routers; for the ATM port adapter on Cisco 7200 series routers)

       interface atm *slot*/*port-adapter*/**0**   (for the ATM port adapter on Cisco 7500 series routers)

To configure a subinterface, use the **interface atm** global configuration command.

       interface atm *number.subinterface-number* {**multipoint** I **point-to-point**} (for the NPM on Cisco 4500 and 4700 routers)

       interface atm *slot*/**0**.*subinterface-number* {**multipoint** I **point-to-point**} (for the AIP on Cisco 7500 series routers; for the ATM port adapter on Cisco 7200 series routers)

       interface atm *slot*/*port-adapter*/**0**.*subinterface-number* {**multipoint** I **point-to-point**} (for the ATM port adapter on Cisco 7500 series routers)

Syntax	Description
number	On Cisco 4500 and Cisco 4700 routers, specifies the NPM number. The numbers are assigned at the factory at the time of installation or when added to a system, and can be displayed with the **show interfaces** command.
port-adapter	ATM port adapter number for the ATM port adapter on Cisco 7500 series routers. The value can be 0 or 1.

Syntax	Description
slot	On the Cisco 7000 series routers with RSP7000 and Cisco 7200 series, specifies the backplane slot number. On the 7000, this value can be **0**, **1**, **2**, **3**, or **4**. On the Cisco 7010, this value can be **0**, **1**, or **2**. The slots are numbered from left to right. On the Cisco 7505, the slot number can be 0, 1, 2, or 3 from bottom to top. On the Cisco 7507, the slot number can be 0 and 1 (CyBus0) and 4 through 6 (Cybus1), from left to right. On the Cisco 7513, the slot numbers are 0 through 5 (CyBus 0) and 8 through 12 (CyBus 1), from left to right.
.subinterface-number	Subinterface number in the range 1 to 4294967293.
multipoint | **point-to-point**	Specifies a multipoint or point-to-point subinterface. There is no default.

Default

None

Command Mode

Global configuration

Usage Guidelines

This command first appeared in Cisco IOS Release 10.0 for the Cisco 7000 family routers. This command first appeared in Cisco IOS Release 11.0 for the Cisco 4500 and 4700 routers.

Example

The following example assigns an IP network address and network mask to the ATM interface in slot 1 on port 0 of a Cisco 7500 series router:

```
interface atm 1/0
  ip address 1.1.1.1.255.255.255.0
```

Related Commands

show interfaces atm

LOOPBACK

Use the following form of the **loopback** interface configuration command, to place one of the following into loopback mode:

- OC-3c, DS3, or E3 interfaces on the Cisco 7500 series AIP
- SONET/SDH OC-3 interface on the Cisco 7200 series routers, and on the second-generation Versatile Interface Processor (VIP2) in Cisco 7500 series routers
- OC-3c interfaces on the Cisco 4500 and Cisco 4700 NPM

Use the **no** form of this command to remove the loopback.

> **loopback [diagnostic | line]**
> **no loopback [diagnostic | line]**

To place E3 or DS3 interfaces on the Cisco 4500 and Cisco 4700 NPM into loopback mode, use the following form of the **loopback** interface configuration command. Use the **no** form of this command to remove the loopback.

> **loopback [cell | diagnostic | line | payload]**
> **no loopback [cell | diagnostic | line | payload]**

Syntax	Description
cell	(Optional) Place the interface into external loopback at cell level.
diagnostic	(Optional) Place the interface into internal loopback at the PLIM.
line	(Optional) Place the interface into external loopback at the line. This is the default.
payload	(Optional) Place the interface into external loopback at the payload level.

Default

The default is **line**; packets loop from the ATM interface back to the ATM network.

Command Mode

Interface configuration

Usage Guidelines

This command first appeared in Cisco IOS Release 11.0.

This command is useful for testing because it loops all packets from the ATM interface back to the ATM interface as well as directing the packets to the network.

Example

The following example loops all packets back to the ATM interface:

```
loopback diagnostic
```

MAP-CLASS ATM

To enter map-class configuration mode to define parameters used to signal a request for an ATM SVC (the SETUP message), use the **map-class atm** global configuration command. The **no** form of this command deletes this class.

> **map-class atm** *class-name*
> **no map-class atm** *class-name*

Command Reference

Syntax   *Description*

class-name   User-assigned name of the traffic parameters table.

Default

No traffic parameters are defined.

Command Mode

Global configuration

Usage Guidelines

This command first appeared in Cisco IOS Release 10.0.

If the ATM map class identified by *class-name* does not already exist, the router creates a new one. In either case, this command specifies the ATM map class to which subsequent ATM commands apply. Configuration of an ATM map class is allowed only if the ATM subsystem is linked.

If parameters are required, it is up to the media-specific routing that uses a static map to ensure that the referenced class exists.

Most parameters specified through an ATM map class are used to dictate the contents of the ATM Traffic Descriptor Information Element (ATD IE) present in a SETUP message used to initiate an SVC (note that this IE was called the User Cell Rate IE in UNI 3.0). These parameters are configured with the following commands:
atm backward-max-burst-size-clp0
atm backward-max-burst-size-clp1
atm backward-peak-cell-rate-clp0
atm backward-peak-cell-rate-clp1
atm backward-sustainable-cell-rate-clp0
atm backward-sustainable-cell-rate-clp1
atm forward-max-burst-size-clp0
atm forward-max-burst-size-clp1
atm forward-peak-cell-rate-clp0
atm forward-peak-cell-rate-clp1
atm forward-sustainable-cell-rate-clp0
atm forward-sustainable-cell-rate-clp1

NOTES

The 1-parameters specify the traffic characteristics of the aggregate of Cell Loss Priority 0 (CLP0) and CLP1 cells; the 0-parameters are CLP0 only.

When possible, Best Effort is signaled. In UNI 3, a Best Effort Indication can be included in the ATD IE only if the contents of the IE consist of forward and backward Peak Cell Rate for CLP 0+1 (and the Best Effort Indication). Therefore, if any of the above commands other than **atm forward-peak-cell-rate-clp1** and **atm backward-peak-cell-rate-clp1** are specified in the map-class, Best Effort cannot be signaled.

It is important that Best Effort is signaled, because this causes a switch to interpret the SETUP as a request for an Unspecified Bit Rate (UBR) connection. UBR requests do not cause bandwidth to be reserved per-connection.

If Best Effort cannot be signaled (one of the other parameters is specified in map-class), then this causes a switch to interpret the SETUP as a request for Non-Real Time Variable Bit Rate (VBR-NRT) service.

All combinations of parameters are allowed in the definition of map-class. The following recommendations can help you to specify a correct set of parameters:

- The maximum length of the contents of the ATD IE is 30 bytes. All of the cell-rate and burst parameters require 4 bytes in the IE. Therefore, no more than seven of the 4-byte parameters should be specified.
- The allowable combinations of cell-rate and burst-size parameters from the UNI 3.0 specification are (per direction) as follows:
  - peak-cell-rate0, peak-cell-rate0+1.
  - peak-cell-rate0+1, sustained-cell-rate0, max-burst0.
  - peak-cell-rate0+1.
  - peak-cell-rate0+1, sustained-cell-rate0+1, max-burst0+1.
- A clp0+1 parameter should be greater than or equal to the clp0 parameter for the same direction.

If default traffic parameters are used in the initiation of an SVC, a Best Effort ATD IE is used. The forward and backward peak-cell-rate0+1 values are 24-bits set to "1" (0xffffff). This is a unique value used to indicate that default-shaping parameters can be applied.

Example

The following example establishes traffic parameters for map class *atmclass1*:

```
map-list atmlist
 ip 172.21.180.121 atm-nsap 12.3456.7890.abcd.0000.00 broadcast class atmclass1
map-class atm atmclass1
 atm forward-peak-cell-rate-clp1 8000
 atm backward-peak-cell-rate-clp1 8000
interface atm 2/0/0
 map-group atmlist
```

Related Commands

show atm map

MAP-GROUP

To associate an ATM map list to an interface or subinterface for either a PVC or SVC, use the **map-group** interface configuration command. The **no** form of this command removes the reference to the map list.

>   **map-group** *name*
>   **no map-group** *name*

Syntax   *Description*

name   Name of the map list identified by the **map-list** command.

Default

No ATM map lists are associated.

Command Mode

Interface configuration

Usage Guidelines

This command first appeared in Cisco IOS Release 10.0.

More than one map group can be configured for an interface.

Example

In the following example, the map list named *atm* is associated with the ATM interface:

```
interface atm 2/0
  map-group atm
```

Related Commands

map-list

MAP-LIST

To define an ATM map statement for either a PVC or SVC, use the **map-list** global configuration command. The **no** form of this command deletes this list and all associated map statements.

>   **map-list** *name*
>   **no map-list** *name*

Syntax   *Description*

name   Name of the map list.

Default

No map statements are defined.

Command Mode

Global configuration

Usage Guidelines

This command first appeared in Cisco IOS Release 10.0.

To allow the router to propagate routing updates and ARP requests, a static map that maps the protocol address and the ATM address of the next-hop ATM station must be configured. The router supports a mapping scheme that identifies the ATM address of remote hosts and routers. This address can be specified either as a virtual circuit descriptor (VCD) for a PVC or an NSAP address for an SVC.

The **map-list** command specifies the map list to which the subsequent map-list configuration commands apply. These map-list configuration commands identify destination addresses. One map list can contain multiple map entries. A map list can be referenced by more than one interface or subinterface.

Examples

In the following example for a PVC, a map list named *atm* is followed by two map statements for protocol addresses being mapped:

```
map-list atm
  ip 172.21.168.112 atm-vc 1 broadcast
  decnet 10.2 atm-vc 2 broadcast
```

In the following example for an SVC, a map list named *atm* includes two map statements for protocol addresses being mapped:

```
map-list atm
  ip 172.21.97.165 atm-nsap BC.CDEF.01.234567.890A.BCDE.F012.3456.7890.1234.13
  ip 172.21.97.166 atm-nsap BC.CDEF.01.234567.890A.BCDE.F012.3456.7890.1234.12
```

Related Commands

atm-nsap
atm-vc
map-group

SHOW ATM ARP-SERVER

To display the ATM ARP server's information about one specific interface or all interfaces, use the **show atm arp-server** user EXEC command.

        show atm arp-server [**atm** *slot/port*[*.subinterface-number*]] (Cisco 7200 series with ATM port adapter; Cisco 7500 series with AIP)

show atm arp-server [**atm** *slot/port-adapter/port*[*.subinterface-number*]] (Cisco 7500 series with ATM port adapter)
show atm arp-server [**atm** *number*[*.subinterface-number*]] (Cisco 4500 and Cisco 4700 routers)

Syntax	*Description*
atm *slot/port*	(Optional) ATM slot and port numbers on the following:
	• Cisco 7200 series with ATM port adapter.
	• Cisco 7500 series with AIP.
atm *slot/port-adapter/port*	(Optional) ATM slot, port adapter, and port numbers on the Cisco 7500 series with ATM port adapter.
atm *number*	(Optional) ATM network processor module (NPM) number on the Cisco 4500 and 4700 routers.
.subinterface-number	(Optional) Subinterface number.

Command Mode

User EXEC

Usage Guidelines

This command first appeared in Cisco IOS Release 11.1.

Sample Displays

The following is sample output from the **show atm arp-server** command when no interface is specified:

```
Router# show atm arp-server
Note that a '*' next to an IP address indicates an active call
     IP Address      TTL     ATM Address
ATM1/0:
   * 4.4.4.2         19:50   ac15336602000000000000000000000000000000
   * 4.4.4.6         19:50   ac15336606000000000000000000000000000000
   * 4.4.4.15        19:14   ac15336615000000000000000000000000000000
ATM1/0.23:
   * 10.0.0.2        19:50   ac15336602000000000000000000000000000023
   * 10.0.0.6        19:50   ac15336606000000000000000000000000000023
```

The following is sample output from the **show atm arp-server** command when a slot and port are specified on the Cisco 7500:

```
Router# show atm arp-server atm 1/0
Note that a '*' next to an IP address indicates an active call
     IP Address      TTL     ATM Address
   * 4.4.4.2         19:00   ac15336602000000000000000000000000000000
   * 4.4.4.6         19:00   ac15336606000000000000000000000000000000
   * 4.4.4.15        19:14   ac15336615000000000000000000000000000000
```

Related Commands

atm arp-server

SHOW ATM INTERFACE ATM

To show ATM-specific information about an ATM interface, use the **show atm interface atm** privileged EXEC command.

show atm interface atm *slot/port* (Cisco 7200 series with ATM port adapter; Cisco 7500 series with AIP)

show atm interface atm *slot/port-adapter/port* (Cisco 7500 series with ATM port adapter)

show atm interface atm *number* (Cisco 4500 and Cisco 4700 routers)

Syntax	*Description*
slot/port	ATM slot number and port number on the following: • Cisco 7200 series with ATM port adapter. • Cisco 7500 series with AIP.
slot/port-adapter/port	ATM slot, port adapter, and port number on the Cisco 7500 series with ATM port adapter.
number	NPM number for Cisco 4500 and Cisco 4700 routers.

Command Mode

Privileged EXEC

Usage Guidelines

The **show atm interface atm** *slot/port* command first appeared in Cisco IOS Release 10.0.
The **show atm interface atm** *slot/port-adapter/port* command first appeared in Cisco IOS Release 11.2 P.
The **show atm interface atm** *number* command first appeared in Cisco IOS Release 11.0.

Sample Display

The following is sample output from the **show atm interface atm** command to display statistics on slot 4, port 0:

```
Router# show atm interface atm 4/0
ATM interface ATM4/0:
AAL enabled: AAL5, Maximum VCs: 1024, Current VCs: 6
Tx buffers 256, Rx buffers 256, Exception Queue: 32, Raw Queue: 32
VP Filter: 0x7B, VCIs per VPI: 1024, Max Datagram Size:4496, MIDs/VC:16
PLIM Type:4B5B - 100Mbps, No Framing, TX clocking: LINE
4897 input, 2900 output, 0 IN fast, 0 OUT fast
Rate-Queue 1 set to 100Mbps, reg=0x4EA DYNAMIC, 1 VCCs
ATM4/0.1:AAL3/4-SMDS address c111.1111.1111 Multicast e222.2222.222
Config. is ACTIVE
```

Table 6–1 describes the fields shown in the display.

Table 6–1 *Show ATM Interface ATM Field Descriptions*

Field	Description
ATM interface	Slot and port number of the interface.
AAL enabled	Type of AAL. If both AAL5 and AAL3/4 are enabled on the interface, the output will include both AAL5 and AAL3/4.
Maximum VCs	Maximum number of virtual circuits this interface can support.
Current VCs	Number of active virtual circuits.
Tx buffers, Rx buffers	Number of buffers configured with the **atm txbuff** or **atm rxbuff** command, respectively.
Exception Queue	Number of buffers configured with the **atm exception-queue** command (AIP only).
Raw Queue	Queue size configured with the **atm rawq-size** command.
VP Filter	Hexadecimal value of the VP filter as configured by the **atm vp-filter** command (AIP only).
VCIs per VPI	Maximum number of VCIs to support per VPI, as configured by the **atm vc-per-vp** command.
Max Datagram Size	The configured maximum number of bytes in the largest datagram.
MIDs/VC	The configured maximum number of message identifiers allowed per virtual circuit on this interface.
PLIM Type	Physical Layer Interface Module (PLIM) type (E3, 4B/5B, or SONET).
Framing	For E3, this might be G.804; otherwise, no framing.
TX clocking	Clocking on the router. For E3 or SONET, this might be INTERNAL, meaning the AIP or NPM generates the clock. Otherwise, LINE indicates that the ATM switch provides the clocking.
input	Number of packets received and process switched.
output	Number of packets sent from process switch.
IN fast	Number of input packets fast-switched.
OUT fast	Number of output packets fast-switched.
Rate-Queue	List of configured rate queues.

Table 6–1   *Show ATM Interface ATM Field Descriptions, Continued*

Field	Description
reg=	Actual register value passed to the AIP to define a specific rate queue (AIP only).
DYNAMIC	Indicates that the rate queue is dynamic and was created automatically by the software. Dynamic rate queues are created when an **atm pvc** command specifies a peak or average rate that does not match any user configured rate queue. The value PERMANENT indicates that the rate queue was user-configured.
VCCs	Number of virtual channel connections (VCCs) dynamically attached to this rate queue.
ATM4/0.1	Indicates that the subinterface supports ATM adaptation layer AAL3/4 and displays the SMDS E.164 unicast address and the SMDS E.164 multicast address assigned to the subinterface.
Config. is	ACTIVE or VALID in *n* SECONDS. ACTIVE indicates that the current AIP or NPM configuration has been loaded into the AIP and is being used. There is a 5-second window when a user changes a configuration and the configuration is sent to the AIP.

Related Commands

atm pvc

SHOW ATM MAP

To display the list of all configured ATM static maps to remote hosts on an ATM network, use the **show atm map** privileged EXEC command.

> show atm map

Syntax Description

This command has no arguments or keywords.

Command Mode

Privileged EXEC

Usage Guidelines

This command first appeared in Cisco IOS Release 10.0.

Sample Displays

The following is sample output from the **show atm map** command:

```
Router# show atm map
Map list atm:

vines 3004B310:0001 maps to VC 4, broadcast
ip 172.21.168.110 maps to VC 1, broadcast
clns 47.0004.0001.0000.0c00.6e26.00 maps to VC 6, broadcast
appletalk 10.1 maps to VC 7, broadcast
decnet 10.1 maps to VC 2, broadcast
```

The following is sample output from the **show atm map** command for a multipoint connection:

```
Router# show atm map
Map list atm_pri : PERMANENT
ip 4.4.4.4 maps to NSAP CD.CDEF.01.234567.890A.BCDE.F012.3456.7890.1234.12, broadcast,
aal5mux, multipoint connection up, VC 6
ip 4.4.4.6 maps to NSAP DE.CDEF.01.234567.890A.BCDE.F012.3456.7890.1234.12, broadcast,
aal5mux, connection up, VC 15, multipoint connection up, VC 6

Map list atm_ipx : PERMANENT
ipx 1004.dddd.dddd.dddd maps to NSAP DE.CDEF.01.234567.890A.BCDE.F012.3456.7890.1234.12,
broadcast, aal5mux, multipoint connection up, VC 8
ipx 1004.cccc.cccc.cccc maps to NSAP CD.CDEF.01.234567.890A.BCDE.F012.3456.7890.1234.12,
broadcast, aal5mux, multipoint connection up, VC 8

Map list atm_apple : PERMANENT
appletalk 62000.5 maps to NSAP CD.CDEF.01.234567.890A.BCDE.F012.3456.7890.1234.12,
broadcast, aal5mux, multipoint connection up, VC 4
appletalk 62000.6 maps to NSAP DE.CDEF.01.234567.890A.BCDE.F012.3456.7890.1234.12,
broadcast, aal5mux, multipoint connection up, VC 4
```

Table 6–2 describes the fields shown in the display.

Table 6–2 *Show ATM Map Field Descriptions*

Field	Description
Map list	Name of map list.
PERMANENT	This map entry was entered from configuration; it was not entered automatically by a process.
protocol address maps to VC *x* or *protocol address* maps to NSAP...	Name of protocol, the protocol address, and the VCD or NSAP to which the address is mapped.
broadcast	Indicates pseudobroadcasting.
aal5mux	Indicates the encapsulation used, a multipoint or point-to-point virtual circuit, and the number of the virtual circuit.
multipoint connection up	Indicates that this is a multipoint virtual circuit.

Table 6–2 *Show ATM Map Field Descriptions, Continued*

Field	Description
VC 6	Number of the virtual circuit.
connection up	Indicates a point-to-point virtual circuit.

Related Commands

atm pvc
map-list

SHOW ATM TRAFFIC

To display current, global ATM traffic information to and from all ATM networks connected to the router, use the **show atm traffic** privileged EXEC command.

> **show atm traffic**

Syntax Description

This command has no arguments or keywords.

Command Mode

Privileged EXEC

Usage Guidelines

This command first appeared in Cisco IOS Release 10.0.

Sample Display

The following is sample output from the **show atm traffic** command:

```
Router# show atm traffic
4915 Input packets
0 Output packets
2913 Broadcast packets
0 Packets for non-existent VC
```

Table 6–3 describes the fields shown in the display.

Table 6–3 *Show ATM Traffic Field Descriptions*

Field	Description
Input packets	Total packets input.
Output packets	Total packets output (nonbroadcast).

Table 6–3 *Show ATM Traffic Field Descriptions, Continued*

Field	Description
Broadcast packets	Total broadcast packets output.
Packets for nonexistent VC	Packets sent to virtual circuits not configured.

Related Commands

atm pvc

SHOW ATM VC

To display all active ATM virtual circuits (PVCs and SVCs) and traffic information, use the **show atm vc** privileged EXEC command.

show atm vc [*vcd*]

Syntax	Description
vcd	(Optional) Specifies which virtual circuit about which to display information.

Command Mode

Privileged EXEC

Usage Guidelines

This command first appeared in Cisco IOS Release 10.0.

If no *vcd* value is specified, the command displays information for all PVCs and SVCs. The output is in summary form (one line per virtual circuit).

Sample Displays

The following is sample output from the **show atm vc** command when no *vcd* value is specified, displaying statistics for all virtual circuits:

```
Router# show atm vc
Intfc.    VCD  VPI  VCI  Type  AAL/Encaps   Peak  Avg.  Burst
ATM4/0.1  1    1    1    PVC   AAL3/4-SMDS  0     0     0
ATM4/0    2    2    2    PVC   AAL5-SNAP    0     0     0
ATM4/0    3    3    3    PVC   AAL5-SNAP    0     0     0
ATM4/0    4    4    4    PVC   AAL5-MUX     0     0     0
ATM4/0    6    6    6    PVC   AAL5-SNAP    0     0     0
ATM4/0    7    7    7    PVC   AAL5-SNAP    0     0     0
```

The following is sample output from the **show atm vc** command when a *vcd* value is specified, displaying statistics for that virtual circuit only:

```
Router# show atm vc 8
ATM4/0: VCD: 8, VPI: 8, VCI: 8, etype:0x0, AAL5 - LLC/SNAP, Flags: 0x30
PeakRate: 0, Average Rate: 0, Burst: 0 *32cells, VCmode: 0xE000
```

```
InPkts: 181061, OutPkts: 570499, InBytes: 757314267, OutBytes: 2137187609
InPRoc: 181011, OutPRoc: 10, Broadcasts: 570459
InFast: 39, OutFast: 36, InAS: 11, OutAS: 6
```

The following is sample output from the **show atm vc** command when a *vcd* value is specified, AAL3/4 is enabled, an ATM SMDS subinterface has been defined, and a range of message identifier numbers (MIDs) has been assigned to the PVC:

```
Router# show atm vc 1
ATM4/0.1: VCD: 1, VPI: 0, VCI: 1, etype:0x1, AAL3/4 - SMDS, Flags: 0x35
PeakRate: 0, Average Rate: 0, Burst: 0 *32cells, VCmode: 0xE200
MID start: 1, MID end: 16
InPkts: 0, OutPkts: 0, InBytes: 0, OutBytes: 0
InPRoc: 0, OutPRoc: 0, Broadcasts: 0
InFast: 0, OutFast: 0, InAS: 0, OutAS: 0
```

The following is sample output from the **show atm vc** command when generation of OAM F5 loop-back cells has been enabled:

```
Router# show atm vc 7
ATM4/0: VCD: 7, VPI: 7, VCI: 7, etype:0x0, AAL5 - LLC/SNAP, Flags: 0x30
PeakRate: 0, Average Rate: 0, Burst: 0 *32cells, VCmode: 0xE000
OAM frequency: 10, InARP DISABLED
InPkts: 0, OutPkts: 0, InBytes: 0, OutBytes: 0
InPRoc: 0, OutPRoc:0, Broadcast:0
InFast:0, OutFast:0, InAS:0, OutAS:0
OAM F5 cells sent: 1, OAM cells received: 0
```

The following is sample output from the **show atm vc** command for an incoming multipoint virtual circuit:

```
Router# show atm vc 3
ATM2/0: VCD: 3, VPI: 0, VCI: 33, etype:0x809B, AAL5 - MUX, Flags: 0x53
PeakRate: 0, Average Rate: 0, Burst: 0, VCmode: 0xE000
OAM DISABLED, InARP DISABLED
InPkts: 6646, OutPkts: 0, InBytes: 153078, OutBytes: 0
InPRoc: 6646, OutPRoc: 0, Broadcasts: 0
InFast: 0, OutFast: 0, InAS: 0, OutAS: 0
interface = ATM2/0, call remotely initiated, call reference = 18082
vcnum = 3, vpi = 0, vci = 33, state = Active
 aal5mux vc, multipoint call
Retry count: Current = 0, Max = 10
timer currently inactive, timer value = never
Root Atm Nsap address: DE.CDEF.01.234567.890A.BCDE.F012.3456.7890.1234.12
```

The following is sample output from the **show atm vc** command for an outgoing multipoint virtual circuit:

```
Router# show atm vc 6
ATM2/0: VCD: 6, VPI: 0, VCI: 35, etype:0x800, AAL5 - MUX, Flags: 0x53
PeakRate: 0, Average Rate: 0, Burst: 0, VCmode: 0xE000
OAM DISABLED, InARP DISABLED
InPkts: 0, OutPkts: 818, InBytes: 0, OutBytes: 37628
InPRoc: 0, OutPRoc: 0, Broadcasts: 818
InFast: 0, OutFast: 0, InAS: 0, OutAS: 0
interface = ATM2/0, call locally initiated, call reference = 3
vcnum = 6, vpi = 0, vci = 35, state = Active
 aal5mux vc, multipoint call
```

```
Retry count: Current = 0, Max = 10
timer currently inactive, timer value = never
Leaf Atm Nsap address: DE.CDEF.01.234567.890A.BCDE.F012.3456.7890.1234.12
Leaf Atm Nsap address: CD.CDEF.01.234567.890A.BCDE.F012.3456.7890.1234.12
```

The following is sample output from the **show atm vc** command for a PPP-over-ATM connection:

```
Router# show atm vc 1
ATM8/0.1: VCD: 1, VPI: 41, VCI: 41, etype:0x8, AAL5 - CISCOPPP, Flags: 0xC38
PeakRate: 155000, Average Rate: 155000, Burst: 96, VCmode: 0xE000
virtual-access: 1, virtual-template: 1
OAM DISABLED, InARP DISABLED
InPkts: 13, OutPkts: 10, InBytes: 198, OutBytes: 156
InPRoc: 13, OutPRoc: 10, Broadcasts: 0
InFast: 0, OutFast: 0, InAS: 0, OutAS: 0
OAM F5 cells sent: 0, OAM cells received: 0
```

The following is sample output from the **show atm vc** command for IP multicast virtual circuits. The display shows the leaf count for multipoint VCs opened by the root. VCD 3 is a root of a multipoint VC with three leaf routers. VCD 4 is a leaf of some other router's multipoint VC. VCD 12 is a root of a multipoint VC with only one leaf router.

```
Router# show atm vc
```

Interface	VCD	VPI	VCI	Type	AAL / Encapsulation	Peak Kbps	Avg. Kbps	Burst Cells	Status
ATM0/0	1	0	5	PVC	AAL5-SAAL	155000	155000	96	ACT
ATM0/0	2	0	16	PVC	AAL5-ILMI	155000	155000	96	ACT
ATM0/0	3	0	124	MSVC-3	AAL5-SNAP	155000	155000	96	ACT
ATM0/0	4	0	125	MSVC	AAL5-SNAP	155000	155000	96	ACT
ATM0/0	5	0	126	MSVC	AAL5-SNAP	155000	155000	96	ACT
ATM0/0	6	0	127	MSVC	AAL5-SNAP	155000	155000	96	ACT
ATM0/0	9	0	130	SVC	AAL5-SNAP	155000	155000	96	ACT
ATM0/0	10	0	131	SVC	AAL5-SNAP	155000	155000	96	ACT
ATM0/0	11	0	132	MSVC-3	AAL5-SNAP	155000	155000	96	ACT
ATM0/0	12	0	133	MSVC-1	AAL5-SNAP	155000	155000	96	ACT
ATM0/0	13	0	134	SVC	AAL5-SNAP	155000	155000	96	ACT
ATM0/0	14	0	135	MSVC-2	AAL5-SNAP	155000	155000	96	ACT
ATM0/0	15	0	136	MSVC-2	AAL5-SNAP	155000	155000	96	ACT

The following is sample output from the **show atm vc** command for an IP multicast virtual circuit. The display shows the owner of the VC and leaves of the multipoint VC. This VC was opened by IP multicast and the three leaf routers' ATM addresses are included in the display. The VC is associated with IP group address 224.1.1.1.

```
Router# show atm vc 11
ATM0/0: VCD: 11, VPI: 0, VCI: 132, etype:0x0, AAL5 - LLC/SNAP, Flags: 0x650
PeakRate: 155000, Average Rate: 155000, Burst Cells: 96, VCmode: 0xE000
OAM DISABLED, InARP DISABLED
InPkts: 0, OutPkts: 12, InBytes: 0, OutBytes: 496
InPRoc: 0, OutPRoc: 0, Broadcasts: 12
InFast: 0, OutFast: 0, InAS: 0, OutAS: 0
OAM F5 cells sent: 0, OAM cells received: 0
Status: ACTIVE, TTL: 2, VC owner: IP Multicast (224.1.1.1)        <<<
interface = ATM0/0, call locally initiated, call reference = 2
vcnum = 11, vpi = 0, vci = 132, state = Active
 aal5snap vc, multipoint call
```

```
Retry count: Current = 0, Max = 10
timer currently inactive, timer value = 00:00:00
Leaf Atm Nsap address: 47.0091810000000002BA08E101.444444444444.02        <<<
Leaf Atm Nsap address: 47.0091810000000002BA08E101.333333333333.02        <<<
Leaf Atm Nsap address: 47.0091810000000002BA08E101.222222222222.02        <<<
```

Table 6–4 describes the fields shown in the displays.

Table 6–4 *Show ATM VC Field Descriptions*

Field	Description
Interface	Interface slot and port.
VCD	Virtual circuit descriptor (virtual circuit number).
VPI	Virtual path identifier.
VCI	Virtual channel identifier.
Type	Type of virtual circuit, either PVC, SVC or MSVC (multipoint SVC): • MSVC (with no -*x*) indicates that VCD is a leaf of some other router's multipoint VC. • MSVC-*x* indicates there are *x* leaf routers for that multipoint VC opened by the root.
AAL/Encapsulation	Type of ATM adaptation layer (AAL) and encapsulation.
etype	Ethernet type.
Flags	Bit mask describing virtual circuit information. The flag values are summed to result in the displayed value: 0x40—SVC. 0x20—PVC. 0x10—ACTIVE. 0x0—AAL5-SNAP. 0x1—AAL5-NLPID. 0x2—AAL5-FRNLPID. 0x3—AAL5-MUX. 0x4—AAL3/4-SMDS. 0x5—QSAAL. 0x6—ILMI. 0x7—AAL5-LANE. 0x8—AAL5-CISCOPPP.

Table 6–4 *Show ATM VC Field Descriptions, Continued*

Field	Description
PeakRate	Kilobits per second transmitted at the peak rate.
Average Rate	Kilobits per second transmitted at the average rate.
Burst Cells	Value that, when multiplied by 32, equals the maximum number of ATM cells the virtual circuit can transmit at peak rate.
VCmode	AIP-specific or NPM-specific register describing the usage of the virtual circuit. This register contains values such as rate queue, peak rate, and AAL mode, which are also displayed in other fields.
virtual-access	Virtual access interface identifier.
virtual-template	Virtual template identifier.
InPkts	Total number of packets received on this virtual circuit. This number includes all silicon-switched, fast-switched, autonomous-switched, and process-switched packets.
OutPkts	Total number of packets sent on this virtual circuit. This number includes all silicon-switched, fast-switched, autonomous-switched, and process-switched packets.
InBytes	Total number of bytes received on this virtual circuit. This number includes all silicon-switched, fast-switched, autonomous-switched, and process-switched bytes.
OutBytes	Total number of bytes sent on this virtual circuit. This number includes all silicon-switched, fast-switched, autonomous-switched, and process-switched bytes.
InPRoc	Number of process-switched input packets.
OutPRoc	Number of process-switched output packets.
Broadcast	Number of process-switched broadcast packets.
InFast	Number of fast-switched input packets.
OutFast	Number of fast-switched output packets.
InAS	Number of autonomous-switched or silicon-switched input packets.
OutAS	Number of autonomous-switched or silicon-switched output packets.
OAM frequency: 10	OAM cells are sent every 10 seconds.
OAM F5 cells sent: 1	Number of OAM cells sent on this virtual circuit.

Table 6–4   *Show ATM VC Field Descriptions, Continued*

Field	Description
OAM cells received: 0	Number of OAM cells received on this virtual circuit.
TTL	Time-to-live in ATM hops across the VC.
VC owner	IP Multicast address of group.

Related Commands

atm-nsap
atm pvc
map-list

SHOW DXI MAP

To display all the protocol addresses mapped to a serial interface, use the **show dxi map** EXEC command.

  show dxi map

Syntax Description

This command has no arguments or keywords.

Command Mode

EXEC

Usage Guidelines

This command first appeared in Cisco IOS Release 10.3.

Sample Display

The following is sample output from the **show dxi map** command. It displays output for several previously defined ATM-DXI maps that defined Apollo, IP, DECnet, CLNS, and AppleTalk protocol addresses as well as various encapsulations and broadcast traffic.

```
Router# show dxi map
Serial0 (administratively down): ipx 123.0000.1234.1234
   DFA 69(0x45,0x1050), static, vpi = 4, vci = 5,
   encapsulation: SNAP
Serial0 (administratively down): appletalk 2000.5
   DFA 52(0x34,0xC40), static, vpi = 3, vci = 4,
   encapsulation: NLPID
Serial0 (administratively down): ip 172.21.177.1
   DFA 35(0x23,0x830), static,
   broadcast, vpi = 2, vci = 3,
   encapsulation: VC based MUX,
   Linktype IP
```

Table 6–5 explains significant fields shown in the display.

Table 6–5 *Show DXI Map Field Descriptions*

Field	Description
DFA	DXI Frame Address, similar to a DLCI for Frame Relay. The DFA is shown in decimal, hexadecimal, and DXI header format. The router computes this address value from the VPI and VCI values.
encapsulation:	Encapsulation type selected by the **dxi pvc** command. Displayed values can be *SNAP, NLPID,* or *VC based MUX.*
Linktype	Value used only with MUX encapsulation and therefore with only a single network protocol defined for the PVC. Maps configured on a PVC with MUX encapsulation must have the same link type.

SHOW DXI PVC

To display the PVC statistics for a serial interface, use the **show dxi pvc** EXEC command.

   show dxi pvc

Syntax Description

This command has no arguments or keywords.

Command Mode

EXEC

Usage Guidelines

This command first appeared in Cisco IOS Release 10.3.

Sample Display

The following is sample output from the **show dxi pvc** command. It displays output for ATM-DXI PVCs previously defined for serial interface 0.

```
Router# show dxi pvc
PVC Statistics for interface Serial0 (ATM DXI)
DFA = 17, VPI = 1, VCI = 1, PVC STATUS = STATIC, INTERFACE = Serial0
  input pkts 0          output pkts 0          in bytes 0
  out bytes 0           dropped pkts 0
DFA = 34, VPI = 2, VCI = 2, PVC STATUS = STATIC, INTERFACE = Serial0
  input pkts 0          output pkts 0          in bytes 0
  out bytes 0           dropped pkts 0
DFA = 35, VPI = 2, VCI = 3, PVC STATUS = STATIC, INTERFACE = Serial0
  input pkts 0          output pkts 0          in bytes 0
  out bytes 0           dropped pkts 0
```

Table 6–6 describes significant fields shown in the display.

Table 6–6 *Show DXI PVC Field Descriptions*

Field	Description
DFA	DXI Frame Address, similar to a DLCI for Frame Relay. The DFA is shown in decimal, hexadecimal, and DXI header format. The router computes this address value from the VPI and VCI values.
PVC STATUS = STATIC	Only static maps are supported. Maps are not created dynamically.
input pkts	Number of packets received.
output pkts	Number of packets transmitted.
in bytes	Number of bytes in all packets received.
out bytes	Number of bytes in all packets transmitted.
dropped pkts	Should display a zero (0) value. A nonzero value indicates a configuration problem, specifically that a PVC does not exist.

SHOW INTERFACES ATM

Use the **show interfaces atm** privileged EXEC command to display information about the ATM interface.

> **show interfaces atm** [*slot/port*] (Cisco 7200 series with ATM port adapter; and Cisco 7500 series with AIP)

> **show interfaces atm** [*slot/port-adapter/port*] (Cisco 7500 series with ATM port adapter)

Syntax	Description
slot	(Optional) ATM slot number for the following:
	• AIP on Cisco 7500 series routers.
	• ATM port adapter on Cisco 7200 series routers and Cisco 7500 series routers.
port-adapter	(Optional) Port adapter number on the VIP2, either 0 or 1.
port	(Optional) Port number; the value must be 0.

Command Mode

Privileged EXEC

Usage Guidelines

This command first appeared in Cisco IOS Release 10.0.

Sample Displays

The following is sample output from the **show interfaces atm** command:

```
Router# show interfaces atm 4/0
ATM4/0 is up, line protocol is up
  Hardware is cxBus ATM
  Internet address is 131.108.97.165, subnet mask is 255.255.255.0
  MTU 4470 bytes, BW 100000 Kbit, DLY 100 usec, rely 255/255, load 1/255
  Encapsulation ATM, loopback not set, keepalive set (10 sec)
  Encapsulation(s): AAL5, PVC mode
  256 TX buffers, 256 RX buffers, 1024 Maximum VCs, 1 Current VCs
  Signalling vc = 1, vpi = 0, vci = 5
  ATM NSAP address: BC.CDEF.01.234567.890A.BCDE.F012.3456.7890.1234.13
  Last input 0:00:05, output 0:00:05, output hang never
  Last clearing of "show interface" counters never
  Output queue 0/40, 0 drops; input queue 0/75, 0 drops
  Five minute input rate 0 bits/sec, 0 packets/sec
  Five minute output rate 0 bits/sec, 0 packets/sec
     144 packets input, 3148 bytes, 0 no buffer
     Received 0 broadcasts, 0 runts, 0 giants
     0 input errors, 0 CRC, 0 frame, 0 overrun, 0 ignored, 0 abort
     154 packets output, 4228 bytes, 0 underruns
     0 output errors, 0 collisions, 1 interface resets, 0 restarts
```

The following is sample output from the **show interfaces atm** command for the ATM port adapter on a Cisco 7500 series router:

```
Router# show interfaces atm 0/0/0
ATM0/0/0 is up, line protocol is up
  Hardware is cyBus ATM
  Internet address is 1.1.1.1/24
  MTU 4470 bytes, sub MTU 4470, BW 156250 Kbit, DLY 80 usec, rely 255/255, load 1/255
  Encapsulation ATM, loopback not set, keepalive set (10 sec)
  Encapsulation(s): AAL5, PVC mode
  256 TX buffers, 256 RX buffers,
  2048 maximum active VCs, 1024 VCs per VP, 1 current VCCs
  VC idle disconnect time: 300 seconds
  Last input never, output 00:00:05, output hang never
  Last clearing of "show interface" counters never
  Queueing strategy: fifo
  Output queue 0/40, 0 drops; input queue 0/75, 0 drops
  5 minute input rate 0 bits/sec, 1 packets/sec
  5 minute output rate 0 bits/sec, 1 packets/sec
     5 packets input, 560 bytes, 0 no buffer
     Received 0 broadcasts, 0 runts, 0 giants
     0 input errors, 0 CRC, 0 frame, 0 overrun, 0 ignored, 0 abort
     5 packets output, 560 bytes, 0 underruns
     0 output errors, 0 collisions, 0 interface resets
     0 output buffer failures, 0 output buffers swapped out
```

Table 6–7 describes the fields shown in both the displays.

Table 6–7 *Show Interfaces ATM Field Descriptions*

Field	Description
ATM... is {up | down} ...is administratively down	Indicates whether the interface hardware is currently active (whether carrier detect is present) and if it has been taken down by an administrator.
line protocol is {up | down | administratively down}	Indicates whether the software processes that handle the line protocol think the line is usable (that is, whether keepalives are successful).
Hardware is	Hardware type.
Internet address is	Internet address and subnet mask.
MTU	Maximum Transmission Unit of the interface.
sub MTU	Maximum Transmission Unit of the subinterface.
BW	Bandwidth of the interface in kilobits per second.
DLY	Delay of the interface in microseconds.
rely	Reliability of the interface as a fraction of 255 (255/255 is 100% reliability), calculated as an exponential average over 5 minutes.
load	Load on the interface as a fraction of 255 (255/255 is completely saturated), calculated as an exponential average over 5 minutes. The calculation uses the value from the **bandwidth** interface configuration command.
Encapsulation	Encapsulation method assigned to interface.
loopback	Indicates whether the interface is configured for loopback testing.
keepalive	Indicates whether keepalives are set or not.
Encapsulation(s)	Type of encapsulation used on the interface (for example, AAL5, and either PVC or SVC mode).
TX buffers	Number of buffers configured with the **atm txbuff** command.
RX buffers	Number of buffers configured with the **atm rxbuff** command.
Maximum active VCs	Maximum number of virtual circuits.
VCs per VP	Number of virtual circuits per virtual path (the default is 1024).
Current VCs	Number of virtual circuit connections currently open.

Table 6-7 *Show Interfaces ATM Field Descriptions, Continued*

Field	Description
VC idle disconnect time	Number of seconds the SVC must be idle before the SVC is disconnected.
Signalling vc	Number of the signaling PVC.
vpi	Virtual path identifier number.
vci	Virtual channel identifier number.
ATM NSAP address	NSAP address of the ATM interface.
Last input	Number of hours, minutes, and seconds since the last packet was successfully received by an interface. Useful for knowing when a dead interface failed.
Last output	Number of hours, minutes, and seconds since the last packet was successfully transmitted by an interface.
output hang	Number of hours, minutes, and seconds (or never) since the interface was last reset because of a transmission that took too long. When the number of hours in any of the "last" fields exceeds 24 hours, the number of days and hours is printed. If that field overflows, asterisks are printed.
Last clearing	The time at which the counters that measure cumulative statistics (such as number of bytes transmitted and received) shown in this report were last reset to zero. Note that variables that might affect routing (for example, load and reliability) are not cleared when the counters are cleared.
	Asterisks (***) indicates the elapsed time is too large to be displayed.
	The time 0:00:00 indicates the counters were cleared more than 2^{31}ms (and less than 2^{32}ms) ago.
Queueing strategy	First-in, first-out queueing strategy (other queueing strategies you might see are priority-list, custom-list, and weighted fair).
Output queue, drops input queue, drops	Number of packets in output and input queues. Each number is followed by a slash, the maximum size of the queue, and the number of packets dropped due to a full queue.
5 minute input rate, 5 minute output rate	Average number of bits and packets transmitted per second in the last 5 minutes.
packets input	Total number of error-free packets received by the system.

Command Reference

Table 6–7 *Show Interfaces ATM Field Descriptions, Continued*

Field	Description
bytes input	Total number of bytes, including data and MAC encapsulation, in the error free packets received by the system.
no buffer	Number of received packets discarded because there was no buffer space in the main system. Compare with ignored count. Broadcast storms on Ethernets and bursts of noise on serial lines are often responsible for no input buffer events.
Received broadcasts	Total number of broadcast or multicast packets received by the interface.
runts	Number of packets that are discarded because they are smaller than the medium's minimum packet size.
giants	Number of packets that are discarded because they exceed the medium's maximum packet size.
input errors	Total number of no buffer, runts, giants, CRCs, frame, overrun, ignored, and abort counts. Other input-related errors can also increment the count, so that this sum may not balance with the other counts.
CRC	Cyclic redundancy checksum generated by the originating LAN station or far end device does not match the checksum calculated from the data received. On a LAN, this usually indicates noise or transmission problems on the LAN interface or the LAN bus itself. A high number of CRCs is usually the result of collisions or a station transmitting bad data. On a serial link, CRCs usually indicate noise, gain hits, or other transmission problems on the data link.
frame	Number of packets received incorrectly having a CRC error and a noninteger number of octets.
overrun	Number of times the serial receiver hardware was unable to hand received data to a hardware buffer because the input rate exceeded the receiver's ability to handle the data.
ignored	Number of received packets ignored by the interface because the interface hardware ran low on internal buffers. These buffers are different than the system bufers mentioned previously in the buffer description. Broadcast storms and bursts of noise can cause the ignored count to be incremented.

Table 6–7   *Show Interfaces ATM Field Descriptions, Continued*

Field	Description
abort	Illegal sequence of one bits the interface. This usually indicates a clocking problem between the interface and the data link equipment.
packets output	Total number of messages transmitted by the system.
bytes	Total number of bytes, including data and MAC encapsulation, transmitted by the system.
underruns	Number of times that the transmitter has been running faster than the router can handle. This may never be reported on some interfaces.
output errors	Sum of all errors that prevented the final transmission of datagrams out of the interface being examined. Note that this may not balance with the sum of the enumerated output errors, as some datagrams may have more than one error, and others may have errors that do not fall into any of the specifically tabulated categories.
collisions	This feature is not applicable for ATM interfaces.
interface resets	Number of times an interface has been completely reset. This can happen if packets queued for transmission were not sent within several seconds. On a serial line, this can be caused by a malfunctioning modem that is not supplying the transmit clock signal, or by a cable problem. If the system notices that the carrier detect line of a serial interface is up, but the line protocol is down, it periodically resets the interface in an effort to restart it. Interface resets can also occur when an interface is looped back or shut down.
output buffer failures	Number of times that a packet was not output from the output hold queue because of a shortage of MEMD shared memory.
output buffers swapped out	Number of packets stored in main memory when the output queue is full; swapping buffers to main memory prevents packets from being dropped when output is congested. The number is high when traffic is bursty.
restarts	Number of times the controller was restarted because of errors.

SHOW SSCOP

To show Service-Specific Connection-Oriented Protocol (SSCOP) details for all ATM interfaces, use the **show sscop** privileged EXEC command.

        show sscop

Syntax Description

This command has no arguments or keywords.

Command Mode

Privileged EXEC

Usage Guidelines

This command first appeared in Cisco IOS Release 10.0.

Sample Display

The following is sample output from the **show sscop** command:

```
Router# show sscop
SSCOP details for interface ATM4/0
    Current State = Data Transfer Ready
    Send Sequence Number: Current = 2,  Maximum = 9
    Send Sequence Number Acked = 3
    Rcv Sequence Number: Lower Edge = 2, Upper Edge = 2, Max = 9
    Poll Sequence Number = 1876, Poll Ack Sequence Number = 2
    Vt(Pd) = 0
    Connection Control:  timer = 1000
    Timer currently Inactive
    Keep Alive Timer = 30000
    Current Retry Count = 0, Maximum Retry Count = 10
        Statistics -
        Pdu's Sent = 0, Pdu's Received = 0, Pdu's Ignored = 0
        Begin = 0/1, Begin Ack = 1/0, Begin Reject = 0/0
        End = 0/0, End Ack = 0/0
        Resync = 0/0, Resync Ack = 0/0
        Sequenced Data = 2/0, Sequenced Poll Data = 0/0
        Poll = 1591/1876, Stat = 0/1591, Unsolicited Stat = 0/0
        Unassured Data = 0/0, Mgmt Data = 0/0, Unknown Pdu's = 0
```

Table 6–8 describes the fields shown in the display. Interpreting this output requires a good understanding of the SSCOP; it is usually displayed by technicians to help diagnose network problems.

Table 6–8 *Show SSCOP Field Descriptions*

Field	Description
SSCOP details for interface	Interface slot and port.
Current State	SSCOP state for the interface.

Table 6–8 *Show SSCOP Field Descriptions, Continued*

Field	Description
Send Sequence Number	Current and maximum send sequence number.
Send Sequence Number Acked	Sequence number of packets already acknowledged.
Rcv Sequence Number	Sequence number of packets received.
Poll Sequence Number	Current poll sequence number.
Poll Ack Sequence Number	Poll sequence number already acknowledged.
Vt(Pd)	Number of sequenced data (SD) frames sent, which triggers a sending of a Poll frame.
Connection Control	Timer used for establishing and terminating SSCOP.
Keep Alive Timer	Timer used to send keepalives on an idle link.
Current Retry Count	Current count of the retry counter.
Maximum Retry Count	Maximum value the retry counter can take.
Pdu's Sent	Total number of SSCOP frames sent.
Pdu's Received	Total number of SSCOP frames received.
Pdu's Ignored	Number of invalid SSCOP frames ignored.
Begin	Number of Begin frames sent/received.
Begin Ack	Number of Begin Ack frames sent/received.
Begin Reject	Number of Begin Reject frames sent/received.
End	Number of End frames sent/received.
End Ack	Number of End Ack frames sent/received.
Resync	Number of Resync frames sent/received.
Resync Ack	Number of Resync Ack frames sent/received.
Sequenced Data	Number of Sequenced Data frames sent/received.
Sequenced Poll Data	Number of Sequenced Poll Data frames sent/received.
Poll	Number of Poll frames sent/received.
Stat	Number of Stat frames sent/received.
Unsolicited Stat	Number of Unsolicited Stat frames sent/received.
Unassured Data	Number of Unassured Data frames sent/received.

Table 6–8 *Show SSCOP Field Descriptions, Continued*

Field	Description
Mgmt Data	Number of Mgmt Data frames sent/received.
Unknown Pdu's	Number of Unknown Pdu's frames sent/received.

SSCOP CC-TIMER

To change the connection control timer, use the **sscop cc-timer** interface configuration command. To restore the default value, use the **no** form of this command.

> **sscop cc-timer** *seconds*
> **no sscop cc-timer**

Syntax   *Description*

seconds   Number of seconds between Begin messages.

Default

10 seconds

Command Mode

Interface configuration

Usage Guidelines

This command first appeared in Cisco IOS Release 10.0.

The connection control timer determines the time between transmission of BGN (establishment), END (release), or RS (resynchronization) protocol data units (PDUs) as long as an acknowledgment has not been received.

Example

In the following example, the connection control timer is set to 15 seconds:

```
sscop cc-timer 15
```

Related Commands

sscop max-cc

SSCOP KEEPALIVE-TIMER

To change the keepalive timer, use the **sscop keepalive-timer** interface configuration command. The **no** form of this command restores the default value.

sscop keepalive-timer *seconds*
no sscop keepalive-timer *seconds*

Syntax	Description
seconds	Number of seconds the router waits between transmission of POLL PDUs when no sequential data (SD) or SDP PDUs are queued for transmission or are outstanding pending acknowledgments.

Default

30 seconds

Command Mode

Interface configuration

Usage Guidelines

This command first appeared in Cisco IOS Release 10.0.

Example

In the following example, the keepalive timer is set to 15 seconds:

```
sscop keepalive-timer 15
```

SSCOP MAX-CC

To change the retry count of connection control, use the **sscop max-cc** interface configuration command. The **no** form of this command restores the default value.

sscop **max-cc** *retries*
no sscop **max-cc**

Syntax	Description
retries	Number of times that SSCOP will retry to transmit BGN (establishment), END (release), or RS (resynchronization) PDUs as long as an acknowledgment has not been received. The valid range is 1 to 6000.

Default

10 retries

Command Mode

Interface configuration

Usage Guidelines

This command first appeared in Cisco IOS Release 10.0.

Example

In the following example, the retry count of the connection control is set to 20:

```
sscop max-cc 20
```

Related Commands

sscop cc-timer

SSCOP POLL-TIMER

To change the poll timer, use the **sscop poll-timer** interface configuration command. The **no** form of this command restores the default value.

> **sscop poll-timer** *seconds*
> **no sscop poll-timer**

Syntax	Description
seconds	Number of seconds the router waits between transmission of POLL PDUs.

Default

10 seconds

Command Mode

Interface configuration

Usage Guidelines

This command first appeared in Cisco IOS Release 10.0.

The poll timer controls the maximum time between transmission of POLL PDUs when SD or SDP PDUs are queued for transmission or are outstanding pending acknowledgments.

Example

In the following example, the poll timer is set to 15 seconds:

```
sscop poll-timer 15
```

SSCOP RCV-WINDOW

To change the receiver window, use the **sscop rcv-window** interface configuration command. The **no** form of this command restores the default value.

> **sscop rcv-window** *packets*
> **no sscop rcv-window**

Syntax   *Description*

packets   Number of packets the interface can receive before it must send an acknowledgment to the ATM switch. The valid range is 1 to 6000.

Default

7 packets

Command Mode

Interface configuration

Usage Guidelines

This command first appeared in Cisco IOS Release 10.0.

Example

In the following example, the receiver's window is set to 10 packets:

```
sscop rcv-window 10
```

SSCOP SEND-WINDOW

To change the transmitter window, use the **sscop send-window** interface configuration command. The **no** form of this command restores the default value.

sscop send-window *packets*
no sscop send-window

Syntax   *Description*

packets   Number of packets the interface can send before it must receive an acknowledgment from the ATM switch. The valid range is 1 to 6000.

Default

7 packets

Command Mode

Interface configuration

Usage Guidelines

This command first appeared in Cisco IOS Release 10.0.

Example

In the following example, the transmitter's window is set to 10 packets:

```
sscop send-window 10
```

CHAPTER 7

Configuring Frame Relay

This chapter describes the tasks required to configure Frame Relay on a router or access server. For a complete description of the Frame Relay commands mentioned in this chapter, refer to Chapter 8, "Frame Relay Commands."

CISCO FRAME RELAY MIB

The Cisco Frame Relay MIB adds extensions to the standard Frame Relay MIB (RFC 1315). It provides additional link-level and virtual circuit-level information and statistics that are mostly specific to Cisco Frame Relay implementation. This MIB provides SNMP network management access to most of the information covered by the **show frame-relay** commands, such as **show frame-relay lmi**, **show frame-relay pvc**, **show frame-relay map**, and **show frame-relay svc**.

CREATING FRAME RELAY HARDWARE CONNECTIONS

You can create Frame Relay connections using one of the following hardware configurations:

- Connect routers and access servers directly to the Frame Relay switch.
- Connect routers and access servers directly to a channel service unit/digital service unit (CSU/DSU), which then connects to a remote Frame Relay switch.

NOTES

Routers can connect to Frame Relay networks either by direct connection to a Frame Relay switch or through CSU/DSUs. However, a single router interface configured for Frame Relay can only be configured for one of these methods.

The CSU/DSU converts V.35 or RS-449 signals to the properly coded T1 transmission signal for successful reception by the Frame Relay network. Figure 7–1 illustrates the connections between the different components.

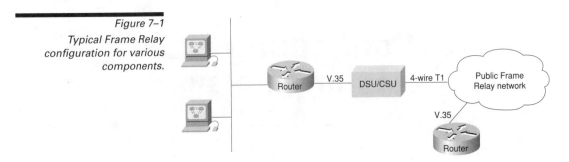

Figure 7–1

Typical Frame Relay configuration for various components.

The Frame Relay interface actually consists of one physical connection between the network server and the switch that provides the service. This single physical connection provides direct connectivity to each device on a network, such as a StrataCom FastPacket wide-area network (WAN).

CONFIGURING FRAME RELAY

You must follow certain required, basic steps to enable Frame Relay for your network. In addition, you can customize Frame Relay for your particular network needs and monitor Frame Relay connections. The following sections outline these tasks.

The tasks in the following list are required:

- Enabling Frame Relay Encapsulation on an Interface
- Configuring Dynamic or Static Address Mapping

The tasks in the following list are optional and are used to customize Frame Relay:

- Configuring the LMI
- Configuring Frame Relay Switched Virtual Circuits
- Configuring Frame Relay Traffic Shaping
- Customizing Frame Relay for Your Network
- Monitoring and Maintaining the Frame Relay Connections

See the "Frame Relay Configuration Examples" section near the end of this chapter for ideas of how to configure Frame Relay on your network. See Chapter 8 for information about the Frame Relay commands listed in the tasks. Use the index or search online for documentation of other commands.

ENABLING FRAME RELAY ENCAPSULATION ON AN INTERFACE

To set Frame Relay encapsulation at the interface level, perform the following tasks beginning in global configuration mode:

Task	Command
Specify the interface, and enter interface configuration mode.	**interface type** *number*
Enable Frame Relay, and specify the encapsulation method.	**encapsulation frame-relay [ietf]**

Frame Relay supports encapsulation of all supported protocols in conformance with RFC 1490, allowing interoperability between multiple vendors. Use the Internet Engineering Task Force (IETF) form of Frame Relay encapsulation if your router or access server is connected to another vendor's equipment across a Frame Relay network. IETF encapsulation is supported either at the interface level or on a per-virtual circuit basis.

For an example of how to enable Frame Relay and set the encapsulation method, see the sections "IETF Encapsulation Examples" and "Static Address Mapping Examples" later in this chapter.

Cisco recommends that you shut down the interface prior to changing encapsulation types. Although this is not required, shutting down the interface ensures the interface is reset for the new encapsulation.

CONFIGURING DYNAMIC OR STATIC ADDRESS MAPPING

Dynamic address mapping uses Frame Relay Inverse ARP to request the next hop protocol address for a specific connection, given its known DLCI. Responses to Inverse ARP requests are entered in an address-to-DLCI mapping table on the router or access server; the table is then used to supply the next hop protocol address or the DLCI for outgoing traffic.

Inverse ARP is enabled by default for all protocols that it supports, but it can be disabled for specific protocol-DLCI pairs. As a result, you can use dynamic mapping for some protocols and static mapping for other protocols on the same DLCI. You can explicitly disable Inverse ARP for a protocol-DLCI pair if you know that the protocol is not supported on the other end of the connection. See the "Disabling or Reenabling Frame Relay Inverse ARP" section later in this chapter for more information.

Configuring Dynamic Mapping

Inverse ARP is enabled by default for all protocols enabled on the physical interface. Packets are not sent out for protocols that are not enabled on the interface.

Because Inverse ARP is enabled by default, no additional command is required to configure dynamic mapping on an interface.

Configuring Static Mapping

A static map links a specified next hop protocol address to a specified DLCI. Static mapping removes the need for Inverse ARP requests; when you supply a static map, Inverse ARP is automatically disabled for the specified protocol on the specified DLCI.

You must use static mapping if the router at the other end either does not support Inverse ARP at all or does not support Inverse ARP for a specific protocol that you want to use over Frame Relay.

To establish static mapping according to your network needs, perform one of the following tasks in interface configuration mode:

Task	Command
Define the mapping between a next hop protocol address and the DLCI used to connect to the address.	**frame-relay map** *protocol protocol-address dlci* [**broadcast**] [**ietf**] [**cisco**]
Define a DLCI used to send International Organization for Standardization (ISO) Connectionless Network Service (CLNS) frames.	**frame-relay map clns** *dlci* [**broadcast**]
Define a DLCI used to connect to a bridge.	**frame-relay map bridge** *dlci* [**broadcast**] [**ietf**]

The supported protocols and the corresponding keywords to enable them are as follows:

- IP—**ip**
- DECnet—**decnet**
- AppleTalk—**appletalk**
- XNS—**xns**
- Novell IPX—**ipx**
- VINES—**vines**
- ISO CLNS—**clns**

You can greatly simplify the configuration for the Open Shortest Path First (OSPF) protocol by adding the optional **broadcast** keyword when doing this task. See the **frame-relay map** command description in Chapter 8 and the examples at the end of this chapter for more information about using the **broadcast** keyword.

For examples of how to establish static address mapping, see the "Static Address Mapping Examples" section later in this chapter.

CONFIGURING THE LMI

Beginning with Cisco IOS Release 11.2, the software supports Local Management Interface (LMI) *autosense*, which enables the interface to determine the LMI type supported by the switch. Support for LMI autosense means that you are no longer required to configure the Local Management Interface (LMI) explicitly.

For information on using Enhanced Local Management Interface with traffic shaping, see "Configuring Frame Relay Traffic Shaping" later in this chapter.

Allowing LMI Autosense to Operate

LMI autosense is active in the following situations:

- The router is powered up or the interface changes state to up.
- The line protocol is down, but the line is up.
- The interface is a Frame Relay DTE.
- The LMI type is not explicitly configured.

Status Requests

When LMI autosense is active, it sends out a full status request, in all three LMI flavors, to the switch. The order is ANSI, ITU, cisco, but it is done in rapid succession. Unlike previous software capability, you can now listen in on both DLCI 1023 (cisco LMI) and DLCI 0 (ANSI and ITU) simultaneously.

Status Messages

One or more of the status requests will elicit a reply (status message) from the switch. The router will decode the format of the reply and configure itself automatically. If more than one reply is received, the router will configure itself with the type of the last received reply. This is to accommodate intelligent switches that can handle multiple formats simultaneously.

LMI Autosense

If LMI autosense is unsuccessful, an intelligent retry scheme is built in. Every N391 interval (default is 60 seconds, which is 6 keep exchanges at 10 seconds each), LMI autosense will attempt to ascertain the LMI type. For more information about N391, see the **frame-relay lmi-n391dte** command in Chapter 8.

The only visible indication to the user that LMI autosense is underway is when **debug frame lmi** is turned on. At each N391 interval, the user will see three rapid status inquiries coming out of the serial interface. One is in ANSI, one is in ITU, and one is in cisco LMI-type.

Configuration Options

No configuration options are provided; this is transparent to the user. You can turn off LMI autosense by explicitly configuring an LMI type. The LMI type must be written into NVRAM so that next time the router powers up, LMI autosense will be inactive. At the end of autoinstall, a **frame-relay lmi-type** *xxx* statement is included within the interface configuration. This configuration is not automatically written to NVRAM; you must explicitly write the configuration to NVRAM by using the **copy running-config** or **copy startup-config** commands.

Explicitly Configuring the LMI

Cisco's Frame Relay software supports the industry-accepted standards for addressing the Local Management Interface (LMI), including the Cisco specification. If you want to configure the LMI and thus deactivate LMI autosense, complete the tasks in the following sections. The first two tasks in the following list are required if you choose to configure the LMI:

- Setting the LMI Type
- Setting the LMI Keepalive Interval
- Setting the LMI Polling and Timer Intervals

Setting the LMI Type

If the router or access server is attached to a public data network (PDN), the LMI type must match the type used on the public network. Otherwise, the LMI type can be set to suit the needs of your private Frame Relay network.

You can set one of three types of LMIs on Cisco devices: ANSI T1.617 Annex D, Cisco, and ITU-T Q.933 Annex A. To do so, perform the following task beginning in interface configuration mode:

Task	Command
Set the LMI type.	**frame-relay lmi-type** {ansi	cisco	q933a}
Exit configuration mode.	end
Write the LMI type to NVRAM.	**copy startup-config** *destination*

For an example of how to set the LMI type, see the "Pure Frame Relay DCE Example" section later in this chapter.

Setting the LMI Keepalive Interval

A keepalive interval must be set to configure the LMI. By default, this interval is 10 seconds and, per the LMI protocol, must be less than the corresponding interval on the switch. To set the keepalive interval, perform the following task in interface configuration mode:

Task	Command
Set the keepalive interval.	**keepalive** *number*

To disable keepalives on networks that don't utilize LMI, use the **no keepalive** interface configuration command. For an example of how to specify an LMI keepalive interval, see the "Two Routers in Static Mode Example" section later in this chapter.

Setting the LMI Polling and Timer Intervals

You can set various optional counters, intervals, and thresholds to fine-tune the operation of your LMI DTE and DCE devices. Set these attributes by performing one or more of the following tasks in interface configuration mode:

Task	Command
Set the DCE and Network-to-Network Interface (NNI) error threshold.	**frame-relay lmi-n392dce** *threshold*
Set the DCE and NNI monitored events count.	**frame-relay lmi-n393dce** *events*
Set the polling verification timer on a DCE or NNI interface.	**frame-relay lmi-t392dce** *timer*
Set a full status polling interval on a DTE or NNI interface.	**frame-relay lmi-n391dte** *keep-exchanges*
Set the DTE or NNI error threshold.	**frame-relay lmi-n392dte** *threshold*
Set the DTE and NNI monitored events count.	**frame-relay lmi-n393dte** *events*

See Chapter 6, "ATM Commands," for details about commands used to set the polling and timing intervals.

CONFIGURING FRAME RELAY SWITCHED VIRTUAL CIRCUITS

Access to Frame Relay networks is made through private leased lines at speeds ranging from 56 Kbps to 45 Mbps. Frame Relay is a connection-oriented, packet-transfer mechanism that establishes virtual circuits between endpoints.

Switched Virtual Circuits

Switched virtual circuits (SVCs) allow access through a Frame Relay network by setting up a path to the destination endpoints only when the need arises and tearing down the path when it is no longer needed.

SVCs can coexist with PVCs in the same sites and routers. For example, routers at remote branch offices might set up PVCs to the central headquarters for frequent communication, but set up SVCs with each other as needed for intermittent communication. As a result, any-to-any communication can be set up without any-to-any PVCs.

On SVCs, quality of service (QOS) elements can be specified on a call-by-call basis to request network resources.

SVC support is offered in the Enterprise image on Cisco platforms that include a serial or HSSI interface (Cisco 7000 series, Cisco 7500 series, Cisco 4500, Cisco 4700, Cisco 4000, Cisco 3000, and Cisco 2500 platforms).

You must have the following services before Frame Relay SVCs can operate:

- Frame Relay SVC support by the service provider—the service provider's switch must be capable of supporting SVC operation.

- Physical loop connection—a leased line or dedicated line must exist between the router (DTE) and the local Frame Relay switch.

Enabling SVC Operation

SVC operation requires that the Data Link layer (Layer 2) be set up and running ITU-T Q.922 Link Access Procedures to Frame mode bearer services (LAPF) prior to signalling for an SVC. Layer 2 sets itself up as soon as SVC support is enabled on the interface if both the line and the line protocol are up. When the SVCs are configured and demand for a path occurs, the Q.933 signalling sequence is initiated. Once the SVC is set up, data transfer begins.

Q.922 provides a reliable link layer for Q.933 operation. All Q.933 call control information is transmitted over DLCI 0; this DLCI is also used for the management protocols specified in ANSI T1.617 Annex D or Q.933 Annex A.

You must enable SVC operation at the interface level. Once it is enabled at the interface level, it is enabled on any subinterfaces on that interface. One signalling channel, DLCI 0, is set up for the interface, and all SVCs are controlled from the physical interface.

Enabling Frame Relay SVC Service

To enable Frame Relay SVC service and set up SVCs, complete the tasks in the following sections. The subinterface tasks are not required, but offer additional flexibility for SVC configuration and operation. The LAPF tasks are not required and not recommended unless you understand thoroughly the impacts on your network. The tasks are shown in the following list:

- Configuring SVCs on a Physical Interface
- Configuring SVCs on a Subinterface (optional)
- Configuring a Map Class
- Configuring a Map Group with E.164 or X.121 Addresses
- Associating the Map Class with Static Protocol Address Maps
- Configuring LAPF Parameters (optional)

See the "SVC Configuration Examples" section at the end of this chapter for more information.

Configuring SVCs on a Physical Interface

To enable SVC operation on a Frame Relay interface, perform the following tasks beginning in global configuration mode:

Task	Command
Specify the physical interface.	**interface** *type number*
Specify the interface IP address, if needed.	**ip address** *ip-address mask*
Enable Frame Relay encapsulation on the interface.	**encapsulation frame-relay**
Assign a map group to the interface.	**map-group** *group-name*
Enable Frame Relay SVC support on the interface.	**frame-relay svc**

Map-group details are specified with the **map-list** command.

Configuring SVCs on a Subinterface

To configure Frame Relay SVCs on a subinterface, perform all the tasks in the previous section, except assigning a map group. After the physical interface is configured, complete the following tasks beginning in global configuration mode:

Task	Command
Specify a subinterface of the main interface configured for SVC operation.	**interface** *type number.subinterface-number* {**multipoint** | **point-to-point**}
Specify the subinterface IP address, if needed.	**ip address** *ip-address mask*
Assign a map group to the subinterface.	**map-group** *group-name*

Configuring a Map Class

To configure a map class, you can perform the following tasks; only the first task is required:

- Specify the map class name.
- Specify a custom queue list for the map class.
- Specify a priority queue list for the map class.
- Enable BECN feedback to throttle the output rate on the SVC for the map class.
- Set nondefault QOS values for the map class.

NOTES

You are not required to set the QOS values; default values are provided.

To configure a map class, perform the following tasks beginning in global configuration mode:

Task	Command
Specify the Frame Relay map class name and enter map class configuration mode.	**map-class frame-relay** *map-class-name*
Specify a custom queue list to be used for the map class.	**frame-relay custom-queue-list** *list-number*
Assign a priority queue to virtual circuits associated with the map class.	**frame-relay priority-group** *list-number*
Enable the type of BECN feedback to throttle the frame-transmission rate.	**frame-relay adaptive-shaping [becn | foresight]**[*]
Specify the inbound committed information rate (CIR).	**frame-relay cir in** *bps*
Specify the outbound committed information rate (CIR).	**frame-relay cir out** *bps*
Set the minimum acceptable incoming CIR.	**frame-relay mincir in** *bps*[†]
Set the minimum acceptable outgoing CIR.	**frame-relay mincir out** *bps*[†]
Set the incoming committed burst size (Bc).	**frame-relay bc in** *bits*[†]
Set the outgoing committed burst size (Bc).	**frame-relay bc out** *bits*[†]
Set the incoming excess burst size (Be).	**frame-relay be in** *bits*[†]
Set the outgoing excess burst size (Be).	**frame-relay be out** *bits*[†]
Set the idle timeout interval.	**frame-relay idle-timer** *duration*[†]

[*] The **frame-relay adaptive-shaping [becn | foresight]** command replaces the **frame-relay becn-response-enable** command, which will be removed in a future Cisco IOS release. If you use the **frame-relay becn-response-enable** command in scripts, you should replace it with the **frame-relay adaptive-shaping becn** command.

[†] The **in** and **out** keywords are optional. Configuring the command without the in and out keywords will apply that value to both the incoming and outgoing traffic values for the SVC setup. For example, **frame-relay cir 56000** applies 56000 to both incoming and outgoing traffic values for setting up the SVC.

You can define multiple map classes. A map class is associated with a static map, not with the interface or subinterface itself. Because of the flexibility this association allows, you can define different map classes for different destinations.

Configuring a Map Group with E.164 or X.121 Addresses

After you have defined a map group for an interface, you can associate the map group with a specific source and destination address to be used. You can specify E.164 addresses or X.121 addresses for the source and destination. To specify the map group to be associated with a specific interface, perform the following task in global configuration mode:

Task	Command
Specify the map group to be associated with specific source address and destination address for the SVC.	map-list *group-name* source-addr {e164	x121} *source-address* dest-addr {e164	x121} *destination-address*

Associating the Map Class with Static Protocol Address Maps

To define the protocol addresses under a **map-list** command and associate each protocol address with a specified map class, use the **class** command. Use this command for each protocol address to be associated with a map class. To associate a map class with a protocol address, perform the following task in map class configuration mode:

Task	Command
Specify a destination protocol address and a Frame Relay map class name from which to derive QOS information.	*protocol protocol-address* **class** *class-name* [ietf] [broadcast [trigger]]

The **ietf** keyword specifies RFC 1490 encapsulation; the **broadcast** keyword specifies that broadcasts must be carried. The **trigger** keyword, which can be configured only if **broadcast** is also configured, enables a broadcast packet to trigger an SVC. If an SVC already exists that uses this map class, the SVC will carry the broadcast.

Configuring LAPF Parameters

Frame Relay Link Access Procedure for Frame Relay (LAPF) commands are used to tune Layer 2 system parameters to work well with the Frame Relay switch. Normally, you do not need to change the default settings.

However, if the Frame Relay network indicates that it does not support the Frame Reject frame (FRMR) at the LAPF Frame Reject procedure, complete the following task in interface configuration mode:

Task	Command
Select not to send FRMR frames at the LAPF Frame Reject procedure.	**no frame-relay lapf frmr**

By default, the Frame Reject frame is sent at the LAPF Frame Reject procedure.

NOTES

Manipulation of Layer 2 parameters is not recommended if you do not understand the resulting functional change. For more information, refer to the ITU-T Q.922 specification for LAPF.

If you must change Layer 2 parameters for your network environment and you understand the resulting functional change, complete the following tasks as needed:

Task	Command
Set the LAPF window size *k*.	**frame-relay lapf k** *number*
Set the LAPF maximum retransmission count *N200*.	**frame-relay lapf n200** *retries*
Set the maximum length of the Information field of the LAPF I frame *N201*.	**frame-relay lapf n201** *number*
Set the LAPF retransmission timer value *T200*.	**frame-relay lapf t200** *tenths-of-a-second*
Set the LAPF link idle timer value *T203* of DLCI 0.	**frame-relay lapf t203** *seconds*

CONFIGURING FRAME RELAY TRAFFIC SHAPING

The following Frame Relay traffic shaping capabilities were introduced with Cisco IOS Release 11.2:

- Rate Enforcement on a Per-Virtual Circuit Basis. This is used to set the peak rate for outbound traffic. The value can be set to match CIR or another value.

- Dynamic Traffic Throttling on a Per-Virtual Circuit Basis. When BECN packets indicate congestion on the network, the outbound traffic rate is automatically stepped down; when congestion eases, the outbound traffic rate is increased. This feature is enabled by default.

- Enhanced Queuing Support on a Per-Virtual Circuit Basis. Either custom queuing or priority queuing can be configured for individual virtual circuits.

NOTES

Frame Relay traffic shaping is not effective for Layer 2 PVC switching using the **frame-relay route** command.

Virtual Circuits for Different Types of Traffic

By defining separate virtual circuits for different types of traffic and specifying queuing and an outbound traffic rate for each virtual circuit, you can provide guaranteed bandwidth for each type of traffic. By specifying different traffic rates for different virtual circuits over the same line, you can perform virtual time division multiplexing. By throttling outbound traffic from high-speed lines in central offices to lower-speed lines in remote locations, you can ease congestion and data loss in the network; enhanced queuing also prevents congestion-caused data loss.

Traffic Shaping Tasks

Traffic shaping applies to both PVCs and SVCs. For information about creating and configuring SVCs, see the "Configuring Frame Relay Switched Virtual Circuits" section earlier in this chapter.

To configure Frame Relay traffic shaping, perform the following tasks:

- Enabling Frame Relay Encapsulation on an Interface (earlier in this chapter)
- Enabling Frame Relay Traffic Shaping on the Interface
- Enabling Enhanced Local Management Interface
- Specify a Traffic Shaping Map Class for the Interface
- Defining a Map Class with Queuing and Traffic Shaping Parameters
- Defining Access Lists
- Defining Priority Queue Lists for the Map Class
- Defining Custom Queue Lists for the Map Class

Enabling Frame Relay Traffic Shaping on the Interface

Enabling Frame Relay traffic shaping on an interface enables both traffic shaping and per-virtual circuit queuing on all the interface's PVCs and SVCs. Traffic shaping enables the router to control the circuit's output rate and react to congestion notification information if also configured.

To enable Frame Relay traffic shaping on the specified interface, complete the following task in interface configuration mode:

Task	Command
Enable Frame Relay traffic shaping and per-virtual circuit queuing.	frame-relay traffic-shaping

Understanding Frame Relay Router ForeSight

ForeSight is the network traffic control software used in Cisco StrataCom switches. The Cisco StrataCom Frame Relay switch can extend ForeSight messages over a User-to-Network Interface (UNI), passing the backward congestion notification for virtual circuits.

The Router ForeSight feature allows Cisco Frame Relay routers to process and react to ForeSight messages and adjust virtual circuit level traffic shaping in a timely manner.

Router ForeSight must be configured explicitly on both the Cisco router and the Cisco StrataCom switch. Router ForeSight is enabled on the Cisco router when Frame Relay traffic shaping is configured. However, the router's response to ForeSight is not applied to any VC until the **frame-relay**

adaptive-shaping foresight command is added to the VCs map-class. When ForeSight is enabled on the StrataCom switch, the switch will periodically send out a ForeSight message based on the time value configured. The time interval can range from 40 to 5000 milliseconds.

When a Cisco router receives a ForeSight message indicating that certain Data Link Connection Identifiers (DLCIs) are experiencing congestion, the Cisco router reacts by activating its traffic shaping function to slow down the output rate. The router reacts as it would if it were to detect the congestion by receiving a packet with the backward explicit congestion notification (BECN) bit set.

Congestion Notification Methods

The difference between the BECN and ForeSight congestion notification methods is that BECN requires a user packet to be sent in the direction of the congested DLCI to convey the signal. The sending of user packets is not predictable and, therefore, not reliable as a notification mechanism. Rather than waiting for user packets to provide the congestion notification, timed ForeSight messages guarantee that the router receives notification before congestion becomes a problem. Traffic can be slowed down in the direction of the congested DLCI.

Router ForeSight Prerequisites

For Router ForeSight to work, the following conditions must exist on the Cisco router:

- Frame Relay traffic shaping must be enabled on the interface.
- The traffic shaping for a circuit is adapted to ForeSight.

The following additional condition must exist on the Cisco StrataCom switch:

- The UNI connecting to the router is Consolidated Link Layer Management (CLLM) enabled, with the proper time interval specified.

Frame Relay Router ForeSight is enabled automatically when you use the **frame-relay traffic-shaping** command. However, you must issue the **map-class frame-relay** command and the **frame-relay adaptive-shaping foresight** command before the router will respond to ForeSight and apply the traffic shaping effect on a specific interface, subinterface, or virtual circuit.

Enabling Enhanced Local Management Interface

When used in conjunction with traffic shaping, the router can respond to changes in the network dynamically. This feature allows the router to learn QOS parameters from the Cisco StrataCom switch and use them for traffic shaping, configuration, or management purposes.

Enhanced Local Management Interface also simplifies the process of configuring traffic shaping on the router. Previously, users had to configure traffic shaping rate enforcement values, possibly for every virtual circuit. Enabling Enhanced Local Management Interface reduces chances of specifying inconsistent or incorrect values when configuring the router.

To enable the Enhanced Local Management Interface feature, you must configure it on the main interface. Perform the following task in interface configuration mode:

Task	Command
Specify the physical interface.	**interface type** *\number*
Enable Frame Relay encapsulation on the interface.	**encapsulation frame-relay** [cisco | ietf]
Enable the Enhanced Local Management Interface feature.	**frame-relay qos-autosense**

NOTES

Enhanced Local Management Interface enables automated exchange of Frame Relay QOS parameter information between the Cisco router and the Cisco StrataCom switch. Routers can base congestion management and prioritization decisions on known QOS values, such as the Committed Information Rate (CIR), Committed Burst Size (Bc), and Excess Burst Size (Be). The router senses Quality of Service (QOS) values from the switch and can be configured to use those values in traffic shaping. This enhancement works between Cisco routers and Cisco StrataCom switches (BPX/AXIS and IGX platforms).

It is not necessary to configure traffic shaping on the interface to enable Enhanced Local Management Interface. You might want to enable it to know the values being used by the switch. If you want the router to respond to the QOS information received from the switch by adjusting the output rate, you must configure traffic shaping on the interface. To configure traffic shaping, use the **frame-relay traffic-shaping** command in interface configuration mode

For an example of how to configure a Frame Relay interface with QOS autosense enabled, see the "Enhanced Local Management Interface Example" section later in this chapter.

Specifying a Traffic Shaping Map Class for the Interface

If you specify a Frame Relay map class for a main interface, all the virtual circuits on its subinterfaces inherit all the traffic shaping parameters defined for the class.

To specify a map class for the specified interface, complete the following task in beginning interface configuration mode:

Task	Command
Specify a Frame Relay map class for the interface.	**frame-relay class** *map-class-name*

You can override the default for a specific DLCI on a specific subinterface by using the **class** virtual circuit configuration command to assign the DLCI explicitly to a different class. See the "Configuring Frame Relay Subinterfaces" section for information about setting up subinterfaces. For an example of assigning some subinterface DLCIs to the default class and assigning others explicitly to a different class, see the "Frame Relay Traffic Shaping Examples" section later in this chapter.

Defining a Map Class with Queuing and Traffic Shaping Parameters

When you define a map class for Frame Relay, you can define the average and peak rates (in bits per second) allowed on virtual circuits associated with the map class. You can also optionally specify *either* a custom queue-list or a priority queue-group to use on virtual circuits associated with the map class.

To define a map class, complete the following tasks beginning in global configuration mode:

Task	Command
Specify a map class to define.	**map-class frame-relay** *map-class-name*
Define the traffic rate for the map class.	**frame-relay traffic-rate** *average* [*peak*]
Specify a custom queue-list.	**frame-relay custom-queue-list** *number*
Specify a priority queue-list.	**frame-relay priority-group** *number*
Select either BECN or ForeSight as the congestion backward-notification mechanism to which traffic shaping will adapt.	**frame-relay adaptive-shaping {becn	foresight}**[*]

[*] The **frame-relay adaptive-shaping** command replaces the **frame-relay becn-response-enable** command, which will be removed in a future Cisco IOS release. If you use the **frame-relay becn-response-enable** command in scripts, you should replace it with the **frame-relay adaptive-shaping** command.

Defining Access Lists

You can specify access lists and associate them with the custom queue-list defined for any map class. The list number specified in the access list and the custom queue list tie them together.

Defining Priority Queue Lists for the Map Class

You can define a priority list for a protocol and you can also define a default priority list. The number used for a specific priority list ties the list to the Frame Relay priority group defined for a specified map class.

For example, if you enter the **frame relay priority-group 2** command for the map class *fast_vcs* and then you enter the **priority-list 2 protocol decnet high** command, that priority list is used for the *fast_vcs* map class. The average and peak traffic rates defined for the *fast_vcs* map class are used for DECnet traffic.

Defining Custom Queue Lists for the Map Class

You can define queue lists for a protocol as well as a default queue list. You can also specify the maximum number of bytes to be transmitted in any cycle. The number used for a specific queue list ties the list to the Frame Relay custom-queue list defined for a specified map class.

For example, if you enter the **frame relay custom-queue-list 1** command for the map class *slow_vcs* and then you enter the **queue-list 1 protocol ip list 100** command, that queue list is used for the *slow_vcs* map class; **access-list 100** definition is also used for that map class and queue. The average and peak traffic rates defined for the *slow_vcs* map class are used for IP traffic that meets the **access list 100** criteria.

CUSTOMIZING FRAME RELAY FOR YOUR NETWORK

Perform the tasks in the following list to customize Frame Relay:

- Configuring Frame Relay Subinterfaces
- Configuring Frame Relay Switching
- Disabling or Reenabling Frame Relay Inverse ARP (multipoint communication only)
- Creating a Broadcast Queue for an Interface
- Configuring Payload Compression
- Configuring Standard-Based FRF.9 Compression
- Configuring TCP/IP Header Compression
- Configuring Real-Time Header Compression with Frame Relay Encapsulation
- Configuring Discard Eligibility
- Configuring DLCI Priority Levels

Configuring Frame Relay Subinterfaces

To understand Frame Relay Subinterfaces, read the following "Understanding Frame Relay Sub-interfaces" section.

To define the Frame Relay subinterface, perform the tasks in the following list:

- Defining Frame Relay Subinterfaces
- Defining Subinterface Addressing

After the subinterface is defined, you can also perform the following optional tasks:

- Configuring Transparent Bridging for Frame Relay
- Configuring a Backup Interface for a Subinterface

For an example of how to define a subinterface, see the section "Subinterface Example" later in this chapter.

Understanding Frame Relay Subinterfaces

Frame Relay subinterfaces provide a mechanism for supporting partially meshed Frame Relay networks. Most protocols assume *transitivity* on a logical network; that is, if station A can talk to station B, and station B can talk to station C, then station A should be able to talk to station C directly. Transitivity is true on LANs, but not on Frame Relay networks unless A is directly connected to C.

Additionally, certain protocols such as AppleTalk and transparent bridging cannot be supported on partially meshed networks because they require "split horizon," in which a packet received on an interface cannot be transmitted out the same interface even if the packet is received and transmitted on different virtual circuits.

Configuring Frame Relay subinterfaces ensures that a *single physical interface* is treated as *multiple virtual interfaces*. This capability allows you to overcome split horizon rules. Packets received on one virtual interface can now be forwarded out another virtual interface, even if they are configured on the same physical interface.

Subinterfaces address the limitations of Frame Relay networks by providing a way to subdivide a partially meshed Frame Relay network into a number of smaller, fully meshed (or point-to-point) subnetworks. Each subnetwork is assigned its own network number and appears to the protocols as if it is reachable through a separate interface. (Note that point-to-point subinterfaces can be unnumbered for use with IP, reducing the addressing burden that might otherwise result.)

For example, suppose you have a five-node Frame Relay network (see Figure 7–2) that is partially meshed (Network A). If the entire network is viewed as a single subnetwork (with a single network number assigned), most protocols assume that node A can transmit a packet directly to node E, when in fact it must be relayed through nodes C and D. This network can be made to work with certain protocols (for example, IP) but will not work at all with other protocols (for example, AppleTalk) because nodes C and D will not relay the packet out the same interface on which it was received. One way to make this network work fully is to create a fully meshed network (Network B), but doing so requires a large number of PVCs, which may not be economically feasible.

Using subinterfaces, you can subdivide the Frame Relay network into three smaller subnetworks (Network C) with separate network numbers. Nodes A, B, and C are connected to a fully meshed network, and nodes C and D, as well as nodes D and E are connected via point-to-point networks. In this configuration, nodes C and D can access two subinterfaces and can therefore forward packets without violating split horizon rules. If transparent bridging is being used, each subinterface is viewed as a separate bridge port.

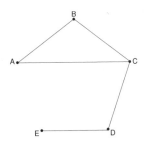

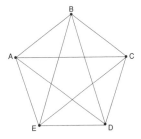

Figure 7–2
Using subinterfaces can provide full connectivity on a partially meshed Frame Relay network.

Network A: Partially Meshed Frame Relay
Network without Full Connectivity

Network B: Fully Meshed Frame Relay
Network with Full Connectivity

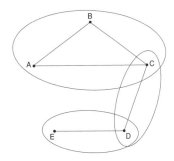

Network C: Partially Meshed Frame Relay Network with Full Connectivity
(configuring subinterfaces)

Defining Frame Relay Subinterfaces

To configure subinterfaces on a Frame Relay network, perform the following tasks beginning in global configuration mode:

Task	Command
Step 1 Specify an interface.	**interface type** *number*
Step 2 Configure Frame Relay encapsulation on the serial interface.	**encapsulation frame-relay**
Step 3 Specify a subinterface.	**interface type** *number.subinterface-number* {**multipoint** | **point-to-point**}

Subinterfaces can be configured for multipoint or point-to-point communication. (There is no default.)

Defining Subinterface Addressing

For point-to-point subinterfaces, the destination is presumed to be known and is identified or implied in the **frame-relay interface-dlci** command. For multipoint subinterfaces, the destinations can be dynamically resolved through the use of Frame Relay Inverse ARP or they can be statically mapped through the use of the **frame-relay map** command.

Addressing on Point-to-Point Subinterfaces

If you specified a point-to-point subinterface in Step 3 of the previous procedure, perform the following task in interface configuration mode:

Task	Command
Associate the selected point-to-point subinterface with a DLCI.	**frame-relay interface-dlci** *dlci* [*option*]

NOTES

This command is typically used on subinterfaces; however, it can also be applied to main interfaces. The **frame-relay interface-dlci** command is used to enable routing protocols on main interfaces that are configured to use Inverse ARP. This command is also helpful for assigning a specific class to a single PVC on a multipoint subinterface.

For an explanation of the many available options, refer to Chapter 6. For an example of how to associate a DLCI with a subinterface, see the section "Subinterface Example," later in this chapter.

If you define a subinterface for point-to-point communication, you cannot reassign *the same subinterface number* to be used for multipoint communication without first rebooting the router or access server. Instead, you can simply avoid using that subinterface number and use a different subinterface number instead.

Addressing on Multipoint Subinterfaces

If you specified a multipoint subinterface in Step 3 under "Define Frame Relay Subinterfaces," perform the one or both of the following tasks:

- Accept Inverse ARP for Dynamic Address Mapping on Multipoint Subinterfaces
- Configuring Static Address Mapping on Multipoint Subinterfaces

You can configure some protocols for dynamic address mapping and others for static address mapping.

Accept Inverse ARP for Dynamic Address Mapping on Multipoint Subinterfaces

Dynamic address mapping uses Frame Relay Inverse ARP to request the next hop protocol address for a specific connection, given a DLCI. Responses to Inverse ARP requests are entered in an address-to-DLCI mapping table on the router or access server; the table is then used to supply the next hop protocol address or the DLCI for outgoing traffic.

Since the physical interface is now configured as multiple subinterfaces, you must provide information that distinguishes a subinterface from the physical interface and associates a specific subinterface with a specific DLCI.

To associate a specific multipoint subinterface with a specific DLCI, perform the following task in interface configuration mode:

Task	Command
Associate a specified multipoint subinterface with a DLCI.	**frame-relay interface-dlci** *dlci*

Inverse ARP is enabled by default for all protocols that it supports, but it can be disabled for specific protocol-DLCI pairs. As a result, you can use dynamic mapping for some protocols and static mapping for other protocols on the same DLCI. You can explicitly disable Inverse ARP for a protocol-DLCI pair if you know the protocol is not supported on the other end of the connection. See the "Disabling or Reenabling Frame Relay Inverse ARP" section later in this chapter for more information.

Because Inverse ARP is enabled by default for all protocols that it supports, no additional command is required to configure dynamic address mapping on a subinterface.

For an example of configuring Frame Relay multipoint subinterfaces with dynamic address mapping, see the "Frame Relay Multipoint Subinterface with Dynamic Addressing Example" section.

Configuring Static Address Mapping on Multipoint Subinterfaces

A static map links a specified next hop protocol address to a specified DLCI. Static mapping removes the need for Inverse ARP requests; when you supply a static map, Inverse ARP is automatically disabled for the specified protocol on the specified DLCI.

You must use static mapping if the router at the other end either does not support Inverse ARP at all or does not support Inverse ARP for a specific protocol that you want to use over Frame Relay.

To establish static mapping according to your network needs, perform one of the following tasks in interface configuration mode:

Task	Command
Define the mapping between a next hop protocol address and the DLCI used to connect to that address.	**frame-relay map** *protocol protocol-address dlci* [**broadcast**] [**ietf**] [**cisco**]
Define a DLCI used to send ISO CLNS frames.	**frame-relay map clns** *dlci* [**broadcast**]
Define a DLCI used to connect to a bridge.	**frame-relay map bridge** *dlci* [**ietf**] **broadcast**

The supported protocols and the corresponding keywords to enable them are as follows:

- IP—**ip**
- DECnet—**decnet**
- AppleTalk—**appletalk**
- XNS—**xns**
- Novell IPX—**ipx**
- VINES—**vines**
- ISO CLNS—**clns**

The **broadcast** keyword is required for routing protocols such as OSI protocols and the Open Short-est Path First (OSPF) protocol. See the **frame-relay map** command description in Chapter 6 and the examples at the end of this chapter for more information about using the **broadcast** keyword.

For an example of how to establish static address mapping, see the sections "Two Routers in Static Mode Example," "DECnet Routing Example," and "IPX Routing Example," later in this chapter.

Configuring Transparent Bridging for Frame Relay

Transparent bridging for Frame Relay encapsulated serial and HSSI interfaces is supported on Cisco routers. Transparent bridging for Frame Relay encapsulated serial interfaces is supported on Cisco access servers.

You can configure transparent bridging for point-to-point or point-to-multipoint subinterfaces.

NOTES

All PVCs configured on a subinterface belong to the same bridge group.

Point-to-Point Subinterfaces

To configure transparent bridging for point-to-point subinterfaces, complete the following tasks beginning in global configuration mode:

Task	Command
Step 1 Specify an interface.	**interface type** *number*
Step 2 Configure Frame Relay encapsulation on the serial interface.	**encapsulation frame-relay**
Step 3 Specify a subinterface.	**interface type** *number:subinterface-number* **point-to-point**
Step 4 Associate a DLCI with the subinterface.	**frame-relay interface-dlci** *dlci* [*option*]
Step 5 Associate the subinterface with a bridge group.	**bridge-group** *bridge-group*

Point-to-Multipoint Interfaces

To configure transparent bridging for point-to-multipoint subinterfaces, complete the following tasks beginning in global configuration mode:

Task	Command
Step 1 Specify an interface.	**interface type** *number*
Step 2 Configure Frame Relay encapsulation on the serial interface.	**encapsulation frame-relay**
Step 3 Specify a subinterface.	**interface type** *number:subinterface-number* **multipoint**
Step 4 Define the mapping between a next hop protocol address and the DLCI used to connect to the address.	**frame-relay map bridge** *dlci* [**broadcast**] [**ietf**]
Step 5 Associate the subinterface with a bridge group.	**bridge-group** *bridge-group*

Configuring a Backup Interface for a Subinterface

Both point-to-point and multipoint Frame Relay subinterfaces can be configured with a backup interface. This approach allows individual PVCs to be backed up in case of failure rather than depending on the entire Frame Relay connection to fail before the backup takes over. You can configure a subinterface for backup on failure only, not for backup based on loading of the line.

If the main interface has a backup interface, it will have precedence over the subinterface's backup interface in the case of complete loss of connectivity with the Frame Relay network. As a result, a subinterface backup is activated only if the main interface is up, or if the interface is down and does not have a backup interface defined. If a subinterface fails while its backup interface is in use, and the main interface goes down, the backup subinterface remains connected.

To configure a backup interface for a Frame Relay subinterface, perform the following tasks, beginning in global configuration mode:

Task	Command
Step 1 Specify the interface.	**interface type** *number*
Step 2 Configure Frame Relay encapsulation.	**encapsulation frame-relay**
Step 3 Configure the subinterface.	**interface type** *number.subinterface-number* **point-to-point**
Step 4 Specify a DLCI for the subinterface.	**frame-relay interface-dlci** *dlci*
Step 5 Specify a backup interface for the subinterface.	**backup interface type** *number*
Step 6 Specify backup enable and disable delay.	**backup delay** *enable-delay disable-delay*

Configuring Frame Relay Switching

Frame Relay switching is a means of switching packets based upon the DLCI, which can be looked upon as the Frame Relay equivalent of a MAC address. You perform the switching by configuring your router or access server as a Frame Relay network. There are two parts to a Frame Relay network: a Frame Relay DTE (the router or access server) and a Frame Relay DCE switch. Figure 7–3 illustrates this concept.

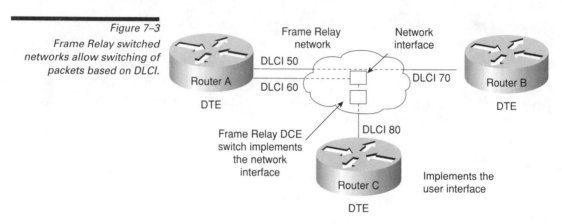

Figure 7–3
Frame Relay switched networks allow switching of packets based on DLCI.

In Figure 7–3, Routers A, B, and C are Frame Relay DTEs connected to each other via a Frame Relay network. Cisco's implementation of Frame Relay switching allows Cisco devices to be used as depicted in this Frame Relay network.

Perform the tasks in the following list, as necessary, to configure Frame Relay switching:

- Enabling Frame Relay Switching
- Configuring a Frame Relay DTE Device, DCE Switch, or NNI Support
- Specifying the Static Route

Enabling Frame Relay Switching

You must enable packet switching before you can configure it on a Frame Relay DTE or DCE, or with Network-to-Network Interface (NNI) support. Do so by performing the following task in global configuration mode before configuring the switch type:

Task	Command
Enable Frame Relay switching.	**frame-relay switching**

For an example of how to enable Frame Relay switching, see the switching examples later in this chapter.

Configuring a Frame Relay DTE Device, DCE Switch, or NNI Support

You can configure an interface as a DTE device, a DCE switch, or as a switch connected to a switch to support NNI connections. (DCE is the default.) To do so, perform the following task in interface configuration mode:

Task	Command
Configure a Frame Relay DTE device or DCE switch.	**frame-relay intf-type [dce	dte	nni]**

For an example of how to configure a DTE device or DCE switch, see the section "Hybrid DTE/DCE PVC Switching Example" later in this chapter.

For an example of how to configure NNI support, see the section "Pure Frame Relay DCE Example," later in this chapter.

Specifying the Static Route

You must specify a static route for PVC switching. To do so, perform the following task in interface configuration mode:

Task	Command
Specify a static route for PVC switching.	**frame-relay route** *in-dlci out-interface out-dlci*

For an example of how to specify a static route, see the section "Pure Frame Relay DCE Example," later in this chapter.

Disabling or Reenabling Frame Relay Inverse ARP

Frame Relay Inverse ARP is a method of building dynamic address mappings in Frame Relay networks running AppleTalk, Banyan VINES, DECnet, IP, Novell IPX, and XNS. Inverse ARP allows the router or access server to discover the protocol address of a device associated with the virtual circuit.

Inverse ARP creates dynamic address mappings, as contrasted with the **frame-relay map** command, which defines static mappings between a specific protocol address and a specific DLCI (see the section "Configuring Dynamic or Static Address Mapping" earlier in this chapter for more information).

Inverse ARP is enabled by default but can be disabled explicitly for a given protocol and DLCI pair. Disable or reenable Inverse ARP under the following conditions:

- Disable Inverse ARP for a selected protocol and DLCI pair when you know that the protocol is not supported on the other end of the connection.

- Reenable Inverse ARP for a protocol and DLCI pair if conditions or equipment change and the protocol is then supported on the other end of the connection.

NOTES

If you change from a point-to-point subinterface to a multipoint subinterface, then change the subinterface number. Frame Relay Inverse ARP will be on by default, and no further action is required.

You do not need to enable or disable Inverse ARP if you have a point-to-point interface, because there is only a single destination and discovery is not required. To select Inverse ARP or disable it, perform one of the following tasks in interface configuration mode:

Task	Command
Enable Frame Relay Inverse ARP for a specific protocol and DLCI pair, only if it was previously disabled.	**frame-relay inverse-arp** *protocol dlci*
Disable Frame Relay Inverse ARP for a specific protocol and DLCI pair.	**no frame relay inverse-arp** *protocol dlci*

Creating a Broadcast Queue for an Interface

Very large Frame Relay networks might have performance problems when many DLCIs terminate in a single router or access server that must replicate routing updates and service advertising updates on each DLCI. The updates can consume access-link bandwidth and cause significant latency variations in user traffic; the updates can also consume interface buffers and lead to higher packet rate loss for both user data and routing updates.

To avoid such problems, you can create a special broadcast queue for an interface. The broadcast queue is managed independently of the normal interface queue, has its own buffers, and has a configurable size and service rate.

A broadcast queue is given a maximum transmission rate (throughput) limit measured in both bytes per second and packets per second. The queue is serviced to ensure that no more than this maximum is provided. The broadcast queue has priority when transmitting at a rate below the configured maximum, and hence has a guaranteed minimum bandwidth allocation. The two transmission rate limits are intended to avoid flooding the interface with broadcasts. The actual transmission rate limit in any second is the first of the two rate limits that is reached.

To create a broadcast queue, complete the following task in interface configuration mode:

Task	Command
Create a broadcast queue for an interface.	**frame-relay broadcast-queue** *size byte-rate packet-rate*

Configuring Payload Compression

You can configure payload compression on point-to-point or multipoint interfaces or subinterfaces. Payload compression uses the stac method to predict what the next character in the frame will be. Because the prediction is done packet-by-packet, the dictionary is not conserved across packet boundaries.

Payload compression on each virtual circuit consumes approximately 40 kilobytes for dictionary memory.

To configure payload compression on a specified multipoint interface or subinterface, complete the following task in interface configuration mode:

Task	Command
Enable payload compression on a multipoint interface.	**frame-relay map** *protocol protocol-address dlci* **payload-compress packet-by-packet**

To configure payload compression on a specified point-to-point interface or subinterface, complete the following task in interface configuration mode:

Task	Command
Enable payload compression on a point-to-point interface.	**frame-relay payload-compress packet-by-packet**

Configuring Standard-Based FRF.9 Compression

Frame Relay compression can now occur on the VIP board, on the Compression Service Adapter (CSA), or on the main CPU of the router. FRF9 is standard-based and, therefore, provides multi-vendor compatibility. FRF.9 compression uses higher compression ratios, allowing more data to be compressed for faster transmission.

The CSA hardware has been in use on the Cisco 7200 series and Cisco 7500 series platforms, but it has had no support for Frame Relay compression. FRF.9 compression provides the ability to maintain multiple decompression/compression histories on a per-DLCI basis.

The CSA can be used in the Cisco 7200 series or in the second-generation Versatile Interface Processor (VIP2) in all Cisco 7500 series routers.

─ **NOTES** ───────────────────────────────────────

The specific VIP2 model required for the CSA is VIP2-40, which has 2 MB of SRAM and 32 MB of DRAM.

How the Router Selects the Compression Method

The router enables compression in the following order:

1. If the router contains a compression service adapter, compression is performed in the CSA hardware (hardware compression).

2. If the CSA is not available, compression is performed in the software installed on the VIP2 card (distributed compression).

3. If the VIP2 card is not available, compression is performed in the router's main processor (software compression).

Configuring FRF.9 Compression Using Map Statements

You can control where you want compression to occur by specifying a specific interface. To enable FRF.9 compression on a specific CSA, VIP CPU, or host CPU, perform the following tasks beginning in global configuration mode:

Task	Command
Step 1 Specify the interface.	interface *type number*
Step 2 Specify Frame Relay as the encapsulation type.	encapsulation frame-relay
Step 3 Enable FRF.9 compression.	frame-relay map payload-compress frf9 stac [csa *csa_number* I distributed I software]

Configuring FRF.9 Compression on the Subinterface

To configure FRF.9 compression on the subinterface, perform the following tasks beginning in global configuration mode:

Task	Command
Step 1 Specify the subinterface type and number.	interface *type number*
Step 2 Specify Frame Relay as the encapsulation type.	encapsulation frame-relay
Step 3 Enable FRF.9 compression.	frame-relay payload-compress frf9 stac [csa *csa_number* I distributed I software]

Configuring TCP/IP Header Compression

TCP/IP header compression, as described by RFC 1144, is designed to improve the efficiency of bandwidth utilization over low-speed serial links. A typical TCP/IP packet includes a 40-byte datagram header. Once a connection is established, the header information is redundant and need not be repeated in every packet that is sent. Reconstructing a smaller header that identifies the connection and indicates the fields that changed and the amount of change reduces the number of bytes transmitted. The average compressed header is 10 bytes long.

For this algorithm to function, packets must arrive in order. If packets arrive out of order, the reconstruction will appear to create regular TCP/IP packets, but the packets will not match the original. Because priority queuing changes the order in which packets are transmitted, enabling priority queueing on the interface is not recommended.

You can configure TCP/IP header compression in either of two ways:

- Configuring an Individual IP Map for TCP/IP Header Compression
- Configuring an Interface for TCP/IP Header Compression

The "Disabling TCP/IP Header Compression" section on the next page describes how to disable this feature.

NOTES

If you configure an interface with Cisco encapsulation and TCP/IP header compression, Frame Relay IP maps inherit the compression characteristics of the interface. However, if you configure the interface with IETF encapsulation, the interface cannot be configured for compression. Frame Relay maps will have to be configured individually to support TCP/IP header compression.

Configuring an Individual IP Map for TCP/IP Header Compression

TCP/IP header compression requires Cisco encapsulation. If you need to have IETF encapsulation on an interface as a whole, you can still configure a specific IP map to use Cisco encapsulation and TCP header compression.

In addition, even if you configure the interface to perform TCP/IP header compression, you can still configure a specific IP map not to compress TCP/IP headers.

You can specify whether TCP/IP header compression is active or passive. Active compression subjects every outgoing packet to TCP/IP header compression. Passive compression subjects an outgoing TCP/IP packet to header compression only if the packet had a compressed TCP/IP header when it was received.

To configure an IP map to use Cisco encapsulation and TCP/IP header compression, perform the following task in interface configuration mode:

Task	Command
Configure an IP map to use Cisco encapsulation and TCP/IP header compression.	**frame-relay map ip** *ip-address dlci* [**broadcast**] **cisco tcp header-compression** {**active** | **passive**}

The default encapsulation is **cisco**.

— **NOTES** ———

An interface that is configured to support TCP/IP header compression cannot also support priority queuing or custom queuing.

For an example of how to configure TCP header compression on an IP map, see the "FRF.9 Compression Configuration Examples" section later in this chapter.

Configuring an Interface for TCP/IP Header Compression

You can configure the interface with active or passive TCP/IP header compression. Active compression, the default, subjects all outgoing TCP/IP packets to header compression. Passive compression subjects an outgoing packet to header compression only if the packet had a compressed TCP/IP header when it was received on that interface.

To apply TCP/IP header compression to an interface, you must perform the following tasks in interface configuration mode:

Task	Command
Configure Cisco encapsulation on the interface.	encapsulation frame-relay
Enable TCP/IP header compression on the interface.	frame-relay ip tcp header-compression [passive]

— **NOTES** ———

If an interface configured with Cisco encapsulation is later configured with IETF encapsulation, all TCP/IP header compression characteristics are lost. To apply TCP/IP header compression over an interface configured with IETF encapsulation, you must configure individual IP maps, as described in the previous section "Configuring an Individual IP Map for TCP/IP Header Compression."

For an example of how to configure TCP header compression on an interface, see the "FRF.9 Compression Configuration Examples" section later in this chapter.

Disabling TCP/IP Header Compression

You can disable TCP/IP header compression by using either of two commands that have different effects, depending on whether Frame Relay IP maps have been explicitly configured for TCP/IP header compression or have inherited their compression characteristics from the interface.

Frame Relay IP maps that have explicitly configured TCP/IP header compression must also have TCP/IP header compression explicitly disabled.

To disable TCP/IP header compression, perform one of the following tasks in interface configuration mode:

Task	Command
Disable TCP/IP header compression on all Frame Relay IP maps that are not explicitly configured for TCP header compression.	no frame-relay ip tcp header-compression
or	
Disable TCP/IP header compression on a specified Frame Relay IP map.	frame-relay map ip *ip-address dlci* nocompress tcp header-compression

For examples of how to turn off TCP/IP header compression, see the section "Disabling Inherited TCP/IP Header Compression Example," and the section "Disabling Explicit TCP/IP Header Compression Example."

Configuring Real-Time Header Compression with Frame Relay Encapsulation

Real-time Transport Protocol (RTP) is a protocol used for carrying packetized audio and video traffic over an IP network. RTP is described in RFC 1889. RTP is not intended for data traffic, which uses TCP or UDP. RTP provides end-to-end network transport functions intended for applications with real-time requirements, such as audio, video, or simulation data over multicast or unicast network services.

Configuring Discard Eligibility

You can specify which Frame Relay packets have low priority or low time sensitivity and will be the first to be dropped when a Frame Relay switch is congested. The mechanism that allows a Frame Relay switch to identify such packets is the discard eligibility (DE) bit.

This feature requires that the Frame Relay network be able to interpret the DE bit. Some networks take no action when the DE bit is set. Other networks use the DE bit to determine which packets to discard. The most desirable interpretation is to use the DE bit to determine which packets should be dropped first and also which packets have lower time sensitivity.

You can define DE lists that identify the characteristics of packets to be eligible for discarding, and you can also specify DE groups to identify the DLCI that is affected. To define a DE list specifying the packets that can be dropped when the Frame Relay switch is congested, perform the following task in global configuration mode:

Task	Command
Define a DE list.	frame-relay de-list *list-number* {protocol *protocol* | interface *type number*} *characteristic*

You can specify DE lists based on the protocol or the interface, and on characteristics such as fragmentation of the packet, a specific TCP or User Datagram Protocol (UDP) port, an access list number, or a packet size. See the **frame-relay de-list** command in Chapter 6 for arguments and other information. To define a DE group specifying the DE list and DLCI affected, perform the following task in interface configuration mode:

Task	Command
Define a DE group.	**frame-relay de-group** *group-number dlci*

Configuring DLCI Priority Levels

DLCI priority levels allow you to separate different types of traffic and can provide a traffic management tool for congestion problems caused by following situations:

- Mixing batch and interactive traffic over the same DLCI.
- Traffic from sites with high-speed access being queued at destination sites with lower speed access.

Before you configure the DLCI priority levels, complete the following tasks:

- Define a global priority list.
- Enable Frame Relay encapsulation, as described earlier in this chapter.
- Define static or dynamic address mapping, as described earlier in this chapter.

— **NOTES** ──

Make sure that you define each of the DLCIs to which you intend to apply levels. You can associate priority-level DLCIs with subinterfaces.

──

- Configure the LMI, as described earlier in this chapter.

— **NOTES** ──

DLCI priority levels provide a way to define multiple parallel DLCIs for different types of traffic. DLCI priority levels do not assign priority queues within the router or access server; in fact, they are independent of the device's priority queues. However, if you enable queuing and use the same DLCIs for queuing, then high-priority DLCIs can be put into high-priority queues.

──

To configure DLCI priority levels, perform the following task in interface configuration mode:

Task	Command
Enable multiple parallel DLCIs for different types of Frame Relay traffic, associate specified DLCIs with the same group, and define their levels.	**frame-relay priority-dlci-group** *group-number high-dlci medium-dlci normal-dlci low-dlci*

NOTES

If you do not explicitly specify a DLCI for each of the priority levels, the last DLCI specified in the command line is used as the value of the remaining arguments. At a minimum, you must configure the high-priority and the medium-priority DLCIs.

MONITORING AND MAINTAINING THE FRAME RELAY CONNECTIONS

To monitor Frame Relay connections, perform any of the following tasks in EXEC mode:

Task	Command
Clear dynamically created Frame Relay maps, which are created by the use of Inverse ARP.	**clear frame-relay-inarp**
Display information about Frame Relay DLCIs and the LMI.	**show interfaces type** *number*
Display LMI statistics.	**show frame-relay lmi** [*type number*]
Display the current Frame Relay map entries.	**show frame-relay map**
Display PVC statistics.	**show frame-relay pvc** [*type number* [*dlci*]]
Display configured static routes.	**show frame-relay route**
Display Frame Relay traffic statistics.	**show frame-relay traffic**
Display information about the status of LAPF.	**show frame-relay lapf**
Display all the SVCs under a specified map list.	**show frame-relay svc maplist**

FRAME RELAY CONFIGURATION EXAMPLES

This section provides examples of Frame Relay configurations. It includes the following examples:

- IETF Encapsulation Examples
- Static Address Mapping Examples
- Subinterface Examples
- SVC Configuration Examples

- Frame Relay Traffic Shaping Examples
- Configuration Providing Backward Compatibility Example
- Booting from a Network Server over Frame Relay Examples
- Frame Relay Switching Examples
- FRF.9 Compression Configuration Examples
- TCP/IP Header Compression Examples
- Disabling TCP/IP Header Compression Examples

IETF Encapsulation Examples

The following example sets IETF encapsulation at the interface level; the keyword **ietf** sets the default encapsulation method for all maps to IETF:

```
encapsulation frame-relay IETF
frame-relay map ip 131.108.123.2 48 broadcast
frame-relay map ip 131.108.123.3 49 broadcast
```

In the following example, IETF encapsulation is configured on a per-DLCI basis. This configuration has the same result as the configuration in the previous example.

```
encapsulation frame-relay
frame-relay map ip 131.108.123.2 48 broadcast ietf
frame-relay map ip 131.108.123.3 49 broadcast ietf
```

Static Address Mapping Examples

The following sections provide examples of static address mapping for the IP, AppleTalk, DECnet, and IPX protocols.

Two Routers in Static Mode Example

The following example illustrates how to configure two routers for static mode:

Configuration for Router 1

```
interface serial 0
 ip address 131.108.64.2 255.255.255.0
 encapsulation frame-relay
 keepalive 10
 frame-relay map ip 131.108.64.1 43
```

Configuration for Router 2

```
interface serial 0
 ip address 131.108.64.1 255.255.255.0
 encapsulation frame-relay
 keepalive 10
 frame-relay map ip 131.108.64.2 43
```

AppleTalk Routing Example

The following example illustrates how to configure two routers to communicate with each other using AppleTalk over a Frame Relay network. Each router has a Frame Relay static address map for the other router. The use of the **appletalk cable-range** command indicates that this is extended AppleTalk (Phase II).

Configuration for Router 1

```
interface Serial0
 ip address 172.21.59.24 255.255.255.0
 encapsulation frame-relay
 appletalk cable-range 10-20 18.47
 appletalk zone eng
 frame-relay map appletalk 18.225 100 broadcast
```

Configuration for Router 2

```
interface Serial2/3
 ip address 172.21.177.18 255.255.255.0
 encapsulation frame-relay
 appletalk cable-range 10-20 18.225
 appletalk zone eng
 clockrate 2000000
 frame-relay map appletalk 18.47 100 broadcast
```

DECnet Routing Example

The following example sends all DECnet packets destined for address 56.4 out on DLCI 101. In addition, any DECnet broadcasts for interface serial 1 will be sent on that DLCI.

```
decnet routing 32.6
!
interface serial 1
 encapsulation frame-relay
 frame-relay map decnet 56.4 101 broadcast
```

IPX Routing Example

The following example illustrates how to send packets destined for IPX address 200.0000.0c00.7b21 out on DLCI 102:

```
ipx routing 000.0c00.7b3b
!
interface ethernet 0
 ipx network 2abc
!
interface serial 0
 ipx network 200
 encapsulation frame-relay
 frame-relay map ipx 200.0000.0c00.7b21 102 broadcast
```

Subinterface Examples

The following sections provide basic Frame Relay subinterface examples and variations appropriate for different routed protocols and for bridging.

Basic Subinterface Examples

In the following example, subinterface 1 models a point-to-point subnet and subinterface 2 models a broadcast subnet. For emphasis, the **multipoint** keyword is used for serial subinterface 2, even though a subinterface is multipoint by default.

```
interface serial 0
 encapsulation frame-relay
interface serial 0.1 point-to-point
 ip address 10.0.1.1 255.255.255.0
 frame-relay interface-dlci 42
 !
interface serial 0.2 multipoint
 ip address 10.0.2.1 255.255.255.0
 frame-relay map 10.0.2.2 18
```

Frame Relay Multipoint Subinterface with Dynamic Addressing Example

The following example configures two multipoint subinterfaces for dynamic address resolution. Each subinterface is provided with an individual protocol address and subnet mask, and the **frame-relay interface-dlci** command associates the subinterface with a specified DLCI. Addresses of remote destinations for each multipoint subinterface will be resolved dynamically.

```
interface Serial0
 no ip address
 encapsulation frame-relay
 frame-relay lmi-type ansi
 !
interface Serial0.103 multipoint
 ip address 172.21.177.18 255.255.255.0
 frame-relay interface-dlci 300
 !
interface Serial0.104 multipoint
 ip address 172.21.178.18 255.255.255.0
 frame-relay interface-dlci 400
```

IPX Routes over Frame Relay Subinterfaces Examples

The following example configures a serial interface for Frame Relay encapsulation and sets up multiple IPX virtual networks corresponding to Frame Relay subinterfaces:

```
ipx routing 0000.0c02.5f4f
 !
interface serial 0
 encapsulation frame-relay
 interface serial 0.1 multipoint
 ipx network 1
 frame-relay map ipx 1.000.0c07.d530 200 broadcast
 ipx network 2
 frame-relay map ipx 2.000.0c07.d530 300 broadcast
 !
```

For subinterface serial 0.1, the router at the other end might be configured as follows:

```
ipx routing
interface serial 2 multipoint
```

```
ipx network 1
frame-relay map ipx 1.000.0c02.5f4f 200 broadcast
```

Unnumbered IP over a Point-to-Point Subinterface Example

The following example sets up unnumbered IP over subinterfaces at both ends of a point-to-point connection. In this example, Router A functions as the DTE, and Router B functions as the DCE. Routers A and B are both attached to Token Ring networks.

Configuration for Router A

```
frame-relay switching
!
interface token-ring 0
 ip address 131.108.177.1 255.255.255.0
!
interface serial 0
 no ip address
 encapsulation frame-relay IETF
!
interface Serial0.2 point-to-point
 ip unnumbered TokenRing0
 ip pim sparse-mode
 frame-relay interface-dlci 20
```

Configuration for Router B

```
frame-relay switching
!
interface token-ring 0
 ip address 131.108.178.1 255.255.255.0
!
interface serial 0
 no ip address
 encapsulation frame-relay IETF
 bandwidth 384
 clockrate 4000000
 frame-relay intf-type dce
!
interface serial 0.2 point-to-point
 ip unnumbered TokenRing1
 ip pim sparse-mode
!
 bandwidth 384
 frame-relay interface-dlci 20
```

Transparent Bridging Using Subinterfaces Example

In the following example, Frame Relay DLCIs 42, 64, and 73 are to be used as separate point-to-point links with transparent bridging running over them. The bridging spanning tree algorithm views each PVC as a separate bridge port, and a frame arriving on the PVC can be relayed back out a separate PVC. Be sure that routing is not enabled when configuring transparent bridging using subinterfaces.

```
interface serial 0
 encapsulation frame-relay
interface serial 0.1 point-to-point
 bridge-group 1
 frame-relay interface-dlci 42
interface serial 0.2 point-to-point
 bridge-group 1
 frame-relay interface-dlci 64
interface serial 0.3 point-to-point
 bridge-group 1
 frame-relay interface-dlci 73
```

SVC Configuration Examples

The following examples provide SVC configuration examples for interfaces and subinterfaces.

Interface Example

The following example configures a physical interface, applies a map-group to the physical interface, and then defines the map-group.

```
interface serial 0
 ip address 172.10.8.6
 encapsulation frame-relay
 map-group bermuda
 frame-relay lmi-type q933a
 frame-relay svc
!
map-list bermuda source-addr E164 123456 dest-addr E164 654321
 ip 131.108.177.100 class hawaii
 appletalk 1000.2 class rainbow
!
map-class frame-relay rainbow
 frame-relay idle-timer 60
!
map-class frame-relay hawaii
 frame-relay cir in 64000
 frame-relay cir out 64000
!
```

Subinterface Example

The following example configures a point-to-point interface for SVC operation. This example assumes that the main serial 0 interface has been configured for signalling, and that SVC operation has been enabled on the main interface.

```
int s 0.1 point-point
! Define the map-group; details are specified under the map-list holiday command.
map-group holiday
!
! Associate the map-group with a specific source and destination.
map-list holiday local-addr X121 <X121-addr> dest-addr E164 <E164-addr>
! Specify destination protocol addresses for a map-class.
 ip 131.108.177.100 class hawaii IETF
```

```
 appletalk 1000.2 class rainbow IETF broadcast
!
! Define a map class and its QOS settings.
map-class hawaii
 frame-relay cir in 2000000
 frame-relay cir out 56000
 frame-relay be 9000
!
! Define another map class and its QOS settings.
map-class rainbow
 frame-relay cir in 64000
 frame-relay idle-timer 2000
```

Frame Relay Traffic Shaping Examples

The following sections provide examples of Frame Relay traffic shaping.

Traffic Shaping with Three Point-to-Point Subinterfaces Example

In this example, the virtual circuits on subinterfaces Serial0.1 and Serial0.2 inherit class parameters from the main interface, namely those defined in *slow_vcs*, but the virtual circuit defined on sub-interface Serial0.2 (DLCI 102) is specifically configured to use map class *fast_vcs*.

Map class *slow_vcs* uses a peak rate of 9,600 and average rate of 4,800 bps. Because BECN feedback is enabled by default, the output rate will be cut back as low as 4,800 bps in response to received BECNs. This map class is configured to use custom queuing using queue-list 1. In this example, queue-list 1 has 3 queues, with the first two being controlled by access lists 100 and 115.

Map class *fast_vcs* uses a peak rate of 64,000 and average rate of 16,000 bps. Because BECN feedback is enabled by default, the output rate will be cut back as low as 4,800 bps in response to received BECNs. This map class is configured to use priority-queuing using priority-group 2.

```
interface Serial0
 no ip address
 encapsulation frame-relay
 frame-relay lmi-type ansi
 frame-relay traffic-shaping
 frame-relay class slow_vcs
!
interface Serial0.1 point-to-point
 ip address 10.128.30.1 255.255.255.248
 ip ospf cost 200
 bandwidth 10
 frame-relay interface-dlci 101
!
interface Serial0.2 point-to-point
 ip address 10.128.30.9 255.255.255.248
 ip ospf cost 400
 bandwidth 10
 frame-relay interface-dlci 102
   class fast_vcs
!
interface Serial0.3 point-to-point
```

```
 ip address 10.128.30.17 255.255.255.248
 ip ospf cost 200
 bandwidth 10
 frame-relay interface-dlci 103
!
map-class frame-relay slow_vcs
 frame-relay traffic-rate 4800 9600
 frame-relay custom-queue-list 1
!
map-class frame-relay fast_vcs
 frame-relay traffic-rate 16000 64000
 frame-relay priority-group 2
!
access-list 100 permit tcp any any eq 2065
access-list 115 permit tcp any any eq 256
!
priority-list 2 protocol decnet high
priority-list 2 ip normal
priority-list 2 default medium
!
queue-list 1 protocol ip 1 list 100
queue-list 1 protocol ip 2 list 115
queue-list 1 default 3
queue-list 1 queue 1 byte-count 1600 limit 200
queue-list 1 queue 2 byte-count 600 limit 200
queue-list 1 queue 3 byte-count 500 limit 200
```

Traffic Shaping with Router ForeSight Example

The following example illustrates a router configuration with traffic shaping enabled. DLCIs 100 and 101 on subinterfaces Serial 13.2 and Serial 13.3 inherit class parameters from the main interface. The traffic shaping for these two VCs will be adaptive to the ForeSight notification.

For Serial 0, the output rate for DLCI 103 will not be affected by the Router ForeSight function.

```
interface Serial0
 no ip address
 encapsulation frame-relay
 frame-relay lmi-type ansi
 frame-relay traffic-shaping
!
interface Serial0.2 point-to-point
 ip address 10.128.30.17 255.255.255.248
 frame-relay interface-dlci 102
 class fast_vcs
!
interface Serial0.3 point-to-point
 ip address 10.128.30.5 255.255.255.248
 ip ospf cost 200
 frame-relay interface-dlci 103
 class slow_vcs
!
interface serial 3
 no ip address
```

```
 encapsulation frame-relay
 frame-relay traffic-shaping
 frame-relay class fast_vcs
!
interface Serial3.2 multipoint
 ip address 100.120.20.13 255.255.255.248
 frame-relay map ip 100.120.20.6 16 ietf broadcast
!
interface Serial3.3 point-to-point
 ip address 100.120.10.13 255.255.255.248
 frame-relay interface-dlci 101
!
map-class frame-relay slow_vcs
 frame-relay adaptive-shaping becn
 frame-relay traffic-rate 4800 9600
!
map-class frame-relay fast_vcs
 frame-relay adaptive-shaping foresight
 frame-relay traffic-rate 16000 64000
 frame-relay cir 56000
 frame-relay bc 64000
```

Enhanced Local Management Interface Example

Figure 7–4 illustrates a Cisco StrataCom switch and a Cisco router, both configured with the Enhanced Local Management Interface feature enabled. The switch sends QOS information to the router, which uses it for traffic rate enforcement.

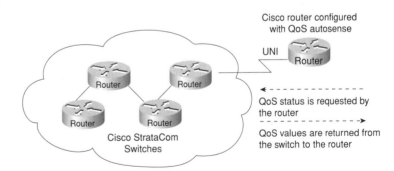

Figure 7–4

Enhanced Local Management Interface can be configured on both the Cisco StrataCom Switch and the Cisco Router.

This configuration example shows a Frame-Relay interface enabled with QOS autosense. The router receives messages from the Cisco StrataCom switch, which is also configured with QOS autosense enabled. When Enhanced Local Management Interface is configured in conjunction with traffic shaping, the router will receive congestion information through BECN or Router ForeSight congestion signaling and reduce its output rate to the value specified in the traffic shaping configuration.

```
interface serial0
  no ip address
```

```
    encapsulation frame-relay
    frame-relay lmi-type ansi
    frame-relay traffic-shaping
    frame-relay qos-autosense
!
interface serial0.1 point-to-point
  no ip address
  frame-relay interface-dlci 101
```

Configuration Providing Backward Compatibility Example

The following configuration provides backward compatibility and interoperability with earlier versions that are not compliant with RFC 1490. The **ietf** keyword is used to generate RFC 1490 traffic. This configuration is possible because of the flexibility provided by separately defining each map entry.

```
    encapsulation frame-relay
    frame-relay map ip 131.108.123.2 48 broadcast ietf
    ! interoperability is provided by IETF encapsulation
    frame-relay map ip 131.108.123.3 49 broadcast ietf
    frame-relay map ip 131.108.123.7 58 broadcast
    ! this line allows the router to connect with a
    ! device running an older version of software
    frame-relay map decnet 21.7 49 broadcast
```

Configure IETF based on map entries and protocol for more flexibility. Use this method of configuration for backward compatibility and interoperability.

Booting from a Network Server over Frame Relay Example

When booting from a Trivial File Transfer Protocol (TFTP) server over Frame Relay, you cannot boot from a network server via a broadcast. You must boot from a specific TFTP host. Also, a **frame-relay map** command must exist for the host from which you will boot.

For example, if file *gs3-bfx* is to be booted from a host with IP address 131.108.126.2, the following commands need to be in the configuration:

```
    boot system gs3-bfx 131.108.126.2
    !
    interface Serial 0
     encapsulation frame-relay
     frame-relay map IP 131.108.126.2 100 broadcast
```

The **frame-relay map** command is used to map an IP address into a DLCI address. To boot over Frame Relay, you must explicitly give the address of the network server to boot from, and a **frame-relay map** entry must exist for that site. For example, if file *gs3-bfx.83-2.0* is to be booted from a host with IP address 131.108.126.111, the following commands must be in the configuration:

```
    boot system gs3-bfx.83-2.0 131.108.13.111
    !
    interface Serial 1
     ip address 131.108.126.200 255.255.255.0
     encapsulation frame-relay
     frame-relay map ip 131.108.126.111 100 broadcast
```

In this case, 100 is the DLCI that can get to host 131.108.126.111.

The remote router must have the following **frame-relay map** entry:

```
frame-relay map ip 131.108.126.200 101 broadcast
```

This entry allows the remote router to return a boot image (from the network server) to the router booting over Frame Relay. Here, 101 is a DLCI of the router being booted.

Frame Relay Switching Examples

The following sections provide several examples of configuring one or more routers as Frame Relay switches:

- PVC Switching Configuration Example. In this example, one router has two interfaces configured as DCEs; the router switches frames from the incoming interface to the outgoing interface on the basis of the DLCI alone.

- Pure Frame Relay DCE Example. In this example, a Frame Relay network is set up with two routers functioning as switches; standard NNI signaling is used between them.

- Hybrid DTE/DCE PVC Switching Example. In this example, one router is configured with both DCE and DTE interfaces (a hybrid DTE/DCE Frame Relay switch). It can switch frames between two DCE ports and between a DCE port and a DTE port.

- Switching over an IP Tunnel Example. In this example, two routers are configured to switch Frame Relay PVCs over a point-to-point IP tunnel.

PVC Switching Configuration Example

You can configure your router as a dedicated, DCE-only Frame Relay switch. Switching is based on DLCIs. The incoming DLCI is examined, and the outgoing interface and DLCI are determined. Switching takes place when the incoming DLCI in the packet is replaced by the outgoing DLCI, and the packet is sent out the outgoing interface.

In the following example, the router switches two PVCs between interface serial 1 and 2. Frames with DLCI 100 received on serial 1 will be transmitted with DLCI 200 on serial 2 (see Figure 7–5).

Figure 7–5

Possible PVC switching configuration for the PVC switching configuration example.

Configuration for Router A

```
frame-relay switching
!
interface Ethernet0
ip address 131.108.160.58 255.255.255.0
!
```

```
interface Serial1
 no ip address
 encapsulation frame-relay
 keepalive 15
 frame-relay lmi-type ansi
 frame-relay intf-type dce
 frame-relay route 100 interface Serial2 200
 frame-relay route 101 interface Serial2 201
 clockrate 2000000
!
interface Serial2
 encapsulation frame-relay
 keepalive 15
 frame-relay intf-type dce
 frame-relay route 200 interface Serial1 100
 frame-relay route 201 interface Serial1 101
 clockrate 64000
```

Pure Frame Relay DCE Example

Using the PVC switching feature, it is possible to build an entire Frame Relay network using Cisco routers. In the following example, Router A and Router C act as Frame Relay switches implementing a two-node network. The standard Network-to-Network Interface (NNI) signaling protocol is used between Router A and Router C (see Figure 7–6).

Figure 7–6

An example of Frame Relay DCE configuration.

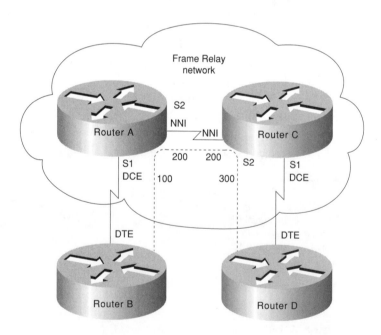

Configuration for Router A

```
frame-relay switching
!
interface ethernet 0
 no ip address
 shutdown :Interfaces not in use may be shut down; shut down is not required.
!
interface ethernet 1
 no ip address
 shutdown
!
interface ethernet 2
 no ip address
 shutdown
!
interface ethernet 3
 no ip address
 shutdown
!
interface serial 0
 ip address 131.108.178.48 255.255.255.0
 shutdown
!
interface serial 1
 no ip address
 encapsulation frame-relay
 frame-relay intf-type dce
 frame-relay lmi-type ansi
 frame-relay route 100 interface serial 2 200
!
interface serial 2
 no ip address
 encapsulation frame-relay
 frame-relay intf-type nni
 frame-relay lmi-type q933a
 frame-relay route 200 interface serial 1 100
 clockrate 2048000
!
interface serial 3
 no ip address
 shutdown
```

Configuration for Router C

```
frame-relay switching
!
interface ethernet 0
 no ip address
 shutdown :Interfaces not in use may be shut down; shut down is not required.
!
interface ethernet1
 no ip address
 shutdown
!
```

```
interface ethernet 2
 no ip address
 shutdown
!
interface ethernet 3
 no ip address
 shutdown
!
interface serial 0
 ip address 131.108.187.84 255.255.255.0
 shutdown
!
interface serial 1
 no ip address
 encapsulation frame-relay
 frame-relay intf-type dce
 frame-relay route 300 interface serial 2 200
!
interface serial 2
 no ip address
 encapsulation frame-relay
 frame-relay intf-type nni
 frame-relay lmi-type q933a
 frame-relay route 200 interface serial 1 300
!
interface serial 3
 no ip address
 shutdown
```

Hybrid DTE/DCE PVC Switching Example

Routers can also be configured as hybrid DTE/DCE Frame Relay switches (see Figure 7–7).

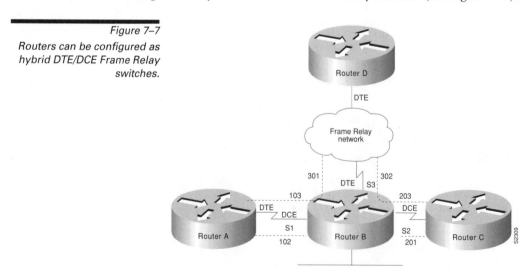

Figure 7–7

Routers can be configured as hybrid DTE/DCE Frame Relay switches.

In the following example, Router B acts as a hybrid DTE/DCE Frame Relay switch. It can switch frames between the two DCE ports and between a DCE port and a DTE port. Traffic from the Frame Relay network can also be terminated locally. In the example, three PVCs are defined, as follows:

- Serial 1, DLCI 102 to serial 2, DLCI 201—DCE switching
- Serial 1, DLCI 103 to serial 3, DLCI 301—DCE/DTE switching
- Serial 2, DLCI 203 to serial 3, DLCI 302—DCE/DTE switching

DLCI 400 is also defined for locally terminated traffic.

Configuration for Router B

```
frame-relay switching
!
interface ethernet 0
 ip address 131.108.123.231 255.255.255.0
!
interface ethernet 1
 ip address 131.108.5.231 255.255.255.0
!
interface serial 0
 no ip address
 shutdown :Interfaces not in use may be shut down; shut down is not required.
!
interface serial 1
 no ip address
 encapsulation frame-relay
 frame-relay intf-type dce
 frame-relay route 102 interface serial 2 201
 frame-relay route 103 interface serial 3 301
!
interface serial 2
 no ip address
 encapsulation frame-relay
 frame-relay intf-type dce
 frame-relay route 201 interface serial 1 102
 frame-relay route 203 interface serial 3 302
!
interface serial 3
 ip address 131.108.111.231
 encapsulation frame-relay
 frame-relay lmi-type ansi
 frame-relay route 301 interface serial 1 103
 frame-relay route 302 interface serial 1 203
 frame-relay map ip 131.108.111.4 400 broadcast
```

Switching over an IP Tunnel Example

You can achieve switching over an IP tunnel by creating a point-to-point tunnel across the internetwork over which PVC switching can take place (see Figure 7–8).

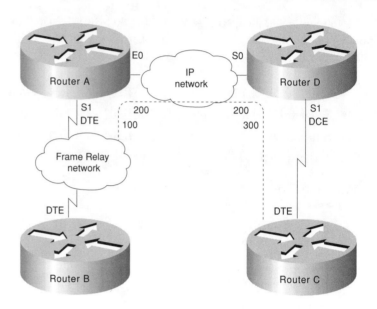

Figure 7–8
A Frame Relay switch can be
created over an IP tunnel.

The following configurations illustrate how to create the IP network depicted in Figure 7–8.

Configuration for Router A

```
frame-relay switching
!
interface Ethernet0
 ip address 108.131.123.231 255.255.255.0
!
interface Ethernet1
 ip address 131.108.5.231 255.255.255.0
!
interface Serial0
 no ip address
 shutdown : Interfaces not in use may be shut down; shutdown is not required.
!
interface Serial1
 ip address 131.108.222.231 255.255.255.0
 encapsulation frame-relay
 frame-relay map ip 131.108.222.4 400 broadcast
 frame-relay route 100 interface Tunnel1 200
!
interface Tunnel1
 tunnel source Ethernet0
 tunnel destination 150.150.150.123
```

Configuration for Router D

```
frame-relay switching
!
interface Ethernet0
```

```
 ip address 131.108.231.123 255.255.255.0
!
interface Ethernet1
 ip address 131.108.6.123 255.255.255.0
!
interface Serial0
 ip address 150.150.150.123 255.255.255.0
 encapsulation ppp
!
interface Tunnel1
 tunnel source Serial0
 tunnel destination 108.131.123.231
!
interface Serial1
 ip address 131.108.7.123 255.255.255.0
 encapsulation frame-relay
 frame-relay intf-type dce
 frame-relay route 300 interface Tunnel1 200
```

FRF.9 Compression Configuration Examples

These examples show how to configure FRF.9 compression. The first example shows FRF.9 compression configuration using the **frame-relay map** command.

Cisco recommends that you shut down the interface or subinterface prior to adding or changing compression techniques. Although this is not required, shutting down the interface ensures the interface is reset for the new data structures.

```
interface Serial2/0/1
 ip address 172.16.1.4 255.255.255.0
 no ip route-cache
 encapsulation frame-relay IETF
 no keepalive
 frame-relay map ip 172.16.1.1 105 IETF payload-compression FRF9 stac
!
```

This second example shows FRF.9 compression configuration for subinterfaces.

```
!
interface Serial2/0/0
 no ip address
 no ip route-cache
 encapsulation frame-relay
 ip route-cache distributed
 no keepalive
!
interface Serial2/0/0.500 point-to-point
 ip address 172.16.1.4 255.255.255.0
 no cdp enable
 frame-relay interface-dlci 500 IETF
 frame-relay payload-compression FRF9 stac
!
```

TCP/IP Header Compression Examples

The following examples show various combinations of TCP/IP header compression and encapsulation characteristics on the interface and the effect on the inheritance of those characteristics on a Frame Relay IP map.

Cisco recommends that you shut down the interface or subinterface prior to adding or changing compression techniques. Although this is not required, shutting down the interface ensures the interface is reset for the new data structures.

IP Map with Inherited TCP/IP Header Compression Example

The following example shows an interface configured for TCP/IP header compression and an IP map that inherits the compression characteristics. Note that the Frame Relay IP map is not explicitly configured for header compression.

```
interface serial 1
 encapsulation frame-relay
 ip address 131.108.177.178 255.255.255.0
 frame-relay map ip 131.108.177.177 177 broadcast
 frame-relay ip tcp header-compression passive
```

Use of the **show frame-relay map** command will display the resulting compression and encapsulation characteristics; the IP map has inherited passive TCP/IP header compression:

```
Router> show frame-relay map

Serial 1    (administratively down): ip 131.108.177.177
            dlci 177 (0xB1,0x2C10), static,
            broadcast,
            CISCO
            TCP/IP Header Compression (inherited), passive (inherited)
```

This example also applies to dynamic mappings achieved with the use of inverse-arp on point-to-point subinterfaces where no Frame Relay maps are configured.

Using an IP Map to Override TCP/IP Header Compression Example

The following example shows the use of a Frame Relay IP map to override the compression set on the interface:

```
interface serial 1
 encapsulation frame-relay
 ip address 131.108.177.178 255.255.255.0
 frame-relay map ip 131.108.177.177 177 broadcast nocompress
 frame-relay ip tcp header-compression passive
```

Use of the **show frame-relay map** command will display the resulting compression and encapsulation characteristics; the IP map has not inherited TCP header compression:

```
Serial 1    (administratively down): ip 131.108.177.177
            dlci 177 (0xB1,0x2C10), static,
            broadcast,
            CISCO
```

Cisco recommends that you shut down the interface or subinterface prior to adding or changing compression techniques. Although this is not required, shutting down the interface ensures the interface is reset for the new data structures.

Disabling TCP/IP Header Compression Examples

The following examples show the use of two different commands to disable TCP/IP header compression.

Cisco recommends that you shut down the interface or subinterface prior to adding or changing compression techniques. Although this is not required, shutting down the interface ensures the interface is reset for the new data structures.

Disabling Inherited TCP/IP Header Compression Example

In this first example, the initial configuration is the following:

```
interface serial 1
 encapsulation frame-relay
 ip address 131.108.177.179 255.255.255.0
 frame-relay ip tcp header-compression passive
 frame-relay map ip 131.108.177.177 177 broadcast
 frame-relay map ip 131.108.177.178 178 broadcast tcp header-compression
```

You enter the following commands:

```
serial interface 1
 no frame-relay ip tcp header-compression
```

Use of the **show frame-relay map** command will display the resulting compression and encapsulation characteristics:

```
Router> show frame-relay map

Serial 1    (administratively down): ip 131.108.177.177 177
            dlci 177(0xB1, 0x2C10), static,
            broadcast
            CISCO
Serial 1    (administratively down): ip 131.108.177.178 178
            dlci 178(0xB2,0x2C20), static
            broadcast
            CISCO
            TCP/IP Header Compression (enabled)
```

As a result, header compression is disabled for the first map (with DLCI 177), which inherited its header compression characteristics from the interface. However, header compression is not disabled for the second map (DLCI 178), which is explicitly configured for header compression.

Disabling Explicit TCP/IP Header Compression Example

In this example, the initial configuration is the same as the previous example, but you enter the following commands:

```
serial interface 1
 no frame-relay ip tcp header-compression
 frame-relay map ip 131.108.177.178 178 nocompress
```

Use of the **show frame-relay map** command will display the resulting compression and encapsulation characteristics:

```
Router> show frame-relay map

Serial 1    (administratively down): ip 131.108.177.177 177
            dlci 177(0xB1,0x2C10), static,
            broadcast
            CISCO
Serial 1    (administratively down): ip 131.108.177.178 178
            dlci 178(0xB2,0x2C20), static
            broadcast
            CISCO
```

The result of the commands is to disable header compression for the first map (with DLCI 177), which inherited its header compression characteristics from the interface, and also explicitly to disable header compression for the second map (with DLCI 178), which was explicitly configured for header compression.

CHAPTER 8

Frame Relay Commands

Use the commands described in this chapter to configure access to Frame Relay networks.

For Frame Relay configuration information and examples, refer to Chapter 7, "Configuring Frame Relay."

NOTES ──

You can use the master indexes or search online to find documentation of related commands.

CLASS (MAP-LIST CONFIGURATION)

To associate a map class with a protocol-and-address combination, use the **class** map-list configuration command.

> *protocol protocol-address* **class** *map-class* [**broadcast**] [**trigger**] [**ietf**]

Syntax	Description
protocol	Supported protocol, bridging, or logical link control keywords: **appletalk**, **bridging**, **clns**, **decnet**, **dlsw**, **ip**, **ipx**, **llc2**, **rsrb**, **vines**, and **xns**.
protocol-address	Protocol address. The **bridge** and **clns** keywords do not use protocol addresses.
class *map-class*	Name of the map class from which to derive quality of service (QOS) information.
broadcast	(Optional) Allows broadcasts on this SVC.

Syntax	Description
trigger	(Optional) Enables a broadcast packet to trigger an SVC. If an SVC already exists that uses this map class, the SVC will carry the broadcast. This keyword can be configured only if **broadcast** is also configured.
ietf	(Optional) Specifies RFC 1490 encapsulation. The default is Cisco encapsulation.

Default

No protocol, protocol address, and map class are defined. If the **ietf** keyword is not specified, the default is Cisco encapsulation. If the **broadcast** keyword is not specified, no broadcasts are sent.

Command Mode

Map-list configuration

Usage Guidelines

This command first appeared in Cisco IOS Release 11.2.

This command is used for Frame Relay switched virtual circuits (SVCs); the parameters within the map class are used to negotiate for network resources.

The class is associated with a static map that is configured under a map list.

Examples

In the following example, if IP triggers the call, the SVC is set up with the QOS parameters defined within the class *hawaii*. However, if AppleTalk triggers the call, the SVC is set up with the QOS parameters defined in the class *rainbow*. An SVC triggered by either protocol results in two SVC maps, one for IP and one for AppleTalk. Two maps are set up because these protocol-and-address combinations are heading for the same destination, as defined by the **dest-addr** keyword and the values following it in the **map-list** command.

```
map-list bermuda source-addr E164 14085551212 dest-addr E164 15085551212
ip 131.108.177.100 class hawaii
appletalk 1000.2 class rainbow
```

In the following example, the **trigger** keyword allows AppleTalk broadcast packets to trigger an SVC:

```
ip 172.21.177.1 class jamaica broadcast ietf
appletalk 1000.2 class jamaica broadcast trigger ietf
```

Related Commands

map-class frame-relay
map-list

CLASS (VIRTUAL CIRCUIT CONFIGURATION)

To associate a map class with a specified data-link connection identifier (DLCI), use the **class** virtual circuit configuration command. To remove the association between the DLCI and the map class, use the **no** form of this command.

    class *name*
    no class *name*

Syntax	*Description*
name	Name of map class to associate with this DLCI.

Default

No map class is defined.

Command Mode

Virtual circuit configuration

Usage Guidelines

This command first appeared in Cisco IOS Release 11.2.

This command applies to DLCIs. The class parameter values are specified with the **map-class frame-relay** command.

Examples

The following example shows how to define map class *slow_vcs* and apply it to DLCI 100:

```
interface serial 0.1 point-to-point
frame-relay interface-dlci 100
  class slow_vcs

map-class frame-relay slow_vcs
frame-relay cir out 9600
```

The following example shows how to apply a map class to a DLCI for which a **frame-relay map** statement exists. The **frame-relay interface-dlci** command must also be used.

```
interface serial 0.2 point-to-multipoint
frame-relay map ip 131.26.13.2 100
frame-relay interface-dlci 100
  class slow_vcs

interface serial 0
frame-relay interface-dlci 100
 class fast_vc

map-class frame-relay fast_vc
 frame-relay traffic-rate 56000 128000
 frame-relay idle-timer 30
```

Command Reference

Related Commands

frame-relay interface-dlci
frame-relay map
map-class frame-relay

CLEAR FRAME-RELAY-INARP

To clear dynamically created Frame Relay maps, which are created by the use of Inverse Address
Resolution Protocol (ARP), use the **clear frame-relay-inarp** EXEC command.

    clear frame-relay-inarp

Syntax Description

This command has no arguments or keywords.

Command Mode

EXEC

Usage Guidelines

This command first appeared in Cisco IOS Release 10.0.

Example

The following example clears dynamically created Frame Relay maps:
```
clear frame-relay-inarp
```

Related Commands

frame-relay inverse-arp
show frame-relay map

ENCAPSULATION FRAME-RELAY

To enable Frame Relay encapsulation, use the **encapsulation frame-relay** interface configuration
command. To disable Frame Relay encapsulation, use the **no** form of this command.

    encapsulation frame-relay [cisco | ietf]
    no encapsulation frame-relay [ietf]

Syntax	*Description*
cisco	(Optional) Uses Cisco's own encapsulation, which is a 4-byte header, with 2 bytes to identify the data-link connection identifier (DLCI) and 2 bytes to identify the packet type. This is the default.

Syntax	Description
ietf	(Optional) Sets the encapsulation method to comply with the Internet Engineering Task Force (IETF) standard (RFC 1490). Use this keyword when connecting to another vendor's equipment across a Frame Relay network.

Default

Enabled

Command Mode

Interface configuration

Usage Guidelines

This command first appeared in Cisco IOS Release 10.0.

Use this command with no keywords to restore the default Cisco encapsulation, which is a 4-byte header with 2 bytes for the DLCI and 2 bytes to identify the packet type.

Cisco recommends that you shut down the interface prior to changing encapsulation types. Although this is not required, shutting down the interface ensures the interface is reset for the new encapsulation.

Examples

The following example configures Cisco Frame Relay encapsulation on interface serial 1:

```
interface serial 1
encapsulation frame-relay
```

Use the **ietf** keyword if your router or access server is connected to another vendor's equipment across a Frame Relay network to conform with RFC 1490:

```
interface serial 1
encapsulation frame-relay ietf
```

FRAME-RELAY ADAPTIVE-SHAPING

Use the **frame-relay adaptive-shaping** map-class subcommand to select the type of backward notification you want to use. Use the **no** form of the command to disable backward notification.

> **frame-relay adaptive-shaping {becn | foresight}**
> **no frame-relay adaptive-shaping**

Syntax	Description
becn	Enables rate adjustment in response to BECN.
foresight	Enables rate adjustment in response to ForeSight messages.

Default

Disabled

Command Mode

Map-class subcommand

Usage Guidelines

This command first appeared in Cisco IOS Release 11.3.

This command replaces the **frame-relay becn-response-enable** command, which will be removed in a future Cisco IOS release. If you use the **frame-relay becn-response-enable** command in scripts, you should replace it with the **frame-relay adaptive-shaping** command.

The **frame-relay adaptive-shaping** command configures a router to respond to either BECN or Fore-Sight backward congestion notification messages.

Include this command in a map-class definition and apply the map class to either the main interface or to a subinterface.

Example

The following example shows the map-class definition for a router configured with traffic shaping and Router ForeSight enabled:

```
interface Serial0
  no ip address
  encapsulation frame-relay
  frame-relay traffic-shaping
  frame-relay class control-A
  map-class frame-relay control-A
    frame-relay adaptive-shaping foresight
    frame-relay cir 56000
    frame-relay bc 64000
```

Related Commands

frame-relay traffic-shaping
map-class frame-relay

FRAME-RELAY BC

To specify the incoming or outgoing committed burst size (Bc) for a Frame Relay virtual circuit, use the **frame-relay bc** map-class configuration command. To reset the committed burst size to the default, use the **no** form of this command.

> **frame-relay bc {in | out}** *bits*
> **no frame-relay bc {in | out}** *bits*

Syntax	Description
in | out	Incoming or outgoing; if neither is specified, both in and out values are set.
bits	Committed burst size, in bits.

Default

7000 bits

Command Mode

Map-class configuration

Usage Guidelines

This command first appeared in Cisco IOS Release 11.2.

The Frame Relay committed burst size is specified within a map class to request a certain burst rate for the circuit. Although it is specified in bits, an implicit time factor is the sampling interval Tc on the switch, which is defined as the burst size Bc divided by the committed information rate (CIR).

Example

In the following example, the serial interface already has a basic configuration, and a map group called *bermuda* has already been defined. The example shows a map-list configuration that defines the source and destination addresses for bermuda, provides IP and IPX addresses, and ties the map list definition to the map class called *jamaica*. Then traffic shaping parameters are defined for the map class.

```
map-list bermuda local-addr X121 31383040703500 dest-addr X121 31383040709000
   ip 172.21.177.26 class jamaica ietf
   ipx 123.0000.0c07.d530 class jamaica ietf

map-class frame-relay jamaica
   frame-relay cir in 2000000
   frame-relay mincir in 1000000
   frame-relay cir out 15000
   frame-relay mincir out 10000
   frame-relay bc in 15000
   frame-relay bc out 9600
   frame-relay be in 10000
   frame-relay be out 10000
   frame-relay idle-timer 30
```

Related Commands

frame-relay be
frame-relay cir

FRAME-RELAY BE

To set the incoming or outgoing excess burst size (Be) for a Frame Relay virtual circuit, use the **frame-relay be** map-class configuration command. To reset the excess burst size to the default, use the **no** form of this command.

    frame-relay be {in | out} *bits*
    no frame-relay be {in | out} *bits*

Command Reference

Syntax	Description
in | out	Incoming or outgoing.
bits	Excess burst size, in bits.

Default

7000 bits

Command Mode

Map-class configuration

Usage Guidelines

This command first appeared in Cisco IOS Release 11.2.

The Frame Relay excess burst size is specified within a map class to request a certain burst rate for the circuit. Although it is specified in bytes, an implicit time factor is the sampling interval Tc on the switch, which is defined as the burst size Bc divided by the committed information rate (CIR).

Example

In the following example, the serial interface already has a basic configuration, and a map group called *bermuda* has already been defined. The example shows a map-list configuration that defines the source and destination addresses for bermuda, provides IP and IPX addresses, and ties the map list definition to the map class called *jamaica*. Then traffic-shaping parameters are defined for the map class.

```
map-list bermuda local-addr X121 31383040703500 dest-addr X121 31383040709000
 ip 172.21.177.26 class jamaica ietf
 ipx 123.0000.0c07.d530 class jamaica ietf

map-class frame-relay jamaica
 frame-relay cir in 2000000
 frame-relay mincir in 1000000
 frame-relay cir out 15000
 frame-relay mincir out 10000
 frame-relay bc in 15000
 frame-relay bc out 9600
 frame-relay be in 10000
 frame-relay be out 10000
 frame-relay idle-timer 30
```

Related Commands

frame-relay bc
frame-relay cir

FRAME-RELAY BECN-RESPONSE-ENABLE

This command has been replaced by the **frame-relay adaptive-shaping** command. If you use the **frame-relay becn-response-enable** command in scripts, you should replace it with the **frame-relay adaptive-shaping** command. This command will be removed from the product in a future release.

FRAME-RELAY BROADCAST-QUEUE

To create a special queue for a specified interface to hold broadcast traffic that has been replicated for transmission on multiple DLCIs, use the **frame-relay broadcast-queue** interface configuration command.

      frame-relay broadcast-queue *size byte-rate packet-rate*

Syntax	Description
size	Number of packets to hold in the broadcast queue.
byte-rate	Maximum number of bytes to be transmitted per second.
packet-rate	Maximum number of packets to be transmitted per second.

Defaults

The default values are as follows:

size—64 packets
byte-rate—256,000 bytes per second
packet-rate—36 packets per second

Command Mode

Interface configuration

Usage Guidelines

This command first appeared in Cisco IOS Release 10.3.

For purposes of the Frame Relay broadcast queue, *broadcast traffic* is defined as packets that have been replicated for transmission on multiple DLCIs. However, the broadcast traffic does not include the original routing packet or service access point (SAP) packet, which passes through the normal queue. Due to timing sensitivity, bridged broadcasts and spanning-tree packets are also sent through the normal queue.

The Frame Relay broadcast queue is managed independently of the normal interface queue. It has its own buffers and a configurable service rate.

A broadcast queue is given a maximum transmission rate (throughput) limit measured in bytes per second and packets per second. The queue is serviced to ensure that only this maximum is provided. The broadcast queue has priority when transmitting at a rate below the configured maximum, and hence has a guaranteed minimum bandwidth allocation. The two transmission rate limits are intended to avoid flooding the interface with broadcasts. The actual limit in any second is the first rate limit that is reached.

Given the transmission rate restriction, additional buffering is required to store broadcast packets. The broadcast queue is configurable to store large numbers of broadcast packets.

The queue size should be set to avoid loss of broadcast routing update packets. The exact size will depend on the protocol being used and the number of packets required for each update. To be safe, set the queue size so that one complete routing update from each protocol and for each DLCI can be stored. As a general rule, start with 20 packets per DLCI.

Generally, the byte rate should be less than both of the following:

- $N/4$ times the minimum remote access rate (measured in *bytes* per second), where N is the number of DLCIs to which the broadcast must be replicated
- 1/4 the local access rate (measured in *bytes* per second)

The packet rate is not critical if you set the byte rate conservatively. As a general rule, set the packet rate assuming 250-byte packets.

Example

The following example specifies a broadcast queue to hold 80 packets, to have a maximum byte transmission rate of 240,000 bytes per second, and to have a maximum packet transmission rate of 160 packets per second:

```
frame-relay broadcast-queue 80 240000 160
```

FRAME-RELAY CIR

To specify the incoming or outgoing committed information rate (CIR) for a Frame Relay virtual circuit, use the **frame-relay cir** map-class configuration command. To reset the CIR to the default, use the **no** form of this command.

> **frame-relay cir {in | out}** *bps*
> **no frame-relay cir {in | out}** *bps*

Syntax	Description
in | out	Incoming or outgoing.
bps	Committed information rate (CIR), in bits per second.

Default

56,000 bits per second

Command Mode

Map-class configuration

Usage Guidelines

This command first appeared in Cisco IOS Release 11.2.

Use this command to specify a CIR for an SVC. The specified CIR value is sent through the SETUP message to the switch, which then attempts to provision network resources to support this value.

Example

The following example sets a higher committed information rate for incoming traffic than for outgoing traffic (which is going out on a slow WAN line):

```
frame-relay cir in 2000000
frame-relay cir out 9600
```

Related Commands

frame-relay bc
frame-relay be

FRAME-RELAY CLASS

To associate a map class with an interface or subinterface, use the **frame-relay class** interface configuration command. To remove the association between in the interface or subinterface and the named map class, use the **no** form of this command.

frame-relay class *name*
no frame-relay class *name*

Syntax	Description
name	Name of the map class to associate with this interface or subinterface.

Default

No map class is defined.

Command Mode

Interface configuration

Usage Guidelines

This command first appeared in Cisco IOS Release 11.2.

This command can apply to interfaces or subinterfaces.

All relevant parameters defined in the *name* map class are inherited by each virtual circuit created on the interface or subinterface. For each virtual circuit, the precedence rules are as follows:

1. Use the map class associated with the virtual circuit if it exists.

2. If not, use the map class associated with the subinterface if the map class exists.

3. If not, use map class associated with interface if the map class exists.

4. If not, use the interface default parameters.

Example

In the following example, the map class *slow_vcs* is associated with the serial 0.1 subinterface and the map class *slow_vcs* is defined to have an outbound CIR value of 9600:

```
interface serial 0.1
frame-relay class slow_vcs

map-class frame-relay slow_vcs
frame-relay cir out 9600
```

If a virtual circuit exists on the serial 0.1 interface and is associated with some other map class, the parameter values of the second map class override those defined in the *slow_vc* map class for that virtual circuit.

Related Commands

map-class frame-relay

FRAME-RELAY CUSTOM-QUEUE-LIST

To specify a custom queue to be used for the virtual circuit queuing associated with a specified map class, use the **frame-relay custom-queue-list** map-class configuration command. To remove the specified queuing from the virtual circuit and cause it to revert to the default first-come-first-served queuing, use the **no** form of this command.

> **frame-relay custom-queue-list** *list-number*
> **no frame-relay custom-queue-list** *list-number*

Syntax	Description
list-number	List number.

Default

If this command is not entered, the default queuing is first come, first served.

Command Mode

Map-class configuration

Usage Guidelines

This command first appeared in Cisco IOS Release 11.2.

Definition of the custom queue takes place in the existing manner (through **queue-list** commands).

Only one form of queuing can be associated with a particular map class; subsequent definitions overwrite previous ones.

Example

The following example configures a custom queue list for the *fast_vcs* map class:

```
map-class frame-relay fast_vcs
  frame-relay custom-queue-list 1

queue-list 1 queue 4 byte-count 100
```

Related Commands

map-class frame-relay

FRAME-RELAY DE-GROUP

To specify the discard eligibility (DE) group number to be used for a specified DLCI, use the **frame-relay de-group** interface configuration command. To disable a previously defined group number assigned to a specified DLCI, use the **no** form of the command with the relevant keyword and arguments.

frame-relay de-group *group-number dlci*
no frame-relay de-group [*group-number*] [*dlci*]

Syntax	Description
group-number	DE group number to apply to the specified DLCI number, in the range from 1 through 10.
dlci	DLCI number.

Default

No DE group is defined.

Command Mode

Interface configuration

Usage Guidelines

This command first appeared in Cisco IOS Release 10.0.

To disable all previously defined group numbers, use the **no** form of this command with no arguments.

This command requires that Frame Relay software be enabled.

The DE bit is not set or recognized by the Frame Relay switching code, but must be recognized and interpreted by the Frame Relay network.

Example

The following example specifies that group number 3 will be used for DLCI 170:

```
frame-relay de-group 3 170
```

Related Commands

frame-relay de-list

FRAME-RELAY DE-LIST

To define a discard eligibility (DE) list specifying the packets that have the DE bit set and thus are eligible for discarding when congestion is experienced on the Frame Relay switch, use the frame-relay de-list global configuration command. To delete a portion of a previously defined DE list, use the no form of this command.

frame-relay de-list *list-number* {protocol *protocol* | interface *type number*} *characteristic*
no frame-relay de-list *list-number* {protocol *protocol* | interface *type number*} *characteristic*

Syntax	Description
list-number	Number of the DE list.
protocol *protocol*	One of the following keywords corresponding to a supported protocol or device: arp—Address Resolution Protocol. apollo—Apollo Domain. appletalk—AppleTalk. bridge—bridging device. clns—ISO Connectionless Network Service. clns_es—CLNS end systems. clns_is—CLNS intermediate systems. compressedtcp—Compressed Transmission Control Protocol (TCP). decnet—DECnet. decnet_node—DECnet end node. decnet_router-L1—DECnet Level 1 (intra-area) router. decnet_router-L2—DECnet Level 2 (interarea) router. ip—Internet Protocol. ipx—Novell Internet Packet Exchange Protocol. vines—Banyan VINES. xns—Xerox Network Systems.
interface *type*	One of the following interface types: serial, null, or ethernet.

Syntax	Description
number	Interface number.
characteristic	One of the following:

fragments—Fragmented IP packets.

tcp *port*—TCP packets to or from a specified port.

udp *port*—User Datagram Protocol (UDP) packets to or from a specified port.

list *access-list-number*—Previously defined access list number.

gt *bytes*—Sets the DE bit for packets larger than the specified number of bytes.

lt *bytes*—Sets the DE bit for packets smaller than the specified number of bytes.

Default

Discard eligibility is not defined.

Command Mode

Global configuration

Usage Guidelines

This command first appeared in Cisco IOS Release 10.0.

To remove an entire DE list, use the **no** form of this command with no options and arguments.

This prioritizing feature requires that the Frame Relay network be able to interpret the DE bit as indicating which packets can be dropped first in case of congestion, or which packets are less time sensitive, or both.

Example

The following example specifies that IP packets larger than 512 bytes will have the DE bit set:

```
frame-relay de-list 1 protocol ip gt 512
```

FRAME-RELAY IDLE-TIMER

To specify the idle timeout interval for a switched virtual circuit, use the **frame-relay idle-timer** map-class configuration command. To reset the idle timer to its default interval, use the **no** form of this command.

frame-relay idle-timer *seconds*
no frame-relay idle-timer *seconds*

Syntax	Description
seconds	Time interval, in seconds, with no frames exchanged on a switched virtual circuit, after which the SVC is released.

Command Reference

Default

120 seconds

Command Mode

Map-class configuration

Usage Guidelines

This command first appeared in Cisco IOS Release 11.2.

The **frame-relay idle-timer** command applies to switched virtual circuits that are associated with the map class where the idle-timer is defined.

The idle timer must be tuned for each application. Routing protocols such as Routing Information Protocol (RIP) might keep the SVC up indefinitely because updates go out every 10 seconds.

Example

The following example defines the traffic rate and idle timer for the *fast_vcs* map class and applies those values to DLCI 100, which is associated with that map class:

```
interface serial 0
frame-relay interface-dlci 100
 class fast_vc

map-class frame-relay fast_vcs
 frame-relay traffic-rate 56000 128000
 frame-relay idle-timer 30
```

Related Commands

map-class frame-relay

FRAME-RELAY INTERFACE-DLCI

To assign a data link connection identifier (DLCI) to a specified Frame Relay subinterface on the router or access server, use the **frame-relay interface-dlci** interface configuration command. To remove this assignment, use the **no** form of this command.

> **frame-relay interface-dlci** *dlci* [ietf | cisco]
> **no frame-relay interface-dlci** *dlci* [ietf | cisco]
> **frame-relay interface-dlci** *dlci* [**protocol ip** *ip-address*] (for a BOOTP server only)

Syntax	Description
dlci	DLCI number to be used on the specified subinterface.
ietf	cisco	(Optional) Encapsulation type: Internet Engineering Task Force (IETF) Frame Relay encapsulation or Cisco Frame Relay encapsulation.

Syntax	Description
protocol ip *ip-address*	(Optional) Indicates the IP address of the main interface of a new router or access server onto which a router configuration file is to be automatically installed over a Frame Relay network. Use this option only when this device will act as the BOOTP server for automatic installation over Frame Relay.

Default

No DLCI is assigned.

Command Mode

Interface configuration

Usage Guidelines

This command first appeared in Cisco IOS Release 10.0.

This command is typically used for subinterfaces; however, it can also be used on main interfaces. Using the **frame-relay interface-dlci** command on main interfaces will enable the use of routing protocols on interfaces that use **Inverse ARP**. The **frame-relay interface-dlci** command on a main interface is also valuable for assigning a specific class to a single PVC where special characteristics are desired. Subinterfaces are logical interfaces associated with a physical interface. You must specify the interface and subinterface before you can use this command to assign any DLCIs and any encapsulation or broadcast options. See the "Example" section for the sequence of commands.

This command is required for all point-to-point subinterfaces; it is also required for multipoint subinterfaces for which dynamic address resolution is enabled. It is not required for multipoint subinterfaces configured with static address mappings.

Use the **protocol ip** *ip-address* option only when this router or access server will act as the BOOTP server for autoinstallation over Frame Relay.

Example

The following example assigns DLCI 100 to serial subinterface 5.17:

```
! Enter interface configuration and begin assignments on interface serial 5
interface serial 5
! Enter subinterface configuration by assigning subinterface 17
interface serial 5.17
! Now assign a DLCI number to subinterface 5.17
frame-relay interface-dlci 100
```

Related Commands

frame-relay class

FRAME-RELAY INTF-TYPE

Use the **frame-relay intf-type** interface configuration command to configure a Frame Relay switch type. Use the **no** form of this command to disable the switch.

    frame-relay intf-type [dce | dte | nni]
    no frame-relay intf-type [dce | dte | nni]

Syntax	Description
dce	(Optional) Router or access server functions as a switch connected to a router.
dte	(Optional) Router or access server is connected to a Frame Relay network. This is the default.
nni	(Optional) Router or access server functions as a switch connected to a switch—it supports Network-to-Network Interface (NNI) connections.

Default

dte

Command Mode

Interface configuration

Usage Guidelines

This command first appeared in Cisco IOS Release 10.0.

This command can be used only if Frame Relay switching has previously been enabled globally by use of the **frame-relay switching** command.

Example

The following example configures a data terminal equipment (DTE) switch type:

```
frame-relay switching
!
interface serial 2
frame-relay intf-type dte
```

FRAME-RELAY INVERSE-ARP

If the Inverse Address Resolution Protocol (Inverse ARP) was previously disabled on a router or access server configured for Frame Relay, use the **frame-relay inverse-arp** interface configuration command to reenable Inverse ARP on a specified interface or subinterface. Use the **no** form of this command to disable this feature.

    frame-relay inverse-arp [*protocol*] [*dlci*]
    no frame-relay inverse-arp [*protocol*] [*dlci*]

Syntax	Description
protocol	Supported protocols: **appletalk, decnet, ip, ipx, vines,** and **xns**.
dlci	One of the DLCI numbers used on the interface. Acceptable numbers are integers in the range 16 through 1007.

Default
Enabled

Command Mode
Interface configuration

Usage Guidelines
This command first appeared in Cisco IOS Release 10.0.

To enable Inverse ARP for all protocols that were enabled before the prior **no frame-relay inverse-arp** command was issued, use the **frame-relay inverse-arp** command without arguments. To disable Inverse ARP for all protocols of an interface, use the **no frame-relay inverse-arp** command without arguments.

To enable or disable Inverse ARP for a specific protocol and DLCI pair, use both the *protocol* and *dlci* arguments. To enable or disable Inverse ARP for all protocols on a DLCI, use only the *dlci* argument. To enable or disable Inverse ARP for a protocol for all DLCIs on the specified interface or subinterface, use only the *protocol* argument.

This implementation of Inverse ARP is based on RFC 1293. It allows a router or access server running Frame Relay to discover the protocol address of a device associated with the virtual circuit.

In Frame Relay, permanent virtual circuits (PVCs) are identified by a DLCI, which is the equivalent of a hardware address. By exchanging signaling messages, a network announces a new virtual circuit, and with Inverse ARP, the protocol address at the other side of the circuit can be discovered.

The **show frame-relay map** command displays the word "dynamic" to flag virtual circuits that are created dynamically by Inverse ARP.

Example
The following example sets Inverse ARP on an interface running AppleTalk:
```
interface serial 0
frame-relay inverse-arp appletalk 100
```

Related Commands
clear frame-relay-inarp
show frame-relay map

FRAME-RELAY IP TCP HEADER-COMPRESSION

To configure an interface to ensure that the associated PVC will always carry outgoing Transmission Control Protocol/Internet Protocol (TCP/IP) headers in compressed form, use the **frame-relay ip tcp header-compression** interface configuration command. To disable compression of TCP/IP packet headers on the interface, use the **no** form of this command.

> frame-relay ip tcp header-compression [passive]
> no frame-relay ip tcp header-compression

Syntax   *Description*

passive   (Optional) Compresses the outgoing TCP/IP packet header only if an incoming packet had a compressed header.

Default

Active TCP/IP header compression; all outgoing TCP/IP packets are subjected to header compression.

Command Mode

Interface configuration

Usage Guidelines

This command first appeared in Cisco IOS Release 10.0.

This command applies to interfaces that support Frame Relay encapsulation, specifically serial ports and High-Speed Serial Interface (HSSI).

Frame Relay must be configured on the interface before this command can be used.

TCP/IP header compression and IETF encapsulation are mutually exclusive. If an interface is changed to IETF encapsulation, all encapsulation and compression characteristics are lost.

When you use this command to enable TCP/IP header compression, every IP map inherits the compression characteristics of the interface, unless header compression is explicitly rejected or modified by use of the **frame-relay map ip tcp header compression** command.

Cisco recommends that you shut down the interface prior to changing encapsulation types. Although this is not required, shutting down the interface ensures the interface is reset for the new encapsulation.

Example

The following example configures serial interface 1 to use the default encapsulation (**cisco**) and passive TCP header compression:

```
interface serial 1
encapsulation frame-relay
frame-relay ip tcp header-compression passive
```

Related Commands

frame-relay map ip tcp header-compression

FRAME-RELAY LAPF FRMR

To resume the default setting of sending the Frame Reject (FRMR) frame at the LAPF Frame Reject procedure after having set the option of not sending the frame, use the **frame-relay frmr** command. To set the option of *not* sending the Frame Reject (FRMR) frame at the LAPF Frame Reject procedure, use the **no frame-relay lapf frmr** interface configuration command.

> **frame-relay frmr**
> **no frame-relay lapf frmr**

Syntax Description

This command has no keywords or arguments.

Default

Send FRMR during the Frame Reject procedure.

Command Mode

Interface configuration command

Usage Guidelines

This command first appeared in Cisco IOS Release 11.2.

If the Frame Relay switch does not support FRMR, use the **no** form of this command to suppress the transmission of FRMR frames.

Example

The following example suppresses the transmission of FRMR frames:

```
no frame-relay lapf frmr
```

FRAME-RELAY LAPF K

To set the Link Access Procedure for Frame Relay (LAPF) window size *k*, use the **frame-relay lapf k** interface configuration command. To reset the maximum window size *k* to the default value, use the **no** form of this command.

> **frame-relay lapf k** *number*
> **no frame-relay lapf k** [*number*]

Syntax	Description
number	Maximum number of information frames that are either outstanding for transmission or are transmitted but unacknowledged, in the range 1 through 127.

Default
7 frames

Command Mode
Interface configuration

Usage Guidelines
This command first appeared in Cisco IOS Release 11.2.

This command is used to tune Layer 2 system parameters to work well with the Frame Relay switch. Normally, you do not need to change the default setting.

Manipulation of Layer 2 parameters is not recommended if you do not fully understand the resulting functional change. For more information, refer to the ITU-T Q.922 specification for LAPF.

Example
The following example resets the LAPF window size *k* to the default value:

```
no frame-relay lapf k
```

Related Commands
frame-relay lapf t203

FRAME-RELAY LAPF N200

To set the LAPF maximum retransmission count *N200*, use the **frame-relay lapf n200** interface configuration command. To reset the maximum retransmission count to the default of 3, use the **no** form of this command.

```
frame-relay lapf n200 retries
no frame-relay lapf n200 [retries]
```

Syntax	Description
retries	Maximum number of retransmissions of a frame.

Default
3 retransmissions

Command Mode

Interface configuration

Usage Guidelines

This command first appeared in Cisco IOS Release 11.2.

This command is used to tune Layer 2 system parameters to work well with the Frame Relay switch. Normally, you do not need to change the default setting.

Manipulation of Layer 2 parameters is not recommended if you do not fully understand the resulting functional change. For more information, refer to the ITU-T Q.922 specification for LAPF.

Example

The following example resets the N200 maximum retransmission count to the default value:

```
no frame-relay lapf n200
```

FRAME-RELAY LAPF N201

To set the LAPF N201 value (the maximum length of the Information field of the LAPF I frame), use the **frame-relay lapf n201** interface configuration command. To reset the maximum length of the Information field to the default of 260 bytes (octets), use the **no** form of this command.

    frame-relay lapf n201 *bytes*
    no frame-relay lapf n201 [*bytes*]

Syntax	Description
bytes	Maximum number of bytes in the Information field of the LAPF I frame, in the range 1 through 16,384.

Default

260 bytes

Command Mode

Interface configuration

Usage Guidelines

This command first appeared in Cisco IOS Release 11.2.

This command is used to tune Layer 2 system parameters to work well with the Frame Relay switch. Normally, you do not need to change the default setting.

Manipulation of Layer 2 parameters is not recommended if you do not fully understand the resulting functional change. For more information, refer to the ITU-T Q.922 specification for LAPF.

Command Reference

Example

The following example resets the N201 maximum information field length to the default value:
```
no frame-relay lapf n201
```

FRAME-RELAY LAPF T200

To set the LAPF retransmission timer value T200, use the **frame-relay lapf t200** interface configuration command. To reset the T200 timer to the default value of 15, use the **no** form of this command.

> **frame-relay lapf t200** *tenths-of-a-second*
> **no frame-relay lapf t200**

Syntax	*Description*
tenths-of-a-second	Time, in tenths of a second, in the range 1 through 100.

Default

15 tenths of a second (1.5 seconds)

Command Mode

Interface configuration

Usage Guidelines

This command first appeared in Cisco IOS Release 11.2.

The retransmission timer value T200 should be less than the link idle timer value T203 (using the same time unit).

This command is used to tune Layer 2 system parameters to work well with the Frame Relay switch. Normally, you do not need to change the default setting.

Manipulation of Layer 2 parameters is not recommended if you do not fully understand the resulting functional change. For more information, refer to the ITU-T Q.922 specification for LAPF.

Example

The following example resets the T200 timer to the default value:
```
no frame-relay lapf t200
```

Related Commands

frame-relay lapf t203

FRAME-RELAY LAPF T203

To set the LAPF link idle timer value T203 of DLCI 0, use the **frame-relay lapf t203** interface configuration command. To reset the link idle timer to the default value, use the **no** form of this command.

> **frame-relay lapf t203** *seconds*
> **no frame-relay lapf t203**

Syntax	Description
seconds	Maximum time allowed with no frames exchanged, in the range 1 through 65,535 seconds.

Default

30 seconds

Command Mode

Interface configuration

Usage Guidelines

This command first appeared in Cisco IOS Release 11.2.

The **frame-relay lapf t203** command applies to the link; that is, it applies to DLCI 0. Circuits other than DLCI 0 are not affected.

The link idle timer value T203 should be greater than the retransmission timer value T200 (using the same time unit).

This command is used to tune Layer 2 system parameters to work well with the Frame Relay switch. Normally, you do not need to change the default setting.

Manipulation of Layer 2 parameters is not recommended if you do not fully understand the resulting functional change. For more information, refer to the ITU-T Q.922 specification for LAPF.

Example

The following example resets the T203 idle link timer to the default value:

```
no frame-relay lapf t203
```

Related Commands

frame-relay lapf k
frame-relay lapf t200

Command Reference

FRAME-RELAY LMI-N391DTE

To set a full status polling interval, use the **frame-relay lmi-n391dte** interface configuration command. To restore the default interval value, assuming an LMI has been configured, use the **no** form of this command.

> **frame-relay lmi-n391dte** *keep-exchanges*
> **no frame-relay lmi-n391dte** *keep-exchanges*

Syntax	Description
keep-exchanges	Number of keep exchanges to be done before requesting a full status message. An acceptable value is any positive integer in the range 1 through 255.

Default

6 keep exchanges

Command Mode

Interface configuration

Usage Guidelines

This command first appeared in Cisco IOS Release 10.0.

Use this command when the interface is configured as data terminal equipment (DTE) or a Network-to-Network Interface (NNI) as a means of setting the full status message polling interval.

Example

In the following example, one out of every four status inquiries generated will request a full status response from the switch. The other three status inquiries will request keepalive exchanges only.

```
interface serial 0
frame-relay intf-type DTE
frame-relay lmi-n391dte 4
```

FRAME-RELAY LMI-N392DCE

To set the DCE and the Network-to-Network Interface (NNI) error threshold, use the **frame-relay lmi-n392dce** interface configuration command. To remove the current setting, use the **no** form of this command.

> **frame-relay lmi-n392dce** *threshold*
> **no frame-relay lmi-n392dce** *threshold*

Syntax	Description
threshold	Error threshold value. An acceptable value is any positive integer in the range 1 through 10.

Default

2 errors

Command Mode

Interface configuration

Usage Guidelines

This command first appeared in Cisco IOS Release 10.0.

In Cisco's implementation, N392 errors must occur within the number defined by the N393 event count in order for the link to be declared down. Therefore, the threshold value for this command must be less than the count value defined in the **frame-relay lmi-n393dce** command.

Example

In the following example, the LMI failure threshold is set to 3. The router acts as a Frame Relay DCE or NNI switch.

```
interface serial 0
frame-relay intf-type DCE
frame-relay lmi-n392dce 3
```

Related Commands

frame-relay lmi-n393dce

FRAME-RELAY LMI-N392DTE

To set the error threshold on a DTE or NNI interface, use the **frame-relay lmi-n392dte** interface configuration command. To remove the current setting, use the **no** form of this command.

    frame-relay lmi-n392dte *threshold*
    no frame-relay lmi-n392dte *threshold*

Syntax	Description
threshold	Error threshold value. An acceptable value is any positive integer in the range 1 through 10.

Default

3 errors

Command Mode

Interface configuration

Usage Guidelines

This command first appeared in Cisco IOS Release 10.0.

Example

In the following example, the LMI failure threshold is set to 3. The router acts as a Frame Relay DTE or NNI switch.

```
interface serial 0
frame-relay intf-type DTE
frame-relay lmi-n392dte 3
```

FRAME-RELAY LMI-N393DCE

To set the DCE and NNI monitored events count, use the **frame-relay lmi-n393dce** interface configuration command. To remove the current setting, use the **no** form of this command.

frame-relay lmi-n393dce *events*
no frame-relay lmi-n393dce *events*

Syntax	Description
events	Monitored events count value. An acceptable value is any positive integer in the range 1 through 10.

Default

2 events

Command Mode

Interface configuration

Usage Guidelines

This command first appeared in Cisco IOS Release 10.0.

This command and the **frame-relay lmi-n392dce** command define the condition that causes the link to be declared down. In Cisco's implementation, N392 errors must occur within the *events* count in order for the link to be declared down. Therefore, the *events* value defined in this command must be greater than the threshold value defined in the **frame-relay lmi-n392dce** command.

Example

In the following example, the LMI monitored events count is set to 3. The router acts as a Frame Relay DCE or NNI switch.

```
interface serial 0
frame-relay intf-type DCE
frame-relay lmi-n393dce 3
```

Related Commands
frame-relay lmi-n392dce

FRAME-RELAY LMI-N393DTE

To set the monitored event count on a DTE or NNI interface, use the **frame-relay lmi-n393dte** interface configuration command. To remove the current setting, use the **no** form of this command.
     frame-relay lmi-n393dte *events*
     no frame-relay lmi-n393dte *events*

Syntax	*Description*
events	Monitored events count value. An acceptable value is any positive integer in the range 1 through 10.

Default
4 events

Command Mode
Interface configuration

Usage Guidelines
This command first appeared in Cisco IOS Release 10.0.

Example
In the following example, the LMI monitored events count is set to 3. The router acts as a Frame Relay DTE or NNI switch.
```
interface serial 0
frame-relay intf-type DTE
frame-relay lmi-n393dte 3
```

FRAME-RELAY LMI-T392DCE

To set the polling verification timer on a DCE or NNI interface, use the **frame-relay lmi-t392dce** interface configuration command. To remove the current setting, use the **no** form of this command.
     frame-relay lmi-t392dce *seconds*
     no frame-relay lmi-t392dce *seconds*

Syntax	*Description*
seconds	Polling verification timer value, in seconds. An acceptable value is any positive integer in the range 5 through 30.

Default

15 seconds

Command Mode

Interface configuration

Usage Guidelines

This command first appeared in Cisco IOS Release 10.0.

The value for the timer must be greater than the DTE or NNI keepalive timer.

Example

The following example indicates a polling verification timer on a DCE or NNI interface set to 20 seconds:

```
interface serial 3
frame-relay intf-type DCE
frame-relay lmi-t392dce 20
```

Related Commands

keepalive

FRAME-RELAY LMI-TYPE

To select the Local Management Interface (LMI) type, use the **frame-relay lmi-type** interface configuration command. To return to the default LMI type, use the **no** form of this command.

> **frame-relay lmi-type {ansi | cisco | q933a}**
> **no frame-relay lmi-type {ansi | q933a}**

Syntax	Description
ansi	Annex D defined by American National Standards Institute (ANSI) standard T1.617.
cisco	LMI type defined jointly by Cisco and three other companies.
q933a	ITU-T Q.933 Annex A.

— **NOTES** ————————————————————————————

The International Telecommunications Union Telecommunications Standardization Sector (ITU-T) carries out the functions of the former Consultative Committee for International Telegraph and Telephone (CCITT).

Default

LMI autosense is active and determines the LMI type by communicating with the switch.

Command Mode

Interface configuration

Usage Guidelines

This command first appeared in Cisco IOS Release 10.0.

Cisco's implementation of Frame Relay supports three LMI types: Cisco, ANSI Annex D, and ITU-T Q.933 Annex A.

The LMI type is set on a per-interface basis and is shown in the output of the **show interfaces** EXEC command.

If you want to deactivate LMI autosense, use this command and the **keepalive** command to configure the LMI. For more information about LMI autosense and configuring the LMI, see Chapter 7.

Example

The following is an example of the commands you might enter to configure an interface for the ANSI Annex D LMI type:

```
interface Serial1
encapsulation frame-relay
frame-relay lmi-type ansi
keepalive 15
```

FRAME-RELAY LOCAL-DLCI

To set the source DLCI for use when the LMI is not supported, use the **frame-relay local-dlci** interface configuration command. To remove the DLCI number, use the **no** form of this command.

> **frame-relay local-dlci** *number*
> **no frame-relay local-dlci**

Syntax	Description
number	Local (source) DLCI number to be used.

Default

No source DLCI is set.

Command Mode

Interface configuration

Usage Guidelines

This command first appeared in Cisco IOS Release 10.0.

If LMI is supported and the multicast information element is present, the network server sets its local DLCI based on information provided via the LMI.

NOTES

The **frame-relay local-dlci** command is provided mainly to allow testing of the Frame Relay encapsulation in a setting where two servers are connected back-to-back. This command is not required in a live Frame Relay network.

Example

The following example specifies 100 as the local DLCI:

```
interface serial 4
frame-relay local-dlci 100
```

FRAME-RELAY MAP

To define the mapping between a destination protocol address and the DLCI used to connect to the destination address, use the **frame-relay map** interface configuration command. Use the **no** form of this command to delete the map entry.

      frame-relay map *protocol protocol-address dlci* [**broadcast**] [**ietf** | **cisco**]
      [**payload-compress** {**packet-by-packet** | **frf9 stac** [*hardware-options*] }]
      no frame-relay map *protocol protocol-address*

Syntax	*Description*
protocol	Supported protocol, bridging, or logical link control keywords: **appletalk, decnet, dlsw, ip, ipx, llc2, rsrb, vines,** and **xns.**
protocol-address	Destination protocol address.
dlci	DLCI number used to connect to the specified protocol address on the interface.
broadcast	(Optional) Forwards broadcasts to this address when multicast is not enabled (see the **frame-relay multicast-dlci** command for more information about multicasts). This keyword also simplifies the configuration of Open Shortest Path First (OSPF) (see the "Usage Guidelines" section for more detail).
ietf	(Optional) Internet Engineering Task Force (IETF) form of Frame Relay encapsulation. Used when the router or access server is connected to another vendor's equipment across a Frame Relay network.
cisco	(Optional) Cisco encapsulation method.
payload-compress packet-by-packet	(Optional) Packet-by-packet payload compression using the Stacker method.

Syntax	Description
payload-compress frf9 stac	(Optional) Enables FRF.9 compression using the Stacker method.
	• If the router contains a compression service adapter (CSA), compression is performed in the CSA hardware (hardware compression).
	• If the CSA is not available, compression is performed in the software installed on the VIP2 (distributed compression).
	• If the VIP2 is not available, compression is performed in the router's main processor (software compression).
hardware-options	**distributed**
	(Optional) Specifies that compression is implemented in the software that is installed in a VIP2. If the VIP2 is not available, compression is performed in the router's main processor (software compression). This option applies only to the Cisco 7500 series.
	software
	(Optional) Specifies that compression is implemented in the Cisco IOS software installed in the router's main processor.
	csa *csa_number*
	(Optional) Specifies the CSA to use for a particular interface. This option applies only to Cisco 7200 series routers.

Default

No mapping is defined.

Command Mode

Interface configuration

Usage Guidelines

This command first appeared in Cisco IOS Release 10.0.

The **payload-compress frf9 stac** keyword first appeared in Cisco IOS Release 11.3.

There can be many DLCIs known by a router or access server that can send data to many different places, but they are all multiplexed over one physical link. The Frame Relay map defines the logical connection between a specific protocol and address pair and the correct DLCI.

The optional **ietf** and **cisco** keywords allow flexibility in the configuration. If no keywords are specified, the map inherits the attributes set with the **encapsulation frame-relay** command. You can also use the encapsulation options to specify that, for example, all interfaces use IETF encapsulation except one, which needs the original Cisco encapsulation method and can be configured through use of the **cisco** keyword with the **frame-relay map** command.

Packet-by-packet compression is Cisco-proprietary and will not interoperate with routers of other manufacturers.

You can disable payload compression by entering the **no frame-relay map payload** command and then entering the **frame-relay map** command again with one of the other encapsulation keywords (**cisco** or **ietf**).

Use the **frame-relay map** command to enable or disable payload compression on multipoint interfaces. Use the **frame-relay payload-compress** command to enable or disable payload compression on point-to-point interfaces.

Cisco recommends that you shut down the interface prior to changing encapsulation types. Although this is not required, shutting down the interface ensures the interface is reset for the new encapsulation.

The **broadcast** keyword provides two functions: It forwards broadcasts when multicasting is not enabled, and it simplifies the configuration of OSPF for nonbroadcast networks that will use Frame Relay.

The **broadcast** keyword might also be required for some routing protocols—AppleTalk for example—that depend on regular routing table updates, especially when the router at the remote end is waiting for a routing update packet to arrive before adding the route.

By requiring selection of a designated router, OSPF treats a nonbroadcast, multiaccess network such as Frame Relay in much the same way as it treats a broadcast network. In previous releases, this required manual assignment in the OSPF configuration using the **neighbor interface** router command. When the **frame-relay map** command is included in the configuration with the **broadcast** keyword, and the **ip ospf network** command (with the **broadcast** keyword) is configured, there is no need to configure any neighbors manually. OSPF will now automatically run over the Frame Relay network as a broadcast network. (Refer to the **ip ospf network** interface command for more detail.)

NOTES

The OSPF broadcast mechanism assumes that IP class D addresses are never used for regular traffic over Frame Relay.

Examples

The following example maps the destination IP address 172.16.123.1 to DLCI 100:
```
interface serial 0
frame-relay map IP 172.16.123.1 100 broadcast
```
OSPF will use DLCI 100 to broadcast updates.

The example shows FRF.9 compression configuration using the **frame-relay map** command.
```
!
interface Serial2/0/1
 ip address 172.16.1.4 255.255.255.0
 no ip route-cache
```

```
encapsulation frame-relay IETF
no keepalive
shutdown
frame-relay map ip 172.16.1.1 105 IETF payload-compression FRF9 stac
!
```

Related Commands

frame-relay payload-compress

FRAME-RELAY MAP BRIDGE

To specify that broadcasts are to be forwarded during bridging, use the **frame-relay map bridge** interface configuration command. Use the **no** form of this command to delete the map entry.

  frame-relay map bridge *dlci* [**broadcast**] [**ietf**]
  no frame-relay map bridge *dlci*

Syntax	*Description*
dlci	DLCI number to be used for bridging on the specified interface or subinterface.
broadcast	(Optional) Broadcasts are forwarded when multicast is not enabled.
ietf	(Optional) IETF form of Frame Relay encapsulation. Use when the router or access server is connected to another vendor's equipment across a Frame Relay network.

Default

No broadcasts are forwarded.

Command Mode

Interface configuration

Usage Guidelines

This command first appeared in Cisco IOS Release 10.0.

Examples

The following example uses DLCI 144 for bridging:

```
interface serial 0
frame-relay map bridge 144 broadcast
```

The following example sets up separate point-to-point links over a subinterface and runs transparent bridging over it:

```
interface serial 0
bridge-group 1
encapsulation frame-relay
interface serial 0.1
bridge-group 1
```

```
frame-relay map bridge 42 broadcast
interface serial 0.2
bridge-group 1
frame-relay map bridge 64 broadcast
interface serial 0.3
bridge-group 1
frame-relay map bridge 73 broadcast
```

DLCI 42 is used as the link.

FRAME-RELAY MAP CLNS

To forward broadcasts when ISO CLNS is used for routing, use the **frame-relay map clns** interface configuration command. Use the **no** form of this interface configuration command to delete the map entry.

> **frame-relay map clns** *dlci* [**broadcast**]
> **no frame-relay map clns** *dlci*

Syntax	Description
dlci	DLCI number to which CLNS broadcasts are forwarded on the specified interface.
broadcast	(Optional) Broadcasts are forwarded when multicast is not enabled.

Default
No broadcasts are forwarded.

Command Mode
Interface configuration

Usage Guidelines
This command first appeared in Cisco IOS Release 10.0.

Example
The following example uses DLCI 125 for ISO CLNS routing:
```
interface serial 0
frame-relay map clns 125 broadcast
```

FRAME-RELAY MAP IP TCP HEADER-COMPRESSION

To assign header compression characteristics to an IP map that differ from the compression characteristics of the interface with which the IP map is associated, use the **frame-relay map ip tcp header-compression** interface configuration command. To remove the IP map, use the **no** form of this command.

frame-relay map ip *ip-address dlci* [broadcast] [cisco I ietf] [nocompress]
   tcp header-compression {active I passive}
   no frame-relay map ip *ip-address dlci*

Syntax	Description
ip-address	IP address.
dlci	DLCI number.
broadcast	(Optional) Forwards broadcasts to the specified IP address.
cisco	(Optional) Uses Cisco's proprietary encapsulation. This is the default.
ietf	(Optional) Uses RFC 1490 encapsulation. No TCP/IP header compression is done if IETF encapsulation is chosen for the IP map or the associated interface.
nocompress	(Optional) Disables TCP/IP header compression for this map.
active	Compresses the header of every outgoing TCP/IP packet.
passive	Compresses the header of an outgoing TCP/IP packet only if an incoming TCP/IP packet had a compressed header.

Default

The default encapsulation is **cisco**.

Command Mode

Interface configuration

Usage Guidelines

This command first appeared in Cisco IOS Release 10.0.

To disable TCP/IP header compression on the IP map, use the **nocompress** form of the command.

IP maps inherit the compression characteristics of the associated interface unless this command is used to provide different characteristics. This command can also reconfigure an IP map that existed before TCP header compression was configured on the associated interface.

When IP maps at both ends of a connection inherit passive compression, the connection will never transfer compressed traffic because neither side will generate a packet with a compressed header.

If you change the encapsulation characteristics of the interface to IETF, you lose the TCP header compression configuration of the associated IP map.

The command **frame-relay map ip** *ip-address dlci* **tcp header-compression active** can also be entered as **frame-relay map ip** *ip-address dlci* **active tcp header-compression**.

Cisco recommends that you shut down the interface prior to changing encapsulation types. Although this is not required, shutting down the interface ensures the interface is reset for the new encapsulation.

Command Reference

Example

The following example illustrates a command sequence configuring an IP map associated with serial interface 1 to enable active TCP/IP header compression:

```
interface serial 1
encapsulation frame-relay
ip address 131.108.177.170 255.255.255.0
frame-relay map ip 131.108.177.180 190 cisco tcp header-compression active
```

Related Commands

frame-relay ip tcp header-compression

FRAME-RELAY MINCIR

To specify the minimum acceptable incoming or outgoing committed information rate (CIR) for a Frame Relay virtual circuit, use the **frame-relay mincir** map-class configuration command. To reset the minimum acceptable CIR to the default, use the **no** form of this command.

frame-relay mincir {in | out} bps

Syntax	Description
**in	out**	Incoming or outgoing.
bps	Committed information rate, in bits per second.

Default

56,000 bps

Command Mode

Map-class configuration

Usage Guidelines

This command first appeared in Cisco IOS Release 11.2.

Rate values greater than 2048 must be entered with trailing zeros. For example, 2,048,000 and 5,120,000.

The network uses the **mincir** value when allocating resources for the SVC. If the **mincir** value cannot be supported, the call is cleared.

Example

The following example defines the peak and average traffic rate, the minimum CIR, and the idle timer for the *fast_vcs* map class and applies those values to DLCI 100, which is associated with that map class:

```
interface serial 0
frame-relay interface-dlci 100
```

```
class fast_vc

map-class frame-relay fast_vc
  frame-relay traffic-rate 56000 128000
  frame-relay idle-timer 30
  frame-relay mincir out 48000
```

Related Commands

map-class frame-relay

FRAME-RELAY MULTICAST-DLCI

Use the **frame-relay multicast-dlci** interface configuration command to define the DLCI to be used for multicasts. Use the **no** form of this command to remove the multicast group.

   frame-relay multicast-dlci *number*
   no frame-relay multicast-dlci

Syntax	*Description*
number	Multicast DLCI.

Default

No DLCI is defined.

Command Mode

Interface configuration

Usage Guidelines

This command first appeared in Cisco IOS Release 10.0.

Use this command when the multicast facility is not supported. Network transmissions (packets) sent to a multicast DLCI are delivered to all network servers defined as members of the multicast group.

NOTES

The **frame-relay multicast-dlci** command is provided mainly to allow testing of the Frame Relay encapsulation in a setting where two servers are connected back-to-back. This command is not required in a live Frame Relay network.

Example

The following example specifies 1022 as the multicast DLCI:

```
interface serial 0
frame-relay multicast-dlci 1022
```

FRAME-RELAY PAYLOAD-COMPRESS

Use the **frame-relay payload-compress** interface configuration command to enable Stacker payload compression on a specified point-to-point interface or subinterface, To disable payload compression on a specified point-to-point interface or subinterface, use the **no** form of this command.

> **frame-relay payload-compress {packet-by-packet | frf9 stac [*hardware-options*]}**
> **no frame-relay payload-compress {packet-by-packet | frf9 stac}**

Syntax	Description
packet-by-packet	Packet-by-packet payload compression, using the Stacker method.
frf9 stac	(Optional) Enables FRF.9 compression using the Stacker method.
	• If the router contains a compression service adapter (CSA), compression is performed in the CSA hardware (hardware compression).
	• If the CSA is not available, compression is performed in the software installed on the VIP2 (distributed compression).
	• If the VIP2 is not available, compression is performed in the router's main processor (software compression).
hardware-options	**distributed**
	(Optional) Specifies that compression is implemented in the software that is installed in a VIP2. If the VIP2 is not available, compression is performed in the router's main processor (software compression). This option applies only to the Cisco 7500 series.
	software
	(Optional) Specifies that compression is implemented in the Cisco IOS software installed in the router's main processor.
	csa *csa_number*
	(Optional) Specifies the CSA to use for a particular interface. This option applies only to Cisco 7200 series routers.

Default

Disabled

Command Mode

Subinterface configuration

Usage Guidelines

The **frame-relay payload-compress** command first appeared in Cisco IOS Release 11.0.
The **packet-by-packet** keyword first appeared in Cisco IOS Release 11.2.
The **frf9 stac** keyword first appeared in Cisco IOS Release 11.3.

Use the **frame-relay payload-compress** command to enable or disable payload compression on a point-to-point interface or subinterface. Use the **frame-relay map** command to enable or disable payload compression on a multipoint interface or subinterface.

Cisco recommends that you shut down the interface prior to changing encapsulation types. Although this is not required, shutting down the interface ensures the interface is reset for the new encapsulation.

Example

This example shows FRF.9 compression configuration for subinterfaces.

```
!
interface Serial2/0/0
 no ip address
 no ip route-cache
 encapsulation frame-relay
 ip route-cache distributed
 no keepalive
 shutdown
!
interface Serial2/0/0.500 point-to-point
 ip address 172.16.1.4 255.255.255.0
 no cdp enable
 frame-relay interface-dlci 500 IETF
 frame-relay payload-compression FRF9 stac
!
```

Related Commands

frame-relay map

FRAME-RELAY PRIORITY-DLCI-GROUP

To prioritize multiple DLCIs based on the type of Frame Relay traffic, use the **frame-relay priority-dlci-group** interface configuration command. Associate the DLCIs to their respective groups and define their priority levels. This command is used for multiple DLCIs, where the source and destination endpoints are the same (parallel paths). This command should not be used on a main interface, or on a point-to-point subintereface, where only a single DLCI is configured.

frame-relay priority-dlci-group *group-number high-dlci medium-dlci normal-dlci low-dlci*

Syntax	Description
group-number	Specific group number.
high-dlci	DLCI that is to have highest priority level.
medium-dlci	DLCI that is to have medium priority level.
normal-dlci	DLCI that is to have normal priority level.
low-dlci	DLCI that is to have lowest priority level.

Default

Disabled

Command Mode

Interface configuration

Usage Guidelines

This command first appeared in Cisco IOS Release 11.0.

This command is applied at the interface or subinterface level.

Levels in descending order are high, medium, normal, and low.

This command allows you to define different DLCIs for different categories of traffic based on traffic priorities. This command does not itself define priority queuing, but it can be used in conjunction with priority queuing.

A global priority list must be defined, and the associated DLCIs must already be applied to the configuration before you enable this command.

A DLCI can only be affiliated with a single priority-group; however, there can be multiple groups per interface or subinterface.

You must configure the *high-priority* and *medium-priority* DLCI values. If you do not explicitly associate a DLCI for the *normal-dlci* and *low-dlci* priority levels, the last DLCI specified in the command line is used as the value of the remaining arguments. For example, the following two commands are equivalent:

```
frame-relay priority-dlci-group 1 40 50
frame-relay priority-dlci-group 1 40 50 50 50
```

When you configure static map entries using **frame-relay map** commands or use Inverse ARP, the high-level DLCI is the only DLCI that is mapped. In the example, DLCI 40 is defined as having the highest priority. Therefore, DLCI 40 is the only DLCI that should be included in the **frame-relay map** command. DLCI 50 should not be included in a **frame-relay map** command.

Examples

The following example shows the **frame-relay priority-dlci-group** command configured on a main interface with a static Frame Relay map entry. Note that DLCI 40 is the high-priority DLCI as defined in the **frame-relay priority-dlci-group** command and the only DLCI included in the **frame-relay map** command.

```
interface serial 1
  ip address 172.21.177.1 255.255.255.0
  encapsulation frame-relay
  frame-relay priority-dlci-group 1 40
  frame-relay map ip 172.21.177.2 40 broadcast
```

The following example shows the **frame-relay priority-dlci-group** command configured on sub-interfaces where multiple priority groups are defined. DLCI 40 is the high-priority DLCI in group 1, and DLCI 80 is the high-priority DLCI in group 2.

```
interface Serial3
 no ip address
 encapsulation frame-relay
!
interface Serial3.2 multipoint
 ip address 172.21.177.1 255.255.255.0
 frame-relay interface-dlci 40
 frame-relay priority-dlci-group 1 40

!
interface Serial3.3 multipoint
 ip address 131.108.177.180 255.255.255.0
 frame-relay priority-dlci-group 2 80 90 100 100
 frame-relay interface-dlci 80
!
interface Serial 4
 no ip address
 encapsulation frame-relay
!
interface serial4.1 multipoint
 ip address 172.16.1.1 255.255.255.0
 frame-relay priority-dlci-group 3 200 210 300 300
 frame-relay priority-dlci-group 4 400 410 410 410
 frame-relay interface-dlci 200
 frame-relay interface-dlci 400
!
```

Related Commands

frame-relay map
priority-list

FRAME-RELAY PRIORITY-GROUP

To assign a priority queue to virtual circuits associated with a map class, use the **frame-relay priority-group** map-class configuration command. To remove the specified queuing from the virtual circuit and cause it to revert to the default first-come-first-served queuing, use the **no** form of this command.

frame-relay priority-group *list-number*
no frame-relay priority-group *list-number*

Syntax	*Description*
list-number	Priority-list number to be associated with the specified map class.

Command Reference

Default

If this command is not entered, the default is first-come-first-served queuing.

Command Mode

Map-class configuration

Usage Guidelines

This command first appeared in Cisco IOS Release 11.2.

Definition of the priority queue takes place in the existing manner (through **priority-list** commands).

Because only one form of queuing can be associated with a particular map class, subsequent definitions overwrite previous ones.

Example

The following example configures a map class for a specified DLCI, specifies a priority list for the map class, and then defines the priority list:

```
interface serial 0
  encapsulation frame-relay
  frame-relay interface-dlci 100
  class pri_vc

  map-class frame-relay pri_vc
  frame-relay priority-group 1

  priority-list 1 protocol ip high
```

Related Commands

class (virtual circuit configuration)
frame-relay interface-dlci
map-class frame-relay
priority-list

FRAME-RELAY QOS-AUTOSENSE

Use the **frame-relay qos-autosense** interface configuration command to enable Enhanced Local Management Interface on the Cisco router. Use the **no** form of this command to disable Enhanced Local Management Interface on the Cisco router.

> **frame-relay qos-autosense**
> **no frame-relay qos-autosense**

Syntax

This command has no arguments or keywords.

Default

Disabled

Command Mode

Interface configuration

Usage Guidelines

This command first appeared in Cisco IOS Release 11.2.

Enhanced Local Management Interface must be configured on both the Cisco router and the Cisco StrataCom switch.

Traffic shaping is optional with Enhanced Local Management Interface. Configure traffic shaping on the interface if you want QOS information to be used by the router for traffic rate enforcement.

Example

This configuration example shows a Frame Relay interface enabled to receive Enhanced Local Management Interface messages from the Cisco StrataCom switch that is also configured with Enhanced Local Management Interface enabled. Traffic shaping is also configured on the interface for traffic rate enforcement and dynamic rate throttling. This allows the router to adjust its output rate based on congestion information it receives from the switch.

```
interface serial0
  no ip address
  encapsulation frame-relay
  frame-relay lmi-type ansi
  frame-relay traffic-shaping
  frame-relay qos-autosense


interface serial0.1 point-to-point
  no ip address
  frame-relay interface-dlci 101
```

Related Commands

encapsulation frame-relay
frame-relay adaptive-shaping
frame-relay traffic-shaping
show frame-relay qos-autosense

FRAME-RELAY ROUTE

Use the **frame-relay route** interface configuration command to specify the static route for PVC switching. Use the **no** form of this command to remove a static route.

    frame-relay route *in-dlci out-interface out-dlci*
    no frame-relay route *in-dlci out-interface out-dlci*

Command Reference

Syntax	Description
in-dlci	DLCI on which the packet is received on the interface.
out-interface	Interface that the router or access server uses to transmit the packet.
out-dlci	DLCI that the router or access server uses to transmit the packet over the specified *out-interface*.

Default

No static route is specified.

Command Mode

Interface configuration

Usage Guidelines

This command first appeared in Cisco IOS Release 10.0.

Examples

The following example configures a static route that allows packets in DLCI 100 and transmits packets out over DLCI 200 on interface serial 2:

```
frame-relay route 100 interface Serial2 200
```

The following example illustrates the commands you enter for a complete configuration that includes two static routes for PVC switching between interface serial 1 and interface serial 2:

```
interface Serial1
no ip address
encapsulation frame-relay
keepalive 15
frame-relay lmi-type ansi
frame-relay intf-type dce
frame-relay route 100 interface Serial2 200
frame-relay route 101 interface Serial2 201
clockrate 2000000
```

FRAME-RELAY SVC

To enable Frame Relay SVC operation on the specified interface, use the **frame-relay svc** interface configuration command. To disable SVC operation on the specified interface, use the **no** form of this command

> **frame-relay svc**
> **no frame-relay svc**

Syntax Description

This command has no keywords or arguments.

Default

Disabled

Command Mode

Interface configuration

Usage Guidelines

This command first appeared in Cisco IOS Release 11.2.

SVC operation can be enabled at the interface level only. Once it is enabled at the interface level, it is enabled on all subinterfaces on the interface. One signaling channel, DLCI 0, is set up for the interface, and all SVCs are controlled from the physical interface.

The first use of this command on the router starts all SVC-related processes on the router. If they are already up and running because SVCs are enabled on another interface, no additional action is taken. These processes are not removed once they are created.

Example

The following example enables Frame Relay SVC operation on serial interface 0 and starts SVC-related processes on the router:

```
interface serial 0
ip address 172.68.3.5 255.255.255.0
encapsulation frame-relay
frame-relay lmi-type q933a
frame-relay svc
```

Related Commands

interface serial
ip address
encapsulation frame-relay
frame-relay lmi-type

FRAME-RELAY SWITCHING

Use the **frame-relay switching** global configuration command to enable PVC switching on a Frame Relay DCE or an NNI. Use the **no** form of this command to disable switching.

> **frame-relay switching**
> **no frame-relay switching**

Syntax Description

This command has no arguments or keywords.

Default

Disabled

Command Mode

Global configuration

Usage Guidelines

This command first appeared in Cisco IOS Release 10.0.

You must add this command to the configuration file before configuring the routes.

Example

The following example shows the simple command that is entered in the configuration file before the Frame Relay configuration commands to enable switching:

```
frame-relay switching
```

FRAME-RELAY TRAFFIC-RATE

To configure all the traffic shaping characteristics of a virtual circuit in a single command, use the **frame-relay traffic-rate** map-class configuration command. To remove the specified traffic shaping from the map class, use the **no** form of this command.

  frame-relay traffic-rate *average* [*peak*]
  no frame-relay traffic-rate *average* [*peak*]

Syntax	Description
average	Average rate, in bits per second; equivalent to specifying the contracted CIR.
peak	(Optional.) Peak rate, in bits per second; equivalent to $CIR + Be/Tc = CIR (1 + Be/Bc) = CIR + EIR$.

Default

If the peak rate is omitted, the default value used is the line rate, which is derived from the **band-width** command.

Command Mode

Map-class configuration

Usage Guidelines

This command first appeared in Cisco IOS Release 11.2.

For SVCs, the configured *peak* and *average* rates are converted to the equivalent CIR, excess burst size (*Be*), and committed burst size (*Bc*) values for use by SVC signaling.

This command lets you configure all the traffic-shaping characteristics of a virtual circuit in a single command. Using it is simpler than the alternative of entering the three subcommands **frame-relay cir out, frame-relay be out,** and **frame-relay bc out,** but offers slightly less flexibility.

Example

The following example associates a map class with specified DLCI and then sets a traffic rate for the map-class (and thus for the DLCI):

```
interface serial 0
frame-relay interface-dlci 100
 class fast_vc

map-class frame-relay fast_vc
 frame-relay traffic-rate 56000 128000
```

Related Commands

frame-relay bc out
frame-relay be out
frame-relay cir out

FRAME-RELAY TRAFFIC-SHAPING

To enable both traffic shaping and per-virtual circuit queuing for all PVCs and SVCs on a Frame Relay interface, use the **frame-relay traffic-shaping** interface configuration command. To disable traffic shaping and per-virtual circuit queuing, use the **no** form of this command.

> **frame-relay traffic-shaping**
> **no frame-relay traffic-shaping**

Syntax Description

This command has no keywords or arguments.

Default

Disabled

Command Mode

Interface configuration

Usage Guidelines

This command first appeared in Cisco IOS Release 11.2.

For virtual circuits for which no specific traffic shaping or queuing parameters are specified, a set of default values are used. The default queuing is performed on a first-come-first-served basis.

Frame Relay traffic shaping is not effective for Layer 2 PVC switching using the **frame-relay route** command.

Example

The following example enables both traffic shaping and per-virtual circuit queuing:

```
frame-relay traffic-shaping
```

Related Commands

frame-relay class
frame-relay custom-queue-list
frame-relay priority-group
frame-relay traffic-rate
map-class frame-relay

KEEPALIVE

To enable the Local Management Interface (LMI) mechanism for serial lines using Frame Relay encapsulation, use the **keepalive** interface configuration command. Use the **no** form of this command to disable this capability.

    keepalive *number*
    no keepalive

Syntax   *Description*

number   Number of seconds that defines the keepalive interval. The interval must be set as a positive integer that is less than the interval set on the switch; see the **frame-relay lmi-t392dce** command description.

Default

10 seconds

Command Mode

Interface configuration

Usage Guidelines

This command first appeared in Cisco IOS Release 11.2.

The **keepalive** command enables the keepalive sequence, which is part of the Local Management Interface (LMI) protocol.

— **NOTES** —————————————————————————

When booting from a network server over Frame Relay, you might need to disable keepalives.

Example

The following example sets the keepalive timer on the server for a period that is two or three seconds faster (shorter interval) than the interval set on the keepalive timer of the Frame Relay switch. The difference in keepalive intervals ensures proper synchronization between the Cisco server and the Frame Relay switch.

```
interface serial 3
keepalive 8
```

Related Commands

frame-relay lmi-t392dce

MAP-CLASS FRAME-RELAY

To specify a map class to define quality of service (QOS) values for an SVC, use the **map-class frame-relay** global configuration command.

map-class frame-relay *map-class-name*

Syntax	*Description*
frame-relay	Keyword specifying the type of map class.
map-class-name	Name of this map class.

Default

Disabled. No default name is defined.

Command Mode

Global configuration

Usage Guidelines

This command first appeared in Cisco IOS Release 11.2.

After you specify the named map class, you can specify the QOS parameters—such as incoming and outgoing CIR, committed burst rate, excess burst rate, and the idle timer—for the map class.

To specify the protocol-and-address combination to which the QOS parameters are to be applied, associate this map class with the static maps under a map list.

Example

The following example specifies a map class called *hawaii* and defines three QOS parameters for it. The *hawaii* map class is associated with a protocol-and-address static map defined under the **map-list** command.

```
map-list bermuda source-addr E164 123456 dest-addr E164 654321
ip 131.108.177.100 class hawaii
```

```
appletalk 1000.2 class hawaii

map-class frame-relay hawaii
 frame-relay cir in 2000000
 frame-relay cir out 56000
 frame-relay be out 9000
```

Related Commands

frame-relay bc
frame-relay be
frame-relay cir
frame-relay idle-timer

MAP-GROUP

To associate a map list with a specific interface, use the **map-group** interface configuration command.

> **map-group** *group-name*

Syntax	Description
group-name	Name used in a **map-list** command.

Default

Disabled. No map group name is defined.

Command Mode

Interface configuration

Usage Guidelines

This command first appeared in Cisco IOS Release 11.2.

A map-group association with an interface is required for SVC operation. In addition, a map list must be configured.

The **map-group** command applies to the interface or subinterface on which it is configured. The associated E.164 or X.121 address is defined by the **map-list** command, and the associated protocol addresses are defined by using the **class** command under the **map-list** command.

Example

The following example configures a physical interface, applies a map group to the physical interface, and then defines the map group:

```
interface serial 0
ip address 172.10.8.6
encapsulation frame-relay
```

```
map-group bermuda
frame-relay lmi-type q933a
frame-relay svc

map-list bermuda source-addr E164 123456 dest-addr E164 654321
ip 131.108.177.100 class hawaii
appletalk 1000.2 class rainbow
```

Related Commands

class (map-list configuration)
map-list

MAP-LIST

To specify a map group and link it to a local E.164 or X.121 source address and a remote E.164 or X.121 destination address for Frame Relay SVCs, use the **map-list** global configuration command. To delete a previous map-group link, use the **no** form of this command.

    map-list *map-group-name* **source-addr** {e164 | x121} *source-address* **dest-addr** {e164 | x121} *destination-address*

    no map-list *map-group-name* **source-addr** {e164 | x121} *source-address* **dest-addr** {e164 | x121} *destination-address*

Syntax	Description
map-group-name	Name of the map group. This map group must be associated with a physical interface.
source-addr {e164	x121}	Type of source address.
source-address	Address of the type specified (E.164 or X.121).
dest-addr {e164	x121}	Type of destination address.
destination-address	Address of the type specified (E.164 or X.121).

Default

Disabled. No default list name and no default address type are defined.

Command Mode

Global configuration

Usage Guidelines

This command first appeared in Cisco IOS Release 11.2.

Use the **map-class** command and its subcommands to define quality of service (QOS) parameters—such as incoming and outgoing CIR, committed burst rate, excess burst rate, and the idle timer—for the static maps defined under a map list.

Each SVC needs to use a source and destination number, in much the same way that a public telephone network needs to use source and destination numbers. These numbers allow the network to route calls from a specific source to a specific destination. This specification is done through map lists.

Based on switch configuration, addressing can take either of two forms: E.164 or X.121.

An X.121 number is 14 digits long and has the following form:

```
Z CC P NNNNNNNNNN
```

Table 8–1 describes the codes in an X.121 number form.

Table 8–1   *X.121 Numbers*

Code	Meaning	Value
Z	Zone code	3 for North America
C	Country code	10–16 for the United States
P	Public data network (PDN) code	Provided by the PDN
N	10-digit number	Set by the network for the specific destination

An E.164 number has a variable length; the maximum length is 15 digits. An E.164 number has the fields shown in Figure 8–1 and described in Table 8–2.

Figure 8–1
E.164 Address Format.

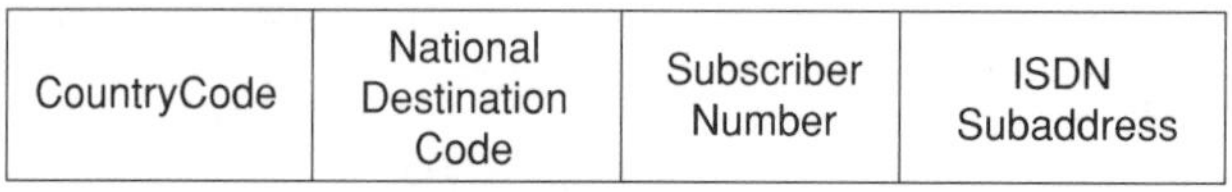

CountryCode	National Destination Code	Subscriber Number	ISDN Subaddress

Table 8–2   *E.164 Address Field Descriptions*

Field	Description
Country Code	Can be 1, 2, or 3 digits long. Some current values are the following: • Code 1—United States of America • Code 44—United Kingdom • Code 61—Australia
National Destination Code + Subscriber Number	Referred to as the National ISDN number; the maximum length is 12, 13, or 14 digits based on the country code.
ISDN Subaddress	Identifies one of many devices at the termination point. An ISDN subaddress is similar to an extension on a PBX.

Example

In the following SVC example, if IP or AppleTalk triggers the call, the SVC is set up with the QOS parameters defined within the class *hawaii*. An SVC triggered by either protocol results in two SVC maps, one for IP and one for AppleTalk. Two maps are set up because these protocol-and-address combinations are heading for the same destination, as defined by the **dest-addr** keyword and the values following it in the **map-list** command.

```
map-list bermuda source-addr E164 123456 dest-addr E164 654321
ip 131.108.177.100 class hawaii
appletalk 1000.2 class hawaii
```

Related Commands

class (map-list configuration)
map-class frame-relay

SHOW FRAME-RELAY IP TCP HEADER-COMPRESSION

To display statistics and TCP/IP header compression information for the interface, use the **show frame-relay ip tcp header-compression** EXEC command.

show frame-relay ip tcp header-compression

Syntax Description

This command has no arguments or keywords.

Command Mode

EXEC

Usage Guidelines

This command first appeared in Cisco IOS Release 10.3.

Sample Display

The following is sample output from the **show frame-relay ip tcp header-compression** command:

```
Router# show frame-relay ip tcp header-compression

DLCI 200          Link/Destination info: ip 131.108.177.200
Interface Serial0:
Rcvd:    40 total, 36 compressed, 0 errors
         0 dropped, 0 buffer copies, 0 buffer failures
Sent:    0 total, 0 compressed
         0 bytes saved, 0 bytes sent
Connect: 16 rx slots, 16 tx slots, 0 long searches, 0 misses, 0% hit ratio
         Five minute miss rate 0 misses/sec, 0 max misses/sec
```

Table 8–3 describes the fields shown in the display.

Table 8–3   *Show Frame-Relay IP TCP Header-Compression Field Descriptions*

Field	Description
Rcvd	
total	Sum of compressed and uncompressed packets received.
compressed	Number of compressed packets received.
errors	Number of errors caused by errors in the header fields (version, total length, or IP checksum).
dropped	Number of packets discarded. Seen only after line errors.
buffer copies	Number of times that a new buffer was needed in which to put the uncompressed packet.
buffer failures	Number of times that a new buffer was needed but was not obtained.
Sent	
total	Sum of compressed and uncompressed packets sent.
compressed	Number of compressed packets sent.
bytes saved	Number of bytes reduced because of the compression.
bytes sent	Actual number of bytes transmitted.
Connect	
rx slots, tx slots	Number of states allowed over one TCP connection. A state is recognized by a source address, a destination address, and an IP header length.
long searches	Number of times that the connection ID in the incoming packet was not the same as the previous one that was processed.
misses	Number of times that a matching entry was not found within the connection table and a new entry had to be entered.
hit ratio	Percentage of times that a matching entry was found in the compression tables and the header was compressed.
Five minute miss rate	Miss rate computed over the most recent five minutes and the maximum per-second miss rate during that period.

SHOW FRAME-RELAY LAPF

To display information about the status of the internals of Frame Relay Layer 2 (LAPF) if SVCs are configured, use the **show frame-relay lapf** EXEC command.

> **show frame-relay lapf**

Syntax Description

This command has no keywords or arguments.

Command Mode

EXEC

Usage Guidelines

This command first appeared in Cisco IOS Release 11.2.

Sample Display

The following is sample output from the **show frame-relay lapf** command.

```
raven# show frame-relay lapf

Interface = Serial1 (up),  LAPF state = TEI_ASSIGNED (down)
SVC disabled, link down cause = LMI down,  #link-reset = 0
T200 = 1.5 sec.,  T203 = 30 sec.,  N200 = 3,  k = 7,  N201 = 260
I xmt = 0, I rcv = 0, I reXmt = 0, I queued = 0
I xmt dropped = 0,  I rcv dropped = 0,  Rcv pak dropped = 0
RR xmt = 0,   RR rcv = 0,  RNR xmt = 0,  RNR rcv = 0
REJ xmt = 0,  REJ rcv = 0,  FRMR xmt = 0,  FRMR rcv = 0
DM xmt = 0,   DM rcv = 0,  DISC xmt = 0,  DISC rcv = 0
SABME xmt = 0,  SABME rcv = 0,  UA xmt = 0,  UA rcv = 0
V(S) = 0,  V(A) = 0,  V(R) = 0,  N(S) = 0,  N(R) = 0
Xmt FRMR at Frame Reject
```

Table 8–4 describes significant fields in this output.

Table 8–4 *Show Frame-Relay LAPF Field Descriptions*

Field	Description
Interface	Identifies the interface and indicates the line status (up, down, or administratively down).
LAPF state	A LAPF state of MULTIPLE FRAME ESTABLISHED or RIMER_RECOVERY indicates that Layer 2 is functional. Others, including TEI_ASSIGNED, AWAITING_ESTABLISHMENT, and AWAITING_RELEASE, indicate that Layer 2 is not functional.
SVC disabled	Indicates whether SVCs are enabled or disabled.
link down cause	Indicates the reason that the link is down. Examples include: N200 error, memory out, peer disconnect, LMI down, line down, or SVC disabled. Many other causes are described in the Q.922 specification.
#link-reset	Number of times the Layer 2 link has been reset.
T200 , T203, N200, k, N201	Values of Layer 2 parameters.

Table 8-4   *Show Frame-Relay LAPF Field Descriptions, Continued*

Field	Description
I xmt, I rcv, I reXmt, I queued	Number of I frames transmitted, received, retransmitted, and queued for transmission, respectively.
I xmt dropped	Number of transmitted I frames that were dropped.
I rcv dropped	Number of I frames received over DLCI 0 that were dropped.
Rcv pak dropped	Number of received packets that were dropped.
RR xmt, RR rcv	Number of RR frames transmitted; number of RR frames received.
RNR xmt, RNR rcv	Number of RNR frames transmitted; number of RNR frames received.
REJ xmt, REJ rcv	Number of REJ frames transmitted; number of REJ frames received.
FRMR xmt, FRMR rcv	Number of FRMR frames transmitted; number of FRMR frames received.
DM xmt, DM rcv	Number of DM frames transmitted; number of DM frames received.
DISC xmt, DISC rcv	Number of DISC frames transmitted; number of DISC frames received.
SABME xmt, SABME rcv	Number of SABME frames transmitted; number of SABME frames received.
UA xmt, UA rcv	Number of UA frames transmitted; number of UA frames received.
V(S) 0, V(A) 0, V(R) 0, N(S) 0, N(R) 0	Layer 2 sequence numbers.
Xmt FRMR at Frame Reject	Indicates whether the FRMR frame is transmitted at Frame Reject.

SHOW FRAME-RELAY LMI

To display statistics about the Local Management Interface (LMI), use the **show frame-relay lmi** EXEC command.

> **show frame-relay lmi** [*type number*]

Syntax	Description
type	(Optional) Interface type; it must be serial.
number	(Optional) Interface number.

Command Mode

EXEC

Usage Guidelines

This command first appeared in Cisco IOS Release 10.0.

Enter the command without arguments to obtain statistics about all Frame Relay interfaces.

Sample Displays

The following is sample output from the **show frame-relay lmi** command when the interface is a DTE:

```
Router# show frame-relay lmi

LMI Statistics for interface Serial1 (Frame Relay DTE) LMI TYPE = ANSI
    Invalid Unnumbered info 0          Invalid Prot Disc 0
    Invalid dummy Call Ref 0           Invalid Msg Type 0
    Invalid Status Message 0           Invalid Lock Shift 0
    Invalid Information ID 0           Invalid Report IE Len 0
    Invalid Report Request 0          Invalid Keep IE Len 0
    Num Status Enq. Sent 9             Num Status msgs Rcvd 0
    Num Update Status Rcvd 0           Num Status Timeouts 9
```

The following is sample output from the **show frame-relay lmi** command when the interface is an NNI:

```
Router# show frame-relay lmi

LMI Statistics for interface Serial3 (Frame Relay NNI) LMI TYPE = CISCO
    Invalid Unnumbered info 0          Invalid Prot Disc 0
    Invalid dummy Call Ref 0           Invalid Msg Type 0
    Invalid Status Message 0           Invalid Lock Shift 0
    Invalid Information ID 0           Invalid Report IE Len 0
    Invalid Report Request 0          Invalid Keep IE Len 0
    Num Status Enq. Rcvd 11            Num Status msgs Sent 11
    Num Update Status Rcvd 0           Num St Enq. Timeouts 0
    Num Status Enq. Sent 10            Num Status msgs Rcvd 10
    Num Update Status Sent 0           Num Status Timeouts 0
```

Table 8–5 describes significant fields shown in the output.

Table 8–5 *Show Frame-Relay LMI Field Descriptions*

Field	Description
LMI Statistics	Signaling or LMI specification: CISCO, ANSI, or ITU-T.
Invalid Unnumbered info	Number of received LMI messages with invalid unnumbered information field.
Invalid Prot Disc	Number of received LMI messages with invalid protocol discriminator.
Invalid dummy Call Ref	Number of received LMI messages with invalid dummy call references.
Invalid Msg Type	Number of received LMI messages with invalid message type.

Table 8–5   *Show Frame-Relay LMI Field Descriptions, Continued*

Field	Description
Invalid Status Message	Number of received LMI messages with invalid status message.
Invalid Lock Shift	Number of received LMI messages with invalid lock shift type.
Invalid Information ID	Number of received LMI messages with invalid information identifier.
Invalid Report IE Len	Number of received LMI messages with invalid Report IE Length.
Invalid Report Request	Number of received LMI messages with invalid Report Request.
Invalid Keep IE Len	Number of received LMI messages with invalid Keep IE Length.
Num Status Enq. Sent	Number of LMI status inquiry messages sent.
Num Status Msgs Rcvd	Number of LMI status messages received.
Num Update Status Rcvd	Number of LMI asynchronous update status messages received.
Num Status Timeouts	Number of times the status message was not received within the keepalive time value.
Num Status Enq. Rcvd	Number of LMI status enquiry messages received.
Num Status Msgs Sent	Number of LMI status messages sent.
Num Status Enq. Timeouts	Number of times the status enquiry message was not received within the T392 DCE timer value.
Num Update Status Sent	Number of LMI asynchronous update status messages sent.

SHOW FRAME-RELAY MAP

To display the current map entries and information about the connections, use the **show frame-relay map** EXEC command.

> **show frame-relay map**

Syntax Description

This command has no arguments or keywords.

Command Mode

EXEC

Usage Guidelines

This command first appeared in Cisco IOS Release 10.0.

Sample Display

The following is sample output from the **show frame-relay map** command:

```
Router# show frame-relay map

Serial 1 (administratively down): ip 131.108.177.177
dlci 177 (0xB1,0x2C10), static,
broadcast,
CISCO
TCP/IP Header Compression (inherited), passive (inherited)
```

Table 8–6 describes significant fields shown in the display.

Table 8–6 *Show Frame-Relay Map Field Descriptions*

Field	Description
Serial 1 (administratively down)	Identifies a Frame Relay interface and its status (up or down).
ip 131.108.177.177	Destination IP address.
dlci 177 (0xB1,0x2C10)	DLCI that identifies the logical connection being used to reach this interface. This value is displayed in three ways: its decimal value (177), its hexadecimal value (0xB1), and its value as it would appear on the wire (0x2C10).
static	Indicates whether this is a static or dynamic entry.
CISCO	Indicates the encapsulation type for this map; either CISCO or IETF.
TCP/IP Header Compression (inherited), passive (inherited)	Indicates whether the TCP/IP header compression characteristics were inherited from the interface or were explicitly configured for the IP map.

Related Commands

show frame-relay pvc

SHOW FRAME-RELAY PVC

To display statistics about PVCs for Frame Relay interfaces, use the **show frame-relay pvc** EXEC command.

> **show frame-relay pvc** [*type number* [*dlci*]]

Syntax	*Description*
type	(Optional) Interface type.
number	(Optional) Interface number.

Syntax	Description
dlci	(Optional) One of the specific DLCI numbers used on the interface. Statistics for the specified PVC display when a DLCI is also specified.

Command Mode

EXEC

Usage Guidelines

This command first appeared in Cisco IOS Release 10.0.

Statistics Reporting

To obtain statistics about PVCs on all Frame Relay interfaces, use this command with no arguments.

Per VC counters are not incremented at all when either autonomous or SSE switching is configured; therefore, PVC values will be inaccurate if either switching method is used.

DCE, DTE, and Logical Interfaces

When the interface is configured as a DCE and the DLCI usage is SWITCHED, the value displayed in the PVC STATUS field is determined by the status of outgoing interfaces (up or down) and the status of the outgoing PVC. The status of the outgoing PVC is updated in the Local Management Interface (LMI) message exchange. PVCs terminated on a DCE interface use the status of the interface to set the PVC STATUS.

In the case of a hybrid DTE switch, the PVC status on the DTE side is determined by the PVC status reported by the external Frame Relay network through the LMI.

If the outgoing interface is a tunnel, the PVC status is determined by what is learned from the tunnel.

Traffic Shaping

Congestion control mechanisms are currently not supported, but the switch passes forward explicit congestion notification (FECN) bits, backward explicit congestion notification (BECN) bits, and discard eligibility (DE) bits unchanged from entry to exit points in the network.

If an LMI status report indicates that a PVC is not active, then it is marked as inactive. A PVC is marked as deleted if it is not listed in a periodic LMI status message.

Sample Displays

The following is sample output from the **show frame-relay pvc** command:

```
Router# show frame-relay pvc
   PVC Statistics for interface Serial (Frame Relay DCE)
DLCI = 22, DLCI USAGE = LOCAL, PVC STATUS = ACTIVE, INTERFACE = Serial3/1:1.1

input pkts 9output pkts 300008in bytes 2754
out bytes 161802283dropped pkts 0in FECN pkts 0
in BECN pkts 1out FECN pkts 0out BECN pkts 0
```

```
   in DE pkts 0out DE pkts 0
   outbcast pkts 0outbcast bytes 0
     Shaping adapts to ForeSight   in ForeSight signals 1304
     pvc create time 1d05h, last time pvc status changed 00:11:00
```

If the circuit is configured for shaping to adapt to BECN, it is indicated in the display:

```
   Shaping adapts to BECN
```

If traffic shaping on the circuit does not adapt to either BECN or ForeSight, nothing extra shows:

```
DLCI = 100, DLCI USAGE = SWITCHED, PVC STATUS = ACTIVE

   input pkts 0output pkts 0in bytes 0
   out bytes 0dropped pkts 0in FECN pkts 0
   in BECN pkts 0out FECN pkts 0out BECN pkts 0
   in DE pkts 0out DE pkts 0
   outbcast pkts 0outbcast bytes 0
   pvc create time 0:03:03 last time pvc status changed 0:03:03
       Num Pkts Switched 0
```

The following is sample output from the **show frame-relay pvc** command for multipoint subinterfaces. The output displays both the subinterface number and the DLCI. This display is the same whether the PVC is configured for static or dynamic addressing.

```
DLCI = 300, DLCI USAGE = LOCAL, PVC STATUS = ACTIVE, INTERFACE = Serial0.103

   input pkts 10output pkts 7in bytes 6222
   out bytes 6034dropped pkts 0in FECN pkts 0
   in BECN pkts 0out FECN pkts 0out BECN pkts 0
   in DE pkts 0out DE pkts 0
   outbcast pkts 0outbcast bytes 0
   pvc create time 0:13:11  last time pvc status changed 0:11:46

DLCI = 400, DLCI USAGE = LOCAL, PVC STATUS = ACTIVE, INTERFACE = Serial0.104

   input pkts 20output pkts 8in bytes 5624
   out bytes 5222dropped pkts 0in FECN pkts 0
   in BECN pkts 0out FECN pkts 0out BECN pkts 0
   in DE pkts 0out DE pkts 0
   outbcast pkts 0outbcast bytes 0
   pvc create time 0:03:57  last time pvc status changed 0:03:48
```

Table 8–7 describes the fields shown in the displays.

Table 8–7 Show Frame-Relay PVC Field Descriptions

Field	Description
DLCI	One of the data link connection identifier (DLCI) numbers for the PVC.
DLCI USAGE	Lists SWITCHED when the router or access server is used as a switch, or LOCAL when the router or access server is used as a DTE.
PVC STATUS	Status of the PVC: ACTIVE, INACTIVE, or DELETED.
INTERFACE = Serial0.103	Specific subinterface associated with this DLCI.
input pkts	Number of packets received on this PVC.
output pkts	Number of packets sent on this PVC.

Table 8–7   *Show Frame-Relay PVC Field Descriptions, Continued*

Field	Description
in bytes	Number of bytes received.
out bytes	Number of bytes sent.
dropped pkts	Number of packets dropped by the router at Frame Relay level because an active outbound DLCI was not found
in FECN pkts	Number of packets received with the FECN bit set.
in BECN pkts	Number of packets received with the BECN bit set.
out FECN pkts	Number of packets sent with the FECN bit set.
out BECN pkts	Number of packets sent with the BECN bit set.
in DE pkts	Number of DE packets received.
out DE pkts	Number of DE packets sent.
outbcast pkts	Number of output broadcast packets.
outbcast bytes	Number of output broadcast bytes.
pvc create time	Time the PVC was created.
last time pvc status changed	Time the PVC changed status (active to inactive).
Num Pkts Switched	Number of packets switched within the router or access server; this PVC is the source PVC.

This sample output shows output from the **show frame-relay pvc** command with no traffic shaping configured on the interface.

```
Router# show frame-relay pvc

PVC Statistics for interface Serial1 (Frame Relay DTE)

DLCI = 100, DLCI USAGE = LOCAL, PVC STATUS = ACTIVE, INTERFACE = Serial1

    input pkts 0           output pkts 0          in bytes 0
    out bytes 0            dropped pkts 0         in FECN pkts 0
    in BECN pkts 0         out FECN pkts 0        out BECN pkts 0
    in DE pkts 0           out DE pkts 0
    out bcast pkts 0        out bcast bytes 0
```

This sample output shows output from the **show frame-relay pvc** command when traffic shaping is in effect:

```
Router# show frame-relay pvc
```

```
PVC Statistics for interface Serial1 (Frame Relay DTE)

DLCI = 101, DLCI USAGE = LOCAL, PVC STATUS = ACTIVE, INTERFACE = Serial1
input pkts 14046    output pkts 4339    in bytes 960362
  out bytes 675566    dropped pkts 0        in FECN pkts 0
  in BECN pkts 148    out FECN pkts 0       out BECN pkts 0
  in DE pkts 44       out DE pkts 0
  out bcast pkts 4034          out bcast bytes 427346
pvc create time 11:59:29, last time pvc status changed 11:59:29
CIR 64000        BC 8000        BE 1600      limit 2000      interval 125
mincir 32000     byte incremen 500          BECN response yes
pkts 9776        bytes 838676   pkts delayed 0       bytes delayed 0
shaping inactive

List   Queue  Args
1      4      byte-count 100
  Output queues: (queue #: size/max/drops)
     0: 0/20/0 1: 0/20/0 2: 0/20/0 3: 0/20/0 4: 0/20/0
     5: 0/20/0 6: 0/20/0 7: 0/20/0 8: 0/20/0 9: 0/20/0
     10: 0/20/0 11: 0/20/0 12: 0/20/0 13: 0/20/0 14: 0/20/0
     15: 0/20/0 16: 0/20/0
```

Table 8–8 describes the additional fields shown in the display when traffic shaping is in effect.

Table 8–8   *Show Frame-Relay PVC Field Descriptions with Traffic Shaping in Effect*

Field	Description
CIR	Current committed information rate (CIR), in bits per second.
BC	Current committed burst size, in bits.
BE	Current excess burst size, in bits.
limit	Maximum number of bytes transmitted per internal interval (excess plus sustained).
interval	Interval being used internally (may be smaller than the interval derived from Bc/CIR; this happens when the router determines that traffic flow will be more stable with a smaller configured interval).
mincir	Minimum committed information rate (CIR) for the PVC.
incremen	Number of bytes that will be sustained per internal interval.
BECN response	Frame Relay has BECN Adaptation configured.
List Queue Args	Identifier and parameter values for a custom queue list defined for the PVC. These identifiers and values correspond to the command **queue-list 1 queue 4 byte-count 100**.
Output queues	Output queues used for the PVC, with the current size, the maximum size, and the number of dropped frames shown for each queue.

The packet and byte values are counts for the number of packets and bytes that have gone through the traffic-shaping system.

SHOW FRAME-RELAY QOS-AUTOSENSE

Use the **show frame-relay qos-autosense** EXEC command to show the QOS values sensed from the switch.

   show frame-relay qos-autosense [interface *number*]

Syntax   *Description*

interface *number*   (Optional) Indicates the number of the physical interface for which you want to display QOS information.

Command Mode

EXEC

Usage Guidelines

This command first appeared in Cisco IOS Release 11.2.

Sample Displays

This sample display shows the output of the **show frame-relay qos-autosense** command when Enhanced Local Management Interface is enabled.

```
router# show frame-relay qos-autosense

ELMI information for interface Serial1
  Connected to switch:FRSM-4T1   Platform:AXIS   Vendor:cisco
                (Time elapsed since last update 00:00:30)

  DLCI = 100
  OUT:  CIR 64000      BC 50000      BE 25000      FMIF 4497
  IN:   CIR 32000      BC 25000      BE 12500      FMIF 4497
  Priority 0    (Time elapsed since last update 00:00:12)

  DLCI = 200
  OUT:  CIR 128000     BC 50000      BE 5100       FMIF 4497
  IN:   CIR Unknown    BC Unknown    BE Unknown    FMIF 4497
  Priority 0    (Time elapsed since last update 00:00:13)
```

Table 8–9 describes the significant fields in the output display.

Table 8–9   *Show Frame-Relay QOS-Autosense Field Descriptions*

Field	Description
ELMI information for interface Serial1	Label indicating the port for which the status is being displayed. It also displays the name, platform, and vendor information about the switch.

Table 8–9 *Show Frame-Relay QOS-Autosense Field Descriptions, Continued*

Field	Description
DLCI	Value that indicates which PVC statistics are being reported.
Out:	Values reporting settings configured for the outgoing Committed Information Rate, Burst Size, Excess Burst Size, and FMIF.
In:	Values reporting settings configured for the incoming Committed Information Rate, Burst Size, Excess Burst Size, and FMIF.
Priority	Value indicating priority level (currently not used).

Related Commands

frame-relay qos-autosense
show frame-relay pvc

SHOW FRAME-RELAY ROUTE

Use the **show frame-relay route** EXEC command to display all configured Frame Relay routes, along with their status.

    show frame-relay route

Syntax Description

This command has no arguments or keywords.

Command Mode

EXEC

Usage Guidelines

This command first appeared in Cisco IOS Release 10.0.

Sample Display

The following is sample output from the **show frame-relay route** command:

```
Router# show frame-relay route

      Input Intf      Input Dlci      Output Intf      Output Dlci  Status
      Serial1         100             Serial2          200          active
      Serial1         101             Serial2          201          active
      Serial1         102             Serial2          202          active
      Serial1         103             Serial3          203          inactive
      Serial2         200             Serial1          100          active
      Serial2         201             Serial1          101          active
      Serial2         202             Serial1          102          active
      Serial3         203             Serial1          103          inactive
```

Table 8–10 describes significant fields shown in the output.

Table 8–10 *Show Frame-Relay Route Field Descriptions*

Field	Description
Input Intf	Input interface and unit.
Input Dlci	Input DLCI number.
Output Intf	Output interface and unit.
Output Dlci	Output DLCI number.
Status	Status of the connection: active or inactive.

SHOW FRAME-RELAY SVC MAPLIST

To display all the SVCs under a specified map list, use the **show frame-relay svc maplist** EXEC command.

> **show frame-relay svc maplist** *name*

Syntax	*Description*
name	Name of the map list.

Command Mode

EXEC

Usage Guidelines

This command first appeared in Cisco IOS Release 11.2.

Sample Output

The following example shows, first, the configuration of the map-list *shank* and, second, the corresponding output of the **show frame-relay svc maplist** command. The following lines show the configuration:

```
map-list shank local-addr X121 87654321 dest-addr X121 12345678
 ip 172.21.177.26 class shank ietf
 ipx 123.0000.0c07.d530 class shank ietf
 !
map-class frame-relay shank
 frame-relay incir 192000
 frame-relay min-incir 19200
 frame-relay outcir 192000
 frame-relay min-outcir 19200
 frame-relay incbr(bytes) 15000
 frame-relay outcbr(bytes) 15000
```

The following lines show the output of the **show frame-relay svc maplist** command for the preceding configuration.

```
Router# show frame-relay svc maplist shank
Map List : shank
Local Address : 87654321          Type: X121
Destination Address: 12345678     Type: X121

Protocol : ip 172.21.177.26
Protocol : ipx 123.0000.0c07.d530
Encapsulation : IETF
Call Reference : 1                     DLCI : 501

Configured Frame Mode Information Field Size :
Incoming : 1500          Outgoing : 1500
Frame Mode Information Field Size :
Incoming : 1500          Outgoing : 1500
Configured Committed Information Rate (CIR) :
Incoming : 192 * (10**3)            Outgoing : 192 * (10**3)
Committed Information Rate (CIR) :
Incoming : 192 * (10**3)            Outgoing : 192 * (10**3)
Configured Minimum Acceptable CIR :
Incoming : 192 * (10**2)            Outgoing : 192 * (10**2)
Minimum Acceptable CIR :
Incoming : 0 * (10**0)        Outgoing : 0 * (10**0)
Configured Committed Burst Rate (bytes) :
Incoming : 15000          Outgoing : 15000
Committed Burst Rate (bytes) :
Incoming : 15000          Outgoing : 15000
Configured Excess Burst Rate (bytes) :
Incoming : 16000          Outgoing : 1200
Excess Burst Rate (bytes) :
Incoming : 16000          Outgoing : 1200
```

Table 8–11 describes significant fields in the output.

Table 8–11   *Show Frame-Relay SVC Maplist Field Descriptions*

Field	Description
Map List	Name of the configured map-list.
Local Address...Type	Configured source address type (E.164 or X.121) for the call.
Destination Address...Type	Configured destination address type (E.164 or X.121) for the call.
Protocol : ip ... Protocol : ipx ...	Destination protocol addresses configured for the map-list.
Encapsulation	Configured encapsulation type (CISCO or IETF) for the specified destination protocol address.
Call Reference	Call identifier.

Table 8–11   *Show Frame-Relay SVC Maplist Field Descriptions, Continued*

Field	Description
DLCI : 501	Number assigned by the switch as the DLCI for the call.
Configured Frame Mode Information Field Size: Incoming : Outgoing : Frame Mode Information Field Size : Incoming : 1500 Outgoing : 1500	Lines that contrast the configured and actual frame mode information field size settings used for the calls.
Configured Committed Information Rate (CIR) : Incoming : 192 * (10**3) Outgoing : 192 * (10**3) Committed Information Rate (CIR) : Incoming : 192 * (10**3) Outgoing : 192 * (10**3)	Lines that contrast the configured and actual committed information rate (CIR) settings used for the calls.
Configured Minimum Acceptable CIR : Incoming : 192 * (10**2) Outgoing : 192 * (10**2) Minimum Acceptable CIR : Incoming : 0 * (10**0) Outgoing : 0 * (10**0)	Lines that contrast the configured and actual minimum acceptable CIR settings used for the calls.
Configured Committed Burst Rate (bytes) : Incoming : 15000 Outgoing : 15000 Committed Burst Rate (bytes) : Incoming : 15000 Outgoing : 15000	Lines that contrast the configured and actual committed burst rate (bytes) settings used for the calls.
Configured Excess Burst Rate (bytes) : Incoming : 16000 Outgoing : 1200 Excess Burst Rate (bytes) : Incoming : 16000 Outgoing : 1200	Lines that contrast the configured and actual excess burst rate (bytes) settings used for the calls.

Related Commands

class (map-list configuration)
frame-relay bc
frame-relay cir
frame-relay mincir
map-class frame-relay
map-list

SHOW FRAME-RELAY TRAFFIC

To display the global Frame Relay statistics since the last reload, use the **show frame-relay traffic** EXEC command.

   show frame-relay traffic

Syntax Description

This command has no arguments or keywords.

Command Mode

EXEC

Usage Guidelines

This command first appeared in Cisco IOS Release 10.0.

Sample Display

The following is sample output from the **show frame-relay traffic** command:

```
Router# show frame-relay traffic

Frame Relay statistics:
ARP requests sent 14, ARP replies sent 0
ARP request recvd 0, ARP replies recvd 10
```

Information shown in the display is self-explanatory.

SHOW INTERFACES SERIAL

Use the **show interfaces serial** EXEC command to display information about a serial interface. When using the Frame Relay encapsulation, use the **show interfaces serial** command to display information about the multicast DLCI, the DLCIs used on the interface, and the DLCI used for the Local Management Interface (LMI).

   show interfaces serial *number*

Syntax	Description
number	Interface number.

Command Mode

EXEC

Usage Guidelines

This command first appeared in Cisco IOS Release 10.0.

Use this command to determine the status of the Frame Relay link. This display also indicates Layer 2 status if SVCs are configured.

Sample Displays

The following is sample output from the **show interfaces serial** command for a serial interface with the CISCO LMI enabled:

```
Router# show interface serial 1

Serial1 is up, line protocol is down
   Hardware is MCI Serial
   Internet address is 131.108.174.48, subnet mask is 255.255.255.0
   MTU 1500 bytes, BW 1544 Kbit, DLY 20000 usec, rely 246/255, load 1/255
   Encapsulation FRAME-RELAY, loopback not set, keepalive set (10 sec)
   LMI enq sent  2, LMI stat recvd 0, LMI upd recvd 0, DTE LMI down
   LMI enq recvd 266, LMI stat sent  264, LMI upd sent  0
   LMI DLCI 1023  LMI type is CISCO  frame relay DTE
   Last input 0:00:04, output 0:00:02, output hang never
   Last clearing of "show interface" counters 0:44:32
   Output queue 0/40, 0 drops; input queue 0/75, 0 drops
   Five minute input rate 0 bits/sec, 0 packets/sec
   Five minute output rate 0 bits/sec, 0 packets/sec
      307 packets input, 6615 bytes, 0 no buffer
      Received 0 broadcasts, 0 runts, 0 giants
      0 input errors, 0 CRC, 0 frame, 0 overrun, 0 ignored, 0 abort
      0 input packets with dribble condition detected
      266 packets output, 3810 bytes, 0 underruns
      0 output errors, 0 collisions, 2 interface resets, 0 restarts
      178 carrier transitions
```

The display shows the statistics for the LMI as the number of status inquiry messages sent (*LMI enq* and *LMI stat sent*), the number of status messages received (*LMI enq* and *LMI stat recvd*), and the number of status updates received (*LMI upd recvd*).

The following is sample output from the **show interfaces serial** command for a serial interface with the ANSI LMI enabled:

```
Router# show interface serial 1
Serial1 is up, line protocol is down
   Hardware is MCI Serial
   Internet address is 131.108.174.48, subnet mask is 255.255.255.0
   MTU 1500 bytes, BW 1544 Kbit, DLY 20000 usec, rely 249/255, load 1/255
   Encapsulation FRAME-RELAY, loopback not set, keepalive set (10 sec)
   LMI enq sent  4, LMI stat recvd 0, LMI upd recvd 0, DTE LMI down
   LMI enq recvd 268, LMI stat sent  264, LMI upd sent  0
   LMI DLCI 0  LMI type is ANSI Annex D  frame relay DTE
   Last input 0:00:09, output 0:00:07, output hang never
   Last clearing of "show interface" counters 0:44:57
   Output queue 0/40, 0 drops; input queue 0/75, 0 drops
   Five minute input rate 0 bits/sec, 0 packets/sec
   Five minute output rate 0 bits/sec, 0 packets/sec
      309 packets input, 6641 bytes, 0 no buffer
      Received 0 broadcasts, 0 runts, 0 giants
      0 input errors, 0 CRC, 0 frame, 0 overrun, 0 ignored, 0 abort
```

```
0 input packets with dribble condition detected
268 packets output, 3836 bytes, 0 underruns
0 output errors, 0 collisions, 2 interface resets, 0 restarts
180 carrier transitions
```

Each display provides statistics and information about the type of LMI configured, either *CISCO* for the Cisco LMI type, *ANSI* for the ANSI T1.617 Annex D LMI type, or *ITU-T* for the ITU-T Q.933 Annex A LMI type. See the **show interfaces** command for a description of the other fields displayed by this command.

Related Commands

show interfaces

CHAPTER 9

Configuring SMDS

The Switched Multimegabit Data Service (SMDS) is a wide-area networking service offered by some Regional Bell Operating Companies (RBOCs) and by MCI. This chapter describes the configuration tasks for the SMDS packet-switched software.

For a complete description of the commands mentioned in this chapter, refer to Chapter 10, "SMDS Commands."

SMDS HARDWARE REQUIREMENTS

You need the following hardware, equipment, and special software to configure SMDS:

- CSC-MCI or CSC-SCI serial interface controller card, a HSSI interface on chassis-based systems, or the serial port on an IGS router

---

NOTES

To operate on CSC-SCI or CSC-MCI cards, SMDS requires that the appropriate microcode version be installed. Version numbers are 1.2 (or later) for CSC-SCI and 1.7 (or later) for CSC-MCI.

- EIA/TIA-449 or V.35 applique on chassis-based systems, or EIA/TIA-449 transition cable on an IGS router
- SMDS data service unit (SDSU) device
- Packet-switched software option with the system software

Figure 9–1 illustrates the connections between the different components.

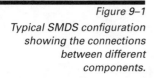
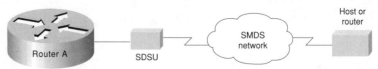

Figure 9–1
Typical SMDS configuration showing the connections between different components.

ASSIGNING SMDS ADDRESSES

All addresses for SMDS service are assigned by the service provider and can be assigned to individuals and groups.

You must enter addresses in the Cisco SMDS configuration software using an E prefix for multicast addresses and a C prefix for unicast addresses.

Cisco IOS software expects the addresses to be entered in E.164 format, which is 64 bits (15-digit addressing). The first 4 bits are the address type, and the remaining 60 bits are the address. If the first 4 bits are 1100 (0xC), the address is a unicast SMDS address which is the address of an individual SMDS host. If the first 4 bits are 1110 (0xE), the address is a multicast SMDS address, which is used to broadcast a packet to multiple end points. The 60 bits of the address are in binary-coded decimal (BCD) format. Each 4 bits of the address field presents a single telephone number digit, allowing for up to 15 digits. At a minimum, you must specify at least 11 digits (44 bits). Unused bits at the end of this field are filled with ones.

— **NOTES** ───

The **arp smds** command supports 48-bit addresses only (C or E followed by 11 digits). The addresses must be entered in dotted notation—for example, C141.5556.1414.

An example of a 15-digit E.164 address follows:
```
C14155561313FFFF
```

— **NOTES** ───

Previous versions of Cisco IOS software supported 48-bit SMDS addresses. If, when using the current version of the software, you write the configuration to NVRAM, the full 64-bit SMDS address is written. Previous versions of the software will no longer be able to read the new SMDS configuration from NVRAM. However, the current version of the software can read previous versions of the configuration in NVRAM.

The addresses can be entered with periods in a manner similar to Ethernet-style notation, or simply as a string of digits.

The following is an example of an individual address entered in Ethernet-style notation:
```
C141.5555.1212.FFFF
```

The following is an example of a group address:
```
E180.0999.9999.FFFF
```

CONFIGURING SMDS

Before you can begin the configuration tasks, you must have already obtained your SMDS addresses from your service provider. You need the following two types of addresses:

- The group address for broadcasts
- The SMDS hardware (individual) address for each router that interfaces directly into the SMDS network (that is, customer premises equipment)

You must perform several basic steps to enable SMDS. In addition, you can customize SMDS for your particular network needs and monitor SMDS connections. Perform the tasks in the following sections:

- Enabling SMDS on the Interface
- Customizing Your SMDS Network
- Monitoring the SMDS Connection

See the "SMDS Configuration Examples" section at the end of this chapter for ideas of how to configure SMDS on your network.

ENABLING SMDS ON THE INTERFACE

You must perform the tasks in the following list to enable SMDS:

- Setting SMDS Encapsulation
- Specifying the SMDS Address
- Establishing Address Mapping
- Mapping a Multicast Address to an SMDS Address
- Enabling ARP
- Enabling Broadcast ARP Messages
- Enabling Dynamic Address Mapping for IPX over SMDS

Setting SMDS Encapsulation

To set SMDS encapsulation at the interface level, perform the following task in interface configuration mode:

Task	Command
Enable SMDS on the interface.	**encapsulation smds**

For examples of enabling SMDS encapsulation, see the examples in the section "SMDS Configuration Examples," later in this chapter.

Specifying the SMDS Address

To specify the SMDS individual address for a particular interface, perform the following task in interface configuration mode:

Task	Command
Enter an individual address provided by the SMDS service provider.	**smds address** *smds-address*

For examples of specifying the SMDS address, see the examples in the section "SMDS Configuration Examples," later in this chapter.

Establishing Address Mapping

Routing tables are configured dynamically when DECnet, extended AppleTalk, IP, IPX, and ISO CLNS routing are configured. However, you can configure static mapping for these protocols, if needed. For other protocols, you must configure a static map between an individual SMDS address and a higher-level protocol address.

To establish address mapping, perform the following task in interface configuration mode:

Task	Command
Define static entries for those routers that are SMDS remote peers.	**smds static-map** *protocol protocol-address smds-address* [**broadcast**]

The supported protocols and the keywords to enable them are as follows:

- AppleTalk—**appletalk**
- Banyan VINES—**vines**
- DECnet—**decnet**
- IP—**ip**
- ISO CLNS—**clns**
- Novell IPX—**ipx**
- XNS—**xns**

For examples of establishing address mapping, see the examples in the section "SMDS Configuration Examples," later in this chapter.

Mapping a Multicast Address to an SMDS Address

You can map an SMDS group address to a broadcast or multicast address used by a higher-level protocol. If you do so, you need not specify the **broadcast** keyword in the **smds static-map** command, and the Cisco IOS software need not replicate each broadcast address.

To map an SMDS group address to a multicast address, perform the following task in interface configuration mode:

Task	Command
Map an SMDS group address to a multicast address used by a higher-level protocol.	**smds multicast** *protocol smds-address*

The protocols supported and the keywords to enable them are as follows:

- AppleTalk—**appletalk**
- AppleTalk ARP address—**aarp**
- Banyan VINES—**vines**
- Bridging—**bridge**

> **NOTES**
>
> Bridging is not a protocol, but the **bridge** keyword is valid for providing a map to a multicast address.

- DECnet—**decnet**
- DECnet multicast address for all Level 1 routers—**decnet_router-L1**
- DECnet multicast address for all Level 2 routers—**decnet_router-L2**
- DECnet multicast address for all end systems—**decnet_node**
- IP—**ip**
- ISO CLNS—**clns**
- Multicast address for all CLNS intermediate systems—**clns_is**
- Multicast address for all CLNS end systems—**clns_es**
- Novell IPX—**ipx**
- XNS—**xns**

For examples of mapping to a multicast address, see the examples in the section "SMDS Configuration Examples," later in this chapter.

Enabling ARP

When you enable the Address Resolution Protocol (ARP), you can choose to enable either a dynamic ARP cache or one built statically. To enable ARP, perform one of the following tasks in the specified configuration mode:

Task	Command
Enable ARP and dynamic address resolution (interface).	**smds enable-arp**
Enable ARP with a static entry for the remote router (global).	**arp** *ip-address smds-address* **smds**

An SMDS network can be thought of in much the same way as an X.25 cloud. The premises equipment (in this case Cisco routers) represents the edge of the cloud. The service provider enables communication across the cloud. However, proper configuration is needed for communication to occur. This configuration will differ between protocol families.

One major difference between protocol families is dynamic versus static routing among the routers (called remote peers) on the periphery of the cloud. For IP, routing across the SMDS cloud is fully dynamic. No action on the user's part is needed to map higher-level protocol addresses to SMDS addresses. Both IP and ARP can be configured and a dynamic ARP routing table enabled.

NOTES

The **arp smds** command requires 12-digit dotted-notation SMDS addresses—for example, C141.5678.9012.

See the section "Configuring Specific Protocols," later in this chapter for more information about configuring higher-level protocols.

Enabling Broadcast ARP Messages

When an ARP server is present in the network, you can enable broadcast ARP messages that are sent to all ARP SMDS addresses or to all IP SMDS multicast addresses when ARP addresses are not present.

To enable broadcast ARP messages, perform the following tasks in interface configuration mode:

Task	Command
Enable ARP and dynamic address resolution.	**smds enable-arp**
Enable broadcast ARP messages.	**smds multicast arp** *smds-address* [*ip-address mask*]

For an example of how to enable broadcast ARP messages, see the section "Typical Multiprotocol Configuration Example," later in this chapter.

Enabling Dynamic Address Mapping for IPX over SMDS

To enable dynamic address mapping for IPX on an SMDS interface, perform the following task in interface configuration mode:

Task	Command
Enable dynamic address mapping for IPX.	**smds glean ipx** [*timeout-value*] [broadcast]

For an example of how to enable dynamic address mapping for IPX over SMDS, see the section "IPX Dynamic Address Mapping Example," later in this chapter.

CUSTOMIZING YOUR SMDS NETWORK

Perform the tasks in the following list, as appropriate, for your network:

- Configuring Specific Protocols
- Enabling Transparent Bridging over SMDS
- Configuring SMDS Subinterfaces for Multiple Logical IP Subnetworks
- Reenabling the Data Exchange Interface Version 3.2 with Heartbeat Support
- Configuring Pseudobroadcasting
- Enabling Fast Switching

Configuring Specific Protocols

Some protocol families are dynamically routed. For IP and CLNS, routing is fully dynamic, and no action is needed on your part to map higher-level protocol addresses to SMDS addresses. But for the other supported protocols, you must make a static entry for each router to communicate with all other peer routers. The static entries need to be made only for those routers that are SMDS remote peers. Nothing additional needs to be done to assure communication with other nodes behind the peer routers.

For an example of how to configure specific protocols, see the section "Typical Multiprotocol Configuration Example," later in this chapter.

Table 9–1 lists protocol families and the multicasts that are needed.

Table 9–1 *Protocol Families and Types of Multicasts Needed*

Protocol Family	Multicasts Needed
IP	IP
DECnet	DECNET, DECNET_NODE, DECNET_ROUTER-L1, DECNET_ROUTER-L2
CLNS	CLNS, CLNS_ES, CLNS_IS

Table 9–1 *Protocol Families and Types of Multicasts Needed, Continued*

Protocol Family	Multicasts Needed
Novell IPX	IPX
XNS	XNS
AppleTalk	APPLETALK, AARP
Banyan VINES	VINES

Configuring ARP and IP

For both IP and ARP, the multicast address must be configured and ARP must be enabled. ARP multicast is required only for ARP servers; the IP multicast is used for ARP and routing updates.

Configuring DECnet

Static maps must be configured for DECnet. In addition, a separate **smds multicast** command is needed for DECNET, DECNET_NODE, DECNET_ROUTER-L1, and DECNET_ROUTER-L2.

Configuring CLNS

Multicasts must be configured for CLNS_ES and CLNS_IS. No static maps are necessary. End system hello (ESH), intermediate system hello (ISH), and router hello packets are sent to the multicast address, and neighbor entries are created automatically.

Configuring IPX

For Novell IPX, the multicast address must be configured. A static map entry can be made for each remote peer, or you can use the **smds glean** command to dynamically map addresses. Static map entries override any dynamic map entries.

Routing Information Protocol (RIP) routing packets, Service Advertisement Protocol (SAP) packets, NetBIOS Name Lookups, directed broadcasts, and traffic to the helper addresses (if that helper address is a broadcast address) are sent to the SMDS IPX multicast address.

Configuring XNS

For XNS, the multicast address must be configured, and a static map entry must be made for each remote peer. Only RIP, directed broadcasts, and helper traffic are sent to the XNS multicast address.

Configuring AppleTalk

The SMDS cloud must be treated by all AppleTalk routers connected to it as either extended or nonextended. The network types cannot be mixed on the same SMDS cloud. Instead, all AppleTalk routers on an SMDS cloud must agree about the network type: extended or nonextended.

If any router in the SMDS cloud uses Cisco IOS Release 10.3(3) (or earlier), use a nonextended AppleTalk configuration for the SMDS cloud. To use nonextended AppleTalk, use the **appletalk address** command and configure static maps.

If all routers in the SMDS cloud use Cisco IOS Release 10.3(4) (or later), you can use extended AppleTalk to support dynamic AARP for SMDS addresses. To use extended AppleTalk, use the **appletalk cable-range** command.

For an example of how to configure AppleTalk, see the section "AppleTalk Configuration Examples," later in this chapter.

Configuring Banyan VINES

For Banyan VINES, the multicast address must be configured. Also note that VINES works only with static maps.

Enabling Transparent Bridging over SMDS

You can enable transparent bridging for SMDS encapsulated serial and HSSI interfaces. Cisco's implementation of IEEE 802.6i transparent bridging for SMDS supports 802.3, 802.5, and FDDI frame formats. The router can accept frames with or without frame check sequence (FCS).

Fast-switched transparent bridging is the default and is not configurable. If a packet cannot be fast switched, it will be process switched.

To enable transparent bridging, perform the following tasks beginning in global configuration mode:

Task		Command
Step 1	Specify a serial or HSSI interface.	**interface** *type number*
Step 2	Configure SMDS encapsulation on the serial interface.	**encapsulation smds**
Step 3	Associate the interface with a bridge group.	**bridge-group** *bridge-group*
Step 4	Configure bridging across SMDS.	**smds multicast bridge** *smds-address*

Configuring SMDS Subinterfaces for Multiple Logical IP Subnetworks

Multiple logical IP subnetworks are supported as defined by RFC 1209. This RFC explains routing IP over an SMDS cloud where each connection is considered a host on one specific private network, and describes cases where traffic must transit from network to network.

This solution allows a single SMDS interface to be treated as multiple logical IP subnetworks and to support routing of packets from one network to the next without using intervening routers. When multiple logical IP subnetworks are enabled, the router performs routing between the subnetworks using IP addresses on an SMDS interface. Each supported subnetwork has an IP address, a unicast SMDS E.164 address, and a multicast SMDS E.164 address configured on the SMDS interface. Broadcast packets are duplicated and transmitted to all IP networks on the specified SMDS interface and use the associated multicast SMDS address for the network.

Only routers that require knowledge of multiple IP networks need to be configured with multipoint subinterfaces that correspond to different networks.

To configure the Cisco IOS software to have multipoint subinterfaces for multiple logical IP subnetworks, perform the following tasks in interface configuration mode:

Task	Command
Step 1 Define a logical subinterface for each IP network.	**interface serial** *number.subinterface-number* **multipoint** **interface serial** *slot/port.subinterface* **multipoint** (for Cisco 7000 series routers[*])
Step 2 Configure the subinterface as an IP network.	**ip address** *ip-address mask*
Step 3 Assign a unicast SMDS E.164 address to the subinterface.	**smds address** *smds-address*
Step 4 Assign a multicast SMDS E.164 address for each protocol supported on the subinterface.	**smds multicast** *protocol smds-address*
Step 5 Enable ARP on the subinterface, if required by the protocol.	**smds enable-arp**

[*] In Cisco IOS Release 11.3, all commands supported on the Cisco 7500 series are also supported on the Cisco 7000 series.

For an example of how to configure multiple logical IP subnetworks, see the "Multiple Logical IP Subnetworks over SMDS Example" section later in this chapter.

Reenabling the Data Exchange Interface Version 3.2 with Heartbeat Support

By default, SMDS provides the Data Exchange Interface (DXI) Version 3.2 *heartbeat* process as specified in the SIG-TS-001/1991 standard. The DXI mechanism encapsulates SMDS packets in a DXI frame before they are transmitted. The heartbeat mechanism automatically generates a heartbeat poll frame every 10 seconds. The Interim Local Management Interface (ILMI) is not supported.

NOTES

If you are running serial lines back-to-back, disable keepalive on SMDS interfaces. Otherwise, DXI declares the link down.

If you find you must reenable the DXI heartbeat, perform the following task in interface configuration mode:

Task	Command
Enable DXI 3.2.	**smds dxi**

Configuring Pseudobroadcasting

Some hosts do not support multicast E.164 addresses. This is a problem in IP where frequent broadcast packets are sent because routing updates are generally broadcast. IP and ARP depend on the use of multicast addresses to determine a route to a destination IP address. A mechanism was needed to artificially support the use of broadcast where multicast E.164 addresses do not exist; the result is *pseudobroadcasting*. If a multicast address is not available to a destination, pseudobroadcasting can be enabled to broadcast packets to those destinations using a unicast address.

To configure pseudobroadcasting, perform the following task in interface configuration mode:

Task	Command
Configure pseudobroadcasting.	**smds static-map ip** *ip-address smds-address* **broadcast**

For an example of how to configure pseudobroadcasting, see the "Pseudobroadcasting Example" section later in this chapter.

Enabling Fast Switching

SMDS fast switching of IP, IPX, and AppleTalk packets provides faster packet transfer on serial links with speeds above 56 Kbps. Use fast switching if you use high-speed, packet-switched, datagram-based WAN technologies such as Frame Relay offered by service providers.

By default, SMDS fast switching is enabled.

To re-enable fast switching, perform the following tasks beginning in interface configuration mode:

Task		Command
Step 1	Define the type and unit number of the interface, and enter interface configuration mode.	**interface** *type number*
Step 2	Set SMDS encapsulation.	**encapsulation smds**
Step 3	Enable the interface for IP fast switching.	**ip route-cache**
Step 4	Enable the interface for IPX fast switching.	**ipx route-cache**
Step 5	Enable the interface for AppleTalk fast switching.	**appletalk route-cache**

MONITORING THE SMDS CONNECTION

To monitor the SMDS connection, perform one or more of the following tasks in EXEC mode:

Task	Command
Monitor ARP activity.	show arp
Display the individual addresses and the interface with which they are associated.	show smds addresses
Display all SMDS addresses that are mapped to higher-level protocol addresses.	show smds map
Display packet traffic activity.	show smds traffic

SMDS CONFIGURATION EXAMPLES

The following section provides typical configuration file examples you can use as models for your network configurations. The following examples are provided:

- Typical Multiprotocol Configuration Example
- Remote Peer on the Same Network Example
- IPX Dynamic Address Mapping Example
- AppleTalk Configuration Examples
- Multiple Logical IP Subnetworks over SMDS Example
- Pseudobroadcasting Example

Typical Multiprotocol Configuration Example

The following example is a typical interface configured for IP, DECnet, ISO CLNS, Novell IPX, XNS, and AppleTalk. DECnet needs to be configured globally and at the interface level:

```
interface serial 4
 ip address 1.1.1.2 255.0.0.0
 decnet cost 4
 appletalk address 92.1
 appletalk zone smds
 clns router igrp FOO
 ipx net 1a
 xns net 17
 encapsulation SMDS
! SMDS configuration follows
 smds address c120.1580.4721
 smds static-map APPLETALK 92.2 c120.1580.4592
 smds static-map APPLETALK 92.3 c120.1580.4593
 smds static-map APPLETALK 92.4 c120.1580.4594
 smds static-map NOVELL 1a.0c00.0102.23ca c120.1580.4792
 smds static-map XNS 17.0c00.0102.23ca c120.1580.4792
```

```
smds static-map NOVELL 1a.0c00.0102.23dd c120.1580.4728
smds static-map XNS 17.0c00.0102.23aa c120.1580.4727
smds multicast NOVELL e180.0999.9999
smds multicast XNS e180.0999.9999
smds multicast ARP e180.0999.9999
smds multicast IP e180.0999.9999
smds multicast APPLETALK e180.0999.9999
smds multicast AARP e180.0999.9999
smds multicast CLNS_IS e180.0999.9990
smds multicast CLNS_ES e180.0999.9990
smds multicast DECNET_ROUTER e180.0999.9992
smds multicast DECNET_NODE e180.0999.9992
smds multicast DECNET e180.0999.9992
smds enable-arp
```

Remote Peer on the Same Network Example

The following example illustrates a remote peer on the same SMDS network. DECnet needs to be configured globally and at the interface level:

```
interface serial 0
ip address 1.1.1.1 255.0.0.0
decnet cost 4
appletalk address 92.2
appletalk zone smds
clns router igrp FOO
ipx net 1a
xns net 17
encapsulation SMDS
! SMDS configuration follows
smds address c120.1580.4792
smds static-map APPLETALK 92.1 c120.1580.4721
smds static-map APPLETALK 92.3 c120.1580.4593
smds static-map APPLETALK 92.4 c120.1580.4594
smds static-map NOVELL 1a.0c00.0102.23cb c120.1580.4721
smds static-map XNS 17.0c00.0102.23cb c120.1580.4721
smds static-map NOVELL 1a.0c00.0102.23dd c120.1580.4728
smds static-map XNS 17.0c00.0102.23aa c120.1580.4727
smds multicast NOVELL e180.0999.9999
smds multicast XNS e180.0999.9999
smds multicast IP e180.0999.9999
smds multicast APPLETALK e180.0999.9999
smds multicast AARP e180.0999.9999
smds multicast CLNS_IS e180.0999.9990
smds multicast CLNS_ES e180.0999.9990
smds multicast DECNET_ROUTER e180.0999.9992
smds multicast DECNET_NODE e180.0999.9992
smds multicast DECNET e180.0999.9992
smds enable-arp
```

IPX Dynamic Address Mapping Example

The following example enables dynamic address mapping for IPX on interface serial 0 and sets the time to live (TTL) to 14 minutes:

```
interface serial 0
 encapsulation smds
 smds address c141.5797.1313
 smds multicast ipx e180.0999.9999
 smds glean ipx 14
```

AppleTalk Configuration Examples

The following two sections provide basic examples of configuration for an extended AppleTalk network and for a nonextended AppleTalk network.

Extended AppleTalk Network Example

If all AppleTalk routers on the SMDS cloud are running Cisco IOS software Release 10.3(4) (or later), you can use an AppleTalk extended network. To do so, use the **appletalk cable-range** interface command.

When SMDS is configured for an extended AppleTalk network, SMDS static maps are not required and not used. Dynamic AARP is supported on the multicast channel. Following is an example using the **appletalk cable-range** command:

```
interface Serial0
 ip address 192.168.200.1 255.255.255.0
 encapsulation smds
 appletalk cable-range 10-10
 appletalk zone SMDS
 smds address c151.0988.1923
 smds static-map ip 192.168.200.2 c151.0988.8770
 smds multicast APPLETALK e151.0988.2232
 smds multicast AARP e151.0988.2232
 smds multicast IP e151.0988.2232
 smds multicast ARP e151.0988.2232
 smds enable-arp
```

Nonextended Appletalk Network Example

When SMDS is configured for a nonextended AppleTalk network, SMDS static maps are required and the **appletalk address** command is used. Dynamic AppleTalk Address Resolution Protocol (AARP) is not supported on the multicast channel. The following example configures SMDS for a nonextended AppleTalk network:

```
interface Serial0
 ip address 192.168.200.1 255.255.255.0
 encapsulation smds
 appletalk address 10.1
 appletalk zone SMDS
 smds address c151.0988.1923
 smds static-map ip 192.168.200.2 c151.0988.8770
 smds static-map appletalk 10.2 c151.0988.8770
 smds multicast APPLETALK e151.0988.2232
 smds multicast IP e151.0988.2232
 smds multicast ARP e151.0988.2232
 smds enable-arp
```

Multiple Logical IP Subnetworks over SMDS Example

In the following example, Routers A, B, and C are connected to an SMDS cloud by means of two logical subnetworks labelled 1 and 2 (see Figure 9–2).

Router A recognizes two IP networks and can communicate with Routers B and C directly. Router B can communicate with Router A directly, and with Router C via Router A. Router C can communicate with Router A directly and with Router B via Router A.

Notice that a packet destined to Router B from Router C must make two hops on the cloud through the same interface on Router A. Notice also that this configuration is nonstandard. This issue was considered when the multiple logical IP subnetworks proposal was made, and was deemed not to be critical.

Figure 9–2
This diagram shows an example of multiple logical IP subnetworks configuration.

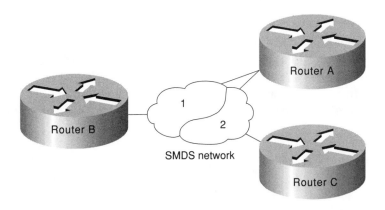

The following examples show all routers as Cisco 7000 routers, but they can be other platforms:

NOTES

In Cisco IOS Release 11.3, all commands supported on the Cisco 7500 series are also supported on the Cisco 7000 series.

Configuration for Router A

```
interface serial 2/0
 encapsulation smds
!
interface serial 2/0.1 multipoint
 smds addr c111.3333.3333
 ip address 2.2.2.1 255.0.0.0
 smds multicast ip e122.2222.2222
 smds enable-arp
 smds multicast ARP e122.2222.2222
```

Configuration for Router B

```
interface serial 4/0
 encapsulation smds
 smds address c111.2222.2222
 ip address 1.1.1.3 255.0.0.0
 smds multicast ip e180.0999.9999
 smds enable-arp
```

Configuration for Router C

```
interface serial 1/0
 encapsulation smds
 smds address c111.4444.4444
 ip address 2.2.2.2 255.0.0.0
 smds multicast ip e122.2222.2222
 smds enable-arp
```

Pseudobroadcasting Example

In the following example, an ARP broadcast from Router A is sent to multicast address
E180.0999.9999.FFFF to Router B and to unicast address C120.1234.5678.FFFF to Router C; the
reply from Router C uses the unicast address C120.1111.2222.FFFF for the return reply if it is the
target of the ARP request. IGRP broadcast updates follow the same rules:

Configuration for Router A

```
interface s 0
 encapsulation smds
 smds address c120.1111.2222
 ip address 172.20.1.30 255.255.255.0
 smds multicast ip e180.0999.9999
 smds static-map ip 172.20.1.10 c120.1234.5678 broadcast
 smds enable-arp
```

Configuration for Router B

```
interface s 4
 smds address c120.9999.8888
 ip address 172.20.1.20
 smds multicast ip e180.0999.9999
 smds enable-arp
```

Configuration for Router C

```
interface serial 2
 smds address c120.1234.5678
 ip address 172.20.1.10
 smds static-map ip 172.20.1.30 c120.1111.2222 broadcast
 smds enable-arp
```

CHAPTER 10

SMDS Commands

Use the commands in this chapter to configure the Switched Multimegabit Data Service (SMDS), a wide-area networking service offered by some Regional Bell Operating Companies (RBOCs) and MCI.

For SMDS configuration information and examples see Chapter 9, "Configuring SMDS."

NOTES

You can use the master indexes or search online to find documentation of related commands.

ARP

Use the following variation of the **arp** global configuration command to enable Address Resolution Protocol (ARP) entries for static routing over the SMDS network. Use the **no** form of this command to disable this capability.

> **arp** *ip-address smds-address* **smds**
> **no arp** *ip-address smds-address* **smds**

Syntax	Description
ip-address	IP address of the remote router.
smds-address	12-digit SMDS address in the dotted notation *nnnn.nnnn.nnnn* (48 bits long).
smds	Enables ARP for SMDS.

Default

Disabled

Command Mode

Global configuration

Usage Guidelines

This command first appeared in Cisco IOS Release 10.3.

This command requires a 12-digit (48-bit) dotted-format SMDS address. It does not support 15-digit SMDS addresses.

Example

The following example creates a static ARP entry that maps the IP address 172.20.173.28 to the SMDS address C141.5797.1313 on interface serial 0:

```
interface serial 0
  arp 172.20.173.28 C141.5797.1313 smds
```

Related Commands

smds enable-arp
smds static-map

ENCAPSULATION SMDS

Use the **encapsulation smds** interface configuration command to enable SMDS service on the desired interface.

> encapsulation smds

Syntax Description

This command has no arguments or keywords.

Default

Disabled

Command Mode

Interface configuration

Usage Guidelines

This command first appeared in Cisco IOS Release 10.0.

The interface to which this command applies must be a serial interface. All subsequent SMDS configuration commands apply only to an interface with encapsulation SMDS.

NOTES

The maximum packet size allowed in the SMDS specifications (TA-772) is 9188. This is larger than the packet size used by servers with most media. The Cisco default maximum transmission unit (MTU) size is 1500 bytes to be consistent with Ethernet. However, on the High Speed Serial Interface (HSSI), the default MTU size is 4470 bytes. If a larger MTU is used, the **mtu** command must be entered before the **encapsulation smds** command.

CAUTION

The Cisco MCI card has buffer limitations that prevent setting the MTU size higher than 2048, and the HSSI card has buffer limitations that prevent setting the MTU size higher than 4500. Configuring higher settings can cause inconsistencies and performance problems.

Example

The following example shows how to configure the SMDS service on serial interface 0:

```
interface serial 0
  encapsulation smds
```

Related Commands

mtu

INTERFACE SERIAL MULTIPOINT

To define a logical subinterface on a serial interface to support multiple logical IP subnetworks over SMDS, use the **interface serial multipoint** interface configuration command.

interface serial *interface.subinterface* **multipoint**

Syntax	Description
interface	Interface number.
subinterface	Number for this subinterface; values in the range 0 to 255.

Default

This command has no default values.

Usage Guidelines

This command first appeared in Cisco IOS Release 10.0.

Use this command only for routers that need knowledge of multiple IP networks. Other routers can be configured with information only about their own networks.

Command Reference

Example

The following example configures serial interface 2 with multipoint logical subinterface 1:

```
interface serial 2.1 multipoint
```

Related Commands

ip address
smds address
smds enable-arp
smds multicast

SHOW ARP

Use the **show arp** privileged EXEC command to display the entries in the ARP table.

    show arp

Syntax Description

This command has no arguments or keywords.

Command Mode

Privileged EXEC

Usage Guidelines

This command first appeared in Cisco IOS Release 10.0.

Sample Display

Following is sample output from the **show arp** command:

```
Router# show arp
Protocol   Address        Age (min)   Hardware Addr    Type   Interface
Internet   172.20.42.112  120         0000.a710.4baf   ARPA   Ethernet3
AppleTalk  4028.5         29          0000.0c01.0e56   SNAP   Ethernet2
Internet   172.20.42.114  105         0000.a710.859b   ARPA   Ethernet3
AppleTalk  4028.9         -           0000.0c02.a03c   SNAP   Ethernet2
Internet   172.20.42.121  42          0000.a710.68cd   ARPA   Ethernet3
Internet   172.20.36.9    -           0000.3080.6fd4   SNAP   TokenRing0
AppleTalk  4036.9         -           0000.3080.6fd4   SNAP   TokenRing0
Internet   172.20.33.9    -           c222.2222.2222   SMDS   Serial0
```

Table 10–1 describes significant fields shown in the first line of output in this display.

Table 10–1 *Show ARP Field Descriptions*

Field	Description
Protocol	Type of network address this entry includes.

Table 10–1   *Show ARP Field Descriptions, Continued*

Field	Description
Address	Network address that is mapped to the media access control (MAC) address in this entry.
Age (min)	Interval (in minutes) since this entry was entered in the table, rather than the interval since the entry was last used. (The timeout value is four hours.)
Hardware Addr	MAC address mapped to the network address in this entry.
Type	Encapsulation type used for the network address in this entry. Possible values include: • ARPA • SNAP • ETLK (EtherTalk) • SMDS
Interface	Interface associated with this network address.

SHOW SMDS ADDRESSES

Use the **show smds addresses** privileged EXEC command to display the individual addresses and the interface with which they are associated.

    show smds addresses

Syntax Description

This command has no arguments or keywords.

Command Mode

Privileged EXEC

Usage Guidelines

This command first appeared in Cisco IOS Release 10.0.

Sample Display

Following is sample output from the **show smds addresses** command:

```
Router# show smds addresses
SMDS address - Serial0   c141.5555.1212.FFFF
```

Table 10–2 describes the fields shown in this display.

Command Reference

Table 10–2 *Show SMDS Addresses Field Descriptions*

Field	Description
Serial0	Interface to which this SMDS address has been assigned.
c141.5555.1212	SMDS address that has been assigned to the interface.

SHOW SMDS MAP

To display all SMDS addresses that are mapped to higher-level protocol addresses, use the **show smds map** privileged EXEC command.

    show smds map

Syntax Description

This command has no arguments or keywords.

Command Mode

Privileged EXEC

Usage Guidelines

This command first appeared in Cisco IOS Release 10.0.

Sample Display

Following is sample output from the **show smds map** command:

```
Router# show smds map
Serial0: ARP maps to e180.0999.9999.FFFF multicast
Serial0: IP maps to e180.0999.9999.FFFF 172.16.42.112 255.255.255.0 multicast
Serial0: XNS 1006.AA00.0400.0C55 maps to c141.5688.1212.FFFF static [broadcast]
Serial0: IPX 1ABC.000.0c00.d8db maps to c111.1111.1111.1111 -- dynamic, TTL: 4 min
```

Table 10–3 describes the fields shown in this output.

Table 10–3 *Show SMDS Map Field Descriptions*

Field	Description
Serial0	Name of interface on which SMDS has been enabled.
ARP maps to	Higher-level protocol address that maps to this particular SMDS address.
e180.0999.9999.FFFF	SMDS address. Includes all SMDS addresses entered with either the **smds static-map** command (static) or **smds multicast** command (multicast).
172.16.42.112	IP address.
255.255.255.0	Subnet mask for the IP address.

Table 10–3 *Show SMDS Map Field Descriptions, Continued*

Field	Description
static/dynamic	The address was obtained from a static map or dynamic map.
TTL	Time to live.

SHOW SMDS TRAFFIC

To display statistics about SMDS packets the router has received, use the **show smds traffic** privileged EXEC command.

    show smds traffic

Syntax Description

This command has no arguments or keywords.

Command Mode

Privileged EXEC

Usage Guidelines

This command first appeared in Cisco IOS Release 10.0.

Sample Display

Following is sample output from the **show smds traffic** command:

```
Router# show smds traffic
624363 Input packets
759695 Output packets
2 DXI heartbeat sent
0 DXI heartbeat received
0 DXI DSU polls received
0 DXI DSU polls sent
0 DXI invalid test frames
0 Bad BA size errors
0 Bad Header extension errors
65 Invalid address errors
1 Bad tag errors
```

Table 10–4 describes the fields shown in this output.

Table 10–4 *Show SMDS Traffic Field Descriptions*

Field	Description
0 Input packets	Number of input packets.
0 Output packets	Number of output packets.

Command Reference

Table 10–4   *Show SMDS Traffic Field Descriptions, Continued*

Field	Description
0 DXI heartbeat sent	Number of Data Exchange Interface (DXI) heartbeat polls transmitted.
0 DXI heartbeat received	Number of DXI heartbeat polls received.
0 DXI DSU polls sent	Number of DXI Data Service Unit (DSU) polls sent.
0 DXI DSU polls received	Number of DXI DSU polls received.
0 DXI invalid test frames	Number of invalid test frames seen.
0 Bad BA size errors	Number of packets that have a size less than 32 bytes or greater than 9188 bytes.
0 DXI Header extension errors	Number of extended SMDS Interface Protocol (SIP) Layer 3 header errors.
0 DXI Invalid address errors	Number of address errors.
0 Bad tag errors	Status indicating the number of errors that occur when there is a mismatch between the Tag value in the header and the BeTag value in the trailer of an SMDS frame. This usually indicates that there is a misconfiguration (that is, a DXI is connected to a non-DXI) or that the SMDS data service unit (SDSU) is scrambling the Layer 2 protocol data units (PDUs).

SMDS ADDRESS

To specify the SMDS individual address for a particular interface, use the **smds address** interface configuration command. To remove the address from the configuration file, use the **no** form of this command.

> **smds address** *smds-address*
> **no smds address** *smds-address*

Syntax	Description
smds-address	Individual address provided by the SMDS service provider. This address is protocol independent.

Default

No address is specified.

Command Mode

Interface configuration

Usage Guidelines

This command first appeared in Cisco IOS Release 10.0.

All addresses for SMDS service are assigned by the service provider; they can be assigned to individuals and groups.

Addresses are entered in the Cisco SMDS configuration software using an E prefix for *multicast* addresses and a C prefix for *unicast* addresses. Cisco IOS software expects the addresses to be entered in E.164 format, which is 64 bits. The first 4 bits are the address type, and the remaining 60 bits are the address. If the first 4 bits are 1100 (0xC), the address is a unicast SMDS address, which is the address of an individual SMDS host. If the first 4 bits are 1110 (0xE), the address is a multicast SMDS address, which is used to broadcast a packet to multiple end points. The 60 bits of the address are in binary-coded decimal (BCD) format. Each 4 bits of the address field presents a single telephone number digit, allowing for up to 15 digits. At a minimum, you must specify at least 11 digits (44 bits). Unused bits at the end of this field are filled with ones.

NOTES

If bridging is enabled on any interface, the SMDS address is erased and must be reentered.

Example

The following example specifies an individual address in Ethernet-style notation:
```
interface serial 0
  smds address c141.5797.1313.FFFF
```

SMDS DXI

To enable the Data Exchange Interface (DXI) version 3.2 support, use the **smds dxi** interface configuration command. To disable the DXI 3.2 support, use the **no** form of this command.

    smds dxi

    no smds dxi

Syntax Description

This command has no arguments or keywords.

Default

Enabled

Command Reference

Command Mode

Interface configuration

Usage Guidelines

This command first appeared in Cisco IOS Release 10.0.

Adding this command to the configuration enables the DXI version 3.2 mechanism and encapsulates SMDS packets in a DXI frame before they are transmitted. DXI 3.2 adds an additional 4 bytes to the SMDS packet header to communicate with the SMDS data service unit (SDSU). These bytes specify the frame type. The interface expects all packets to arrive with DXI encapsulation.

The DXI 3.2 support also includes the *heartbeat* process as specified in the SIG-TS-001/1991 standard, revision 3.2. The heartbeat (active process) is enabled when both DXI and keepalives are enabled on the interface. The *echo* (passive process) is enabled when DXI is enabled on the interface. The heartbeat mechanism automatically generates a heartbeat poll frame every 10 seconds. This default value can be changed with the **keepalive** command.

The Interim Local Management Interface (ILMI) is not supported.

— **NOTES** ————————————————————————————————

If you are running serial lines back-to-back, disable keepalive on SMDS interfaces. Otherwise, DXI declares the link down.

— **NOTES** ————————————————————————————————

Switching in or out of DXI mode causes the IP cache to be cleared. This clearing process is necessary to remove all cached IP entries for the serial line being used. Stale entries must be removed to allow the new media access control (MAC) header with or without DXI framing to be installed in the cache. This clearing process is not frequently done and is not considered to be a major performance penalty.

Fast switching of DXI frames is also supported.

Example

The following example enables DXI 3.2 on interface HSSI 0:

```
interface hssi 0
  encapsulation smds
  smds dxi
  smds address C120.1111.2222.FFFF
  ip address 172.20.1.30 255.255.255.0
  smds multicast ip E180.0999.9999
  smds enable-arp
```

Related Commands

keepalive

SMDS ENABLE-ARP

To enable dynamic Address Resolution Protocol (ARP), use the **smds enable-arp** interface configuration command. The multicast address for ARP must be set before this command is issued. Once ARP has been enabled, use the **no** form of this command to disable the interface.

    smds enable-arp
    no smds enable-arp

Syntax Description

This command has no arguments or keywords.

Default

Disabled

Command Mode

Interface configuration

Usage Guidelines

This command first appeared in Cisco IOS Release 10.0.

Example

The following example enables the dynamic ARP routing table:

```
interface serial 0
 ip address 172.20.1.30 255.255.255.0
 smds multicast IP E180.0999.9999.2222
 smds enable-arp
```

Related Commands

arp

SMDS GLEAN

To enable dynamic address mapping for IPX over SMDS, use the **smds glean** interface configuration command. To disable dynamic address mapping for IPX over SMDS, use the **no** form of this command.

    smds glean *protocol* [*timeout value*] [**broadcast**]
    no smds glean *protocol*

Command Reference

Syntax	*Description*
protocol	Protocol type. Only IPX is supported.
timeout value	(Optional) Time to live (TTL) value. This value can be from 1 to 65535 minutes. The default is 5 minutes. This value indicates how long a gleaned dynamic map is stored in the SMDS map table.
broadcast	(Optional) This marks the gleaned protocol address as a candidate for broadcast packets. All broadcast requests are sent to the unicast SMDS address.

Default

Disabled

Command Mode

Interface configuration

Usage Guidelines

This command first appeared in Cisco IOS Release 11.1.

The **smds glean** command uses incoming packets to dynamically map SMDS addresses to higher-level protocol addresses. Therefore, the need for static map configuration for the IPX protocol is optional rather than mandatory. However, any static map configuration overrides the dynamic maps.

If a map is gleaned and it already exists as a dynamic map, the timer for the dynamic map is reset to either the default value or the user-specified value.

Example

The following example enables dynamic address mapping for IPX on interface serial 0 and sets the time to live (TTL) to 14 minutes:

```
interface serial 0
  encapsulation smds
  smds address c141.5797.1313.FFFF
  smds multicast ipx e1800.0999.9999.FFFF
  smds glean ipx 14
```

SMDS MULTICAST

To assign a multicast SMDS E.164 address to a higher-level protocol, use the **smds multicast** interface configuration command. To remove an assigned multicast address, use the **no** form of this command with the appropriate address.

    smds multicast *protocol smds-address*
    no smds multicast *protocol smds-address*

Syntax	Description
protocol	Protocol type. See Table 10–5 for a list of supported protocols and their keywords.
smds-address	SMDS address. Because SMDS does not incorporate broadcast addressing, a group address for a particular protocol must be defined to serve the broadcast function.

Default

No mapping is defined.

Command Mode

Interface configuration

Usage Guidelines

This command first appeared in Cisco IOS Release 10.0.

When configuring DECnet, you must enter all four DEC keywords (**decnet, decnet_router-L1, decnet_router-L2,** and **decnet_node**) in the configuration.

Table 10–5 lists the high-level protocols supported by the **smds multicast** command.

Table 10–5   *SMDS Multicast Supported Protocols*

Keyword	Protocol
aarp	AppleTalk Address Resolution Protocol
appletalk	AppleTalk
arp	Address Resolution Protocol
bridge	Transparent bridging
clns	International Organization for Standardization (ISO) Connectionless Network Service (CLNS)
clns_es	Multicast address for all CLNS end systems
clns_is	Multicast address for all CLNS intermediate systems
decnet	DECnet
decnet_node	DECnet multicast address for all end systems
decnet_router-L1	DECnet multicast address for all Level 1 (intra-area) routers
decnet_router-L2	DECnet multicast address for all Level 2 (interarea) routers
ip	Internet Protocol (IP)
ipx	Novell IPX

Command Reference

Table 10–5   *SMDS Multicast Supported Protocols, Continued*

Keyword	Protocol
vines	Banyan VINES
xns	Xerox Network Systems (XNS)

For IP, the IP NETwork and MASK fields are no longer required. The Cisco IOS software accepts these arguments, but ignores the values. These were required commands for the previous multiple logical IP subnetworks configuration. The software continues to accept the arguments to allow for backward compatibility, but ignores the contents.

Example

The following example maps the IP broadcast address to the SMDS group address E180.0999.9999:

```
interface serial 0
 smds multicast IP E180.0999.9999.FFFF
```

SMDS MULTICAST ARP

To map the SMDS address to a multicast address, use the **smds multicast arp** interface configuration command. Use the **no** form of this command to disable this feature.

> **smds multicast arp** *smds-address* [*ip-address mask*]
> **no smds multicast arp** *smds-address* [*ip-address mask*]

Syntax	Description
smds-address	SMDS address in E.164 format.
ip-address	(Optional) IP address.
mask	(Optional) Subnet mask for the IP address.

Default

No mapping is defined.

Command Mode

Interface configuration

Usage Guidelines

This command first appeared in Cisco IOS Release 10.0.

This command is used only when an Address Resolution Protocol (ARP) server is present on a network. When broadcast ARPs are sent, SMDS first attempts to send the packet to all multicast ARP SMDS addresses. If none exist in the configuration, broadcast ARPs are sent to all multicast IP

SMDS multicast addresses. If the optional ARP multicast address is missing, each entered IP multicast command is used for broadcasting.

Example

The following example configures broadcast ARP messages:
```
interface serial 0
  smds multicast arp E180.0999.9999.2222
```

Related Commands

smds multicast ip

SMDS MULTICAST BRIDGE

To enable spanning tree updates, use the **smds multicast bridge** interface configuration command. Use the **no** form of this command to disable this function.

> **smds multicast bridge** *smds-address*
> **no smds multicast bridge** *smds-address*

Syntax	Description
smds-address	SMDS multicast address in E.164 format.

Default

No multicast SMDS address is defined. Spanning tree updates are disabled for transparent bridging across SMDS networks.

Command Mode

Interface configuration

Usage Guidelines

This command first appeared in Cisco IOS Release 10.0.

To allow transparent bridging of packets across serial and HSSI interfaces in an SMDS network, the SMDS interface must be added to an active bridge group. Also, standard bridging commands are necessary to enable bridging on an SMDS interface.

When the **smds multicast bridge** command is added to the configuration, broadcast packets are encapsulated with the specified SMDS multicast address configured for bridging. Two broadcast ARP packets are sent to the multicast address. One is sent with a standard (SMDS) ARP encapsulation, while the other is sent with the ARP packet encapsulated in an 802.3 MAC header. The native ARP is sent as a regular ARP broadcast.

Cisco's implementation of IEEE 802.6i transparent bridging for SMDS supports 802.3, 802.5, and FDDI frame formats. The router can accept frames with or without frame check sequence (FCS).

Fast-switched transparent bridging is the default and is not configurable. If a packet cannot be fast switched, it is process switched.

In Cisco IOS Release 10.2 software (or earlier), bridging over multiple logical IP subnetworks is not supported. Bridging of IP packets in a multiple logical IP subnetwork environment is unpredictable.

Example

In the following example, all broadcast bridge packets are sent to the configured SMDS multicast address:

```
interface hssi 0
 encapsulation smds
 smds address C120.1111.2222.FFFF
 ip address 172.16.0.0 255.255.255.0
 smds multicast bridge E180.0999.9999.FFFF
 bridge-group 5
```

Related Commands

bridge-group

SMDS MULTICAST IP

To map an SMDS group address to a secondary IP address, use the smds multicast ip interface configuration command. Use the no form of this command to remove the address map.

    smds multicast ip *smds-address* [*ip-address mask*]
    no smds multicast ip *smds-address* [*ip-address mask*]

Syntax	Description
smds-address	SMDS address in E.164 format.
ip-address	(Optional) IP address.
mask	(Optional) Subnet mask for the IP address.

Defaults

The IP address and mask default to the primary address of the interface if they are left out of the configuration.

Command Mode

Interface configuration

Usage Guidelines

This command first appeared in Cisco IOS Release 10.0.

This command allows a single SMDS interface to be treated as multiple logical IP subnetworks. If taking advantage of the multiple logical IP subnetworks support in SMDS, you can use more than one multicast address on the SMDS interface (by entering multiple commands). However, each **smds multicast ip** command entry must be associated with a different IP address on the SMDS interface.

Broadcasts can be sent on the SMDS interface by means of the multicast address. By sending broadcasts in this manner, the router is not required to replicate broadcast messages to every remote host.

In addition, the higher-level protocols such as Open Shortest Path First (OSPF) and Intermediate System-to-Intermediate System (IS-IS) can use the multicast capability by sending one update packet or routing packet to the multicast address.

If the optional IP address and mask arguments are not present, the SMDS address and multicast address are associated with the primary IP address of the interface. This association allows the command to be backward compatible with earlier versions of the software.

If an Address Resolution Protocol (ARP) multicast address is missing, each entered IP multicast command is used for broadcasting. The ARP multicast command has the same format as the IP multicast command and is typically used only when an ARP server is present in the network.

NOTES

All routers at the other end of the SMDS cloud must have the multiple logical IP subnetworks capability enabled. If you allocate a different SMDS subinterface for each logical IP subnetwork on the SMDS interface, you do not have to configure secondary IP addresses.

Example

The following example configures an interface with two subinterfaces to support two different IP subnets with different multicast addresses to each network:

```
interface serial 2/0
 encapsulation smds
 smds address C120.1111.2222.4444
interface serial 2/0.1 multipoint
 smds addr c111.3333.3333.3333
 ip address 2.2.2.1 255.0.0.0
 smds multicast ip e222.2222.2222.2222
 smds enable-arp
interface serial 2/0.2 multipoint
 smds addr c111.2222.3333.3333.3333
 ip address 2.3.3.3 255.0.0.0
 smds multicast ip E180.0999.9999.FFFF
 smds enable-arp
```

Related Commands

smds multicast arp

SMDS STATIC-MAP

To configure a static map between an individual SMDS address and a higher-level protocol address, use the **smds static-map** interface configuration command. Use the **no** form of this command with the appropriate arguments to remove the map.

    smds static-map *protocol protocol-address smds-address* [**broadcast**]
    no smds static-map *protocol protocol-address smds-address* [**broadcast**]

Syntax	Description
protocol	Higher-level protocol. It can be one of the following values: **appletalk, clns, decnet, ip, ipx, vines,** or **xns**.
protocol-address	Address of the higher-level protocol.
smds-address	SMDS address to complete the mapping.
broadcast	(Optional) Marks the specified protocol address as a candidate for broadcast packets. All broadcast requests are sent to the unicast SMDS address.

Default

No mapping is defined.

Command Mode

Interface configuration

Usage Guidelines

This command first appeared in Cisco IOS Release 10.0.

The **smds static-map** command provides *pseudobroadcasting* by allowing the use of broadcasts on those hosts that cannot support SMDS multicast addresses.

Examples

This example illustrates how to enable pseudobroadcasting. The router at address C120.4444.9999 will receive a copy of the broadcast request because the broadcast keyword is specified with the **smds static-map** command. The host at address 172.16.1.15 is incapable of receiving multicast packets. The multicasting is simulated with this feature. This is accomplished by the following code:

```
interface hssi 0
 encapsulation smds
 smds address C120.1111.2222.FFFF
 ip address 172.16.1.30 255.255.255.0
 smds static-map ip 172.16.1.15 C120.4444.9999.FFFF broadcast
 smds enable-arp
```

This example illustrates how to enable multicasting. In addition to IP and ARP requests to E100.0999.9999, the router at address C120.4444.9999 will also receive a copy of the multicast request. The host at address 172.16.1.15 is incapable of receiving broadcast packets. The code needed to accomplish this is as follows:

```
interface hssi 0
 encapsulation smds
 smds address C120.1111.2222.FFFF
 ip address 172.16.1.30 255.255.255.0
 smds multicast ip E100.0999.999.FFFF
 smds static-map ip 172.16.1.15 C120.4444.9999.FFFF
 smds enable-arp
```

CHAPTER 11

Configuring X.25 and LAPB

This chapter describes how to configure connections through X.25 networks and Link Access Procedure, Balanced (LAPB) connections. LAPB procedures are presented first for those users who only want to configure a simple, reliable serial encapsulation method. This chapter also describes how to configure Defense Data Network (DDN) X.25 and the Blacker Front End (BFE). It includes coverage of how to create X.29 access lists as well.

For a complete description of the commands mentioned in this chapter, refer to Chapter 12, "X.25 and LAPB Commands."

NOTES

To locate documentation of other commands that appear in this chapter, use the command reference master index or search online.

LAPB CONFIGURATION TASK LIST

You can only use LAPB as a serial encapsulation method if you have a private serial line. You must use one of the X.25 packet-level encapsulations when attaching to an X.25 network.

The LAPB standards distinguish between two types of hosts: data terminal equipment (DTE) and data circuit-terminating equipment (DCE). At Level 2, or the data link layer in the OSI model, LAPB allows for orderly and reliable exchange of data between a DTE and a DCE. A router using LAPB encapsulation can act as a DTE or DCE device at the protocol level, which is distinct from the hardware DTE or DCE identity.

Using LAPB under noisy conditions can result in greater throughput than High-Level Data Link Control (HDLC) encapsulation. When LAPB detects a missing frame, the router retransmits the frame instead of waiting for the higher layers to recover the lost information. This behavior is good only if the host timers are relatively slow. In the case of quickly expiring host timers, however, you will discover that LAPB is spending much of its time transmitting host retransmissions. If the line is not noisy, the lower overhead of HDLC encapsulation is more efficient than LAPB. When you are using long-delay satellite links, for example, the lock-step behavior of LAPB makes HDLC encapsulation a better choice.

To configure LAPB, complete the tasks in the following list. The first task in the following list is required; the remaining tasks are optional:

- Configuring an LAPB Datagram Transport
- Modifying LAPB Protocol Parameters
- Configuring Priority and Custom Queuing for LAPB
- Configuring Transparent Bridging over Multiprotocol LAPB
- Monitoring and Maintaining LAPB and X.25

Examples of LAPB configurations are given at the end of this chapter.

CONFIGURING AN LAPB DATAGRAM TRANSPORT

To set the appropriate LAPB encapsulation to run datagrams over a serial interface, perform the following task in global configuration mode. One end of the link must be DTE, and the other must be DCE.

Task	Command
Specify a serial interface.	**interface serial** *number*

Because the default serial encapsulation is HDLC, you must explicitly configure an LAPB encapsulation method.

NOTES

Cisco recommends that you shut down an interface before changing the encapsulation.

To select an encapsulation and the protocol if using a single protocol, or to select the multiple protocol operation, perform one or more of the following tasks in interface configuration mode:

Task	Command
Enable encapsulation of a single protocol on the line using DCE operation.	**encapsulation lapb dce** [*protocol*]*
Enable encapsulation of a single protocol on the line using DTE operation.	**encapsulation lapb dte** [*protocol*]*

Task	Command
Enable multiple protocols on the line using DCE operation.	**encapsulation lapb dce multi**
Enable multiple protocols on the line using DTE operation.	**encapsulation lapb dte multi**[††]

* Single protocol LAPB defaults to IP encapsulation.
† Multiprotocol LAPB does not support source-route bridging or TCP/IP header compression, but does support transparent bridging.
‡ A multiprotocol LAPB encapsulation supports all of the protocols available to a single protocol LAPB encapsulation plus transparent bridging.

For an example of configuring LAPB operation, see the section "Typical LAPB Configuration Example," later in this chapter.

Configuring Compression of LAPB Data

You can configure point-to-point software compression on serial interfaces that use a LAPB or multi-LAPB encapsulation. Compression reduces the size of a LAPB or multi-LAPB frame via lossless data compression. Compression is performed in software and can significantly affect system performance. Cisco recommends that you disable compression if the router CPU load exceeds 65 percent. To display the CPU load, use the **show process cpu** EXEC command.

Predictor compression is recommended when the bottleneck is caused by the load on the router or access server; Stacker compression is recommended when the bottleneck is the result of line bandwidth. Compression is not recommended if the majority of your traffic already consists of compressed files. Compression is also not recommended for line speeds greater than T1 because the added processing time slows performance on fast lines.

To configure compression over LAPB, perform the following tasks in interface configuration mode:

Task	Command
Step 1 Enable encapsulation of a single protocol on the serial line.	**encapsulation lapb** [*protocol*]
Step 2 Enable compression.	**compress** [predictor | stac]

To configure compression over multi-LAPB, perform the following tasks in interface configuration mode:

Task	Command
Step 1 Enable encapsulation of multiple protocols on the serial line.	**encapsulation lapb multi**
Step 2 Enable compression.	**compress** [predictor | stac]

When you are using compression, adjust the maximum transmission unit (MTU) for the serial interface and the LAPB N1 parameter (as in the following example) to avoid informational diagnostics regarding excessive MTU or N1 sizes:

```
interface serial 0
encapsulation lapb
compress predictor
mtu 1509
lapb n1 12072
```

For information about configuring X.25 TCP/IP header compression and X.25 payload compression, see the "Setting X.25 TCP/IP Header Compression" and "Configuring X.25 Payload Compression" sections later in this chapter.

MODIFYING LAPB PROTOCOL PARAMETERS

X.25 Level 2, or LAPB, operates at the data link layer of the OSI reference model. LAPB specifies methods for exchanging data (in units called *frames*); it detects out-of-sequence or missing frames, retransmitting frames, and acknowledging frames. Several protocol parameters can be modified to change LAPB protocol performance on a particular link. Because X.25 operates the Packet Level Protocol (PLP) on top of the LAPB protocol, these tasks apply to both X.25 links and LAPB links. The parameters and their default values are summarized in Table 11–1.

Table 11–1   *LAPB Parameters*

Task (LAPB Parameter)	Command	Values or Ranges	Default
Set the modulo.	**lapb modulo** *modulus*	8 or 128	8
Set the window size (K).	**lapb k** *window-size*	1- (modulo minus 1) frames	7
Set the maximum bits per frame (N1).	**lapb n1** *bits*	Bits (must be a multiple of 8)	Based on hardware MTU and protocol overhead
Set the count for sending frames (N2).	**lapb n2** *tries*	1–255 tries	20
Set the retransmission timer (T1).	**lapb t1** *milliseconds*	1–64000 milliseconds	3000
Set the hardware outage period.	**lapb interface-outage** *milliseconds*		0 (disabled)
Set the idle link period (T4).	**lapb t4** *seconds*		0 (disabled)

Additional explanation of the commands in the previous table is provided in the following list:

- LAPB Modulo and LAPB K—The LAPB modulo determines the operating mode. Modulo 8 (basic mode) is widely available because it is required for all standard LAPB implementations, and it is sufficient for most links. Modulo 128 (extended mode) can achieve greater throughput on high-speed links that have a low error rate (some satellite links, for example) by increasing the number of frames that can be transmitted before waiting for acknowledgment (as configured by the LAPB window parameter, k). By its design, LAPB's k parameter can be at most one less than the operating modulo. Modulo 8 links can typically send seven frames before an acknowledgment must be received; modulo 128 links can set k to a value as large as 127. By default, LAPB links use the basic mode with a window of 7.

- LAPB N1—When connecting to an X.25 network, use the N1 parameter value set by the network administrator. This value is the maximum number of bits in an LAPB frame, which determines the maximum size of an X.25 packet. When you are using LAPB over leased lines, the N1 parameter should be eight times the hardware maximum transmission unit (MTU) size plus any protocol overhead. The LAPB N1 range is dynamically calculated by the Cisco IOS software whenever an MTU change, an L2/L3 modulo change, or a compression change occurs on a LAPB interface.

CAUTION

The LAPB N1 parameter provides little benefit beyond the interface MTU, and can easily cause link failures if misconfigured. Cisco recommends that this parameter be left at its default value.

- LAPB N2—The transmit counter (N2) is the number of unsuccessful transmit attempts that are made before the link is declared down.

- LABP T1—The retransmission timer (T1) determines how long a transmitted frame can remain unacknowledged before the Cisco IOS software polls for an acknowledgment. For X.25 networks, the retransmission timer setting should match that of the network. For leased-line circuits, the T1 timer setting is critical because the design of LAPB assumes that a frame has been lost if it is not acknowledged within period T1. The timer setting must be large enough to permit a maximum-sized frame to complete one round trip on the link. If the timer setting is too small, the software will poll before the acknowledgment frame can return, which may result in duplicated frames and severe protocol problems. If the timer setting is too large, the software waits longer than necessary before requesting an acknowledgment, which reduces bandwidth.

- LAPB interface outage—Another LAPB timer function allows brief hardware failures while the protocol is up without requiring a protocol reset. When a brief hardware outage occurs, the link will continue uninterrupted if the outage is corrected before the specified hardware outage period expires.

- LAPB T4—The LAPB standards define a timer to detect unsignaled link failures (T4). The T4 timer is reset every time a frame is received from the partner on the link. If the T4 timer expires, a Receiver Ready frame with the Poll bit set is sent to the partner, which is required to respond. If the partner does not respond, the standard polling mechanism is used to determine whether the link is down. The period of T4 must be greater than the period of T1.

For an example of configuring the LAPB T1 timer, see the section "Typical LAPB Configuration Example," later in this chapter.

CONFIGURING PRIORITY AND CUSTOM QUEUING FOR LAPB

Cisco priority queuing and custom queuing are available for LAPB to allow you to improve a link's responsiveness to a given type of traffic by specifying the handling of that type of traffic for transmission on the link.

Priority queuing is a mechanism that classifies packets based on certain criteria and then assigns the packets to one of four output queues with high, medium, normal, or low priority. Custom queuing similarly classifies packets and assigns them to one of 10 output queues, and controls the percentage of an interface's available bandwidth that is used for a queue.

For example, you can use priority queuing to ensure that all Telnet traffic is processed promptly and that Simple Mail Transfer Protocol (SMTP) traffic is sent only when there is no other traffic to send. Priority queuing in this example can starve the non-Telnet traffic; custom queuing can be used instead to ensure that some traffic of all categories is sent.

Both priority queuing and custom queuing can be defined, but only one method can be assigned to a given interface.

To configure priority and custom queuing for LAPB, perform the following tasks:

1. Perform the standard priority and custom queuing tasks *except* the task of assigning a priority or custom group to the interface.

2. Perform the standard LAPB encapsulation tasks, as specified in the "Configuring an LAPB Datagram Transport" section of this chapter.

3. Assign either a priority group or a custom queue to the interface.

— **NOTES** ———

The **lapb hold-queue** command is no longer supported, but the same functionality is provided by the standard queue control command **hold-queue** *size* **out**.

CONFIGURING TRANSPARENT BRIDGING OVER MULTIPROTOCOL LAPB

To configure transparent bridging over multiprotocol LAPB, perform the following tasks beginning in global configuration mode:

Task	Command
Specify the serial interface, and enter interface configuration mode.	**interface serial** *number*
Assign no IP address to the interface.	**no ip address**
Configure multiprotocol LAPB encapsulation.	**encapsulation lapb multi**
Assign the interface to a bridge group.	**bridge-group** *bridge-group*
Define the type of spanning tree protocol.	**bridge** *bridge-group* **protocol** {ieee	dec}

NOTES

This feature requires use of the **encapsulation lapb multi** command. You cannot use the **encapsulation lapb** *protocol* command with a **bridge** keyword to configure this feature.

For an example of configuring transparent bridging over multiprotocol LAPB, see the section "Transparent Bridging for Multiprotocol LAPB Encapsulation Example," later in this chapter.

X.25 CONFIGURATION TASK LIST

To configure X.25, complete the tasks in one or more of the tasks in the following list, depending upon the X.25 application or task required for your network. The interface, datagram transport, and routing tasks are divided into sections based generally on how common the feature is and how often it is used. Those features and parameters that are relatively uncommon are found in the "Additional" sections. LAPB frame parameters can be modified to optimize X.25 operation, as described earlier in this chapter.

- Configuring an X.25 Interface
- Configuring Additional X.25 Interface Parameters
- Configuring an X.25 Datagram Transport
- Configuring Additional X.25 Datagram Transport Features
- Configuring Priority Queuing or Custom Queuing for X.25
- Configuring X.25 Routing
- Configuring Additional X.25 Routing Features
- Configuring CMNS Routing
- Configuring DDN or BFE X.25
- Creating X.29 Access Lists
- Creating an X.29 Profile Script
- Monitoring and Maintaining LAPB and X.25

All these features can coexist on an X.25 interface.

Default parameters are provided for X.25 operation; however, you can change the settings to meet the needs of your X.25 network or as defined by your X.25 service supplier. Cisco also provides additional configuration settings to optimize your X.25 usage.

NOTES

If you connect a router to an X.25 network, use the parameters set by your network administrator for the connection; these parameters will typically be those described in the "Configuring an X.25 Interface" and "Modifying LAPB Protocol Parameters" sections. Also, note that the X.25 Level 2 parameters described in the "Modifying LAPB Protocol Parameters" section affect X.25 Level 3 operations.

See the end of this chapter for examples of configuring X.25.

CONFIGURING AN X.25 INTERFACE

To configure an X.25 interface, perform the tasks in the following list:

- Setting the X.25 Mode
- Setting the Virtual Circuit Ranges
- Setting the Packet Numbering Modulo
- Setting the X.121 Address
- Setting the Default Flow Control Values

These tasks describe the parameters that are essential for correct X.25 behavior. The first task is required. The others might be required or optional, depending on what the router is expected to do with the X.25 attachment.

You can also configure other, less common parameters, as specified in the "Configuring Additional X.25 Interface Parameters" section later in this chapter.

Setting the X.25 Mode

A router using X.25 Level 3 encapsulation can act as a DTE or DCE protocol device (according to the needs of your X.25 service supplier), use Defense Data Network (DDN) or Blacker Front End (BFE) encapsulation, or use the Internet Engineering Task Force (IETF) standard encapsulation, as specified by RFC 1356.

Because the default serial encapsulation is HDLC, you must explicitly configure an X.25 encapsulation method.

NOTES

Cisco recommends that you shut down an interface before changing the encapsulation.

To configure the mode of operation and one of these encapsulation types for a specified interface, perform the following task in interface configuration mode:

Task	Command
Set the X.25 mode of operation.	encapsulation x25 [dte | dce] [[ddn | bfe] | [ietf]]

Typically, a PDN will require attachment as a DTE. (This requirement is distinct from the hardware interface DTE or DCE identity.) The default mode of operation is DTE, and the default encapsulation method is Cisco's pre-IETF method. If either DDN or BFE operation is needed, it must be explicitly configured.

For an example of configuring X.25 DTE operation, see the section "Typical X.25 Configuration Example," later in this chapter.

Setting the Virtual Circuit Ranges

The X.25 protocol maintains multiple connections over one physical link between a DTE and a DCE. These connections are called *virtual circuits* (VCs) or *logical channels* (LCs). X.25 can maintain up to 4095 virtual circuits numbered 1 through 4095. You identify an individual virtual circuit by giving its logical channel identifier (LCI) or virtual circuit number (VCN). Many documents use the terms *virtual circuit* and *LC, VCN, LCN,* and *LCI* interchangeably. Each of these terms refers to the virtual circuit number.

An important part of X.25 operation is the range of virtual circuit numbers. Virtual circuit numbers are broken into four ranges (listed here in numerically increasing order):

1. Permanent virtual circuits (PVCs)
2. Incoming-only circuits
3. Two-way circuits
4. Outgoing-only circuits

The incoming-only, two-way, and outgoing-only ranges define the virtual circuit numbers over which a switched virtual circuit (SVC) can be established by the placement of an X.25 call, much like a telephone network establishes a switched voice circuit when a call is placed.

The rules about DCE and DTE devices initiating calls are as follows:

- Only the DCE device can initiate a call in the incoming-only range.
- Only the DTE device can initiate a call in the outgoing-only range.
- Both the DCE device and the DTE device can initiate a call in the two-way range.

(The ITU-T Recommendation X.25 defines "incoming" and "outgoing" in relation to the DTE or DCE interface role; Cisco's documentation uses the more intuitive sense. Unless the ITU-T sense is explicitly referenced, a call received from the interface is an *incoming call* and a call sent out the interface is an *outgoing call*.)

NOTES

The ITU-T carries out the functions of the former Consultative Committee for International Telegraph and Telephone (CCITT).

There is no difference in the operation of the SVCs in the different ranges except the restrictions on which device can initiate a call. These ranges can be used to prevent one side from monopolizing the virtual circuits, which can be useful for X.25 interfaces with a small total number of SVCs available.

Six X.25 parameters define the upper and lower limit of each of the three SVC ranges. A PVC must be assigned a number less than the numbers assigned to the SVC ranges. An SVC range is not allowed to overlap another range.

NOTES

Because the X.25 protocol requires the DTE and DCE to have identical virtual circuit ranges, changes you make to the virtual circuit range limits when the interface is up are held until the X.25 protocol restarts the packet service.

To configure X.25 virtual circuit ranges, complete the following tasks in interface configuration mode as appropriate for your configuration:

Task	Command	Default
Set the lowest incoming-only circuit number.	**x25 lic** *circuit-number*	0
Set the highest incoming-only circuit number.	**x25 hic** *circuit-number*	0
Set the lowest two-way circuit number.	**x25 ltc** *circuit-number*	1
Set the highest two-way circuit number.	**x25 htc** *circuit-number*	1024—for X.25 4095—for CMNS
Set the lowest outgoing-only circuit number.	**x25 loc** *circuit-number*	0
Set the highest outgoing-only circuit number.	**x25 hoc** *circuit-number*	0

Each of these parameters can range from 1 to 4095, inclusively. Note that the values for these parameters must be the same on both ends of an X.25 link. For connection to a public data network, these values must be set to the values assigned by the network. An SVC range is unused if its lower and upper limits are set to 0; other than this use for marking unused ranges, virtual circuit 0 is not available.

For an example of configuring virtual circuit ranges, see the section "Virtual Circuit Ranges Example," later in this chapter.

Setting the Packet Numbering Modulo

Cisco's implementation of X.25 supports both modulo 8 and modulo 128 packet sequence numbering; module 8 is the default.

To set the packet numbering modulo, perform the following task in interface configuration mode:

Task	Command
Set the packet numbering modulo (the default is 8).	**x25 modulo** {8	128}

NOTES

Because the X.25 protocol requires the DTE and DCE to have identical modulos, changes you make to the modulo when the interface is up are held until the X.25 protocol restarts the packet service.

The X.25 modulo and the LAPB modulo are distinct and serve different purposes. LAPB modulo 128 (or extended mode) can be used to achieve higher throughput across the DTE or DCE interface; it affects only the local point of attachment. X.25 Packet-Level Protocol (PLP) modulo 128 can be used to achieve higher end-to-end throughput for virtual circuits by allowing more data packets to be in transit through the X.25 network.

Setting the X.121 Address

If your router does not originate or terminate calls but only participates in X.25 switching, this task is optional. However, if the router is attached to a PDN, you must set the interface X.121 address assigned by the X.25 network service provider. Interfaces that use the DDN or BFE mode will have an X.121 address generated from the interface IP address; for correct DDN or BFE operation, any such X.121 address must not be modified.

To set the X.121 address, perform the following task in interface configuration mode:

Task	Command
Set the X.121 address.	**x25 address** *x121-address*

For an example of configuring the X.25 interface address, see the section "Typical X.25 Configuration Example," later in this chapter.

Setting the Default Flow Control Values

Setting correct default flow control parameters of window size and packet size is essential for correct operation of the link because X.25 is a strongly flow controlled protocol. However, it is easy to overlook this task because many networks use standard default values. Mismatched default flow control values will cause X.25 local procedure errors, evidenced by Clear and Reset events.

To configure flow control parameters, complete the tasks in the following list. These tasks are optional if your X.25 attachment uses the standard default values for maximum packet sizes (128 bytes incoming and outgoing) and window sizes (2 packets incoming and outgoing).

- Setting Default Window Sizes
- Setting Default Packet Sizes

NOTES ——

Because the X.25 protocol requires the DTE and DCE to have identical default maximum packet sizes and default window sizes, changes made to the window and packet sizes when the interface is up are held until the X.25 protocol restarts the packet service.

Setting Default Window Sizes

X.25 networks have a default input and output window size (the default is 2) that is defined by your network administrator. You must set the Cisco IOS software default input and output window sizes to match those of the network. These defaults are the values that an SVC takes on if it is set up without explicitly negotiating its window sizes. Any PVC also uses these default values unless different values are configured.

To set the default window sizes, perform the following tasks in interface configuration mode:

Task	Command
Set the default virtual circuit receive window size.	**x25 win** *packets*
Set the default virtual circuit transmit window size.	**x25 wout** *packets*

For an example of setting the default window sizes, see the sections "Typical X.25 Configuration Example" and "DDN X.25 Configuration Example," later in this chapter.

Setting Default Packet Sizes

X.25 networks have a default maximum input and output packet size (the default is 128) that is defined by your network administrator. You must set the Cisco IOS software default input and output maximum packet sizes to match those of the network. These defaults are the values that an SVC takes on if it is set up without explicitly negotiating its maximum packet sizes. Any PVC also uses these default values unless different values are configured.

To set the default input and output maximum packet sizes, perform the following tasks in interface configuration mode:

Task	Command
Set the default input maximum packet size.	**x25 ips** *bytes*
Set the default output maximum packet size.	**x25 ops** *bytes*

To send a packet larger than the agreed-on X.25 packet size over an X.25 virtual circuit, the Cisco IOS software must break the packet into two or more X.25 packets with the M-bit ("more data" bit) set. The receiving device collects all packets in the M-bit sequence and reassembles them into the original packet.

It is possible to define default packet sizes that cannot be supported by the lower layer (see the description of the LAPB N1 parameter earlier in this chapter). However, the router will negotiate lower maximum packet sizes for all SVCs so the agreed-on sizes can be carried. The Cisco IOS software will also refuse a PVC configuration if the resulting maximum packet sizes cannot be supported by the lower layer.

For an example of setting the default maximum packet sizes, see the sections "Typical X.25 Configuration Example" and "DDN X.25 Configuration Example," later in this chapter.

CONFIGURING ADDITIONAL X.25 INTERFACE PARAMETERS

Some X.25 applications have less common uses. Several X.25 parameters are available to modify the X.25 protocol behavior for these applications.

To configure less common X.25 interface parameters for special needs, perform the tasks in the following list as needed:

- Configuring the X.25 Level 3 Timers
- Configuring X.25 Addresses
- Establishing a Default Virtual Circuit Protocol
- Disabling Packet-Level Protocol (PLP) Restarts

Configuring the X.25 Level 3 Timers

The X.25 Level 3 event timers determine how long the Cisco IOS software waits for acknowledgment of control packets. You can set these timers independently. Only those timers that apply to the interface are configurable. (A DTE interface does not have the T1*x* timers, and a DCE interface does not have the T2*x* timers.)

To set the event timers, perform any of the following tasks in interface configuration mode:

Task	Command
Set DTE T20 Restart Request timeout.	**x25 t20** *seconds*
Set DCE T10 Restart Indication timeout.	**x25 t10** *seconds*

Task	Command
Set DTE T21 Call Request timeout.	**x25 t21** *seconds*
Set DCE T11 Incoming Call timeout.	**x25 t11** *seconds*
Set DTE T22 Reset Request timeout.	**x25 t22** *seconds*
Set DCE T12 Reset Indication timeout.	**x25 t12** *seconds*
Set DTE T23 Clear Request timeout.	**x25 t23** *seconds*
Set DCE T13 Clear Indication timeout.	**x25 t13** *seconds*

For an example of setting the event timers, see the section "DDN X.25 Configuration Example," later in this chapter.

Configuring X.25 Addresses

When establishing SVCs, X.25 uses addresses in the form defined by the ITU-T *Recommendation X.121* (or simply an "X.121 address"). An X.121 address has from 0 to 15 digits. Because of the importance of addressing to call setup, several interface addressing features are available for X.25.

To configure X.25 addresses, perform the tasks in the following list:

- Understanding Normal X.25 Addressing
- Understanding X.25 Subaddresses
- Configuring an Interface Alias Address
- Suppressing or Replacing the Calling Address
- Suppressing the Called Address

Understanding Normal X.25 Addressing

An X.25 interface's X.121 address is used when it is the source or destination of an X.25 call. The X.25 call setup procedure identifies both the calling (source) and the called (destination) X.121 addresses. When an interface is the source of a call, it encodes the interface X.121 address as the source address. An interface determines that it is the destination of a received call if the destination address matches the interface's address.

Cisco's X.25 software can also route X.25 calls, which involves placing and accepting calls, but the router is neither the source nor the destination for these calls. Routing X.25 does not modify the source or destination addresses, thus preserving the addresses specified by the source host. Routed (switched) X.25 simply connects two logical X.25 channels to complete an X.25 virtual circuit. An X.25 virtual circuit, then, is a connection between two hosts (the source host and the destination host) that is switched between zero or more routed X.25 links.

The null X.121 address (the X.121 address that has zero digits) is a special case. The router acts as the destination host for any call it receives that has the null destination address.

Understanding X.25 Subaddresses

A subaddress is an X.121 address that matches the digits defined for the interface's X.121 address, but has one or more additional digits after the base address. X.25 acts as the destination host for an incoming packet assembler/disassembler (PAD) call with a destination that is a subaddress of the interface's address; the trailing digits specify which line a PAD connection is requesting. Other calls that use a subaddress can be accepted if the trailing digit or digits are zeros; otherwise, the router will not act as the call's destination host.

Configuring an Interface Alias Address

You can supply alias X.121 addresses for an interface. This allows the interface to act as the destination host for calls having a destination address that is neither the interface's address, an allowed subaddress of the interface, nor the null address.

Local processing (for example, IP encapsulation) can be performed only for incoming calls whose destination X.121 address matches the serial interface or alias of the interface.

To configure an alias, perform the following task in configuration mode:

Task	Command
Supply an alias X.121 address for the interface.	**x25 alias** *x121-address-pattern* [**cud** *pattern*]

Suppressing or Replacing the Calling Address

Some attachments require that no calling (source) address be presented in outgoing calls; this requirement is called *suppressing the calling address*.

When attached to a PDN, X.25 may need to ensure that outgoing calls only use the assigned X.121 address for the calling (source) address. Routed X.25 normally uses the original source address. Although individual X.25 route configurations can modify the source address, Cisco provides a simple command to force the use of the interface address in all calls sent; this requirement is called *replacing the calling address*.

To suppress or replace the calling address, perform the appropriate task in interface configuration mode:

Task	Command
Suppress the calling (source) X.121 address in outgoing calls.	**x25 suppress-calling-address**
Replace the calling (source) X.121 address in switched calls.	**x25 use-source-address**

Suppressing the Called Address

Some attachments require that no called (destination) address be presented in outgoing calls; this requirement is called *suppressing the called address*.

To suppress the called address, perform the following task in interface configuration mode:

Task	Command
Suppress the called (destination) X.121 address in outgoing calls.	x25 suppress-called-address

Establishing a Default Virtual Circuit Protocol

The Call Request packet that sets up a virtual circuit can encode a field called the *Call User Data (CUD)* field. Typically, the first few bytes of the CUD field identify which high-level protocol is carried by the virtual circuit. The router, when acting as a destination host, normally refuses a call if the CUD is absent or the protocol identification isn't recognized. The PAD protocol, however, specifies that unidentified calls be treated as PAD connection requests. Other applications require that they be treated as IP encapsulation connection requests, per RFC 877.

To configure either PAD or IP encapsulation treatment of unidentified calls, perform the following task in interface configuration mode:

Task	Command
Establish a default virtual circuit protocol.	x25 default {ip | pad}

Disabling Packet-Level Protocol (PLP) Restarts

By default, a Packet-Level Protocol (PLP) restart is performed when the link level resets (for example, when LAPB reconnects). Although PLP restarts can be disabled for those few networks that do not allow restarts, Cisco does not recommended disabling these restarts because doing so can cause anomalous packet layer behavior.

> **CAUTION**
>
> Very few networks require this feature; Cisco does not recommend that it be enabled except when attaching to a network that requires it.

To disable PLP restarts, perform the following task in interface configuration mode:

Task	Command
Disable packet-level restarts.	no x25 linkrestart

CONFIGURING AN X.25 DATAGRAM TRANSPORT

X.25 support is most commonly configured as a transport for datagrams across an X.25 network. Datagram transport (or *encapsulation*) is a cooperative effort between two hosts communicating across an X.25 network. You configure datagram transport by establishing a mapping on the encapsulating interface between the far host's protocol address (for example, IP or DECnet) and its X.121 address. Because the call identifies the protocol that the virtual circuit will carry (by encoding a Protocol Identifier, or PID, in the first few bytes of the CUD field), the terminating host can accept the call if it is configured to exchange the identified traffic with the source host.

Figure 11–1 illustrates two routers sending datagrams across an X.25 public data network.

Figure 11–1
Two routers transporting LAN protocols across an X.25 PDN.

Perform the tasks in the following list, as necessary, to complete the X.25 configuration for your network needs:

- Configuring Subinterfaces
- Mapping Protocol Addresses to X.121 Addresses
- Establishing an Encapsulation PVC
- Setting X.25 TCP/IP Header Compression
- Configuring X.25 Bridging

Configuring the X.25 parameters and special features, including payload compression and X.25 user facilities, are described in the section "Configuring Additional X.25 Datagram Transport Features," later in this chapter.

Configuring Subinterfaces

Subinterfaces are virtual interfaces that can be used to connect several networks to each other through a single physical interface. Subinterfaces are made available on Cisco routers because routing protocols, especially those using the split horizon principle, may need help to determine which hosts need a routing update. The split horizon principle, which allows routing updates to be distributed to other routed interfaces except the interface on which the routing update was received, works well in a LAN environment in which other routers reached by the interface have already received the routing update.

However, in a WAN environment using connection-oriented interfaces (like X.25 and Frame Relay), other routers reached by the same physical interface might not have received the routing update. Rather than forcing you to connect routers by separate physical interfaces, Cisco provides subinterfaces that are treated as separate interfaces. You can separate hosts into subinterfaces on a physical interface so that the X.25 protocol is unaffected. Routing processes recognize each sub-interface as a separate source of routing updates so that all subinterfaces are eligible to receive routing updates.

Understanding Point-to-Point and Multipoint Subinterfaces

There are two types of subinterfaces: point-to-point and multipoint. Subinterfaces are implicitly multipoint unless configured as point-to-point.

A point-to-point subinterface is used to encapsulate one or more protocols between two hosts. An X.25 point-to-point subinterface will accept only a single encapsulation command (such as the **x25 map** or **x25 pvc** commands) for a given protocol, so there can be only one destination for the protocol. (However, you can use multiple encapsulation commands, one for each protocol, or multiple protocols for one map or PVC.) All protocol traffic routed to a point-to-point subinterface is forwarded to the one destination host defined for the protocol. (Because only one destination is defined for the interface, the routing process need not consult the destination address in the datagrams.)

A multipoint subinterface is used to connect one or more hosts for a given protocol. There is no restriction on the number of encapsulation commands that can be configured on a multipoint subinterface. Because the hosts appear on the same subinterface, they are not relying on the router to distribute routing updates between them. When a routing process forwards a datagram to a multipoint subinterface, the X.25 encapsulation process must be able to map the datagram's destination address to a configured encapsulation command. If the routing process cannot find a map for the datagram destination address, the encapsulation will fail.

--- **NOTES** ---

Because of the complex operations dependent on a subinterface and its type, the router will not allow a subinterface's type to be changed, nor can a subinterface with the same number be re-established once it has been deleted. After a subinterface has been deleted, you must reload the Cisco IOS software (by using the **reload** command) to remove all internal references. However, you can easily re-constitute the deleted subinterface by using a different subinterface number.

Creating and Configuring X.25 Subinterfaces

To create and configure a subinterface, complete the first task, and one or both of the remaining tasks, in the following table beginning in global configuration mode:

Task	Command
Create a point-to-point or multipoint subinterface.	**interface serial** *number.subinterface-number* [**point-to-point** | **multipoint**]
Configure an X.25 encapsulation map for the subinterface.	**x25 map** *protocol address* [*protocol2 address2* [... [*protocol9 address9*]]] *x121-address* [*option*]
and/or	
Establish an encapsulation PVC for the subinterface.	**x25 pvc** *circuit protocol address* [*protocol2 address2* [...[*protocol9 address9*]]] *x121-address* [*option*]

For an example of configuring an X.25 subinterface and using multiple encapsulation commands for a single destination address, see the "Point-to-Point Subinterface Configuration Example" section later in this chapter.

NOTES

When configuring IP routing over X.25, you might need to make adjustments to accommodate split horizon effects. By default, split horizon is enabled for X.25 attachments.

Mapping Protocol Addresses to X.121 Addresses

This section describes the X.25 single-protocol and multiprotocol encapsulation options that are available and describes how to map protocol addresses to an X.121 address for a remote host. This section also includes reference information about how protocols are identified.

Understanding Protocol Encapsulation for Single-Protocol and Multiprotocol Virtual Circuits

Cisco has long supported encapsulation of a number of datagram protocols across X.25, using a standard method when available or a proprietary method when necessary. These traditional methods assign a protocol to each virtual circuit. If more than one protocol is carried between the router and a given host, each active protocol will have at least one virtual circuit dedicated to carrying its datagrams.

Cisco also supports a newer standard, RFC 1356, which standardizes a method for encapsulating most datagram protocols over X.25. It also specifies how one virtual circuit can carry datagrams from more than one protocol.

The Cisco IOS software can be configured to use any of the available encapsulation methods with a particular host.

After you establish an encapsulation virtual circuit using any method, the Cisco IOS software sends and receives a datagram by simply fragmenting it into, and reassembling it from, an X.25 complete packet sequence. An X.25 complete packet sequence is one or more X.25 data packets that have the M-bit set in all but the last packet. A virtual circuit that can carry multiple protocols includes protocol identification data as well as the protocol data at the start of each complete packet sequence.

Understanding Protocol Identification

The various methods and protocols used in X.25 SVC encapsulation are identified in a specific field of the call packet; this field is defined by X.25 to carry Call User Data (CUD). Only PVCs do not use CUD to identify their encapsulation (since PVCs do not use the X.25 call setup procedures).

The primary difference between the available Cisco and IETF encapsulation methods is the specific value used to identify a protocol. When any of the methods establishes a virtual circuit for carrying a single protocol, the protocol is identified in the call packet by the CUD.

Table 11–2 summarizes the values used in the CUD field to identify protocols.

Table 11–2 *Protocol Identification in the Call User Data (CUD) Field*

Protocol	Cisco Protocol Identifier	IETF RFC 1356 Protocol Identifier
Apollo Domain	0xD4	0x80 (5-byte SNAP encoding[*])
AppleTalk	0xD2	0x80 (5-byte SNAP encoding)
Banyan VINES	0xC0 00 80 C4[†]	0x80 (5-byte SNAP encoding)
Bridging	0xD5	(Not implemented)
ISO CLNS	0x81	0x81[‡]
Compressed TCP	0xD8	0x00 (Multiprotocol)[**]
DECnet	0xD0	0x80 (5-byte SNAP encoding)
IP	0xCC	0xCC [††] or 0x80 (5-byte SNAP encoding)
Novell IPX	0xD3	0x80 (5-byte SNAP encoding)
PAD	0x01 00 00 00[‡‡]	0x01 00 00 00
QLLC	0xC3	(Not available)
XNS	0xD1	0x80 (5-byte SNAP encoding)
Multiprotocol	(Not available)	0x00

[*] Subnetwork Access Protocol (SNAP) encoding is defined from the Assigned Numbers RFC; Cisco's implementation recognizes only the IETF organizational unique identifier (OUI) 0x00 00 00 followed by a 2-byte Ethernet protocol type.
[†] The use of 0xC0 00 80 C4 for Banyan VINES is defined by Banyan.
[‡] The use of 0x81 for CLNS is compatible with ISO/IEC 8473-3:1994.
[**] Compressed TCP traffic has two types of datagrams, so IETF encapsulation requires a multiprotocol virtual circuit.
[††] The use of 0xCC for IP is backwards-compatible with RFC 877.
[‡‡] The use of 0x01 00 00 00 for PAD is defined by ITU-T Recommendation X.29.

Once a multiprotocol virtual circuit has been established, datagrams on the virtual circuit have protocol identification data before the actual protocol data; the protocol identification values are the same used by RFC 1356 in the CUD field for an individual protocol.

NOTES

IP datagrams can be identified with a one-byte identification (0xCC) or a six-byte identification (0x80 followed by the five-byte SNAP encoding). The one-byte encoding is used by default, although the SNAP encoding can be configured.

Mapping Datagram Addresses to X.25 Hosts

Encapsulation is a cooperative process between the router and another X.25 host. Because X.25 hosts are reached with an X.121 address (an X.121 address has between 0 and 15 decimal digits), the router must have a means to map a host's protocols and addresses to its X.121 address.

Each encapsulating X.25 interface must be configured with the relevant datagram parameters. For example, an interface that encapsulates IP will typically have an IP address.

A router set up for DDN or BFE service uses a dynamic mapping technique to convert between IP and X.121 addresses. These techniques have been designed specifically for attachment to the DDN network and to Blacker encryption equipment. Their design, restrictions, and operation make them work well for these specific applications, but not for other networks.

You must also establish the X.121 address of an encapsulating X.25 interface using the **x25 address** interface configuration command. This X.121 address is the address to which the encapsulation calls are directed. This is also the source X.121 address used for originating an encapsulation call and is used by the destination host to map the source host and protocol to the protocol address. An encapsulation virtual circuit must be a mapped at both the source and destination host interfaces. A DDN or BFE interface will have an X.121 address generated from the interface IP address, which for proper operation, should not be modified.

For each X.25 interface, you must explicitly map each destination host's protocols and addresses to its X.121 address. If needed, and the destination host has the capability, one host map can be configured to support several protocols; alternatively, you can define one map for each supported protocol.

To establish a map, perform the following task in interface configuration mode:

Task	Command
Map one or more host protocol addresses to the host's X.121 address.	**x25 map** *protocol address* [*protocol2 address2* [...[*protocol9 address9*]]] *x121-address* [*option*]

For example, if you are encapsulating IP over a given X.25 interface, you must define an IP address for the interface and, for each of the desired destination hosts, map the host's IP address to its X.121 address.

NOTES

You can map an X.121 address to as many as nine protocol addresses, but each protocol can be mapped only once in the command line.

An individual host map can use the following keywords to specify the following protocols:

- **apollo**—Apollo Domain
- **appletalk**—AppleTalk
- **bridge**—Bridging
- **clns**—OSI Connectionless Network Service
- **compressedtcp**—TCP/IP header compression
- **decnet**—DECnet
- **ip**—IP
- **ipx**—Novell IPX
- **pad**—Packet Assembler/Disassembler
- **qllc**—IBM's QLLC
- **vines**—Banyan VINES
- **xns**—XNS

Each mapped protocol, except bridging and CLNS, takes a datagram address. All bridged datagrams are either broadcast to all bridging destinations or are sent to a specific destination's X.121 address, and CLNS uses the mapped X.121 address as the SNPA, which is referenced by a **clns neighbor** command. The configured datagram protocol(s) and their relevant address are mapped to the destination host's X.121 address. All protocols that are supported for RFC 1356 operation can be specified in a single map. (Bridging and QLLC are not supported for RFC 1356 encapsulation.) If IP and TCP/IP header compression are both specified, the same IP address must be given for both protocols.

When setting up the address map, you can include options such as enabling broadcasts, specifying the number of virtual circuits allowed, and defining various user facility settings.

NOTES

Multiprotocol maps, especially those configured to carry broadcast traffic, can result in significantly larger traffic loads, requiring a larger hold queue, larger window sizes, or multiple virtual circuits.

You can simplify the configuration for the Open Shortest Path First (OSPF) protocol by adding the optional **broadcast** keyword. See the **x25 map** command description in Chapter 12 for more information.

Configuring PAD Access

By default, Packet Assembler/Disassembler (PAD) connection attempts are processed for session creation or protocol translation (subject to the configuration of those functions) from all hosts. To restrict PAD connections to only statically mapped X.25 hosts, perform the following tasks in interface configuration mode:

Task	Command
Restrict PAD access.	**x25 pad-access**
Configure a host for PAD access.	**x25 map pad** *x121-address* [*option*]

You can configure outgoing PAD access using the optional features of the **x25 map pad** command without restricting incoming PAD connections to the configured hosts.

Establishing an Encapsulation PVC

Permanent virtual circuits (PVCs) are the X.25 equivalent of leased lines; they are never disconnected. You do not need to configure an address map before defining a PVC; an encapsulation PVC implicitly defines a map.

To establish a PVC, perform the following task in interface configuration mode:

Task	Command
Set an encapsulation PVC.	**x25 pvc** *circuit protocol address* [*protocol2 address2* [...[*protocol9 address9*]]] *x121-address* [*option*]

The **x25 pvc** command uses the same protocol keywords as the **x25 map** command. See the "Mapping Datagram Addresses to X.25 Hosts" section of this chapter for a list of protocol keywords. Encapsulation PVCs also use a subset of the options defined for the **x25 map** command.

The user may establish multiple, parallel PVCs that carry the same set of encapsulation traffic by specifying the identical mappings for each PVC. Additionally, the user can permit a mixture of SVCs and PVCs to carry the traffic set by using the **x25 map** command to specify an **nvc** *count* that exceeds the number of configured PVCs. The total number of VCs, of whatever type, can never exceed 8.

For an example of configuring a PVC, see the section "PVC Used to Exchange IP Traffic Example," later in this chapter.

Setting X.25 TCP/IP Header Compression

Cisco supports RFC 1144 TCP/IP Header Compression (THC) on serial lines using HDLC and X.25 encapsulation. THC encapsulation is only slightly different from other encapsulation traffic, but these differences are worth noting. The implementation of compressed TCP over X.25 uses one virtual circuit to pass the compressed packets. Any IP traffic (including standard TCP) is separate from THC traffic; it is carried over separate IP encapsulation virtual circuits or identified separately in a multiprotocol virtual circuit.

NOTES

If you specify both **ip** and **compressedtcp** in the same **x25 map compressedtcp** command, they must both specify the same IP address.

To set up a separate virtual circuit for X.25 TCP/IP header compression, perform the following task in interface configuration mode:

Task	Command
Allow a separate virtual circuit for compressed packets.	**x25 map compressedtcp** *ip-address* [*protocol2 address2* [...[*protocol9 address9*]]] *x121-address* [*option*]

Configuring X.25 Bridging

Cisco's transparent bridging software supports bridging over X.25 virtual circuits. Bridging is not supported for RFC 1356 operation. Bridge maps must include the **broadcast** option for correct operation.

To enable the X.25 bridging capability, perform the following task in interface configuration mode:

Task	Command
Define bridging of X.25 frames.	**x25 map bridge** *x121-address* **broadcast** [*option*]

CONFIGURING ADDITIONAL X.25 DATAGRAM TRANSPORT FEATURES

The Cisco IOS software allows you to configure additional X.25 datagram transport features, including various user facilities defined for X.25 call setup.

This section describes the X.25 datagram transport features you can configure by using the options in the **x25 map** or **x25 pvc** encapsulation commands (or by setting an interface default). The tasks you perform depend upon your needs, the structure of your network, and the requirements of the service provider.

To configure the optional parameters, user facilities, and special features, perform one or more of the tasks described in the following list:

- Configuring X.25 Payload Compression
- Configuring the Encapsulation Virtual Circuit Idle Time
- Increasing the Number of Virtual Circuits Allowed
- Configuring the Ignore Destination Time
- Establishing the Packet Acknowledgment Policy
- Configuring X.25 User Facilities
- Defining the Virtual Circuit Packet Hold Queue Size
- Restricting Map Usage

Configuring X.25 Payload Compression

For increased efficiency on relatively slow networks, the Cisco IOS software supports X.25 payload compression of outgoing encapsulation traffic.

The following restrictions apply to X.25 payload compression:

- The compressed virtual circuit must connect two Cisco routers, because X.25 payload compression is not standardized. The data packets conform to the X.25 protocol rules, so a compressed virtual circuit can be switched through standard X.25 equipment. However, only Cisco routers can compress and decompress the data.

- Only datagram traffic can be compressed, although all the encapsulation methods supported by Cisco routers are available (for example, an IETF multiprotocol virtual circuit can be compressed). Switched virtual circuits (SVCs) cannot be translated between compressed and uncompressed data, nor can PAD data be compressed.

- X.25 payload compression must be applied carefully. Each compressed virtual circuit requires significant memory resources (for a dictionary of learned data patterns) and computation resources (every data packet received is decompressed and every data packet sent is compressed). Excessive use of compression can cause unacceptable overall performance.

- X.25 compression must be explicitly configured for a map command. A received call that specifies compression will be rejected if the corresponding host map does not specify the **compress** option. An incoming call that does not specify compression can, however, be accepted by a map that specifies compression.

To enable payload compression over X.25, perform the following task in interface configuration mode:

Task	Command
Enable payload compression over X.25.	**x25 map** *protocol address* [*protocol2 address2* [...[*protocol9 address9*]]] *x121-address* **compress** [*option*]

This command specifies that X.25 compression is to be used between the two hosts. Because each virtual circuit established for compressed traffic uses significant amounts of memory, compression should be used with careful consideration of its impact on the performance.

The **compress** option may be specified for an encapsulation PVC.

Configuring the Encapsulation Virtual Circuit Idle Time

The Cisco IOS software can clear a datagram transport or PAD SVC after a set period of inactivity. Routed SVCs are not timed for inactivity.

To set the time, perform the following tasks in interface configuration mode:

Task	Command
Set an idle time for clearing encapsulation.	**x25 idle** *minutes*
Specify an idle time for clearing a map's SVCs.	**x25 map** *protocol address* [*protocol2 address2* [...[*protocol9 address9*]]] *x121-address* **idle** *minutes*

For an example of configuring the SVC idle timer, see the section "Typical X.25 Configuration Example" later in this chapter. See the section "Monitoring and Maintaining LAPB and X.25," later in this chapter for additional commands that clear virtual circuits.

Increasing the Number of Virtual Circuits Allowed

For X.25 datagram transport, you can establish up to eight VCs to one host for each map.

To increase the number of virtual circuits allowed, perform one or both of the following tasks in interface configuration mode:

Task	Command
Specify the default maximum number of SVCs that can be open simultaneously to one host for each map.	**x25 nvc** *count*
Specify the maximum number of SVCs allowed for a map.	**x25 map** *protocol address* [*protocol2 address2* [...[*protocol9 address9*]]] *x121-address* **nvc** *count*

For an example of increasing the number of virtual circuits allowed, see the sections "Typical X.25 Configuration Example" and "DDN X.25 Configuration Example," later in this chapter.

Configuring the Ignore Destination Time

Upon receiving a Clear for an outstanding datagram transport Call Request, the X.25 encapsulation code immediately tries another Call Request if it has more traffic to send. This action can overrun some X.25 switches.

To define the number of minutes the Cisco IOS software will prevent calls from going to a previously failed destination, perform the following task in interface configuration mode (incoming calls will still be accepted and will cancel the timer):

Task	Command
Configure the ignore destination time.	**x25 hold-vc-timer** *minutes*

Establishing the Packet Acknowledgment Policy

You can instruct the Cisco IOS software to send an acknowledgment packet when it has received a threshold of data packets it has not acknowledged, instead of waiting until its input window is full. A value of 1 sends an acknowledgment for each data packet received if it cannot be acknowledged in an outgoing data packet. This approach improves line responsiveness at the expense of bandwidth. A value of 0 restores the default behavior of waiting until the input window is full.

To establish the acknowledgment threshold, perform the following task in interface configuration mode:

Task	Command
Establish the threshold at which to acknowledge data packets.	**x25 threshold** *packet-count*

The packet acknowledgment threshold also applies to encapsulation PVCs.

Configuring X.25 User Facilities

The X.25 software provides commands to support X.25 user facilities—options specified by the creators of the X.25 Recommendation—that allow you to use network features such as reverse charging, user identification, and flow control negotiation. You can choose to configure facilities on a per-map basis or on a per-interface basis. In the following table, the **x25 map** commands configure facilities on a per-map basis; the **x25 facility** commands specify the values sent for all encapsulation calls originated by the interface. Routed calls are not affected by the facilities specified for the outgoing interface.

To set the supported X.25 user facilities, perform one or more of the following tasks in interface configuration mode:

Task	Command
Select the closed user group.	**x25 facility cug** *group-number* or **x25 map** *protocol address* [*protocol2 address2* [...[*protocol9 address9*]]] *x121-address* **cug** *group-number*
Set flow control parameter negotiation values to request on outgoing calls.	**x25 facility packetsize** *in-size out-size* or **x25 map** *protocol address* [*protocol2 address2* [...[*protocol9 address9*]]] *x121-address* **packetsize** *in-size out-size* **x25 facility windowsize** *in-size out-size* or **x25 map** *protocol address* [*protocol2 address2*[...[*protocol9 address9*]]] *x121-address* **windowsize** *in-size out-size*
Set reverse charging.	**x25 facility reverse** or **x25 map** *protocol address* [*protocol2 address2* [...[*protocol9 address9*]]] *x121-address* **reverse**
Allow reverse charging acceptance.	**x25 accept-reverse** or **x25 map** *protocol address* [*protocol2 address2* [...[*protocol9 address9*]]] *x121-address* **accept-reverse**
Select throughput class negotiation.	**x25 facility throughput** *in out* or **x25 map** *protocol address* [*protocol2 address2* [...[*protocol9 address9*]]] *x121-address* **throughput** *in out*
Select transit delay.	**x25 facility transit-delay** *milliseconds* or **x25 map** *protocol address* [*protocol2 address2* [...[*protocol9 address9*]]] *x121-address* **transit-delay** *milliseconds*
Set the Recognized Operating Agency (ROA) to use.	**x25 facility roa** *name* or **x25 map** *protocol address* [*protocol2 address2* [...[*protocol9 address9*]]] *x121-address* **roa** *name*
Set the Cisco standard network user identification.	**x25 map** *protocol address* [*protocol2 address2* [...[*protocol9 address9*]]] *x121-address* **nuid** *username password*

Task	Command
Set a user-defined network user identification allowing the format to be determined by your network administrator.	**x25 map** *protocol address* [*protocol2 address2* [...[*protocol9 address9*]]] *x121-address* **nudata** *string*

The **windowsize** and **packetsize** options are supported for PVCs, although they have a slightly different meaning because PVCs do not use the call setup procedure. If the PVC does not use the interface defaults for the flow control parameters, these options must be used to specify the values. Not all networks will allow a PVC to be defined with arbitrary flow control values.

Additionally, the D-bit is supported, if negotiated. PVCs allow the D-bit procedure because there is no call setup to negotiate its use. Both restricted and unrestricted fast select are also supported and are transparently handled by the software. No configuration is required for use of the D-bit or fast select facilities.

Defining the Virtual Circuit Packet Hold Queue Size

To define the maximum number of packets that can be held while a virtual circuit is unable to send data, perform the following task in interface configuration mode:

Task	Command
Define the virtual circuit packet hold queue size.	**x25 hold-queue** *queue-size*

An encapsulation virtual circuit's hold queue size is determined when it is created; the **x25 hold-queue** command does not affect existing virtual circuits. This command also defines the hold queue size of encapsulation PVCs.

Restricting Map Usage

An X.25 map can be restricted so that it will not be used to place calls or so that it will not be considered when incoming calls are mapped.

To restrict X.25 map usage, use the following map options as needed in interface configuration mode:

Task	Command
Restrict incoming calls from a map.	**x25 map** *protocol address* [*protocol2 address2* [...[*protocol9 address9*]]] *x121-address* **no-incoming**
Restrict outgoing calls from a map.	**x25 map** *protocol address* [*protocol2 address2* [...[*protocol9 address9*]]] *x121-address* **no-outgoing**

CONFIGURING PRIORITY QUEUING OR CUSTOM QUEUING FOR X.25

Two types of output queuing are available for X.25:

- Priority queuing—Classifies packets based on certain criteria and then assigns the packets to one of four output queues with high, medium, normal, or low priority.

- Custom queuing—Classifies packets, assigns them to one of 16 output queues, and controls the percentage of an interface's available bandwidth that is used for a queue.

Understanding the Effect of X.25 Flow Control on Queuing

Output queuing for X.25 interfaces differs subtly from its use with other protocols because X.25 is a strongly flow-controlled protocol. Each X.25 virtual circuit has an authorized number of packets it can send before it must suspend transmission to await acknowledgment of one or more of the packets that were sent.

Queue processing is also subject to a virtual circuit's ability to send data; a high priority packet on a virtual circuit that cannot send data will not stop other packets from being sent if they are queued for a virtual circuit that can send data. In addition, a datagram that is in the process of being fragmented and sent may have its priority artificially promoted if higher priority traffic is blocked by the fragmentation operation.

Configuring Queuing

Both priority queuing and custom queuing can be defined, but only one method can be active on a given interface.

To configure priority queuing and custom queuing for X.25, perform the following tasks:

Step 1	Perform the standard priority and custom queuing tasks *except* the task of assigning a priority or custom group to the interface.
Step 2	Perform the standard X.25 encapsulation tasks, as specified in the "Configuring an X.25 Datagram Transport" section earlier in this chapter.
Step 3	Assign either a priority group or a custom queue to the interface.

NOTES

Connection-oriented virtual circuits (for example, QLLC, PAD, switched X.25) will use the interface's default queue. To maintain the correct order, all connection-oriented VCs use a single output queue for sending data.

CONFIGURING X.25 ROUTING

The X.25 software implementation allows virtual circuits to be routed from one X.25 interface to another, and from one router to another. The routing behavior can be controlled with switching and X.25-over-TCP (XOT) configuration commands, based on a locally built table.

X.25 encapsulation can share an X.25 serial interface with the X.25 switching support. Switching or forwarding of X.25 virtual circuits can be done in the following two ways:

- Incoming calls received from a local serial interface running X.25 can be forwarded to another local serial interface running X.25. This is known as *local X.25 switching* because the router handles the complete path. It does not matter whether the interfaces are configured as DTE or DCE devices, because the software takes the appropriate actions.

- An incoming call can also be forwarded using the *XOT* service (previously *remote switching* or *tunneling*). Upon receipt of an incoming X.25 call, a TCP connection is established to the destination XOT host (for example, another Cisco router) that will, in turn, handle the call using its own criteria. All X.25 packets are sent and received over the reliable TCP data stream. Flow control is maintained end-to-end. It does not matter whether the interface is configured for DTE or DCE, because the software takes the appropriate actions.

Running X.25 over TCP/IP provides a number of benefits. The datagram containing the X.25 packet can be switched by other routers using their high-speed switching abilities. X.25 connections can be sent over networks running only the TCP/IP protocols. The TCP/IP protocol suite runs over many different networking technologies, including Ethernet, Token Ring, T1 serial, and FDDI. Thus X.25 data can be forwarded over these media to another router, where it can, for example, be switched to an X.25 interface.

When the connection is made locally, the switching configuration is used; when the connection is across a LAN, the XOT configuration is used. The basic function is the same for both types of connections, but different configuration commands are required for each type of connection.

The X.25 switching subsystem supports the following facilities and parameters:

- D-bit negotiation (data packets with the D-bit set are passed through transparently)
- Variable-length interrupt data (if not operating as a DDN or BFE interface)
- Flow control parameter negotiation:
  - Window size up to 7, or 127 for modulo 128 operation
  - Packet size up to 4096 (if the LAPB layers used are capable of handling the requested size)
- Basic closed user group selection
- Throughput class negotiation
- Reverse charging and fast select

The handing of these facilities is described in Appendix A, "X.25 Facility Handling."

To configure X.25 routing, perform the tasks in the following list:

- Enabling X.25 Routing
- Configuring an X.25 Route

- Configuring a PVC Switched between X.25 Interfaces
- Configuring X.25 Switching between PVCs and SVCs

You may also need to configure additional X.25 routing features, as required for your network. Each task is described in a following section.

Enabling X.25 Routing

You must enable X.25 routing to use switch VCs.

To enable X.25 routing, perform the following task in global configuration mode:

Task	Command
Enable X.25 routing.	**x25 routing [use-tcp-if-defs]**

The **use-tcp-if-defs** keyword is used by some routers that receive remote routed calls from older versions of XOT; it might be needed if the originating router cannot be migrated to a new software release. The use of this keyword is described in the "Configuring XOT to Use Interface Default Flow Control Values" section later in this chapter.

For an example of configuring X.25 routing, see the sections "X.25 Route Address Pattern Matching Example" and "X.25 Routing Examples," later in this chapter.

Configuring an X.25 Route

An X.25 route table enables you to control which destination is selected for several applications. When an X.25 service receives a call that must be forwarded, the X.25 route table determines which X.25 service (X.25, CMNS, or XOT) and destination should be used. When a PAD call is originated by the router, either from a user request or a protocol translation event, the route table similarly determines what X.25 service and destination should be used.

You create the X.25 route table and add route entries to it. You can optionally specify the entry's order in the table, the criteria to match against the virtual circuit information, and whether to modify the destination or source addresses. Each entry must specify the disposition of the virtual circuit (that is, what is done with the virtual circuit). Each route can also specify XOT keepalive options.

The route table is used as follows:

- Virtual circuit information is matched against selection criteria specified for each route.
- The table is scanned sequentially from the top.
- The first matching route determines how the virtual circuit is handled.
- Once a matching entry is found, the call addresses can be modified and the call is disposed of (forwarded or cleared) as instructed by the entry.

Each application can define special conditions if a route will not be used or what occurs if no route matches. For instance, switched X.25 will skip a route if the disposition interface is down and clear a call if no route matches.

To configure an X.25 route (thus adding the route to the X.25 routing table), perform the following task in global configuration mode:

Task	Command
Configure an X.25 route.	**x25 route** [#*position*] {[*selection*] [*modification*]} *disposition* [*xot-keepalive*]

The following options offer versatility and flexibility when you use the **x25 route** command:

- #*position* —Position in the table. You can use the optional #*position* element to indicate the number of the entry in the route table. For example, #9 indicates the ninth entry from the top. The route table is always searched sequentially from the top, and the first match found will be used.

- *selection*—Criteria to define to which virtual circuits the route will apply. You can match against zero to four of the following optional *selection* elements:
  - *destination-pattern*
  - **source** *source-pattern*
  - **dest-ext** *nsap-destination-pattern*
  - **cud** *user-data-pattern*

- *modification*—Modifications to the source or destination address for address translation. You can use none, one, or both of the following optional *modification* elements to change the source or destination address before forwarding the call to the destination:
  - **substitute-source** *rewrite-source*
  - **substitute-dest** *rewrite-destination*

— **NOTES**

You must include a selection option or a modification option in an **x25 route** command.

- *disposition*—Where the virtual circuit will be forwarded, or if it will be cleared. You are required to use one of the following *disposition* elements:
  - **interface** *serial-interface*

    A route to a specific *serial-interface* will send the virtual circuit to an X.25 service on a synchronous serial interface.
  - **interface** *cmns-interface* **mac** *mac-address*

A route to a broadcast interface will send the virtual circuit to a CMNS partner reachable on a broadcast medium at a specified MAC address. The CMNS interface can be an Ethernet, Token Ring, or FDDI interface.

○ **xot** *ip-address* [*ip2-address* [...[*ip6-address*]]] [**xot-source** *interface*]

A route to an **xot** destination (formerly called a remote or tunneled configuration) will send the virtual circuit to the XOT service for establishment of a TCP connection across which the XOT virtual circuit packets will travel. An **xot** disposition may specify alternate destinations to try if a TCP connection cannot be established for all preceding destinations.

○ clear

A route to a **clear** destination will deny further service to the virtual circuit by shutting down the connection.

- *xot-keepalive*—Options. You can use none, one, or both of the following optional *xot-keepalive* elements:
  ○ **xot-keepalive-period** *seconds*
  ○ **xot-keepalive-tries** *count*

Configuring a PVC Switched between X.25 Interfaces

You can configure an X.25 PVC in the X.25 switching software. As a result, DTEs that require permanent circuits can be connected to a router acting as an X.25 switch and have a properly functioning connection. X.25 resets will be sent to indicate when the circuit comes up or goes down. Both interfaces must define complementary locally switched PVCs.

To configure a locally switched PVC, perform the following task in interface configuration mode:

Task	Command
Configure a locally switched PVC.	**x25 pvc** *number1* **interface** *type number* **pvc** *number2* [*option*]

The command options are **packetsize** *in out* and **windowsize** *in out*; they allow a PVC's flow control values to be defined if they differ from the interface defaults.

For an example of configuring a locally switched PVC, see the section "PVC Switching on the Same Router Example" later in this chapter.

To ensure that these TCP sessions remain connected in the absence of XOT traffic, perform the following task in global configuration mode:

Task	Command
Enable keepalives for TCP sessions sent and received to ensure timely detection of a connection failure.	**service tcp-keepalives-in** **service tcp-keepalives-out**

TCP keepalives also inform a router when an XOT SVC's session is not active, thus freeing router resources.

For examples of enabling keepalives, see the "Simple Switching of a PVC over XOT Example" and "PVC Switching over XOT Example" sections later in this chapter.

Configuring X.25 Switching between PVCs and SVCs

To configure PVC to SVC switching between two serial interfaces, both interfaces must already be configured for X.25. In addition, X.25 switching must be enabled using the **x25 routing** global configuration command. The PVC interface must be a serial interface configured with X.25 encapsulation. (The SVC interface may use X.25, XOT, or CMNS.)

Once the interfaces have been configured for X.25 switching, perform the following task in interface configuration mode:

Task	Command
Configure the PVC whose traffic is to be forwarded to an SVC.	**x25 pvc** *number1* **svc** *x121-address* [*flow-control-options*] [*call-control-options*]

To display information about the switched PVC to SVC circuit, perform the following task in EXEC mode:

Task	Command
Display information about the active SVCs and PVCs.	**show x25 vc** [*lcn*]

For an example of configuring switching between a PVC and SVC, see the section "X.25 Switching between PVCs and SVCs Example," later in this chapter.

CONFIGURING ADDITIONAL X.25 ROUTING FEATURES

To configure other, less common, X.25 routing features, perform the tasks in the following list:

- Configuring XOT to Use Interface Default Flow Control Values
- Substituting Addresses in an X.25 Route
- Configuring XOT Alternate Destinations

Configuring XOT to Use Interface Default Flow Control Values

When setting up a connection, the source and destination XOT implementations need to cooperate to determine the flow control values that apply to the SVC. The source XOT ensures cooperation by encoding the X.25 flow control facilities (the window sizes and maximum packet sizes) in the X.25 Call packet; the far host's XOT implementation can then correctly negotiate the flow control values at the destination interface and, if needed, indicate the final values in the X.25 Call Confirm packet.

When XOT receives a call that leaves one or both flow control values unspecified, it supplies the values. The values supplied are a window size of 2 packets and maximum packet size of 128 bytes; according to the standards, any SVC can be negotiated to use these values. Thus, when XOT receives a call from an older XOT implementation, it can specify in the Call Confirm packet that these flow control values must revert to the lowest common denominator.

What the older XOT implementations required was that the source and destination XOT router use the same default flow control values on the two X.25 interfaces that connect the SVC. Consequently, connections with mismatched flow control values were created when this assumption was not true, which resulted in mysterious problems. The current implementation's practice of signaling the values in the Call Confirm packet avoids these problems.

Occasionally, the older XOT implementation will be connected to a piece of X.25 equipment that cannot handle modification of the flow control parameters in the Call Confirm packet. These configurations should be upgraded to use a more recent version of XOT; when upgrade is not possible, XOT's behavior causes a migration problem. In this situation, you may configure the Cisco IOS software to cause XOT to obtain unspecified flow control facility values from the destination interface's default values.

To configure this behavior, add the option **use-tcp-if-defs** when enabling X.25 routing in global configuration mode:

Task	Command
Enable X.25 routing; optionally modify XOT's source of unencoded flow control values.	x25 routing [use-tcp-if-defs]

Substituting Addresses in an X.25 Route

When interconnecting two separate X.25 networks, you must sometimes provide for address substitution for routes. The **x25 route** command supports modification of X.25 source and destination addresses.

To modify addresses, perform either or both of the following tasks in global configuration mode:

Task	Command
Modify the X.25 source address.	**x25 route** [#*position*] *destination-pattern* [**source** *source-pattern*] [**substitute-source** *rewrite-source*] **interface** *interface number*
Modify the X.25 destination address.	**x25 route** [#*position*] *destination-pattern* [**source** *source-pattern*] [**substitute-dest** *rewrite-dest*] **interface** *interface number*

Address substitution is available for all applications of X.25 routes.

Configuring XOT Alternate Destinations

Routes to XOT hosts can be configured with alternate destination hosts. On routing a call, XOT will try each XOT destination host in sequence; if the TCP connection attempt fails, the next destination will be attempted. Up to six XOT destination addresses can be entered.

To configure an XOT route with alternate destinations (thus adding it to the X.25 routing table), perform the following task in global configuration mode:

Task	Command
Configure an XOT route; optionally define alternate XOT destination hosts.	**x25 route** [#*position*] *destination-pattern* **xot** *ip-address* [*ip-address2*... [*ip-address6*]]

The sequence of alternate destination XOT host addresses is simply added to the normal XOT route configuration command.

— **NOTES**

It can take up to 50 seconds to try an alternate route due to TCP timings.

For an example of constructing the routing table, see the section "X.25 Routing Examples" later in this chapter.

CONFIGURING CMNS ROUTING

The Connection-Mode Network Service (CMNS) provides a mechanism through which X.25 services can be extended to nonserial media through the use of packet-level X.25 over frame-level LLC2.

Cisco's CMNS implementation permits most X.25 services to be extended across a LAN, although datagram encapsulation and QLLC operations are not available. For example, a DTE host and a Sun workstation can be interconnected via the router's LAN interfaces *and* to a remote OSI-based DTE through a WAN interface to an X.25 Packet-Switched Network (PSN).

Implementing CMNS routing involves completing the tasks in the following list:

- Enabling CMNS on an Interface
- Configuring a Route to a CMNS Host

Enabling CMNS on an Interface

To enable CMNS on a nonserial interface, perform the following task in interface configuration mode:

Task	Command
Enable CMNS.	cmns enable

For an example of enabling CMNS on an interface, see the section "CMNS Switching Example" later in this chapter.

Configuring a Route to a CMNS Host

Once CMNS is enabled on a nonserial interface, the router can forward calls over that medium by configuring **x25 route** commands that define the MAC address of each CMNS host that can be reached.

To define routes to CMNS hosts, perform the following task in interface configuration mode:

Task	Command
Define a route to a CMNS host.	**x25 route** *match-criteria* **interface** *cmns-interface* **mac** *mac-address*

CONFIGURING DDN OR BFE X.25

The Defense Data Network (DDN) X.25 protocol has two versions: Basic Service and Standard Service. Cisco's X.25 implementation supports only the Standard Service and also includes Blacker Front End (BFE) and Blacker Emergency Mode operation.

DDN X.25 Standard Service requires that the X.25 data packets carry IP datagrams. The DDN Packet Switching Nodes (PSNs) can extract the IP datagram from within the X.25 packet and pass data to another Standard Service host.

The DDN X.25 Standard is the required protocol for use with DDN PSNs. The Defense Communications Agency (DCA) has certified Cisco's DDN X.25 Standard implementation for attachment to the Defense Data Network. As part of the certification, Cisco IOS software is required to provide a scheme for dynamically mapping Internet addresses to X.121 addresses. See the following section, "Understanding DDN X.25 Dynamic Mapping," for details on that scheme.

To enable DDN X.25 service, perform the tasks in the following list:

- Enabling DDN X.25
- Defining IP Precedence Handling

To enable BFE X.25 service, perform the following task:

- Configuring Blacker Front End (BFE) X.25

Understanding DDN X.25 Dynamic Mapping

The DDN X.25 standard implementation includes a scheme for dynamically mapping all classes of IP addresses to X.121 addresses without a table. This scheme requires that the IP and X.121 addresses conform to the formats shown in Figure 11–2 and Figure 11–3. These formats segment the IP addresses into network (N), host (H), logical address (L), and PSN (P) portions. For the BFE encapsulation, the IP address is segmented into Port (P), Domain (D), and BFE ID number (B). The DDN algorithm requires that the host value be less than 64.

Figure 11–2
DDN IP address conventions.

| Class A: | Net.Host.LH.PSN→ 0000 0 PPPHH00 |
| Bits: | 8   8   8   8 |

| Class B: | Net.Net.Host.PSN → 0000 0 PPPHH00 |
| Bits: | 8   8   8   8 |

| Class C: | Net.Net.Net.Host.PSN→ 0000 0 PPPHH00 |
| Bits: | 8   8   8   4   4 |

Figure 11–3
BFE IP address conventions.

| BFE Class A : | Net.unused.Port.Domain.BFE→ 0000 0 PDDDBBB |
| Bits: | 8   1   3   10   10 |

The DDN conversion scheme uses the host and PSN portions of an IP address to create the corresponding X.121 address. The DDN conversion mechanism is limited to Class A IP addresses; however, the Cisco IOS software can convert Class B and Class C addresses as well. As indicated, this method uses the last two octets of a Class B address as the host and PSN identifiers, and the upper and lower four bits in the last octet of a Class C address as the host and PSN identifiers, respectively. The BFE conversion scheme requires a Class A IP address.

The DDN conversion scheme uses a physical address mapping if the host identifier is numerically less than 64. (This limit derives from the fact that a PSN cannot support more than 64 nodes.) If the host identifier is numerically larger than 64, the resulting X.121 address is called a *logical address*. The DDN does not use logical addresses.

The format of physical DDN X.25/X.121 addresses is ZZZZFIIIHHZZ(SS). Each character represents a digit and is described in the following list:

- ZZZZ represents four zeros.
- F is zero to indicate a physical address.
- III represents the PSN octet from the IP address padded with leading zeros.
- HH is the host octet from the IP address padded with leading zeros.
- ZZ represents two zeros.
- (SS) represents the optional and unused subaddress.

The physical and logical mappings of the DDN conversion scheme always generate a 12-digit X.121 address. Subaddresses are optional; when added to this scheme, the result is a 14-digit X.121 address. The DDN does not use subaddressing.

Packets using routing and other protocols that require broadcast support can successfully traverse X.25 networks, including the DDN. This traversal requires the use of network protocol-to-X.121 maps, because the router must know explicitly where to deliver broadcast datagrams. (X.25 does not support broadcasts.) You can mark network protocol-to-X.121 map entries to accept broadcast packets; the router then sends broadcast packets to hosts with marked entries. For DDN or BFE operation, the router generates the interface X.121 addresses from the interface IP address using the DDN or BFE mapping technique.

Enabling DDN X.25

Both DCE and DTE operation causes the Cisco IOS software to specify the Standard Service facility in the Call Request packet, which notifies the PSNs to use Standard Service.

To enable DDN X.25, perform one of the following tasks in interface configuration mode, as appropriate for your network:

Task	Command
Set DDN X.25 DTE operation.	**encapsulation x25 ddn**
Set DDN X.25 DCE operation.	**encapsulation x25 dce ddn**

For an example of enabling DDN X.25, see the section "DDN X.25 Configuration Example," later in this chapter.

Defining IP Precedence Handling

Using Standard Service, the DDN can be configured to provide separate service for datagrams with high precedence values. When IP precedence handling is enabled, the router uses a separate X.25 SVC to handle each of four precedence classes of IP traffic—routine, priority, immediate, and other. An IP datagram is transmitted across an SVC that is carrying the appropriate precedence only.

By default, the DDN X.25 software opens one virtual circuit for all types of service values. You can enable the precedence-sensitivity feature by performing the following task in interface configuration mode:

Task	Command
Allow a new virtual circuit based on the type of service (TOS) field.	x25 ip-precedence

Verify that your host does not send nonstandard data in the TOS field. Nonstandard data can cause multiple, wasteful virtual circuits to be created.

Configuring Blacker Front End (BFE) X.25

For environments that require a high level of security, the Cisco IOS software supports attachment to Defense Data Network Blacker Front End equipment and Blacker Emergency Mode operation.

Blacker Emergency Mode allows your BFE device and your router to function in emergency situations. When the router is configured to participate in emergency mode and the BFE device is in emergency mode, the Cisco IOS software sends address translation information to the BFE device to assist it in sending information.

Cisco's implementation of Blacker Emergency Mode adheres to the specifications outlined in the *DCA Blacker Interface Control* document, published March 21, 1989.

Your BFE device can be configured to respond in one of the following ways:

- Enters emergency mode when requested to by the network. If the Cisco IOS software is configured to respond to a BFE device in emergency mode, or if the EXEC command **bfe enter** is used, the software sends address translation information to the BFE device.

- Never enters emergency mode.

- Notifies the router that the emergency mode window is open and waits for the router to signal it to enter emergency mode. If the software is configured to respond to a BFE in emergency mode, or if the EXEC command **bfe enter** is used, the software sends a special address translation packet to the BFE device. The "special" data includes a command to the BFE to enter emergency mode.

To configure Blacker Emergency Mode, complete the tasks in the following list:

- Setting BFE Encapsulation
- Providing Address Translation
- Defining Emergency Conditions
- Entering Blacker Emergency Mode

For an example of configuring Blacker Emergency mode, see the section "Blacker Emergency Mode Example," at the end of this chapter.

Setting BFE Encapsulation

BFE encapsulation operates to map between Class A IP addresses and the X.121 addresses expected by the BFE encryption device.

To set BFE encapsulation on the router attached to a BFE device, perform the following task in interface configuration mode:

Task	Command
Set BFE encapsulation on the router attached to a BFE device.	**encapsulation x25 bfe**

Providing Address Translation

You must set up a table that provides the address translation information the router sends to the BFE device when the BFE device is in emergency mode.

To provide address translation information to the BFE device, perform the following task in interface configuration mode:

Task	Command
Set up the table that lists the BFE nodes (host or gateways) to which the router will send packets.	**x25 remote-red** *host-ip-address* **remote-black** *blacker-ip-address*

Defining Emergency Conditions

To define the circumstances under which the router participates in emergency mode and how it will participate, perform the following tasks in interface configuration mode:

Task	Command
Define the circumstances under which the router will participate in emergency mode.	**x25 bfe-emergency** {**never** | **always** | **decision**}
Define how a router configured as **x25 bfe-emergency decision** will participate in emergency mode.	**x25 bfe-decision** {**no** | **yes** | **ask**}

Entering Blacker Emergency Mode

To set the router to participate in emergency mode or to end participation in emergency mode when your router is so configured, perform the following task in EXEC mode:

Task	Command
Set router to participate in emergency mode.	**bfe** {**enter**	**leave**} *type number*

CREATING X.29 ACCESS LISTS

Protocol translation software supports access lists, which make it possible to limit access to the access server from X.25 hosts. Access lists take advantage of the message field defined by Recommendation X.29, which describes procedures for exchanging data between two PADs or between a PAD and a DTE device.

To define X.29 access lists, perform the following tasks:

Step 1   Create an X.29 access list.

Step 2   Apply an access list to a virtual terminal line or to protocol translation.

These tasks are described in the following sections.

When configuring protocol translation, you can specify an access list number with each **translate** command. When translation sessions result from incoming PAD connections, the corresponding X.29 access list is used.

For an example of defining an X.29 access list, see the section "X.29 Access List Example," at the end of this chapter.

Creating an Access List

To specify the access conditions, perform the following global configuration task:

Task	Command
Restrict incoming and outgoing connections between a particular virtual terminal line (into a Cisco access server) and the addresses in an access list.	**x29 access-list** *access-list-number* {**deny**	**permit**} *x121-address*

An access list can contain any number of lines. The lists are processed in the order in which you type the entries. The first match causes the permit or deny condition. If an X.121 address does not match any of the entries in the access list, access is denied.

Applying an Access List to a Line

To apply an access list to a virtual line, perform the following task in line configuration mode:

Task	Command
Restrict incoming and outgoing connections between a particular virtual terminal line (into a Cisco access server) and the addresses in an access list.	**access-class** *access-list-number* **in**

The access list number is used for incoming TCP access, incoming local-area transport (LAT) access, and for incoming PAD access. For TCP access, the protocol translator uses the defined IP access lists. For LAT access, the protocol translator uses the defined LAT access list. For incoming PAD connections, an X.29 access list is used. If you want to have access restrictions only on one of the protocols, then you can create an access list that permits all addresses for the other protocol.

CREATING AN X.29 PROFILE SCRIPT

You can create an X.29 profile script for use by the **translate** command. When an X.25 connection is established, the protocol translator then acts as if an X.29 Set Parameter packet had been sent that contained the parameters and values set by this command.

To create an X.29 profile script, perform the following global configuration task:

Task	Command
Create an X.29 profile script.	**x29 profile** {**default**	*name*} *parameter:value* [*parameter:value*]

For an example of a profile script, see the section "X.29 Profile Script Example," at the end of this chapter.

MONITORING AND MAINTAINING LAPB AND X.25

To monitor and maintain X.25 and LAPB, perform any of the following tasks in EXEC mode:

Task	Command
Clear an SVC, restart an X.25 or CMNS service, or reset a PVC.	**clear x25** {**serial** *number*	*cmns-interface mac-address*} [*vc-number*]
Clear an XOT SVC or reset an XOT PVC.	**clear xot remote** *ip-address port* **local** *ip-address port*
Display CMNS information.	**show cmns** [*type number*]
Display operation statistics for an interface.	**show interfaces serial** *number*
Display CMNS connections over LLC2.	**show llc2**

Task	Command
Display information about VCs on an X.25 interface (a serial interface) or a CMNS interface (an Ethernet, Token Ring, or FDDI interface).	**show x25 interface** [**serial** *number* | *cmns-interface* **mac** *mac-address*]
Display the protocol-to-X.121 address map.	**show x25 map**
Display the one-to-one mapping of the host IP addresses and the remote BFE device's IP addresses.	**show x25 remote-red**
Display routes assigned by the **x25 route** command.	**show x25 route**
Display information about X.25 services.	**show x25 services**
Display details of active virtual circuits.	**show x25 vc** [*lcn*]
Display information for all XOT virtual circuits or, optionally, for the virtual circuits that match a specified set of criteria.	**show x25 xot** [**local** *ip-address* [**port** *port*]] [**remote** *ip-address* [**port** *port*]]

X.25 AND LAPB CONFIGURATION EXAMPLES

The following sections provide examples to help you understand how to configure LAPB and X.25 for your network. The provided examples are the following:

- Typical LAPB Configuration Example
- Transparent Bridging for Multiprotocol LAPB Encapsulation Example
- Typical X.25 Configuration Example
- Virtual Circuit Ranges Example
- PVC Switching on the Same Router Example
- X.25 Route Address Pattern Matching Example
- X.25 Routing Examples
- PVC Used to Exchange IP Traffic Example
- Point-to-Point Subinterface Configuration Example
- Simple Switching of a PVC over XOT Example
- PVC Switching over XOT Example
- X.25 Switching between PVCs and SVCs Example
- CMNS Switching Example
- CMNS Switched over a PDN Example
- CMNS Switched over Leased Lines Example
- DDN X.25 Configuration Example
- Blacker Emergency Mode Example

- X.25 Configured to Allow Ping Support over Multiple Lines Example
- Booting from a Network Server over X.25 Example
- X.29 Access List Example
- X.29 Profile Script Example

Typical LAPB Configuration Example

In the following example, the frame size (N1), window size (k), and maximum retransmission (N2) parameters retain their default values. The **encapsulation** interface configuration command sets DCE operation to carry a single protocol, IP by default. The **lapb t1** interface configuration command sets the retransmission timer to 4,000 milliseconds (4 seconds) for a link with a long delay or slow connecting DTE device.

```
interface serial 3
 encapsulation lapb dce
 lapb t1 4000
```

Transparent Bridging for Multiprotocol LAPB Encapsulation Example

The following example configures transparent bridging for multiprotocol LAPB encapsulation:

```
no ip routing
!
interface Ethernet 1
 no ip address
 no mop enabled
 bridge-group 1
!
interface serial 0
 no ip address
 encapsulation lapb multi
 bridge-group 1
!
bridge 1 protocol ieee
```

Typical X.25 Configuration Example

The following example shows the complete configuration for a serial interface connected to a commercial X.25 PDN for routing the IP protocol. The IP subnetwork address 172.25.9.0 has been assigned for the X.25 network.

─── **NOTES** ──

When you are routing IP over X.25, you must treat the X.25 network as a single IP network or subnetwork. Map entries for routers with addresses on subnetworks other than the one on which the interface's IP address is stored are ignored by the routing software. Additionally, all routers using the subnet number must have map entries for all others routers. Moreover, using the broadcast option with dynamic routing can result in significantly larger traffic loads, thus requiring a larger hold queue, larger window sizes, or multiple virtual circuits.

```
interface serial 2
 ip address 172.25.9.1 255.255.255.0
!
 encapsulation X25
!
! The "bandwidth" command is not part of the X.25
! configuration; it is especially important to understand that it does not
! have any connection with the X.25 entity of the same name.
! "bandwidth" commands are used by IP routing processes (currently only IGRP)
! to determine which lines are the best choices for traffic.
! Since the default is 1544 Kbaud, and X.25 service at that rate is not generally
! available, most X.25 interfaces that are being used with IGRP in a
! real environment will have "bandwidth" settings.
!
! This is a 9.6 Kbaud line:
!
 bandwidth 10
! You must specify an X.121 address to be assigned to the X.25 interface by the PDN.
!
 x25 address 31370054065
!
! The following Level 3 parameters have been set to match the network.
! You generally need to change some Level 3 parameters, most often
! those listed below. You might not need to change any Level 2
! parameters, however.
!
 x25 htc 32
!
! These Level 3 parameters are default flow control values; they need to
! match the PDN defaults. The values used by an SVC are negotiable on a per-call basis:
!
 x25 win 7
 x25 wout 7
 x25 ips 512
 x25 ops 512
!
!
! The following commands configure the default behavior for our encapsulation
! SVCs
!
 x25 idle 5
 x25 nvc 2
!
! The following commands configure the X.25 map. If you want to exchange
! routing updates with any of the routers, they would need
! "broadcast" flags.
! If the X.25 network is the only path to the routers, static routes are
! generally used to save on packet charges. If there is a redundant
! path, it might be desirable to run a dynamic routing protocol.
!
 x25 map IP 172.25.9.3 31370019134 ACCEPT-REVERSE
! ACCEPT-REVERSE allows collect calls
 x25 map IP 172.25.9.2 31370053087
!
```

```
! If the PDN cannot handle fast back-to-back frames, use the
!"transmitter-delay" command to slow down the interface.
!
 transmitter-delay 1000
```

Virtual Circuit Ranges Example

The following example sets the virtual circuit ranges of 5 to 20 for incoming calls only (from the DCE to the DTE) and 25 to 1024 for either incoming or outgoing calls. It also specifies that no virtual circuits are reserved for outgoing calls (from the DTE to the DCE). Up to four permanent virtual circuits can be defined on virtual circuits 1 through 4.

```
x25 lic 5
x25 hic 20
x25 ltc 25
```

PVC Switching on the Same Router Example

In the following example, a PVC is connected between two serial interfaces on the same router. In this type of interconnection configuration, the destination interface must be specified along with the PVC number on that interface. To make a working PVC connection, two commands must be specified, each pointing to the other.

```
interface serial 0
 encapsulation x25
 x25 ltc 5
 x25 pvc 1 interface serial 1 pvc 4
!
interface serial 1
 encapsulation x25
 x25 ltc 5
 x25 pvc 4 interface serial 0 pvc 1
```

X.25 Route Address Pattern Matching Example

The following example shows how to route X.25 calls with addresses whose first four Data Network Identification Code (DNIC) digits are 1111 to interface serial 3, and to change the DNIC field in the addresses presented to the equipment connected to that interface to 2222. The \1 in the rewrite pattern indicates the portion of the original address matched by the digits following the 1111 DNIC.

```
x25 route ^1111(.*) substitute-dest 2222\1 interface serial 3
```

Figure 11–4 shows a more contrived command intended to illustrate the power of the rewriting scheme.

The command in Figure 11–4 causes all X.25 calls with 14-digit called addresses to be routed through interface serial 0. The incoming DNIC field is moved to the end of the address. The fifth, sixth, ninth, and tenth digits are deleted, and the thirteenth and fourteenth are moved before the eleventh and twelfth.

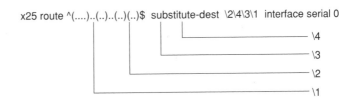

Figure 11–4
An example of X.25 route
address pattern matching.

X.25 Routing Examples

The following examples illustrate how to enable the X.25 switch service, and how to configure a router on a Tymnet/PAD switch to accept and forward calls.

This first example shows how to enable X.25 switching, as well as how to enter routes into the X.25 routing table:

```
! Enable X.25 forwarding
x25 routing
!
! Enter routes into the table. Without a positional parameter, entries
! are appended to the end of the table
x25 route ^100$ interface serial 0
x25 route 100 cud ^pad$ interface serial 2
x25 route 100 interface serial 1
x25 route ^3306 interface serial 3
x25 route .* ip 10.2.0.2
```

The routing table forwards calls for X.121 address 100 out interface serial 0. Otherwise, calls are forwarded onto serial 1 if the X.121 address contains 100 anywhere within it and contains no call user data (CUD), or if the CUD is not the string *pad*. If the X.121 address contains the digits 100 and the CUD is the string *pad*, the call is forwarded onto serial 2. All X.121 addresses that do not match the first three routes are checked for a DNIC of 3306 as the first four digits. If they do match, they are forwarded over serial 3. All other X.121 addresses will match the fifth entry, which is a match-all pattern and will have a TCP connection established to the IP address 10.2.0.2. The router at 10.2.0.2 will then handle the call according to its configuration.

This second example configures a router that sits on a Tymnet/PAD switch to accept calls and have them forwarded to a DEC VAX system. This feature permits running an X.25 network over a generalized existing IP network, thereby making another physical line for one protocol unnecessary. The router positioned next to the DEC VAX system is configured with X.25 routes as follows:

```
x25 route vax-x121-address interface serial 0
x25 route .* ip cisco-on-tymnet-ipaddress
```

These commands route all calls to the DEC VAX X.121 address out to serial 0, where the VAX is connected running PSI. All other X.121 addresses are forwarded to the *cisco-on-tymnet* address through its IP address. As a result, all outgoing calls from the VAX are sent to *cisco-on-tymnet* for further processing.

On the router named *cisco-on-tymnet*, you enter these commands:

```
x25 route vax-x121-address ip cisco-on-vax
x25 route .* interface serial 0
```

These commands force all calls with the VAX X.121 address to be sent to the router with the VAX connected to it. All other calls with X.121 addresses are forwarded out to Tymnet. If Tymnet can route them, a Call Accepted packet is returned, and everything proceeds normally. If Tymnet cannot handle the calls, it clears each call and the Clear Request packet is forwarded back toward the VAX.

PVC Used to Exchange IP Traffic Example

The following example, illustrated in Figure 11–5, demonstrates how to use the PVC to exchange IP traffic between Router X and Router Y.

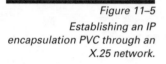

Figure 11–5

Establishing an IP encapsulation PVC through an X.25 network.

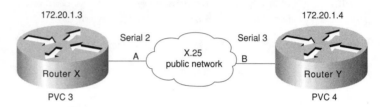

Configuration for Router X

```
interface serial 2
  ip address 172.20.1.3 255.255.255.0
  x25 pvc 4 ip 172.20.1.4
```

Configuration for Router Y

```
interface serial 3
  ip address 172.20.1.4 255.255.255.0
  x25 pvc 3 ip 172.20.1.3
```

In this example, the PDN has established a PVC through its network connecting PVC number 3 of access point A to PVC number 4 of access point B. On Router X, a connection is established between Router X and Router Y's IP address, 172.20.1.4. On Router Y, a connection is established between Router Y and Router X's IP address, 172.20.1.3.

Point-to-Point Subinterface Configuration Example

The following example creates a point-to-point subinterface, maps IP and AppleTalk to a remote host, and creates an encapsulating PVC for DECnet to the same remote host, identified by the X.121 address in the commands:

```
interface Serial0.1 point-to-point
  x25 map ip 172.20.170.90 170090 broadcast
  x25 map appletalk 4.50 170090 broadcast
  x25 pvc 1 decnet 1.2 170090 broadcast
```

Simple Switching of a PVC over XOT Example

In the following simple example, a connection is established between two PVCs across a LAN. Because the connection is remote (across the LAN), the XOT service is used. This example establishes a PVC between Router X, Serial 0, PVC 1 and Router Y, Serial 1, PVC 2. Keepalives are enabled to maintain connection notification. Figure 11–6 provides a visual representation of the configuration.

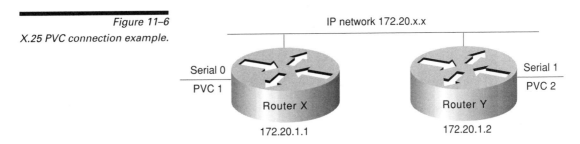

Figure 11–6
X.25 PVC connection example.

Configuration for Router X
```
service tcp-keepalives-in
service tcp-keepalives-out
interface serial 0
  x25 pvc 1 xot 172.20.1.2 interface serial 1 pvc 2
```

Configuration for Router Y
```
service tcp-keepalives-in
service tcp-keepalives-out
interface serial 1
  x25 pvc 2 xot 172.20.1.1 interface serial 0 pvc 1
```

PVC Switching over XOT Example

In the more complex example shown in Figure 11–7, the connection between points A and B is switched, and the connections between point C and points A and B are made using XOT. Keepalives are enabled to maintain connection notification.

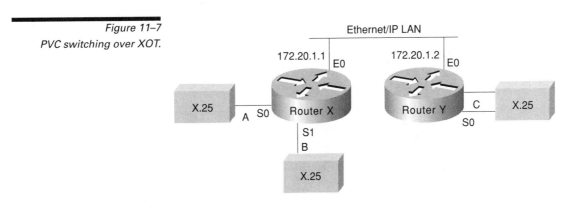

Figure 11–7
PVC switching over XOT.

Configuration for Router X
```
service tcp-keepalives-in
service tcp-keepalives-out
interface ethernet 0
 ip address 172.20.1.1 255.255.255.0
 !
interface serial 0
 x25 ltc 5
 x25 pvc 1 interface serial 1 pvc 1
 x25 pvc 2 xot 172.20.1.2 interface serial 0 pvc 1
 !
interface serial 1
 x25 ltc 5
 x25 pvc 1 interface serial 0 pvc 1
 x25 pvc 2 xot 172.20.1.2 interface serial 0 pvc 2
```

Configuration for Router Y
```
service tcp-keepalives-in
service tcp-keepalives-out
interface ethernet 0
 ip address 172.20.1.2 255.255.255.0
 !
interface serial 0
 x25 ltc 5
 x25 pvc 1 xot 172.20.1.1 interface serial 0 pvc 2
 x25 pvc 2 xot 172.20.1.1 interface serial 1 pvc 2
```

X.25 Switching between PVCs and SVCs Example

The following example allows X.25 switching between a PVC on the first interface and an SVC on the second interface. X.25 traffic arriving on PVC 20 on serial interface 0 will cause a call to be placed to 000000160100, if one does not already exist.
```
x25 routing
interface serial0
 encapsulation x25
 x25 address 000000180100
 x25 ltc 128
 x25 pvc 20 svc 000000160100 packetsize 128 128 windowsize 2 2

interface serial2
 encapsulation x25 dce
 x25 route ^000000160100$ interface Serial2
 x25 route ^000000180100$ interface Serial0
```

The **x25 route** command adds the two X.121 addresses to the X.25 routing table. Data traffic received on PVC 20 on serial interface 0 will cause a call to be placed with a Called (destination) Address of 000000160100; this call will be routed to serial interface 2. Alternatively, an X.25 call received with a Called Address of 000000180100 and a Calling Address of 000000160100 will be associated with PVC 20 on serial interface 0. In either case, subsequent X.25 traffic on either the SVC or the PVC will be forwarded to the other circuit. Because no idle timeout has been specified for the interface or for the circuit, the router will not clear the call.

CMNS Switching Example

The following example illustrates enabling CMNS and configuring X.25 routes to the available CMNS host and the PDN connectivity:

```
interface ethernet 0
 cmns enable
!
interface serial 0
 encapsulation x25
!
interface serial 1
 encapsulation x25
!
x25 route dest-ext ^38.8261.1000.0150.1000.17 interface Ethernet0 mac 0000.0c00.ff89
! Above maps NSAP to MAC-address on Ethernet0
!
x25 route dest-ext ^38.8261.1000.0150.1000.18 substitute-dest 3110451 interface Serial0
! Above maps NSAP to X.121-address on Serial0 assuming the link is over a PDN
!
x25 route dest-ext ^38.8261.1000.0150.1000.20 interface Serial1
! Above specifies cmns support for Serial1
! assuming that the link is over a leased line
```

CMNS Switched over a PDN Example

The following example depicts switching CMNS over a packet-switched PDN. Figure 11–8 illustrates the general network topology for a CMNS switching application where calls are being made between resources on opposite sides of a remote link to Host A (on an Ethernet) and Host B (on a Token Ring), with a PDN providing the connection.

Figure 11–8

Example network topology for switching CMNS over a PDN.

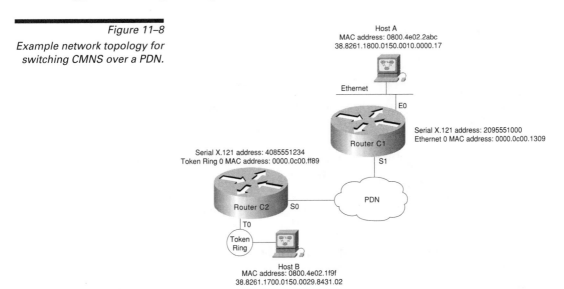

Host A
MAC address: 0800.4e02.2abc
38.8261.1800.0150.0010.0000.17

Ethernet

E0

Router C1

Serial X.121 address: 2095551000
Ethernet 0 MAC address: 0000.0c00.1309

S1

Serial X.121 address: 4085551234
Token Ring 0 MAC address: 0000.0c00.ff89

Router C2   S0

PDN

T0

Token Ring

Host B
MAC address: 0800.4e02.1f9f
38.8261.1700.0150.0029.8431.02

The following configuration listing allows resources on either side of the PDN to call Host A or Host B. This configuration allows traffic intended for the remote NSAP address specified in the **x25 route** commands (for the serial ports) to be switched through the serial interface for which CMNS is configured.

Configuration for Router C2

```
interface token 0
 cmns enable
!
interface serial 0
 encapsulation x25
 x25 address 4085551234
!
x25 route dest-ext ^38.8261.17 interface Token0 mac 0800.4e02.1f9f
!
! The line above specifies that any traffic from any other interface
! intended for any NSAP address with NSAP prefix 38.8261.17 will be
! switched to MAC address 0800.4e02.1f9f through Token Ring 0
!
x25 route dest-ext ^38.8261.18 substitute-dest 2095551000 interface Serial0
!
! The line above specifies that traffic from any other interface
! on Cisco Router C2 that is intended for any NSAP address with
! NSAP-prefix 38.8261.18 will be switched to
! X.121 address 2095551000 through Serial 0
```

Configuration for Router C1

```
interface ethernet 0
 cmns enable
!
interface serial 1
 encapsulation x25
 x25 address 2095551000
!
x25 route dest-ext ^38.8261.18 interface Ethernet0 mac 0800.4e02.2abc
!
! The line above specifies that any traffic from any other
! interface intended for any NSAP address with NSAP 38.8261.18
! will be switched to MAC address 0800.4e02.2abc through Ethernet 0
!
x25 route dest-ext ^38.8261.17 substitute-dest 4085551234 interface Serial1
!
! The line above specifies that traffic from any other interface
! on Cisco Router C1 that is intended for any NSAP address with
! NSAP-prefix 38.8261.17 will be switched to X.121 address
! 4085551234 through Serial 1
```

CMNS Switched over Leased Lines Example

The following example illustrates switching CMNS over a leased line. Figure 11–9 illustrates the general network topology for a CMNS switching application where calls are being made by resources on the opposite sides of a remote link to Host C (on an Ethernet) and Host B (on a Token Ring), with a dedicated leased line providing the connection.

The following configuration listing allows resources on either side of the leased line to call Host C or Host B. This configuration allows traffic intended for the remote NSAP address specified in the **x25 route** commands (for the serial ports) to be switched through the serial interface for which CMNS is configured.

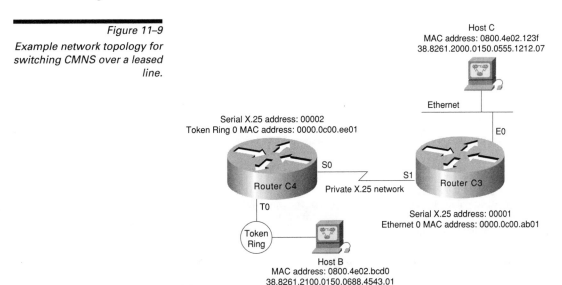

Figure 11–9

Example network topology for switching CMNS over a leased line.

A key difference for this configuration compared with the previous example is that with no PDN, the substitution of the destination X.121 address in the **x25 route** command is not necessary. The specification of an X.25 address also is not needed, but is included for symmetry with the previous example.

Configuration for Router C4

```
interface token 0
 cmns enable
!
interface serial 0
 encapsulation x25
 x25 address 4085551234
!
x25 route dest-ext ^38.8261.17 interface Token0 mac 0800.4e02.1f9f
!
! The line above specifies that any traffic from any other interface
! intended for any NSAP address with NSAP prefix 38.8261.17 will be
! switched to MAC address 0800.4e02.1f9f through Token Ring 0
!
x25 route dest-ext ^38.8261.18 interface Serial0
```

```
!
! The line above specifies that traffic from any other interface
! on Cisco Router C2 that is intended for any NSAP address with
! NSAP-prefix 38.8261.18 will be switched to
! X.121 address 2095551000 through Serial 0
```

Configuration for Router C3

```
interface ethernet 0
 cmns enable
!
interface serial 1
 encapsulation x25
 x25 address 2095551000
!
x25 route dest-ext ^38.8261.18 interface Ethernet0 mac 0800.4e02.2abc
!
! The line above specifies that any traffic from any other
! interface intended for any NSAP address with NSAP 38.8261.18
! will be switched to MAC address 0800.4e02.2abc through Ethernet 0
!
x25 route dest-ext ^38.8261.17 interface Serial1
!
! The line above specifies that traffic from any other interface
! on Cisco Router C1 that is intended for any NSAP address with
! NSAP-prefix 38.8261.17 will be switched to X.121 address
! 4085551234 through Serial 1
```

DDN X.25 Configuration Example

The following example illustrates how to configure a router interface to run DDN X.25:

```
interface serial 0
 ip address 192.31.7.50 255.255.255.240
 encapsulation x25 ddn
 x25 win 6
 x25 wout 6
 x25 ips 1024
 x25 ops 1024
 x25 t20 10
 x25 t21 10
 x25 t22 10
 x25 t23 10
 x25 nvc 2
 x25 map IP 192.31.7.49 000000010300 BROADCAST
```

Blacker Emergency Mode Example

In the following example, interface serial 0 is configured to require an EXEC command from you or your network administrator before it participates in emergency mode. The host IP address is 21.0.0.12, and the address of the remote BFE unit is 21.0.0.1. When the BFE enters emergency mode, the router prompts for the EXEC command **bfe enter** to direct the router to participate in emergency mode.

```
interface serial 0
 ip address 21.0.0.2 255.0.0.0
 encapsulation x25 bfe
 x25 bfe-emergency decision
 x25 remote-red 21.0.0.12 remote-black 21.0.0.1
 x25 bfe-decision ask
```

X.25 Configured to Allow Ping Support over Multiple Lines Example

For **ping** commands to work in an X.25 environment (when load sharing over multiple serial lines), you must include entries for all adjacent interface IP addresses in the **x25 map** command for each serial interface. The following example illustrates this point.

Consider two routers, Router A and Router B, communicating with each other over two serial lines via an X.25 PDN (see Figure 11–10) or over leased lines. In either case, all serial lines must be configured for the same IP subnet address space. The configuration that follows allows for successful **ping** commands. A similar configuration is required for the same subnet IP addresses to work across X.25.

Figure 11–10

Communicating via parallel serial lines to an X.25 network.

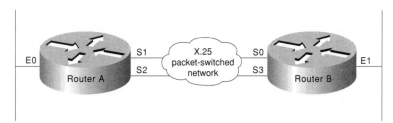

NOTES

All four serial ports configured for the two routers in the following configuration example must be assigned to the same IP subnet address space. In this case, the subnet is 172.20.170.0.

Configuration for Router A

```
interface serial 1
 ip 172.20.170.1 255.255.255.0
 x25 address 31370054068
 x25 alias ^31370054069$
 x25 map ip 172.20.170.3 31370054065
 x25 map ip 172.20.170.4 31370054065
!
interface serial 2
 ip 172.20.170.2 255.255.255.0
 x25 address 31370054069
 x25 alias ^31370054068$
 x25 map ip 172.20.170.4 31370054067
 x25 map ip 171.20.170.3 31370054067
! allow either destination address
```

Configuration for Router B

```
interface serial 0
 ip 172.20.170.3 255.255.255.0
 x25 address 31370054065
 x25 alias ^31370054067$
 x25 map ip 172.20.170.1 31370054068
 x25 map ip 172.20.170.2 31370054068
 !
interface serial 3
 ip 172.20.170.4 255.255.255.0
 x25 address 31370054067
 x25 alias ^31370054065$
 x25 map ip 172.20.170.2 31370054069
 x25 map ip 172.20.170.1 31370054069
 ! allow either destination address
```

Booting from a Network Server over X.25 Example

You cannot boot the router over an X.25 network using broadcasts. Instead, you must boot from a specific host. Also, an **x25 map** command must exist for the host from which you boot. The **x25 map** command is used to map an IP address into an X.121 address. There must be an **x25 map** command that matches the IP address given on the **boot system** command line. The following is an example of such a configuration:

```
boot system gs3-k.100 172.18.126.111
!
interface Serial 1
 ip address 172.18.126.200 255.255.255.0
 encapsulation X25
 x25 address 10004
 x25 map IP 172.18.126.111 10002 broadcast
 lapb n1 12040
 clockrate 56000
```

In this case, 10002 is the X.121 address of the remote router that can get to host 172.18.126.111.

The remote router must have the following **x25 map** entry:

```
x25 map IP 172.18.126.200 10004 broadcast
```

This entry allows the remote router to return a boot image from the host to the router booting over X.25.

X.29 Access List Example

The following example illustrates an X.29 access list. Incoming permit conditions are set for all IP hosts and LAT nodes that have specific characters in their names. All X.25 connections to a printer are denied. Outgoing connections are list restricted.

```
!Permit all IP hosts and LAT nodes beginning with "VMS".
!Deny X.25 connections to the printer on line 5.
!
access-list 1 permit 0.0.0.0 255.255.255.255
 lat access-list 1 permit ^VMS.*
 x29 access-list 1 deny .*
```

```
!
line vty 5
 access-class 1 in
!
!Permit outgoing connections for other lines.
!
!Permit IP access with the network 172.30
 access-list 2 permit 172.30.0.0 0.0.255.255
!
!Permit LAT access to the boojum/snark complexes.
 lat access-list 2 permit ^boojum$
 lat access-list 2 permit ^snark$
!
!Permit X.25 connections to Infonet hosts only.
 x29 access-list 2 permit ^31370
!
line vty 0 16
 access-class 2 out
```

X.29 Profile Script Example

The following profile script turns local edit mode on when the connection is made and establishes local echo and line termination upon receipt of a Return. The name *linemode* is used with the **translate** command to effect use of this script.

```
x29 profile linemode 2:1 3:2 15:1
translate tcp 172.30.1.26 x25 55551234 profile linemode
```

CHAPTER 12

X.25 and LAPB Commands

Use the commands in this chapter to configure Link Access Procedure, Balanced (LAPB), X.25 services (X.25, XOT, and CMNS), Defense Data Network (DDN) X.25, and the Blacker Front End (BFE). X.25 provides remote terminal access; encapsulation for the IP, DECnet, XNS, ISO CLNS, AppleTalk, Novell IPX, Banyan VINES, and Apollo Domain protocols; and bridging.

X.25 virtual circuits can also be switched as follows:

- Between interfaces—for local routing
- Between two routers—for remote routing using X.25-over-TCP (XOT)
- Over nonserial media—for Connection-Mode Network Service (CMNS)

For X.25 and LAPB configuration information and examples, see Chapter 11, "Configuring X.25 and LAPB."

— **NOTES**

You can use the master indexes or search online to find documentation of related commands.

ACCESS-CLASS

To configure an incoming access class on virtual terminals, use the **access-class** line configuration command.

> **access-class** *access-list-number* **in**

Syntax	Description
access-list-number	An integer between 1 and 199 that you select for the access list.
in	Restricts incoming connections between a particular access server and the addresses in the access list.

Default

No incoming access class is defined.

Command Mode

Line configuration

Usage Guidelines

This command first appeared in Cisco IOS Release 10.3.

The access list number is used for both incoming Transmission Control Protocol (TCP) access and incoming packet assembler/disassembler (PAD) access. In the case of TCP access, the access server uses the Internet Protocol (IP) access list defined with the **access-list** command. For incoming PAD connections, the same numbered X.29 access list is referenced. If you only want to have access restrictions on one of the protocols, you can create an access list that permits all addresses for the other protocol.

Example

The following example configures an incoming access class on virtual terminal line 4:

```
line vty 4
  access-class 4 in
```

Related Commands

access-list
line vty
x29 access-list

BFE

To allow the router to participate in emergency mode or to end participation in emergency mode when the interface is configured for **x25 bfe-emergency decision** and **x25 bfe-decision ask**, use the **bfe** EXEC command.

     bfe {**enter** | **leave**} *type number*

Syntax	Description
enter	Causes the Cisco IOS software to send a special address translation packet that includes an **enter emergency mode** command to the Blacker Front End (BFE) if the emergency mode window is open. If the BFE is already in emergency mode, this command enables the sending of address translation information.
leave	Disables the sending of address translation information from the Cisco IOS software to the BFE when the BFE is in emergency mode.
type	Interface type.
number	Interface number.

Command Mode

EXEC

Usage Guidelines

This command first appeared in Cisco IOS Release 10.3.

Example

The following example enables an interface to participate in BFE emergency mode:
```
bfe enter serial 0
```

Related Commands

encapsulation x25 bfe
x25 bfe-decision
x25 bfe-emergency

CLEAR X25

Use the **clear x25** privileged EXEC command to restart an X.25 or CMNS service, to clear an SVC, or to reset a PVC.

   clear x25 {**serial** *number* | *cmns-interface mac-address*} [*vc-number*]

Syntax	Description
serial *number*	Local serial interface being used for X.25 service.
cmns-interface mac-address	Local CMNS interface (an Ethernet, Token Ring, or FDDI interface) and MAC address of the remote device; this information identifies a CMNS service.
vc-number	(Optional) SVC or PVC number, in the range 1 to 4095. If specified, the SVC is cleared or the PVC is reset. If not specified, the X.25 or CMNS service is restarted.

Command Reference

Command Mode
Privileged EXEC

Usage Guidelines
This command first appeared in Cisco IOS Release 11.2 F. (This command replaces the **clear x25-vc** command, which first appeared in Cisco IOS Release 8.3.)

This command form is used to disrupt service forcibly on an individual circuit or on all circuits using a specific X.25 service or CMNS service. If this command is used without the *vc-number* value, a restart event is initiated, which implicitly clears all SVCs and resets all PVCs.

Examples
The following command clears the SVC or resets the PVC specified:

```
clear x25 serial 0 1
```

The following command forces an X.25 restart, which implicitly clears all SVCs and resets all PVCs using the interface:

```
clear x25 serial 0
```

The following command restarts the specified CMNS service (if active), which implicitly clears all SVCs using the service:

```
clear x25 ethernet 0 0001.0002.0003
```

Related Commands
clear xot
show x25 services

CLEAR X25-VC

This command is replaced by the **clear x25** command.

CLEAR XOT

To clear an XOT SVC or reset an XOT PVC, use the **clear xot** EXEC command.

clear xot remote *ip-address port* **local** *ip-address port*

Syntax	Description
remote *ip-address port*	Remote IP address and port number of an XOT connection ID.
local *ip-address port*	Local IP address and port number of an XOT connection ID.

Command Mode
EXEC

Usage Guidelines

This command first appeared in Cisco IOS Release 11.2 F.

Each SVC or PVC supported by the XOT service uses a TCP connection to communicate X.25 packets. A TCP connection is uniquely identified by the data quartet: remote IP address, remote TCP port, local IP address, and local TCP port. This command form is used to forcibly disrupt service on an individual XOT circuit.

XOT connections are sent to TCP port 1998, so XOT connections originated by the router will have that remote port number, and connections received by the router will have that local port number.

Example

The following command will clear or reset, respectively, the SVC or PVC using the TCP connection identified:

```
clear xot remote 1.1.1.1 1998 local 2.2.2.2 2000
```

Related Commands

show x25 services

CMNS ENABLE

To enable the Connection-Mode Network Service (CMNS) on a nonserial interface, use the **cmns enable** interface configuration command. To disable this capability, use the **no** form of this command.

> **cmns enable**
> **no cmns enable**

Syntax Description

This command has no arguments or keywords.

Default

Each nonserial interface must be explicitly configured to use CMNS.

Command Mode

Interface configuration

Usage Guidelines

This command first appeared in Cisco IOS Release 10.0.

After this command is processed on the LAN interfaces—Ethernet, Fiber Distributed Data Interface (FDDI), and Token Ring—all the X.25-related interface configuration commands are made available.

Example

The following example enables CMNS on Ethernet interface 0:

Command Reference

```
interface ethernet 0
cmns enable
```

Related Commands

x25 route

ENCAPSULATION LAPB

To exchange datagrams over a serial interface using LAPB encapsulation, use the **encapsulation lapb** interface configuration command.

> **encapsulation lapb** [**dte** | **dce**] [**multi** | *protocol*]

Syntax	Description
dte	(Optional) Specifies operation as a data terminal equipment (DTE) device. This is the default LAPB mode.
dce	(Optional) Specifies operation as a data communications equipment (DCE) device.
multi	(Optional) Specifies use of multiple local-area network (LAN) protocols to be carried on the LAPB line.
protocol	(Optional) A single protocol to be carried on the LAPB line. A single protocol can be one of the following: **apollo, appletalk, clns** (ISO CLNS), **decnet, ip, ipx** (Novell IPX), **vines,** and **xns.** IP is the default protocol.

Defaults

The default serial encapsulation is High-Level Data Link Control (HDLC). You must explicitly configure a LAPB encapsulation method.

DTE operation is the default LAPB mode. IP is the default protocol.

Command Mode

Interface configuration

Usage Guidelines

This command first appeared prior to Cisco IOS Release 10.0.
The **dte, dce, multi,** and *protocol* argument forms first appeared in Cisco IOS Release 10.3.

LAPB encapsulations are appropriate only for private connections, where you have complete control over both ends of the link. Connections to X.25 networks should use an X.25 encapsulation configuration, which operates the X.25 Layer 3 protocol above an LAPB Layer 2. One end of the link must be a logical DCE, and the other end a logical DTE. (This assignment is independent of the interface's hardware DTE or DCE identity.)

Both ends of the LAPB link must specify the same protocol encapsulation.

LAPB encapsulation is supported on serial lines configured for dial-on-demand routing (DDR). It can be configured on DDR synchronous serial and Integrated Services Digital Network (ISDN) interfaces and on DDR dialer rotary groups. It is not supported on asynchronous dialer interfaces.

A single-protocol LAPB encapsulation exchanges datagrams of the given protocol, each in a separate LAPB information frame. You must configure the interface with the protocol-specific parameters needed—for example, a link that carries IP traffic will have an IP address defined for the interface.

A multiprotocol LAPB encapsulation can exchange any or all of the protocols allowed for a LAPB interface. It exchanges datagrams, each in a separate LAPB information frame. Two bytes of protocol identification data precede the protocol data. You need to configure the interface with all the protocol-specific parameters needed for each protocol carried.

Beginning with Cisco IOS Release 11.0, *multiprotocol* LAPB encapsulation supports transparent bridging. This feature requires the use of the **encapsulation lapb multi** command followed by the **bridge-group** command, which identifies the bridge group associated with multiprotocol LAPB encapsulation. This feature does *not* support use of the **encapsulation lapb** *protocol* command with a **bridge** keyword.

Beginning with Release 10.3, LAPB encapsulation supports the priority and custom queueing features.

Example

The following example sets the operating mode as DTE and specifies that AppleTalk protocol traffic will be carried on the LAPB line:

```
interface serial 1
  encapsulation lapb dte appletalk
```

Related Commands

bridge-group

ENCAPSULATION X25

To specify a serial interface's operation as an X.25 device, use the **encapsulation x25** interface configuration command.

    encapsulation x25 [dte | dce] [ddn | bfe] | [ietf]

Syntax	Description
dte	(Optional) Specifies operation as a DTE. This is the default X.25 mode.
dce	(Optional) Specifies operation as a DCE.
ddn	(Optional) Specifies DDN encapsulation on an interface using DDN X.25 Standard Service.
bfe	(Optional) Specifies BFE encapsulation on an interface attached to a BFE device.
ietf	(Optional) Specifies that the interface's datagram encapsulation defaults to the use of the Internet Engineering Task Force (IETF) standard method, as defined by RFC 1356.

Command Reference

Defaults

The default serial encapsulation is HDLC. You must explicitly configure an X.25 encapsulation method.

DTE operation is the default X.25 mode. Cisco's traditional X.25 encapsulation method is the default.

Command Mode

Interface configuration

Usage Guidelines

This command first appeared prior to Cisco IOS Release 10.0. The **dte, dce, ddn, bfe,** and **ietf** keywords first appeared in Cisco IOS Release 10.3.

One end of an X.25 link must be a logical DCE and the other end a logical DTE. (This assignment is independent of the interface's hardware DTE or DCE identity.) Typically, when connecting to a public data network (PDN), the customer equipment acts as the DTE and the PDN attachment acts as the DCE.

Cisco has long supported the encapsulation of a number of datagram protocols, using a standard means when available, and a proprietary means when necessary. More recently, the IETF adopted a standard, RFC 1356, for encapsulating most types of datagram traffic over X.25. X.25 interfaces use Cisco's traditional method unless explicitly configured for IETF operation; if the **ietf** keyword is specified, that standard is used unless Cisco's traditional method is explicitly configured. For details, see the **x25 map** command.

You can configure a router attaching to the Defense Data Network (DDN) or to a Blacker Front End (BFE) device to use their respective algorithms to convert between IP and X.121 addresses by using the **ddn** or **bfe** option, respectively. An IP address must be assigned to the interface, from which the algorithm will generate the interface's X.121 address. For proper operation, this X.121 address must not be modified.

A router DDN attachment can operate as either a DTE or a DCE device. A BFE attachment can operate only as a DTE device. The **ietf** option is not available if either the **ddn** or **bfe** option is selected.

Example

The following example configures the interface for connection to a BFE device:

```
interface serial 0
  encapsulation x25 bfe
```

Related Commands

x25 map

LAPB INTERFACE-OUTAGE

To specify a period during which a link will remain connected, even if a brief hardware outage occurs, use the **lapb interface-outage** interface configuration command.

    lapb interface-outage *milliseconds*

Syntax	*Description*
milliseconds	Number of milliseconds a hardware outage can last without having the protocol disconnect the service.

Default

0 ms, which disables this feature.

Command Mode

Interface configuration

Usage Guidelines

This command first appeared in Cisco IOS Release 10.0.

If a hardware outage lasts longer than the LAPB hardware outage period you set, normal protocol operations will occur. The link will be declared down and, when it is restored, a link setup will be initiated.

Example

The following example sets the interface outage period to 100 ms. The link remains connected for outages equal to or shorter than that period.

```
encapsulation lapb dte ip
lapb interface-outage 100
```

LAPB K

To specify the maximum permissible number of outstanding frames, called the *window size*, use the **lapb k** interface configuration command.

    lapb k *window-size*

Syntax	*Description*
window-size	Frame count. It can be a value from 1 to the modulo size minus 1 (the maximum is 7 if the modulo size is 8; it is 127 if the modulo size is 128).

Default

7 frames

Command Mode

Interface configuration

Usage Guidelines

This command first appeared prior to Cisco IOS Release 10.0.

If the window size is changed while the protocol is up, the new value takes effect only when the protocol is reset. You will be informed that the new value will not take effect immediately.

When using the LAPB modulo 128 mode (extended mode), you must increase the window parameter *k* to send a larger number of frames before acknowledgment is required. This increase is the basis for the router's ability to achieve greater throughput on high-speed links that have a low error rate.

This configured value must match the value configured in the peer X.25 switch. Nonmatching values will cause repeated LAPB reject (REJ) frames.

Example

The following example sets the LAPB window size (the *k* parameter) to 10 frames:

```
interface serial 0
  lapb modulo
  lapb k 10
```

Related Commands

lapb modulo

LAPB MODULO

To specify the LAPB basic (modulo 8) or extended (modulo 128) protocol mode, use the **lapb modulo** interface configuration command.

lapb modulo *modulus*

Syntax	Description
modulus	Either 8 or 128. The value 8 specifies LAPB's basic mode; the value 128 specifies LAPB's extended mode.

Default

Modulo 8

Command Mode

Interface configuration

Usage Guidelines

This command first appeared prior to Cisco IOS Release 10.0.

The modulo parameter determines which of LAPB's two modes is to be used. The modulo values derive from the fact that basic mode numbers information frames between 0 and 7, whereas extended mode numbers them between 0 and 127. Basic mode is widely available and is sufficient for most links. Extended mode is an optional LAPB feature that may achieve greater throughput on high-speed links that have a low error rate.

The LAPB operating mode may be set on X.25 links as well as LAPB links. The X.25 modulo is independent of the LAPB layer modulo. Both ends of a link must use the same LAPB mode.

When using modulo 128 mode, you must increase the window parameter k to send a larger number of frames before acknowledgment is required. This increase is the basis for the router's ability to achieve greater throughput on high-speed links that have a low error rate.

If the modulo value is changed while the protocol is up, the new value takes effect only when the protocol is reset. You will be informed that the new value will not take effect immediately.

Example

The following example configures a high-speed X.25 link to use LAPB's extended mode:

```
interface serial 1
  encapsulation x25
  lapb modulo 128
  lapb k 40
  clock rate 2000000
```

Related Commands

lapb k

LAPB N1

To specify the maximum number of bits a frame can hold (the LAPB N1 parameter), use the **lapb n1** interface configuration command.

    lapb n1 *bits*

Syntax	Description
bits	Maximum number of bits in multiples of eight. The minimum and maximum range is dynamically set. Use the question mark (**?**) to view the range.

Defaults

The largest (maximum) value available for the particular interface is the default. The Cisco IOS software dynamically calculates N1 whenever you change the maximum transmission unit (MTU), the L2/L3 modulo, or compression on a LAPB interface.

Command Mode

Interface configuration

Usage Guidelines

This command first appeared prior to Cisco IOS Release 10.0.

CAUTION

The LAPB N1 parameter provides little benefit beyond the interface MTU and can easily cause link failures if misconfigured. Cisco recommends that this parameter be left at its default value.

The Cisco IOS software uses the following formula to determine the minimum N1 value:

(128 (default packet size) + LAPB overhead + X.25 overhead + 2 bytes of CRC) * 8

The Cisco IOS software uses the following formula to determine for the maximum N1 value:

(hardware MTU + LAPB overhead + X.25 overhead + 2 bytes of CRC) * 8

LAPB overhead is 2 bytes for modulo 8 and 3 bytes for modulo 128.

X.25 overhead is 3 bytes for modulo 8 and 4 bytes for modulo 128.

You need not set N1 to an exact value to support a particular X.25 data packet size. The N1 parameter prevents the processing of any huge frames that result from a "jabbering" interface, which is an unlikely event. In addition, the various standards bodies specify that N1 be given in bits rather than bytes. While some equipment can be configured in bytes or will automatically adjust for some of the overhead information present, Cisco devices are configured using the true value, in bits, of N1.

You cannot set the N1 parameter to a value less than that required to support an X.25 data packet size of 128 bytes. All X.25 implementations must be able to support 128-byte data packets. Moreover, if you configure N1 to be less than 2104 bits, you receive a warning message that X.25 might have problems because some nondata packets can use up to 259 bytes.

You cannot set the N1 parameter to a value larger than the default unless the hardware MTU size is first increased.

The X.25 software accepts default packet sizes and calls that specify maximum packet sizes greater than those the LAPB layer supports, but negotiates the calls placed on the interface to the largest value that can be supported. For switched calls, the packet size negotiation takes place end-to-end through the router so the call will not have a maximum packet size that exceeds the capability of either of the two interfaces involved.

Examples

The following example shows how to use the question mark (?) command to display the minimum and maximum N1 value. In this example, X.25 encapsulation has both the LAPB and X.25 modulo set to 8. Any violation of this N1 range results in an "Invalid input" error message.

```
router# interface serial 1
router(config)# lapb n1 ?
  <1080-12056> LAPB N1 parameter (bits; multiple of 8)
```

The following example sets the N1 bits to 16440:

```
interface serial 0
  lapb n1 16440
  mtu 2048
```

Related Commands

mtu

LAPB N2

To specify the maximum number of times a data frame can be transmitted (the LAPB N2 parameter), use the **lapb n2** interface configuration command.

    lapb n2 *tries*

Syntax   Description

tries   Transmission count. It can be a value from 1 to 255.

Default

20 transmissions

Command Mode

Interface configuration

Usage Guidelines

This command first appeared prior to Cisco IOS Release 10.0.

Example

The following example sets the N2 tries to 50:

```
interface serial 0
  lapb n2 50
```

LAPB PROTOCOL

This command is obsolete. It has been replaced by the [*protocol* | **multi**] option of the **encapsulation lapb** command.

LAPB T1

To set the retransmission timer period (the LAPB T1 parameter), use the **lapb t1** interface configuration command.

    lapb t1 *milliseconds*

Syntax	*Description*
milliseconds	Time in milliseconds. It can be a value from 1 to 64,000.

Default

3000 ms

Command Mode

Interface configuration

Usage Guidelines

This command first appeared prior to Cisco IOS Release 10.0.

The retransmission timer determines how long a transmitted frame can remain unacknowledged before the LAPB software polls for an acknowledgment. The design of the LAPB protocol specifies that a frame is presumed to be lost if it is not acknowledged within T1; a T1 value that is too small may result in duplicated control information, which can severely disrupt service.

To determine an optimal value for the retransmission timer, use the privileged EXEC command **ping** to measure the round-trip time of a maximum-sized frame on the link. Multiply this time by a safety factor that takes into account the speed of the link, the link quality, and the distance. A typical safety factor is 1.5. Choosing a larger safety factor can result in slower data transfer if the line is noisy. However, this disadvantage is minor compared to the excessive retransmissions and effective bandwidth reduction caused by a timer setting that is too small.

Example

The following example sets the T1 retransmission timer to 2000 ms:

```
interface serial 0
 lapb t1 2000
```

LAPB T4

To set the T4 idle timer, after which the Cisco IOS software sends out a Poll packet to determine whether the link has suffered an unsignaled failure, use the **lapb t4** interface configuration command.

    lapb t4 *seconds*

Syntax	Description
seconds	Number of seconds between reception of the last frame and the transmission of the outgoing Poll.

Default

0 seconds, which disables the T4 timer feature.

Command Mode

Interface configuration

Usage Guidelines

This command first appeared in Cisco IOS Release 10.0.

Any nonzero T4 duration must be greater than T1, which is the LAPB retransmission timer period.

Example

The following example will poll the other end of an active link if it has been 10 seconds since the last frame was received. If the far host has failed, the service will be declared down after **n2** tries are timed out.

```
interface serial0
  encapsulation x25
  lapb t4 10
```

Related Commands

lapb n2
lapb t1

SERVICE PAD

To enable all packet assembler/disassembler (PAD) commands and connections between PAD devices and access servers, use the **service pad** global configuration command. Use the **no** form of this command to disable this service.

```
service pad [cmns]
no service pad [cmns]
```

Syntax	Description
cmns	(Optional) Specifies sending and receiving of PAD calls over CMNS.

Default

All PAD commands and associated connections are enabled. PAD services over XOT or CMNS are not enabled.

Command Mode

Global configuration

Usage Guidelines

This command first appeared in Cisco IOS Release 10.0. The **cmns** option first appeared in Cisco IOS Release 11.3.

Examples

If **service pad** is disabled, the EXEC **pad** command and all PAD related configurations, such as X.29, are unrecognized, as shown in the following example:

```
Router(config)# no service pad
Router(config)# x29 ?
% Unrecognized command
Router(config)# exit
Router# pad ?
% Unrecognized command
```

If **service pad** is enabled, the EXEC **pad** command and access to an X.29 configuration is granted as shown in the following example:

```
Router# config terminal
Enter configuration commands, one per line. End with CNTL/Z.
Router(config)# service pad
Router(config)# x29 ?
access-list        Define an X.29 access list
inviteclear-time   Wait for response to X.29 Invite Clear message
profile            Create an X.3 profile
Router# pad ?
WORD   X121 address or name of a remote system
```

In the following example, PAD services over CMNS are enabled:

```
! Enable CMNS on a nonserial interface
interface ethernet0
 cmns enable
!
!Enable inbound and outbound PAD over CMNS service
service pad cmns
!
! Specify an X.25 route entry pointing to an interface's CMNS destination MAC address
x25 route ^2193330 interface Ethernet0 mac 00e0.b0e3.0d62

Router# show x25 vc

SVC 1,  State: D1,  Interface: Ethernet0
    Started 00:00:08, last input 00:00:08, output 00:00:08

    Line: 0  con 0   Location: console Host: 2193330
     connected to 2193330 PAD <--> CMNS Ethernet0 00e0.b0e3.0d62

    Window size input: 2, output: 2
    Packet size input: 128, output: 128
    PS: 2  PR: 3  ACK: 3  Remote PR: 2  RCNT: 0  RNR: no
    P/D state timeouts: 0  timer (secs): 0
    data bytes 54/19 packets 2/3 Resets 0/0 RNRs 0/0 REJs 0/0 INTs 0/0
```

Related Commands

cmns enable
show x25 vc
x29 access-list
x29 profile

SERVICE PAD FROM-XOT

To permit incoming XOT Calls to be accepted as a PAD session, use the **service pad from-xot** global configuration command. Use the **no** form of this command to disable this service.

> service pad from-xot
> no service pad from-xot

Syntax Description

This command has no arguments or keywords.

Default

Incoming XOT connections are ignored.

Command Mode

Global configuration

Usage Guidelines

This command first appeared in Cisco IOS Release 11.2 F.

If **service pad from-xot** is enabled, the Calls received using the XOT service may be accepted for processing a PAD session.

Example

The following example prevents incoming XOT Calls from being accepted as a PAD session:

```
no service pad from-xot
```

Related Commands

x29 access-list
x29 profile
x25 route

SERVICE PAD TO-XOT

To permit outgoing PAD sessions to use routes to an XOT destination, use the **service pad to-xot** global configuration command. Use the **no** form of this command to disable this service.

service pad to-xot
no service pad to-xot

Syntax Description

This command has no arguments or keywords.

Default

XOT routes pointing to XOT are not considered.

Command Mode

Global configuration

Usage Guidelines

This command first appeared in Cisco IOS Release 11.2 F.

Example

If **service pad to-xot** is enabled, the configured routes to XOT destinations may be used when the router determines where to send a PAD Call, as show in the following example:

```
service pad to-xot
```

Related Commands

x29 access-list
x29 profile
x25 route

SHOW CMNS

To display X.25 Level 3 parameters for LAN interfaces (such as Ethernet or Token Ring) and other information pertaining to Connection-Mode Network Service (CMNS) traffic activity, use the **show cmns** EXEC command.

    show cmns [*type number*]

Syntax	Description
type	(Optional) Interface type.
number	(Optional) Interface number.

Command Mode

EXEC

Usage Guidelines

This command first appeared in Cisco IOS Release 10.0.

Sample Display

The following is sample output from the **show cmns** command for an Ethernet interface:

```
Router# show cmns
Ethernet1 is administratively down, line protocol is down
  Hardware address is 0000.0c02.5f4c, (bia 0000.0c2.5f4c), state R1
    Modulo 8, idle 0, timer 0, nvc 1
    Window size: input 2, output 2, Packet size: input 128, output 128
    Timer: TH 0
    Channels: Incoming-only none, Two-way 1-4095, Outgoing-only none
    RESTARTs 0/0 CALLs 0+0/0+0/0+0 DIAGs 0/0
```

Table 12–1 describes significant fields shown in the display.

Table 12–1 *Show SMNS Field Descriptions*

Field	Description
Ethernet1 is administratively down	Interface is currently active and inserted into network (up) or inactive and not inserted (down), or disabled (administratively down).
line protocol is {up | down}	Indicates whether the software processes that handle the line protocol recognize the interface as usable.
Hardware address	Media access control (MAC) address for this interface.
bia	Burned-in address.
state R1	State of the interface. R1 is normal ready state. (The state should always be R1.)
Modulo 8	Modulo value; determines the packet sequence numbering scheme used.
idle 0	Number of minutes the Cisco IOS software waits before closing idle virtual circuits.
timer 0	Value of the interface time; should always be zero.
nvc 1	Maximum number of simultaneous virtual circuits permitted to and from a single host for a particular protocol.
Window size:	Default window sizes (in packets) for the interface. (CMNS cannot originate or terminate calls.)
input 2	Default input window size is two packets.
output 2	Default output window size is two packets.

Table 12–1 *Show SMNS Field Descriptions, Continued*

Field	Description
Packet size:	Default packet sizes for the interface. (CMNS cannot originate or terminate calls.)
input 128	Default input maximum packet size is 128 bytes.
output 128	Default output maximum packet size is 128 bytes.
TH 0	X.25 delayed acknowledgment threshold. Should always be zero.
Channels: Incoming-only none, Two-way 1-4095, Outgoing-only none	Virtual circuit ranges for this interface per Logical Link Control, type 2 (LLC2) connection.
RESTARTs 0/0	Restarts sent/received.
CALLs 0+0/0+0/0+0	Successful calls + failed calls/calls sent + calls failed/calls received + calls failed.
DIAGs 0/0	Diagnostic messages sent and received.

Related Commands

show interfaces serial

SHOW INTERFACES SERIAL

To display information about a serial interface, use the **show interfaces serial** EXEC command.

   show interfaces serial *number*

Syntax	*Description*
number	Interface port number.

Command Mode

EXEC

Usage Guidelines

This command first appeared in Cisco IOS Release 10.0.

Sample Displays

The following is a partial sample output from the **show interfaces serial** command for a serial interface using LAPB encapsulation:

```
Router# show interfaces serial 1
LAPB state is SABMSENT, T1 3000, N1 12056, N2 20, k7,Protocol ip
VS 0, VR 0, RCNT 0, Remote VR 0, Retransmissions 2
IFRAMEs 0/0 RNRs 0/0 REJs 0/0 SABMs 3/0 FRMRs 0/0 DISCs 0/0
```

Table 12–2 shows the fields relevant to all LAPB connections.

Table 12–2 *Show Interfaces Serial Fields Descriptions when LAPB Is Enabled*

Field	Description
LAPB state is	State of the LAPB protocol.
T1 3000, N1 12056,...	Current parameter settings.
Protocol	Protocol encapsulated on a LAPB link; this field is not present on interfaces configured for multiprotocol LAPB or X.25 encapsulations.
VS	Modulo 8 frame number of the next outgoing information frame.
VR	Modulo 8 frame number of the next information frame expected to be received.
RCNT	Number of received information frames that have not yet been acknowledged.
Remote VR	Number of the next information frame the remote device expects to receive.
Retransmissions	Count of current retransmissions due to expiration of T1.
Window is closed	No more frames can be transmitted until some outstanding frames have been acknowledged. This message should be displayed only temporarily.
IFRAMEs	Count of information frames in the form of sent/received.
RNRs	Count of Receiver Not Ready frames in the form of sent/received.
REJs	Count of Reject frames in the form of sent/received.
SABMs	Count of Set Asynchronous Balanced Mode commands in the form of sent/received.
FRMRs	Count of Frame Reject frames in the form of sent/received.
DISCs	Count of Disconnect commands in the form of sent/received.

The following is a partial sample output from the **show interfaces** command for a serial X.25 interface:

```
Router# show interfaces serial 1
X25 address 000000010100, state R1, modulo 8, idle 0, timer 0, nvc 1
  Window size: input 2, output 2, Packet size: input 128, output 128
  Timers: T20 180, T21 200, T22 180, T23 180, TH 0
  Channels: Incoming-only none, Two-way 1-1024, Outgoing-only none
(configuration on RESTART: modulo 8,
  Window size: input 2 output 2, Packet size: input 128, output 128
  Channels: Incoming-only none, Two-way 5-1024, Outgoing-only none)
  RESTARTs 3/2 CALLs 1000+2/1294+190/0+0/ DIAGs 0/0
```

The stability of the X.25 protocol requires that some parameters not be changed without a restart of the protocol. Any change to these parameters are held until a restart is sent or received. If any of these parameters change, the configuration on restart information will be output as well as the values that are currently in effect.

Table 12–3 describes significant fields shown in the display.

Table 12–3   *Show Interfaces X25 Field Descriptions*

Field	Description
X25 address 000000010100	Address used to originate and accept calls.
state R1	State of the interface. Possible values are: • R1 is the normal ready state • R2 is the DTE restarting state • R3 is the DCE restarting state If the state is R2 or R3, the interface is awaiting acknowledgment of a Restart packet.
modulo 8	Modulo value; determines the packet sequence numbering scheme used.
idle 0	Number of minutes the Cisco IOS software waits before closing idle virtual circuits that it originated or accepted.
timer 0	Value of the interface timer, which is zero unless the interface state is R2 or R3.
nvc 1	Default maximum number of simultaneous virtual circuits permitted to and from a single host for a particular protocol.
Window size: input 2, output 2	Default window sizes (in packets) for the interface. The **x25 facility** interface configuration command can be used to override these default values for the switched virtual circuits originated by the router.
Packet size: input 128, output 128	Default maximum packet sizes (in bytes) for the interface. The **x25 facility** interface configuration command can be used to override these default values for the switched virtual circuits originated by the router.

Table 12–3 *Show Interfaces X25 Field Descriptions, Continued*

Field	Description
Timers: T20 180, T21 200, T22 180, T23 180	Values of the X.25 timers: • T10 through T13 for a DCE device • T20 through T23 for a DTE device
TH0	Packet acknowledgment threshold (in packets). This value determines how many packets are received before an explicit acknowledgment is sent. The default value (0) sends an explicit acknowledgment only when the incoming window is full.
Channels: Incoming-only none Two-way 5-1024 Outgoing-only none	Displays the virtual circuit ranges for this interface.
RESTARTs 3/2	Shows Restart packet statistics for the interface using the format Sent/Received.
CALLs 1000+2/1294+190/ 0+0	Successful calls sent + failed calls/calls received + calls failed/calls forwarded + calls failed. Calls forwarded are counted as calls sent.
DIAGs 0/0	Diagnostic messages sent and received.

Related Commands

show cmns

SHOW LLC2

To display active Logical Link Control, type 2 (LLC2) connections, use the **show llc2** EXEC command.

> show llc2c

Syntax Description

This command has no arguments or keywords.

Command Mode

EXEC

Usage Guidelines

This command first appeared in Cisco IOS Release 10.0.

Sample Display

The following is sample output from the **show llc2** command:

```
Router# show llc2

TokenRing0 DTE=1000.5A59.04F9,400022224444 SAP=04/04, State=NORMAL
V(S)=5, V(R)=5, Last N(R)=5, Local Window=7, Remote Window=127
ack-max=3, n2=8, Next timer in 7768
xid-retry timer 0/60000 ack timer 0/1000
p timer 0/1000 idle timer 7768/10000
rej timer 0/3200 busy timer 0/9600
ack-delay timer 0/3200
CMNS Connections to:
Address 1000.5A59.04F9 via Ethernet2
Protocol is up
Interface type X25-DCE RESTARTS 0/1
Timers: T10 1 T11 1 T12 1 T13 1
```

The display includes a CMNS addendum, indicating that LLC2 is running with CMNS. When LLC2 is not running with CMNS, the **show llc2** command does not display a CMNS addendum.

Table 12–4 describes significant fields shown in the display.

Table 12–4 *Show LLC2 Field Descriptions*

Field	Description
TokenRing0	Name of interface on which the session is established.
DTE=1000.5A59.04 F9, 400022224444	Address of the station to which the router is transmitting on this session. (The address is the MAC address of the interface on which the connection is established, except when Local Acknowledgment or SDLLC is used, in which case the address used by the router is shown as in this example, following the DTE address and separated by a comma.)
SAP=04/04	Other station's and router's (remote/local) service access point (SAP) for this connection. The SAP is analogous to a "port number" on the router and allows for multiple sessions between the same two stations.
State=	Current state of the LLC2 session, which can be any of the following: • ADM—Asynchronous Disconnect Mode—A connection is not established, and either end can begin one. • SETUP—Request to begin a connection has been sent to the remote station, and this station is waiting for a response to that request. • RESET—A previously open connection has been reset because of some error by this station, and this station is waiting for a response to that reset command.

Table 12–4 *Show LLC2 Field Descriptions, Continued*

Field	Description
	• D_CONN—This station has requested a normal, expected end of communications with the remote station, and is waiting for a response to that disconnect request.
	• ERROR—This station has detected an error in communications and has told the other station about it. This station is waiting for a reply to its posting of this error.
	• NORMAL—Connection between the two sides is fully established, and normal communication is occurring.
	• BUSY—Normal communication state exists, except that busy conditions on this station prevent this station from receiving information frames from the other station at this time.
	• REJECT—Out-of-sequence frame has been detected on this station, and this station has requested that the other resend this information.
	• AWAIT—Normal communication exists, but this station has had a timer expire, and is trying to recover from it (usually by resending the frame that started the timer).
	• AWAIT_BUSY—A combination of the AWAIT and BUSY states.
	• AWAIT_REJ—A combination of the AWAIT and REJECT states.
V(S)=5	Sequence number of the next information frame this station will send.
V(R)=5	Sequence number of the next information frame this station expects to receive from the other station.
Last N(R)=5	Last sequence number of this station's transmitted frames acknowledged by the remote station.
Local Window=7	Number of frames this station may send before requiring an acknowledgment from the remote station.
Remote Window=127	Number of frames this station can accept from the remote station.
ack-max=3, n2=8	Value of these parameters, as given in the previous configuration section.
Next timer in 7768	Number of milliseconds before the next timer, for any reason, goes off.

Table 12–4 *Show LLC2 Field Descriptions, Continued*

Field	Description
xid-retry timer 0/60000	A series of timer values in the form of next-time/time-between, where "next-time" is the next time, in milliseconds, that the timer will wake, and "time-between" is the time, in milliseconds, between each timer wakeup. A "next-time" of zero indicates that the given timer is not enabled, and will never wake.
CMNS Connections to	CMNS addendum when LLC2 is running with the CMNS protocol contains the following: • Address 1000.5A59.04F9 via Ethernet2—MAC address of remote station. • Protocol is up—Up indicates the LLC2 and X.25 protocols are in a state in which incoming and outgoing Call Requests can be made on this LLC2 connection. • Interface type X25-DCE—One of the following: X25-DCE, X25-DTE, or X25-DXE (either DTE or DCE). • RESTARTS 0/1—Restarts sent/received on this LLC2 connection. • Timers: T10, T11, T12, T13 (or T20, T21, T22, T23 for DTE). These are Request packet timers and are similar in function to X.25 parameters of the same name.

SHOW X25 INTERFACE

To display information about VCs that use an X.25 interface and, optionally, about a specified virtual circuit, use the **show x25 interface** EXEC command.

   show x25 interface [**serial** *number* | *cmns-interface* **mac** *mac-address*]

Syntax

serial *number*

cmns-interface **mac** *mac-address*

Description

(Optional) Keyword **serial** and number of the serial interface used for X.25.

(Optional) Local CMNS interface type and number, plus the MAC address of the remote device. CMNS interface types are Ethernet, Token Ring, or FDDI. The interface numbering scheme depends on the router interface hardware.

Command Mode

EXEC

Usage Guidelines

This command first appeared in Cisco IOS Release 11.2 F.

Sample Display

The following **show x25 interface** sample output displays X.25 information about VCs on serial interface 0:

```
Router# show x25 interface serial 0

SVC 1,  State: D1,  Interface: Serial0
  Started 00:13:52, last input 00:00:05, output never
  Connects 3334 <-> ip 3.3.3.4
  Call PID ietf, Data PID none
  Window size input: 7, output: 7
  Packet size input: 512, output: 512
  PS: 0  PR: 6  ACK: 1  Remote PR: 0  RCNT: 5  RNR: no
  P/D state timeouts: 0  timer (secs): 0
  data bytes 0/2508 packets 0/54 Resets 0/0 RNRs 0/0 REJs 0/0 INTs 0/0
SVC 32,  State: D1,  Interface: Serial0.11
  Started 00:16:53, last input 00:00:37, output 00:00:28
  Connects 3334 <-> clns
  Call PID cisco, Data PID none
  Window size input: 7, output: 7
  Packet size input: 512, output: 512
  PS: 5  PR: 4  ACK: 4  Remote PR: 4  RCNT: 0  RNR: no
  P/D state timeouts: 0  timer (secs): 0
  data bytes 378/360 packets 21/20 Resets 0/0 RNRs 0/0 REJs 0/0 INTs 0/0
```

SHOW X25 MAP

To display information about configured address maps, use the **show x25 map** EXEC command.

    show x25 map

Syntax Description

This command has no arguments or keywords.

Command Mode

EXEC

Usage Guidelines

This command first appeared in Cisco IOS Release 10.0.

The **show x25 map** command shows information about the following:

- Configured maps (defined by the **x25 map** command)
- Maps implicitly defined by encapsulation PVCs (defined by the **x25 pvc** command)
- Dynamic maps (from the X.25 DDN or BFE operations)
- Temporary maps (from unconfigured CMNS endpoints)

Command Reference

Sample Display

The following is sample output from the **show x25 map** command:

```
Router# show x25 map

Serial0: X.121 1311001 <--> ip 172.20.170.1
  PERMANENT, BROADCAST, 2 VCS: 3 4*
Serial0: X.121 1311005 <--> appletalk 128.1
  PERMANENT
Serial1: X.121 2194441 cud hello <--> pad
  PERMANENT, windowsize 5 5, accept-reverse, idle 5
Serial1: X.121 1311005 <--> bridge
  PERMANENT, BROADCAST
Serial2: X.121 001003 <--> apollo 1.3,
        appletalk 1.3,
        ip 172.20.1.3,
        decnet 1.3,
        novell 1.0000.0c04.35df,
        vines 00000001:0003,
        xns 1.0000.0c04.35df,
        clns
  PERMANENT, NVC 8, 1 VC: 1024
```

The display shows that four maps have been configured for a router: two for serial interface 0, one for serial interface 1, and one for the serial interface 2 (which maps eight protocols to the host).

Table 12–5 describes fields shown in the display.

Table 12–5 *Show X25 Map Field Descriptions*

Field	Description
Serial0	Interface on which this map is configured.
X.121 1311001	X.121 address of the mapped encapsulation host.
ip 172.20.170.1	Type and address of the higher-level protocol(s) mapped to the remote host. Bridge maps do not have a higher-level address; all bridge datagrams are sent to the mapped X.121 address. CLNS maps refer to a configured neighbor as identified by the X.121 address.
PERMANENT	Address-mapping type that has been configured for the interface in this entry. Possible values include the following: • CONSTRUCTED—Derived with the DDN or BFE address conversion scheme. • PERMANENT—Map was entered with the **x25 map** interface configuration command. • PVC—Map was configured with the **x25 pvc** interface command. • TEMPORARY—A temporary map was created for an incoming unconfigured CMNS connection.

Table 12–5 *Show X25 Map Field Descriptions, Continued*

Field	Description
BROADCAST	If any options are configured for an address mapping, they are listed; the example shows a map that is configured to forward datagram broadcasts to the mapped host.
2 VCs:	If the map has any active virtual circuits, they are identified.
3 4*	Identifies the circuit number of the active virtual circuits. The asterisk (*) marks the virtual circuit last used to send data.
	Note that a single protocol virtual circuit can be associated with a multiprotocol map.

SHOW X25 REMOTE-RED

To display the one-to-one mapping of the host IP addresses and the remote BFE device's IP addresses, use the **show x25 remote-red** EXEC command.

> **show x25 remote-red**

Syntax Description

This command has no arguments or keywords.

Command Mode

EXEC

Usage Guidelines

This command first appeared in Cisco IOS Release 10.0.

Sample Display

The following is sample output from the **show x25 remote-red** command:

```
Router# show x25 remote-red
Entry      REMOTE-RED     REMOTE-BLACK   INTERFACE
1          21.0.0.3       21.0.0.7       serial3
2          21.0.0.10      21.0.0.6       serial1
3          21.0.0.24      21.0.0.8       serial3
```

Table 12–6 describes significant fields shown in the display.

Table 12–6 *Show X25 Remote-Red Display Field Descriptions*

Field	Description
Entry	Address mapping entry.

Command Reference

Table 12–6　*Show X25 Remote-Red Display Field Descriptions, Continued*

Field	Description
REMOTE-RED	Host IP address.
REMOTE-BLACK	IP address of the remote BFE device.
INTERFACE	Name of interface through which communication with the remote BFE device will take place.

SHOW X25 ROUTE

To display the X.25 routing table, use the **show x25 route** EXEC command.

    show x25 route

Syntax Description

This command has no arguments or keywords.

Command Mode

EXEC

Usage Guidelines

This command first appeared in Cisco IOS Release 10.0.

Sample Display

The following is sample output from the **show x25 route** command:

```
Router# show x25 route

# Match                      Substitute              Route To
1 ^1311001$                                          Serial0, 0 uses
2 ^1311002$                                          xot 172.20.170.10
```

Table 12–7 describes significant fields shown in the display.

Table 12–7　*Show X25 Route Display Field Descriptions*

Field	Description
#	Number identifying the entry in the X.25 routing table.
Match	The match criteria and patterns associated with this entry.
Route To	Destination to which the router will forward a Call; X.25 destinations identify an interface, CMNS destinations identify an interface and host MAC address, and XOT destinations identify one (or more) IP addresses.

Related Commands

x25 route

SHOW X25 SERVICES

To display information pertaining to the X.25 services, use the **show x25 services** EXEC command.

    show x25 services

Syntax Description

This command has no arguments or keywords.

Command Mode

EXEC

Usage Guidelines

This command first appeared in Cisco IOS Release 11.2 F.

This command is the default form of the **show x25** command.

Sample Display

The following is sample output from the **show x25 services** command:

```
Router# show x25 services

X.25 software, Version 3.0.0.
  3 configurations supporting 3 active contexts
  VCs allocated, freed and in use: 7 - 0 = 7
  VCs active and idle: 4, 3
XOT software, Version 2.0.0.
  VCs allocated, freed and in use: 2 - 1 = 1
  connections in-progress: 0 outgoing and 0 incoming
  active VCs: 1, connected to 1 remote hosts
```

Related Commands

show x25 interface
show x25 map
show x25 route
show x25 vc

SHOW X25 VC

To display information about active switched virtual circuits (SVCs) and permanent virtual circuits (PVCs), use the **show x25 vc** EXEC command.

    show x25 vc [*lcn*]

Syntax	Description
lcn	(Optional) Logical channel number (LCN).

Command Mode

EXEC

Usage Guidelines

This command first appeared prior to Cisco IOS Release 8.3.

To examine a particular virtual circuit number, add an LCN argument to the **show x25 vc** command.

This command displays information about virtual circuits. Virtual circuits may be used for a number of purposes, such as the following:

- Encapsulation traffic
- Traffic switched between X.25 services (X.25, CMNS, and XOT)
- PAD traffic
- QLLC traffic

The connectivity information displayed will vary according to the traffic carried by the virtual circuit. For multiprotocol circuits, the output varies depending on the number and identity of the protocols mapped to the X.121 address and the encapsulation method selected for the circuit.

Sample Display for Encapsulated Traffic

The following is sample output from the **show x25 vc** command used on an encapsulated traffic circuit:

```
Router# show x25 vc 1024

SVC 1024, State: D1, Interface: Serial0
  Started 0:00:31, last input 0:00:31, output 0:00:31
  Connects 170090 <-->
     compressedtcp 172.20.170.90
     ip 172.20.170.90
  Call PID multi, Data PID ietf
  Reverse charged
  Window size input: 2, output: 2
  Packet size input: 128, output: 128
  PS: 5 PR: 5 ACK: 4 Remote PR: 5 RCNT: 1 RNR: FALSE
  Window is closed
  P/D state timeouts: 0 Timer (secs): 0
   data bytes 505/505 packets 5/5 Resets 0/0 RNRs 0/0 REJs 0/0 INTs 0/0
```

Table 12–8 describes the fields shown in the sample output that are typical for virtual circuits.

Table 12–8 *Show X25 VC Typical Field Descriptions*

Field	Description
SVC *n* or PVC *n*	Identifies the type of virtual circuit (switched or permanent) and its LCN (also called its "virtual circuit number").
State	State of the virtual circuit (which is independent of the states of other virtual circuits); D1 is the normal ready state. See the International Telecommunication Union Telecommunication Standardization Sector (ITU-T)[*] X.25 Recommendation for a description of virtual circuit states.
Interface	Interface or subinterface on which the virtual circuit is established.
Started	Time elapsed since the virtual circuit was created.
last input	Time of last input.
output	Shows time of last output.
Connects...<-->...	Describes the traffic-specific connection information. See Table 12–9, Table 12–10, Table 12–11, and Table 12–12 for more information.
D-bit permitted	Indicates that the X.25 D-bit (Delivery Confirmation) may be used on this circuit (displayed as needed).
Fast select VC	Indicates that the Fast Select facility was present on the incoming call (displayed as needed).
Reverse charged	Indicates reverse charged virtual circuit (displayed as needed).
Window size	Window sizes for the virtual circuit.
Packet size	Maximum packet sizes for the virtual circuit.
PS	Current send sequence number.
PR	Current receive sequence number.
ACK	Last acknowledged incoming packet.
Remote PR	Last receive sequence number received from the other end of the circuit.
RCNT	Count of unacknowledged input packets.
RNR	State of the Receiver Not Ready flag; this field is true if the network sends a Receiver-not-Ready packet.
Window is closed	This line appears if the router cannot transmit any more packets until the X.25 Layer 3 peer has acknowledged some outstanding packets.

Table 12–8 *Show X25 VC Typical Field Descriptions, Continued*

Field	Description
P/D state timeouts	Number of times a supervisory packet (Reset or Clear) has been retransmitted.
Timer	A nonzero time value indicates that a control packet has not been acknowledged yet or that the virtual circuit is being timed for inactivity.
Reassembly	Number of bytes received and held for reassembly. Packets with the M-bit set are reassembled into datagrams for encapsulation virtual circuits; switched X.25 traffic is not reassembled (displayed only when values are non-zero).
Held Fragments/Packets	Number of X.25 data fragments to transmit to complete an outgoing datagram, and the number of datagram packets waiting for transmission (displayed only when values are non-zero).
data bytes m/n packets p/q	Total number of data bytes sent (m), data bytes received (n), data packets sent (p), and data packets received (q) since the circuit was established.
Resets t/r	Total number of Reset packets transmitted/received since the circuit was established.
RNRs t/r	Total number of Receiver Not Ready packets transmitted/received since the circuit was established.
REJs t/r	Total number of Reject packets transmitted/received since the circuit was established.
INTs t/r	Total number of Interrupt packets transmitted/received since the circuit was established.

*The ITU-T carries out the functions of the former Consultative Committee for International Telegraph and Telephone (CCITT).

Table 12–9 describes the connection fields specific for encapsulation traffic.

Table 12–9 *Show X25 VC Encapsulation Traffic Field Descriptions*

Field	Description
170090	The X.121 address of the remote host.
ip 172.20.170.90	The higher-level protocol and address values that are mapped to the virtual circuit.

Table 12–9 *Show X25 VC Encapsulation Traffic Field Descriptions, Continued*

Field	Description
Call PID	Identifies the method used for the protocol identification (PID) in the Call User Data (CUD) field. Because PVCs are not set up using a Call packet, this field is not displayed for encapsulation PVCs. The available methods are as follows: • cisco—Cisco's traditional method was used to set up a single protocol virtual circuit. • ietf—The IETF's standard RFC 1356 method was used to set up a single protocol virtual circuit. • snap—The IETF's Subnetwork Access Protocol (SNAP) method for IP encapsulation was used. • multi—The IETF's multiprotocol encapsulation method was used.
Data PID	Identifies the method used for protocol identification (PID) when sending datagrams. The available methods are as follows: • none—The virtual circuit is a single-protocol virtual circuit; no PID is used. • ietf—The IETF's standard RFC 1356 method for identifying the protocol is used. • snap—The IETF's SNAP method for identifying IP datagrams is used.

Sample Display for Locally Switched X.25 Traffic

The following is sample output from the **show x25 vc** command used on a virtual circuit carrying locally switched X.25 traffic:

```
Router# show x25 vc

PVC 1, State: D1, Interface: Serial2
  Started 0:01:26, last input never, output never
  PVC <--> Serial1 PVC 1, connected
  Window size input: 2, output: 2
  Packet size input: 128, output: 128
  PS: 0 PR: 0 ACK: 0 Remote PR: 0 RCNT: 0 RNR: FALSE
  P/D state timeouts: 0 Timer (secs): 0
  data bytes 0/0 packets 0/0 Resets 0/0 RNRs 0/0 REJs 0/0 INTs 0/0

SVC 5, State: D1, Interface: Serial2
  Started 0:00:16, last input 0:00:15, output 0:00:15
  Connects 170093 <--> 170090 from Serial1 VC 5
  Window size input: 2, output: 2
  Packet size input: 128, output: 128
  PS: 5 PR: 5 ACK: 4 Remote PR: 5 RCNT: 1 RNR: FALSE
  P/D state timeouts: 0 Timer (secs): 0
  data bytes 505/505 packets 5/5 Resets 0/0 RNRs 0/0 REJs 0/0 INTs 0/0
```

Table 12–10 describes the connection fields for virtual circuits carrying locally switched X.25 traffic.

Command Reference

Table 12–10 *Show X25 VC Local Traffic Field Descriptions*

Field	Description
PVC <-->	Indicates a switched connection between two PVCs.
Serial1 PVC 1	Identifies the other half of a local PVC connection.
connected	Identifies connection status for a switched connection between two PVCs. See Table 12–11 for PVC status messages.
170093	Identifies the Calling (source) Address of the connection. If a Calling Address Extension was encoded in the call facilities, it is also displayed. If the source host is a CMNS host, its MAC address is also displayed.
170090	Identifies the Called (destination) Address of the connection. If a Called Address Extension was encoded in the call facilities, it is also displayed. If the destination host is a CMNS host, its MAC address is also displayed.
from Serial1	Indicates the direction of the call and the connecting interface.
VC 5	Identifies the circuit type and LCN for the connecting interface. VC indicates an SVC, and PVC indicates a PVC. If the connecting host is a CMNS host, its MAC address is also displayed.

Sample Display for Locally Switched X.25 Traffic between PVCs and SVCs

The following is sample output from the **show x25 vc** command used on a virtual circuit carrying locally switched PVC to SVC X.25 traffic:

```
Router# show x25 vc

PVC 5,  State: D1,  Interface: Serial0
  Started 4d21h, last input 00:00:14, output 00:00:14
  Connects 101600 <--> 201700 from Serial2 VC 700
  D-bit permitted
  Window size input: 2, output: 2
  Packet size input: 128, output: 128
  PS: 5  PR: 5  ACK: 4  Remote PR: 5  RCNT: 1  RNR: no
  P/D state timeouts: 0  timer (secs): 0
  data bytes 1000/1000 packets 10/10 Resets 1/0 RNRs 0/0 REJs 0/0 INTs 0/0
  SVC 700,  State: D1,  Interface: Serial2
    Started 00:00:16, last input 00:00:16, output 00:00:16
    Connects 101600 <--> 201700 from Serial0 PVC 5
    Window size input: 2, output: 2
    Packet size input: 128, output: 128
    PS: 5  PR: 5  ACK: 5  Remote PR: 4  RCNT: 0  RNR: no
    P/D state timeouts: 0  timer (secs): 103
    data bytes 500/500 packets 5/5 Resets 0/0 RNRs 0/0 REJs 0/0 INTs 0/0
```

Table 12–11 describes the connection fields for virtual circuits carrying locally switched X.25 traffic between PVCs and SVCs.

Table 12–11 *Show X25 VC Locally Switched PVC to SVC Traffic Field Descriptions*

Field	Description
101600	Identifies the Calling (source) Address of the connection. If a Calling Address Extension was encoded in the call facilities, it is also displayed. If the source host is a CMNS host, its MAC address is also displayed.
201700	Identifies the Called (destination) Address of the connection. If a Called Address Extension was encoded in the call facilities, it is also displayed. If the destination host is a CMNS host, its MAC address is also displayed.
from Serial2	Indicates the direction of the call and the connecting interface.
VC 700	Identifies the circuit type and LCN for the connecting interface. VC indicates an SVC and PVC indicates a PVC. If the remote host is a CMNS host, its MAC address is also displayed.

Sample Display for Remotely Switched X.25 Traffic

The following is sample output from the **show x25 vc** command used on a virtual circuit carrying remotely switched X.25 traffic:

```
Router# show x25 vc

PVC 2, State: D1, Interface: Serial2
  Started 0:01:25, last input never, output never
  PVC <--> [172.20.165.92] Serial2/0 PVC 1 connected
  XOT between 171.20.165.91, 1998 and 172.20.165.92, 27801
  Window size input: 2, output: 2
  Packet size input: 128, output: 128
  PS: 0 PR: 0 ACK: 0 Remote PR: 0 RCNT: 0 RNR: FALSE
  P/D state timeouts: 0 Timer (secs): 0 Reassembly (bytes): 0
  Held Fragments/Packets: 0/0
  data bytes 0/0 packets 0/0 Resets 0/0 RNRs 0/0 REJs 0/0 INTs 0/0

SVC 6, State: D1, Interface: Serial2
  Started 0:00:04, last input 0:00:04, output 0:00:04
  Connects 170093 <--> 170090 from
  XOT between 172.20.165.91, 1998 and 172.20.165.92, 27896
  Window size input: 2, output: 2
  Packet size input: 128, output: 128
  PS: 5 PR: 5 ACK: 4 Remote PR: 5 RCNT: 1 RNR: FALSE
  P/D state timeouts: 0 Timer (secs): 0 Reassembly (bytes): 0
  Held Fragments/Packets: 0/0
  data bytes 505/505 packets 5/5 Resets 0/0 RNRs 0/0 REJs 0/0 INTs 0/0
```

Table 12–12 describes the connection fields for virtual circuits carrying remotely switched X.25 traffic.

Table 12–12 *Show X25 VC Remote X.25 Traffic Field Descriptions*

Field	Description
PVC	Flags PVC information.

Table 12–12 *Show X25 VC Remote X.25 Traffic Field Descriptions, Continued*

Field	Description
[172.20.165.92]	Indicates the IP address of the router remotely connecting the PVC.
Serial 2/0 PVC 1	Identifies the remote interface and PVC number.
connected	Identifies connection status for a switched connection between two PVCs. See Table 12–13 for PVC status messages.
170093	Identifies the Calling (source) Address of the connection. If a Calling Address Extension was encoded in the call facilities, it is also displayed.
170090	Identifies the Called (destination) Address of the connection. If a Called Address Extension was encoded in the call facilities, it is also displayed.
from	Indicates the direction of the call.
XOT between...	Identifies the IP addresses and port numbers of the X.25-over-TCP (XOT) connection.

Table 12–13 lists the PVC states that can be reported. These states are also reported by the **debug x25** command in PVC-SETUP packets (for remote PVCs only) as well as in the PVCBAD system error message. Some states apply only to remotely switched PVCs.

Table 12–13 *X.25 PVC States*

Status Message	Description
awaiting PVC-SETUP reply	A remote PVC has initiated an XOT TCP connection and is waiting for a reply to the setup message.
can't support flow control values	The window sizes or packet sizes of the PVC cannot be supported by one of its two interfaces.
connected	The PVC is up.
dest. disconnected	The other end disconnected the PVC.
dest. interface is not up	The target interface's X.25 service is down.
dest. PVC config mismatch	The targeted PVC is already connected.
mismatched flow control values	The configured flow control values do not match.
no such dest. interface	The remote destination interface was reported to be in error by the remote router.
no such dest. PVC	The targeted PVC does not exist.
non-X.25 dest. interface	The target interface is not configured for X.25.

Table 12-13 *X.25 PVC States, Continued*

Status Message	Description
PVC/TCP connect timed out	A remote PVC XOT TCP connection attempt timed out.
PVC/TCP connection refused	A remote PVC XOT TCP connection was tried and refused.
PVC/TCP routing error	A remote PVC XOT TCP connection routing error was reported.
trying to connect via TCP	A remote PVC XOT TCP connection is established and is in the process of connecting.
waiting to connect	The PVC is waiting to be processed for connecting.

SHOW X25 XOT

To display information for all XOT virtual circuits that match a given criterion, use the **show x25 xot** EXEC command.

    show x25 xot [**local** *ip-address* [**port** *port*]] [**remote** *ip-address* [**port** *port*]]

Syntax	*Description*
local *ip-address* [**port** *port*]	Local IP address and optional port number.
remote *ip-address* [**port** *port*]	Remote IP address and optional port number.

Command Mode

EXEC

Usage Guidelines

This command first appeared in Cisco IOS Release 11.2 F.

Sample Display

The following **show x25 xot** sample output displays information about all XOT virtual circuits:

```
Router> show x25 xot

SVC 11,  State: D1,  Interface: [2.2.2.2,1998/2.2.2.1,11002]
  Started 00:00:08, last input 00:00:08, output 00:00:08
  Line: 0   con 0   Location: Host: 5678
  111 connected to 5678 PAD <--> XOT 2.2.2.2,1998
  Window size input: 2, output: 2
  Packet size input: 128, output: 128
  PS: 2  PR: 3  ACK: 3  Remote PR: 2  RCNT: 0  RNR: no
  P/D state timeouts: 0  timer (secs): 0
  data bytes 54/18 packets 2/3 Resets 0/0 RNRs 0/0 REJs 0/0 INTs 0/0
```

Related Commands

show x25 interface
show x25 services

X25 ACCEPT-REVERSE

To configure the Cisco IOS software to accept all reverse charge calls, use the **x25 accept-reverse** interface configuration command. To disable this facility, use the **no** form of this command.

 x25 accept-reverse
 no x25 accept-reverse

Syntax Description

This command has no arguments or keywords.

Default

Disabled

Command Mode

Interface configuration

Usage Guidelines

This command first appeared prior to Cisco IOS Release 10.0.

This command causes the interface to accept reverse charge calls by default. You can also configure this behavior for each peer with the **x25 map** interface configuration command.

Example

The following example sets acceptance of reverse charge calls:

```
interface serial 0
 x25 accept-reverse
```

Related Commands

x25 map

X25 ADDRESS

To set the X.121 address of a particular network interface, use the **x25 address** interface configuration command.

 x25 address *x121-address*

Syntax	Description
x121-address	Variable-length X.121 address. The address is assigned by the X.25 network service provider.

Default

DDN and BFE encapsulations have a default interface address generated from the interface IP address; for proper DDN or BFE operation, this generated X.121 address must not be changed. Standard X.25 encapsulations do not have a default.

Command Mode

Interface configuration

Usage Guidelines

This command first appeared prior to Cisco IOS Release 10.0.

When you are connecting to a public data network (PDN), the PDN administrator will assign the X.121 address to be used. Other applications (for example, a private X.25 service) may assign arbitrary X.121 addresses as required by the network and service design. X.25 interfaces that engage in X.25 switching only do not need to assign an X.121 address.

Example

The following example sets the X.121 address for the interface:

```
interface serial 0
  encapsulation x25
  x25 address 00000123005
```

The address must match that assigned by the X.25 network service provider.

X25 ALIAS

To configure an interface alias address that will allow this interface to accept calls with other destination addresses, use the **x25 alias** interface configuration command.

  x25 alias *destination-pattern* [**cud** *cud-pattern*]

Syntax	Description
destination-pattern	Regular expression used to match against the destination address of a received call.
cud *cud-pattern*	(Optional) Call user data (CUD) pattern, a regular expression of ASCII text. The CUD field might be present in a call packet. The first few bytes (commonly 4 bytes long) identify a protocol; the specified pattern is applied to any user data after the protocol identification.

Command Reference

Default

No alias is configured.

Command Mode

Interface configuration

Usage Guidelines

This command first appeared in Cisco IOS Release 11.2 F. It replaces the functionality that was provided by the **alias** keyword of the **x25 route** command.

Encapsulation, PAD, and QLLC calls are normally accepted when the destination address is that of the interface (or the zero-length address). Those calls will also be accepted when the destination address matches a configured alias.

Example

An X.25 call may be addressed to the receiving interface; calls addressed to the receiving interface are eligible for acceptance as a datagram encapsulation, PAD or QLLC connection, and may not be routed. In the following example, serial interface 0 is configured with a native address of 0000123 and a destination alias for any address that starts with 1111123. That is, serial interface 0 can accept its own calls and calls for any destination that starts with 1111123.

```
interface serial 0
 encapsulation x25
 x25 address 0000123
 x25 alias ^1111123.*
```

X25 BFE-DECISION

To specify how a router configured for **x25 bfe-emergency decision** will participate in emergency mode, use the **x25 bfe-decision** interface configuration command.

    x25 bfe-decision {no | yes | ask}

Syntax   *Description*

no   Prevents the router from participating in emergency mode and from sending address translation information to the BFE device.

yes   Allows the router to participate in emergency mode and to send address translation information to the BFE when the BFE enters emergency mode. This information is obtained from the table created by the **x25 remote-red** command.

ask   Configures the Cisco IOS software to prompt you to enter the **bfe** EXEC command.

Default

The router does not participate in emergency mode.

Command Mode

Interface configuration

Usage Guidelines

This command first appeared in Cisco IOS Release 10.0.

Example

The following example configures serial interface 0 to require an EXEC command from you before it participates in emergency mode. The host IP address is 21.0.0.12, and the address of the remote BFE unit is 21.0.0.1. When the BFE enters emergency mode, the Cisco IOS software prompts you for the EXEC command **bfe enter** to direct the router to participate in emergency mode.

```
interface serial 0
 x25 bfe-emergency decision
 x25 remote-red 21.0.0.12 remote-black 21.0.0.1
 x25 bfe-decision ask
```

Related Commands

bfe
x25 bfe-emergency
x25 remote-red

X25 BFE-EMERGENCY

To configure the circumstances under which the router participates in emergency mode, use the **x25 bfe-emergency** interface configuration command.

    x25 bfe-emergency {never | always | decision}

Syntax	Description
never	Prevents the router from sending address translation information to the Blacker Front End (BFE). If it does not receive address translation information, the BFE cannot open a new connection for which it does not know the address.
always	Allows the router to pass address translations to the BFE when it enters emergency mode and an address translation table has been created.
decision	Directs the router to wait until it receives a diagnostic packet from the BFE device indicating that the emergency mode window is open. The window is only open when a condition exists that allows the BFE to enter emergency mode. When the diagnostic packet is received, the participation in emergency mode depends on how the router is configured with the **x25 bfe-decision** command.

Default

No address translation information is sent to the BFE.

Command Mode

Interface configuration

Usage Guidelines

This command first appeared in Cisco IOS Release 10.0.

Example

The following example configures serial interface 0 to require an EXEC command from you before it participates in emergency mode. The host IP address is 21.0.0.12, and the address of the remote BFE unit is 21.0.0.1. When the BFE enters emergency mode, the Cisco IOS software prompts you for the EXEC command **bfe enter** to direct the router to participate in emergency mode.

```
interface serial 0
 x25 bfe-emergency decision
 x25 remote-red 21.0.0.12 remote-black 21.0.0.1
 x25 bfe-decision ask
```

Related Commands

bfe
x25 bfe-decision

X25 DEFAULT

To set a default protocol, use the **x25 default** interface configuration command. To remove the default protocol specified, use the **no** form of this command.

> **x25 default** *protocol*
> **no x25 default** *protocol*

Syntax	Description
protocol	Specifies the protocol to assume; may be **ip** or **pad**.

Default

No default protocol is set.

Command Mode

Interface configuration

Usage Guidelines

This command first appeared in Cisco IOS Release 10.0.

This command specifies the protocol assumed by the Cisco IOS software for incoming calls with unknown or missing protocol identifier in the Call User Data (CUD). If you do not use the **x25 default** interface configuration command, the software clears any incoming calls with unrecognized CUD.

Example

The following example establishes IP as the default protocol for X.25 calls:

```
interface serial 0
  x25 default ip
```

Related Commands

x25 map

X25 FACILITY

To force facilities on a per-call basis for calls originated by the router (switched calls are not affected), use the **x25 facility** interface configuration command. To disable a facility, use the **no** form of this command.

> **x25 facility** *facility-keyword value*
> **no x25 facility** *facility-keyword value*

Syntax	Description
facility-keyword	User facility.
value	Facility value; see Table 12–14 for a list of supported facilities and their values.

Default

No facility is sent.

Command Mode

Interface configuration

Usage Guidelines

This command first appeared prior to Cisco IOS Release 10.0.

Table 12–14 lists X.25 user facilities.

Table 12–14 *X.25 User Facilities*

User Facility	Description
cug *number*	Specifies a Closed User Group (CUG) number; CUGs in the range of 1 to 9999 are allowed. CUGs can be used by a Public Data Network (PDN) to create a virtual private network within the larger network and to restrict access.

Table 12–14 *X.25 User Facilities, Continued*

User Facility	Description
packetsize *in-size out-size*	Proposes input maximum packet size *(in-size)* and output maximum packet size *(out-size)* for flow control parameter negotiation. The sizes must be one of the following values: 16, 32, 64, 128, 256, 512, 1024, 2048, or 4096.
windowsize *in-size out-size*	Proposes the packet count for input windows *(in-size)* and output windows *(out-size)* for flow control parameter negotiation. The size values must be in the range 1 to 127 and must not be greater than or equal to the value set for the **x25 modulo** command.
reverse	Specifies reverses charging on all calls originated by the interface.
throughput *in out*	Sets the requested throughput class negotiation values for input *(in)* and output *(out)* throughput across the network. Values for *in* and *out* are in bits per second (bps) and range from 75 to 64000 bps.
transit-delay *value*	Specifies a network transit delay to request for the duration of outgoing calls for networks that support transit delay. The transit delay value can be between 0 and 65534 milliseconds.
roa *name*	Specifies the name defined by the **x25 roa** command for a list of transit Recognized Operation Agencies (ROAs) to use in outgoing Call Request packets.

Examples

The following example specifies a transit delay value in an X.25 configuration:

```
interface serial 0
 x25 facility transit-delay 24000
```

The following example sets an ROA name and then sends the list via the X.25 user facilities:

```
x25 roa green_list 23 35 36
interface serial 0
 x25 facility roa green_list
```

Related Commands

x25 roa

X25 HIC

To set the highest incoming-only virtual circuit number, use the **x25 hic** interface configuration command.

    x25 hic *circuit-number*

Syntax   *Description*

circuit-number   Virtual circuit number from 1 to 4095, or 0 if there is no incoming-only
                       virtual circuit range.

Default

0

Command Mode

Interface configuration

Usage Guidelines

This command first appeared prior to Cisco IOS Release 10.0.

This command is applicable only if you have the X.25 switch configured for an incoming-only virtual circuit range. *Incoming* is from the perspective of the X.25 DTE. If you do not want any outgoing calls from your DTE, configure both ends to disable the two-way range (set the values of **x25 ltc** and **x25 htc** to 0) and configure an incoming-only range. Any incoming-only range must come before (that is, must be numerically less than) any two-way range. Any two-way range must come before any outgoing-only range.

Example

The following example sets a valid incoming-only virtual circuit range of 1 to 5:

```
interface serial 0
  x25 lic 1
  x25 hic 5
```

Related Commands

x25 lic

X25 HOC

To set the highest outgoing-only virtual circuit number, use the **x25 hoc** interface configuration command.

    x25 hoc *circuit-number*

Syntax   *Description*

circuit-number   Virtual circuit number from 1 to 4095, or 0 if there is no outgoing-only
                       virtual circuit range.

Default

0

Command Mode

Interface configuration

Usage Guidelines

This command first appeared prior to Cisco IOS Release 10.0.

This command is applicable only if you have the X.25 switch configured for an outgoing-only virtual circuit range. *Outgoing* is from the perspective of the X.25 DTE. If you do not want any incoming calls on your DTE, disable the two-way range (set the values of **x25 ltc** and **x25 htc** to 0) and configure an outgoing-only range. Any outgoing-only range must come after (that is, be numerically greater than) any other range.

Example

The following example sets a valid outgoing-only virtual circuit range of 2000 to 2005:

```
interface serial 0
 x25 loc 2000
 x25 hoc 2005
```

Related Commands

x25 loc

X25 HOLD-QUEUE

To set the maximum number of packets to hold until a virtual circuit is able to transmit, use the **x25 hold-queue** interface configuration command. To remove this command from the configuration file and restore the default value, use the **no** form of this command without an argument.

> **x25 hold-queue** *packets*
> **no x25 hold-queue** [*packets*]

Syntax	Description
packets	Number of packets. A hold queue value of 0 allows an unlimited number of packets in the hold queue. This argument is optional for the **no** form of this command.

Default

10 packets

Command Mode

Interface configuration

Usage Guidelines

This command first appeared prior to Cisco IOS Release 10.0.

If you set the *queue-size* to 0 when using the **no x25 hold-queue** command, there will be no hold queue limit. While this setting will prevent drops until the router runs out of memory, it is only rarely appropriate. A virtual circuit hold queue value is determined when it is created; changing this parameter will not affect the hold queue limits of the existing virtual circuits.

Example

The following example sets the X.25 hold queue to hold 25 packets:

```
interface serial 0
x25 hold-queue 25
```

Related Commands

ip mtu
x25 ips
x25 ops

X25 HOLD-VC-TIMER

To start the timer that prevents additional calls to a destination for a given period of time (thus preventing overruns on some X.25 switches caused by Call Request packets), use the **x25 hold-vc-timer** interface configuration command. To restore the default value for the timer, use the **no** form of this command.

　　x25 hold-vc-timer *minutes*
　　no x25 hold-vc-timer

Syntax	*Description*
minutes	Number of minutes to prevent calls from going to a previously failed destination. Incoming calls are still accepted.

Default

0 minutes

Command Mode

Interface configuration

Usage Guidelines

This command first appeared prior to Cisco IOS Release 10.0.

Only Call Requests that the router originates are held down; routed X.25 Call Requests are not affected by this parameter. Upon receiving a Clear Request for an outstanding Call Request, the

X.25 support code immediately tries another Call Request if it has more traffic to send, and this action might cause overrun problems.

Example

The following example sets this timer to 3 minutes:

```
interface serial 0
  x25 hold-vc-timer 3
```

X25 HOST

To define a static host name-to-address mapping, use the **x25 host** global configuration command. Use the **no** form of the command to remove the host name.

> **x25 host** *name x121-address* [**cud** *call-user-data*]
> **no x25 host** *name*

Syntax	Description
name	Host name.
x121-address	The X.121 address.
cud *call-user-data*	(Optional) Sets the Call User Data (CUD) field in the X.25 Call Request packet.

Default

No static host name-to-address mapping is defined.

Command Mode

Global configuration

Usage Guidelines

This command first appeared prior to Cisco IOS Release 10.0.

Examples

The following example specifies a static address mapping:

```
x25 host Willard 4085551212
```

The following example removes a static address mapping:

```
no x25 host Willard
```

X25 HTC

To set the highest two-way virtual circuit number, use the **x25 htc** interface configuration command.

> **x25 htc** *circuit-number*

Syntax	Description
circuit-number	Virtual circuit number from 1 to 4095, or 0 if there is no two-way virtual circuit range.

Defaults

1024 for X.25 network service interfaces; 4095 for CMNS network service interfaces.

Command Mode

Interface configuration

Usage Guidelines

This command first appeared prior to Cisco IOS Release 10.0.

This command is applicable if the X.25 switch is configured for a two-way virtual circuit range. Any two-way virtual circuit range must come after (that is, be numerically larger than) any incoming-only range, and must come before any outgoing-only range.

Example

The following example sets a valid two-way virtual circuit range of 5 to 25:

```
interface serial 0
  x25 ltc 5
  x25 htc 25
```

Related Commands

cmns enable
x25 ltc

X25 IDLE

To define the period of inactivity after which the router can clear a switched virtual circuit (SVC), use the **x25 idle** interface configuration command.

   x25 idle *minutes*

Syntax	Description
minutes	Idle period in minutes.

Default

0 (the SVC is kept open indefinitely)

Command Mode

Interface configuration

Usage Guidelines

This command first appeared prior to Cisco IOS Release 10.0.

Calls originated and terminated by the router are cleared; PAD and switched virtual circuits are not affected. To clear one or all virtual circuits at once, use the privileged EXEC command **clear x25**.

Example

The following example sets a 5-minute wait period before an idle circuit is cleared:
```
interface serial 2
  x25 idle 5
```

Related Commands

clear x25

X25 IP-PRECEDENCE

To enable the Cisco IOS software to use the IP precedence value when it opens a new virtual circuit, use the **x25 ip-precedence** interface configuration command. To cause the Cisco IOS software to ignore the precedence value when opening virtual circuits, use the **no** form of this command.
   x25 ip-precedence
   no x25 ip-precedence

Syntax Description

This command has no arguments or keywords.

Default

The router opens one virtual circuit for all types of service.

Command Mode

Interface configuration

Usage Guidelines

This command first appeared prior to Cisco IOS Release 10.0.

This feature is useful only for DDN or BFE encapsulations, because only these methods have an IP precedence facility defined to allow the source and destination devices to both use the virtual circuit for traffic of the given IP priority.

Verify that your host does not send nonstandard data in the IP Type Of Service (TOS) field because it can cause wasteful multiple virtual circuits to be created. Four virtual circuits may be opened based on IP precedence to encapsulate routine, priority, immediate, and all higher precedences.

The **x25 map nvc** limit or the default **x25 nvc** limit still applies.

Example

The following example allows new IP encapsulation virtual circuits based on the IP precedence:
```
interface serial 3
  x25 ip-precedence
```

X25 IPS

To set the interface default maximum input packet size to match that of the network, use the **x25 ips** interface configuration command.

    x25 ips *bytes*

Syntax	Description
bytes	Byte count. It can be one of the following values: 16, 32, 64, 128, 256, 512, 1024, 2048, or 4096.

Default

128 bytes

Command Mode

Interface configuration

Usage Guidelines

This command first appeared prior to Cisco IOS Release 10.0.

X.25 network connections have a default maximum input packet size set by the network administrator. Larger packet sizes require less overhead processing. To send a packet larger than the X.25 packet size over an X.25 virtual circuit, the Cisco IOS software must break the packet into two or more X.25 packets with the more data bit (M-bit) set. The receiving device collects all packets with the M-bit set and reassembles the original packet.

NOTES

Set the **x25 ips** and **x25 ops** commands to the same value unless your network supports asymmetric input and output packet sizes.

Command Reference

Example

The following example sets the default maximum packet sizes to 512:

```
interface serial 1
  x25 ips 512
  x25 ops 512
```

Related Commands

x25 facility
x25 ops

X25 LIC

To set the lowest incoming-only virtual circuit number, use the **x25 lic** interface configuration command.

   x25 lic *circuit-number*

Syntax	Description
circuit-number	Virtual circuit number from 1 to 4095, or 0 if there is no incoming-only virtual circuit range.

Default

0

Command Mode

Interface configuration

Usage Guidelines

This command first appeared prior to Cisco IOS Release 10.0.

This command is applicable only if you have the X.25 switch configured for an incoming-only virtual circuit range. *Outgoing* is from the perspective of the X.25 DTE. If you do not want any incoming calls on your DTE, disable the two-way range (set the values of **x25 ltc** and **x25 htc** to 0) and configure an outgoing-only range. Any outgoing-only range must come after (that is, be numerically greater than) any other range.

This command is applicable if you have the X.25 switch configured for two-way virtual circuit range.

Example

The following example sets a valid incoming-only virtual circuit range of 1 to 5 and sets the lowest two-way virtual circuit number:

```
interface serial 0
  x25 lic 1
  x25 hic 5
  x25 ltc 6
```

Related Commands

x25 hic

X25 LINKRESTART

To force X.25 Level 3 (packet level) to restart when Level 2 (LAPB, the link level) resets, use the **x25 linkrestart** interface configuration command. To disable this function, use the **no** form of this command.

> x25 linkrestart
> no x25 linkrestart

Syntax Description

This command has no arguments or keywords.

Default

Forcing packet-level restarts is the default and is necessary for networks that expect this behavior.

Command Mode

Interface configuration

Usage Guidelines

This command first appeared prior to Cisco IOS Release 10.0.

Example

The following example disables the link-level restart:

```
interface serial 3
  no x25 linkrestart
```

X25 LOC

To set the lowest outgoing-only virtual circuit number, use the **x25 loc** interface configuration command.

> x25 loc *circuit-number*

Syntax	*Description*
circuit-number	Virtual circuit number from 1 to 4095, or 0 if there is no outgoing-only virtual circuit range.

Default

0

Command Mode

Interface configuration

Usage Guidelines

This command first appeared prior to Cisco IOS Release 10.0.

This command is applicable only if you have the X.25 switch configured for an outgoing-only virtual circuit range. *Outgoing* is from the perspective of the X.25 DTE. If you do not want any incoming calls from your DTE, configure the values of **x25 loc** and **x25 hoc** and set the values of **x25 ltc** and **x25 htc** to 0.

Example

The following example sets a valid outgoing-only virtual circuit range of 2000 to 2005:

```
interface serial 0
  x25 loc 2000
  x25 hoc 2005
```

Related Commands

x25 hoc

X25 LTC

To set the lowest two-way virtual circuit number, use the **x25 ltc** interface configuration command.

x25 ltc *circuit-number*

Syntax	Description
circuit-number	Virtual circuit number from 1 to 4095, or 0 if there is no two-way virtual circuit range.

Default

1

Command Mode

Interface configuration

Usage Guidelines

This command first appeared prior to Cisco IOS Release 10.0.

This command is applicable if you have the X.25 switch configured for a two-way virtual circuit range. Any two-way virtual circuit range must come after (that is, be numerically larger than) any incoming-only range, and must come before any outgoing-only range.

Example

The following example sets a valid two-way virtual circuit range of 5 to 25:
```
interface serial 0
  x25 ltc 5
  x25 htc 25
```

Related Commands

x25 htc

X25 MAP

To set up the LAN protocols-to-remote host mapping, use the **x25 map** interface configuration command. To retract a prior mapping, use the **no** form of this command with the appropriate network protocol(s) and X.121 address argument.

> **x25 map** *protocol address* [*protocol2 address2*[...[*protocol9 address9*]]] *x121-address* [*option*]
>
> **no x25 map** *protocol address x121-address*

Syntax	Description
protocol	Protocol type, entered by keyword. Supported protocols are entered by keyword, as listed in Table 12–15. As many as nine protocol and address pairs can be specified in one command line.
address	Protocol address.
x121-address	X.121 address of the remote host.
option	(Optional) Additional functionality that can be specified for originated calls. This option can be any of the options listed in Table 12–16.

Default

No LAN protocol-to-remote host mapping is set up.

Command Mode

Interface configuration

Usage Guidelines

This command first appeared prior to Cisco IOS Release 10.0.

Because no defined protocol can dynamically determine LAN protocol-to-remote host mappings, you must enter all the information for each host with which the router may exchange X.25 encapsulation traffic.

Two methods are available to encapsulate traffic: Cisco's long-available encapsulation method and the IETF's standard method (defined in RFC 1356). The latter method allows hosts to exchange several protocols over a single virtual circuit. Cisco's encapsulation method is the default (for backward compatibility) unless the interface configuration command specifies **ietf**.

When you configure multiprotocol maps, you can specify a maximum of nine protocol and address pairs in an **x25 map** command. However, you can specify a protocol only once. For example, you can specify the IP protocol and an IP address, but you cannot specify another IP address. If **compressedtcp** and **ip** are both specified, the same IP address must be used.

Bridging is supported only if you are using Cisco's traditional encapsulation method. For correct operation, bridging maps must specify the **broadcast** option.

Since most datagram routing protocols rely on broadcasts or multicasts to send routing information to their neighbors, the **broadcast** keyword is needed to run such routing protocols over X.25.

Encapsulation maps might also specify that traffic between the two hosts should be compressed, thus increasing the effective bandwidth between them at the expense of memory and computation time. Because each compression virtual circuit requires memory and computation resources, compression must be used with care and monitored to maintain acceptable resource usage and overall performance.

OSPF treats a nonbroadcast, multiaccess network such as X.25 in much the same way as it treats a broadcast network by requiring the selection of a designated router. In previous releases, this required manual assignment in the OSPF configuration using the **neighbor** router configuration command. When the **x25 map** command is included in the configuration with the broadcast, and the **ip ospf network** command (with the **broadcast** keyword) is configured, there is no need to configure any neighbors manually. OSPF will now run over the X.25 network as a broadcast network. (Refer to the **ip ospf network** interface configuration command for more detail.)

— ◖ **NOTES** ◗ ───

The OSPF broadcast mechanism assumes that IP class D addresses are never used for regular traffic over X.25.

───

You can modify the options of an **x25 map** command by restating the complete set of protocols and addresses specified for the map, followed by the desired options. To delete a map command, you must also specify the complete set of protocols and addresses; the options can be omitted when deleting a map.

Once defined, a map's protocols and addresses cannot be changed. This requirement exists because the Cisco IOS software cannot determine whether you want to add to, delete from, or modify an existing map's protocol and address specification, or simply mistyped the command. To change a map's protocol and address specification, you must delete it and create a new map.

A given protocol-address pair cannot be used in more than one map on the same interface.

Table 12–15 lists the protocols supported by X.25.

Table 12–15 *Protocols Supported by X.25*

Keyword	Protocol
apollo	Apollo Domain
appletalk	AppleTalk
bridge	Bridging[*]
clns	ISO Connectionless Network Service
compressedtcp	TCP/IP header compression
decnet	DECnet
ip	IP
ipx	Novell IPX
pad	PAD links[†]
qllc	System Network Architecture (SNA) encapsulation in X.25[‡]
vines	Banyan VINES
xns	XNS

[*] Bridging traffic is supported only for Cisco's traditional encapsulation method, so a bridge map cannot specify other protocols.

[†] Packet Assembly/Disassembly (PAD) maps are used to configure session and protocol translation access, therefore, this protocol is not available for multiprotocol encapsulation.

[‡] Qualified Logical Link Control (QLLC) is not available for multiprotocol encapsulation.

The CMNS map form is obsolete; its function is replaced by the enhanced **x25 route** command. Table 12–16 lists the map options supported by X.25.

Table 12–16 *X.25 Map Options*

Option	Description
compress	Specifies that X.25 payload compression be used for mapping the traffic to this host. Each virtual circuit established for compressed traffic uses a significant amount of memory (for a table of learned data patterns) and for computation (for compression and decompression of all data). Cisco recommends that compression be used with careful consideration to its impact on overall performance.
method {cisco | ietf | snap | multi}	Specifies the encapsulation method. The choices are as follows: • **cisco**—Cisco's proprietary encapsulation; not available if more than one protocol is to be carried.

Table 12–16   *X.25 Map Options, Continued*

Option	Description
	• **ietf**—Default RFC 1356 operation: protocol identification of single-protocol virtual circuits and protocol identification within multiprotocol virtual circuits use the standard encoding, which is compatible with RFC 877. Multiprotocol virtual circuits are used only if needed. • **snap**—RFC 1356 operation where IP is identified with SNAP rather than the standard IETF method (the standard method is compatible with RFC 877). • **multi**—Forces a map that specifies a single protocol to set up a multiprotocol virtual circuit when a call is originated; also forces a single-protocol PVC to use multiprotocol data identification methods for all datagrams sent and received.
no-incoming	Use the map only to originate calls.
no-outgoing	Do not originate calls when using the map.
idle *minutes*	Specifies an idle timeout for calls other than the interface default; 0 minutes disables the idle timeout.
reverse	Specifies reverse charging for outgoing calls.
accept-reverse	Causes the Cisco IOS software to accept incoming reverse-charged calls. If this option is not present, the Cisco IOS software clears reverse-charged calls unless the interface accepts all reverse-charged calls.
broadcast	Causes the Cisco IOS software to direct any broadcasts sent through this interface to the specified X.121 address. This option also simplifies the configuration of OSPF.
cug *group-number*	Specifies a closed user group number (from 1 to 9999) for the mapping in an outgoing call.
nvc *count*	Sets the maximum number of virtual circuits for this map or host. The default *count* is the **x25 nvc** setting of the interface. A maximum number of eight virtual circuits can be configured for each map. Compressed TCP may use only 1 virtual circuit.
packetsize *in-size out-size*	Proposes maximum input packet size (*in-size*) and maximum output packet size (*out-size*) for an outgoing call. Typically, both sizes are the same and must be one of the following values: 16, 32, 64, 128, 256, 512, 1024, 2048, or 4096.
windowsize *in-size out-size*	Proposes the packet count for input window (*in-size*) and output window (*out-size*) for an outgoing call. Typically, both sizes are the same, must be in the range 1 to 127, and must be less than the value set by the **x25 modulo** command.

Table 12–16 *X.25 Map Options, Continued*

Option	Description
throughput *in out*	Sets the requested throughput class values for input (*in*) and output (*out*) throughput across the network for an outgoing call. Values for *in* and *out* are in bits per second (bps) and range from 75 to 48000 bps.
transit-delay *milliseconds*	Specifies the transit delay value in milliseconds (0 to 65534) for an outgoing call for networks that support transit delay.
nuid *username password*	Specifies that a Network User ID (NUID) facility be sent in the outgoing call with the specified Terminal Access Controller Access Control System (TACACS) username and password (in a format defined by Cisco). This option should be used only when connecting to another Cisco router. The combined length of the username and password should not exceed 127 characters. This option only works if the router is configured as an X.25 DTE.
nudata *string*	Specifies the network user identification in a format determined by the network administrator (as allowed by the standards). This option is provided for connecting to non-Cisco equipment that requires an NUID facility. The string should not exceed 130 characters and must be enclosed in quotation marks ("") if there are any spaces present. This option only works if the router is configured as an X.25 DTE.
roa *name*	Specifies the name defined by the **x25 roa** command for a list of transit Recognized Operating Agencies (ROAs, formerly called Recognized Private Operating Agencies or RPOAs) to use in outgoing Call Request packets.
passive	Specifies that the X.25 interface should send compressed outgoing TCP datagrams only if they were already compressed when they were received. This option is available only for compressed TCP maps.

Examples

The following example maps IP address 172.20.2.5 to X.121 address 000000010300. The **broadcast** keyword directs any broadcasts sent through this interface to the specified X.121 address.

```
interface serial 0
    x25 map ip 171.20.2.5 000000010300 broadcast
```

The following example specifies an ROA name to be used for originating connections:

```
x25 roa green_list 23 35 36
interface serial 0
    x25 map ip 172.20.170.26 10 roa green_list
```

The following example specifies a NUID facility to send on calls originated for the address map:

```
interface serial 0
    x25 map ip 172.20.174.32 2 nudata "Network User ID 35"
```

Strings can be quoted, but quotation marks are not required unless embedded blanks are present.

Related Commands

ip ospf network
show x25 map
x25 facility
x25 map bridge
x25 map compressedtcp
x25 map pad
x25 route
x25 roa

X25 MAP BRIDGE

To configure an Internet-to-X.121 address mapping for bridging over X.25, use the **x25 map bridge** interface configuration command.

> **x25 map bridge** *x121-address* **broadcast** [*option*]

Syntax	Description
x121-address	The X.121 address.
broadcast	Required keyword for bridging over X.25.
option	(Optional) Services that can be added to this map; the same options as the **x25 map** command; see Table 12–16 earlier in this chapter.

Default

No bridging over X.25 is configured.

Command Mode

Interface configuration

Usage Guidelines

This command first appeared prior to Cisco IOS Release 10.0.

Example

The following example configures transparent bridging over X.25 between two Cisco routers using a maximum of six virtual circuits:

```
interface serial 1
 x25 map bridge 000000010300 broadcast nvc 6
```

Related Commands

x25 map

X25 MAP CMNS

The enhanced **x25 route** command replaces the **x25 map cmns** command. Refer to the description of the **x25 route** command for more information.

X25 MAP COMPRESSEDTCP

To map compressed TCP traffic to an X.121 address, use the **x25 map compressedtcp** interface configuration command. To delete a TCP/IP header compression map for the link, use the **no** form of this command.

> **x25 map compressedtcp** *ip-address* [*protocol2 address2* [...[*protocol9 address9*]]]
> **x121-address** [*option*]
> **no x25 map compressedtcp** *address* [*protocol2 address2* [...[*protocol9 address9*]]]
> *x121-address*

Syntax	Description
ip-address	IP address.
protocol	(Optional) Protocol type, entered by keyword. Supported protocols are entered by keyword, as listed in Table 12–15. As many as nine protocol and address pairs can be specified in one command line.
address	(Optional) Protocol address.
x121-address	X.121 address.
option	(Optional) The same options as those for the **x25 map** command; see Table 12–16 earlier in this chapter.

Default

No mapping is configured.

Command Mode

Interface configuration

Usage Guidelines

This command first appeared prior to Cisco IOS Release 10.0.

Cisco supports RFC 1144 TCP/IP Header Compression (THC) on serial lines using HDLC and X.25 encapsulation. THC encapsulation is only slightly different from other encapsulation traffic, but these differences are worth noting. The implementation of compressed TCP over X.25 uses one virtual circuit to pass the compressed packets. Any IP traffic (including standard TCP) is separate from TCH traffic; it is carried over separate IP encapsulation virtual circuits or identified separately in a multiprotocol virtual circuit.

If you specify both **ip** and **compressedtcp** in the same **x25 map compressedtcp** command, they must both specify the same IP address.

The **nvc** map option cannot be used for TCP/IP header compression, because only one virtual circuit can carry compressed TCP/IP header traffic to a given host.

Example

The following example establishes a map for TCP/IP header compression on serial interface 4:

```
interface serial 4
 ip tcp header-compression
 x25 map compressedtcp 172.20.2.5 000000010300
```

Related Commands

x25 map

X25 MAP PAD

To configure an X.121 address mapping for PAD access over X.25, use the **x25 map pad** interface configuration command.

    x25 map pad *x121-address* [*option*]

Syntax	Description
x121-address	X.121 address of the interface.
option	(Optional.) Services that can be added to this map—the same options as the **x25 map** command (see Table 12–16 earlier in this chapter).

Default

No specific options are used for PAD access.

Command Mode

Interface configuration

Usage Guidelines

This command first appeared in Cisco IOS Release 10.2.

Use a PAD map to configure optional X.25 facility use for PAD access. When used with the **x25 pad-access** interface configuration command, the **x25 map pad** command restricts incoming PAD access to those statically mapped hosts.

Example

The following example configures an X.25 interface to restrict incoming PAD access to the single mapped host. This example requires that both incoming and outgoing PAD access use the NUID user authentication.

```
interface serial 1
  x25 pad-access
  x25 map pad 000000010300 nuid johndoe secret
```

Related Commands

x25 map
x25 pad-access

X25 MODULO

To set the window modulus, use the **x25 modulo** interface configuration command.

    x25 modulo *modulus*

Syntax	Description
modulus	Either 8 or 128. The value of the modulo parameter must agree with that of the device on the other end of the X.25 link.

Default

8

Command Mode

Interface configuration

Usage Guidelines

This command first appeared prior to Cisco IOS Release 10.0.

X.25 supports flow control with a sliding window sequence count. The window counter restarts at zero upon reaching the upper limit, which is called the *window modulus*. Modulo 128 operation is also referred to as *extended packet sequence numbering*, which allows larger packet windows.

Example

The following example sets the window modulus to 128:

```
interface serial 0
  x25 modulo 128
```

Related Commands

x25 facility
x25 win
x25 wout

X25 NVC

To specify the maximum number of virtual circuits that a protocol can have open simultaneously to one host, use the **x25 nvc** interface configuration command. To increase throughput across networks, you can establish up to eight virtual circuits to a host and protocol.

    x25 nvc *count*

Syntax   Description

count   Circuit count from 1 to 8. A maximum of eight virtual circuits can be configured for each protocol-host pair. Protocols that do not tolerate out-of-order delivery, such as encapsulated TCP/IP header compression, will use only one virtual circuit despite this value. The default is 1. Permitting more than one VC may help throughput on slow networks.

Default

1

Command Mode

Interface configuration

Usage Guidelines

This command first appeared prior to Cisco IOS Release 10.0.

When the windows and output queues of all existing connections to a host are full, a new virtual circuit will be opened to the designated circuit count. If a new connection cannot be opened, the data is dropped.

NOTES

The *count* value specified for **x25 nvc** affects the default value for the number of VCs. It does not affect the **nvc** option for any **x25 map** commands that are configured.

Example

The following example sets the default maximum number of VCs that each map can have open simultaneously to 4:

```
interface serial 0
x25 nvc 4
```

X25 OPS

To set the interface default maximum output packet size to match that of the network, use the **x25 ops** interface configuration command.

    x25 ops *bytes*

Syntax	Description
bytes	Byte count that is one of the following: 16, 32, 64, 128, 256, 512, 1024, 2048, or 4096.

Default

128 bytes

Command Mode

Interface configuration

Usage Guidelines

This command first appeared prior to Cisco IOS Release 10.0.

X.25 networks use maximum output packet sizes set by the network administrator. Larger packet sizes are better because smaller packets require more overhead processing. To send a packet larger than the X.25 packet size over an X.25 virtual circuit, the Cisco IOS software must break the packet into two or more X.25 packets with the more data bit (M-bit) set. The receiving device collects all packets with the M-bit set and reassembles the original packet.

NOTES

Set the **x25 ips** and **x25 ops** commands to the same value unless your network supports asymmetry between input and output packets.

Example

The following example sets the default maximum packet sizes to 512:

```
interface serial 1
  x25 ips 512
  x25 ops 512
```

Related Commands

x25 ips

X25 PAD-ACCESS

Use the **x25 pad-access** interface configuration command to cause the PAD software to accept PAD connections only from statically mapped X.25 hosts. To disable checking maps on PAD connections, use the **no** form of this command.

x25 pad-access
no x25 pad-access

Command Reference

Syntax Description

This command has no arguments or keywords.

Default

Accept PAD connections from any host.

Command Mode

Interface configuration

Usage Guidelines

This command first appeared in Cisco IOS Release 10.2.

By default, all PAD connection attempts are processed for session creation or protocol translation, subject to the configuration of those functions. If you use the **x25 pad-access** command, PAD connections are processed only for incoming calls with a source address that matches a statically mapped address configured with the **x25 map pad** interface configuration command. PAD connections are refused for any incoming calls with a source address that has not been statically mapped.

Example

The following example restricts incoming PAD access on the interface to attempts from the host with the X.121 address 000000010300:

```
interface serial 1
 x25 pad-access
 x25 map pad 000000010300
```

Related Commands

service pad
x25 map pad
x29 access-list
x29 profile

X25 PVC (ENCAPSULATING)

To establish an encapsulation Permanent Virtual Circuit (PVC), use the encapsulating version of the **x25 pvc** interface configuration command. To delete the PVC, use the **no** form of this command with the appropriate channel number.

    x25 pvc *circuit protocol address* [*protocol2 address2*[...[*protocol9 address9*]]] *x121-address* [*option*]
    no x25 pvc *circuit*

Syntax	Description
circuit	Virtual-circuit channel number, which must be less than the virtual circuits assigned to the Switched Virtual Circuits (SVCs).
protocol	Protocol type, entered by keyword. Supported protocols are listed in Table 12–17. As many as nine protocol and address pairs can be specified in one command line.
address	Protocol address of the host at the other end of the PVC.
x121-address	X.121 address.
option	(Optional) Provides additional functionality or allows X.25 parameters to be specified for the PVC. This can be any of the options listed in Table 12–18.

Default

No encapsulation PVC is established. The PVC window and maximum packet sizes default to the interface default values.

Command Mode

Interface configuration

Usage Guidelines

This command first appeared prior to Cisco IOS Release 10.0.

PVCs are not supported for ISO CMNS.

You no longer need to specify a datagram protocol-to-address mapping before you can set up a PVC; a map is implied from the PVC configuration. Configurations generated by the router will no longer specify a map for encapsulating PVCs.

When configuring a PVC to carry CLNS traffic, use the X.121 address as the SubNetwork Point of Attachment (SNPA) to associate the PVC with a CLNS neighbor configuration. When configuring a PVC to carry transparent bridge traffic, the X.121 address is required to identify the remote host to the bridging function. Other encapsulation PVCs do not require an X.121 address.

Table 12–17 lists supported protocols.

Table 12–17 *Protocols Supported by X.25 PVCs*

Keyword	Protocol
apollo	Apollo Domain
appletalk	AppleTalk
bridge	Bridging[*]
clns	OSI Connectionless Network Service

Table 12–17   *Protocols Supported by X.25 PVCs, Continued*

Keyword	Protocol
compressedtcp	TCP/IP header compression
decnet	DECnet
ip	IP
ipx	Novell IPX
qllc	SNA encapsulation in X.25[†]
vines	Banyan VINES
xns	XNS

[*] Bridging traffic is supported only for Cisco's traditional encapsulation method, so a bridge PVC cannot specify other protocols.
[†] QLLC is not available for multiprotocol encapsulation.

Table 12–18 lists supported X.25 PVC options.

Table 12–18   *X.25 PVC Options*

Option	Description
broadcast	Causes the Cisco IOS software to direct any broadcasts sent through this interface to this PVC. This option also simplifies the configuration of OSPF.
method {cisco | ietf | snap | multi}	Specifies the encapsulation method. The choices are as follows: • **cisco**—Single protocol encapsulation; not available if more than one protocol is carried. • **ietf**—Default RFC 1356 operation; single-protocol encapsulation unless more than one protocol is carried, and protocol identification when more than one protocol is carried. • **snap**—RFC 1356 operation where IP is identified when more than one protocol is carried using the SNAP encoding. • **multi**—Multiprotocol encapsulation used on the PVC.
packetsize *in-size out-size*	Maximum input packet size (*in-size*) and output packet size (*out-size*) for the PVC. Typically, both sizes are the same and must be one of the following values: 16, 32, 64, 128, 256, 512, 1024, 2048, or 4096.
passive	Specifies that transmitted TCP datagrams will be compressed only if they were received compressed. This option is available only for PVCs carrying compressed TCP/IP header traffic.

Table 12-18 *X.25 PVC Options, Continued*

Option	Description
windowsize *in-size* *out-size*	Packet count for input window (*in-size*) and output window (*out-size*) for the PVC. Typically, both sizes are the same, must be in the range 1 to 127, and must be less than the value set for the **x25 modulo** command.

Example

The following example establishes a PVC on channel 2 to encapsulate VINES and IP with the far host:

```
interface serial 0
  x25 ltc 5
  x25 pvc 2 vines 60002A2D:0001 ip 172.20.170.91 11110001
```

Related Commands

x25 map

X25 PVC (SWITCHED)

To configure a switched PVC for a given interface, use the switched version of the **x25 pvc** interface configuration command.

    x25 pvc *number1* **interface** *type number* pvc *number2* [*option*]

Syntax	Description
number1	PVC number that will be used on the local interface (as defined by the primary interface command).
interface	Required keyword to specify an interface.
type	Remote interface type.
number	Remote interface number.
pvc	Required keyword to specify a switched PVC.
number2	PVC number that will be used on the remote interface.
option	(Optional) Adds certain features to the mapping specified; can be either option listed in Table 12–19.

Default

No switched PVC is configured. The PVC window and maximum packet sizes default to the interface default values.

Command Mode

Interface configuration

Usage Guidelines

This command first appeared prior to Cisco IOS Release 10.0.

You can configure X.25 PVCs in the X.25 switching software. As a result, DTEs that require permanent circuits can be connected to the router acting as an X.25 switch and have a properly functioning connection. X.25 resets will be sent to indicate when the circuit comes up or goes down.

PVC circuit numbers must come before (that is, be numerically smaller than) the circuit numbers allocated to any SVC range.

Table 12–19 lists the switched PVC options supported by X.25.

Table 12–19 *Switched PVC Options*

Option	Description
packetsize *in-size* *out-size*	Maximum input packet size (*in-size*) and output packet size (*out-size*) for the PVC. Both sizes must be one of the following values: 16, 32, 64, 128, 256, 512, 1024, 2048, or 4096.
windowsize *in-size* *out-size*	Packet count for input window (*in-size*) and output window (*out-size*) for the PVC. Both values should be the same, must be in the range 1 to 127, and must not be greater than the value set for the **x25 modulo** command.

Example

The following example configures a PVC connected between two serial interfaces on the same router. In this type of interconnection configuration, the alternate interface must be specified along with the PVC number on that interface. To make a working PVC connection, two commands must be specified, each pointing to the other, as this example illustrates:

```
interface serial 0
 encapsulation x25
 x25 ltc 5
 x25 pvc 1 interface serial 1 pvc 1
interface serial 1
 encapsulation x25
 x25 ltc 5
 x25 pvc 1 interface serial 0 pvc 1
```

X25 PVC (SWITCHED PVC TO SVC)

To configure a switched PVC to SVC circuit for a given interface, use the switched version of the **x25 pvc** interface configuration command.

  x25 pvc *number1* **svc** *x121-address* [*flow-control-options*] [*call-control-options*]

Syntax	Description
number1	Logical channel ID of the PVC. This value must be lower than any range of circuit numbers defined for SVCs.
svc	Specifies a switched virtual circuit type.
x121-address	Destination X.121 address for opening an outbound switched virtual circuit and source X.121 address for matching an inbound switched virtual circuit.
flow-control-options	(Optional) Adds certain features to the mapping specified; this can be any of the options listed in Table 12–20.
call-control-options	(Optional) Adds certain features to the mapping specified; this can be any of the options listed in Table 12–21.

Default

No switched PVC is configured. The PVC window and maximum packet sizes default to the interface default values.

The default idle time comes from the interface on which the **x25 pvc** command is configured, not the interface on which the call is sent/received.

Command Mode

Interface configuration

Usage Guidelines

This command first appeared in Cisco IOS Release 11.2 F.

PVC circuit numbers must come before (that is, be numerically smaller than) the circuit numbers allocated to any SVC range.

On an outgoing call, the packet size facilities and window size facilities will be included. The call will be cleared if the call accepted packet specifies different values.

On an incoming call, requested values that do not match the configured values will be refused.

Table 12–20 lists the flow control options supported by X.25 during PVC to SVC switching.

Table 12–20 *Flow Control Options*

Option	Description
packetsize *in-size* *out-size*	Maximum input packet size (*in-size*) and output packet size (*out-size*) for both the PVC and SVC. Values may differ but must be one of the following: 16, 32, 64, 128, 256, 512, 1024, 2048, or 4096.

Command Reference

Table 12–20   *Flow Control Options, Continued*

Option	Description
windowsize *in-size* *out-size*	Packet count for input window (*in-size*) and output window (*out-size*) for both the PVC and SVC. The values may differ but must be in the range 1 to 127 and must be less than the value set for the **x25 modulo** command.

Table 12–21 lists the call control options supported by X.25 during PVC to SVC switching.

Table 12–21   *Call Control Options*

Option	Description
idle *minutes*	Idle time-out for the SVC. This option will override the interface's **x25 idle** command value only for this circuit.
no-incoming	Establishes a switched virtual circuit to the specified X.121 address when data is received from the permanent virtual circuit, but does not accept calls from this X.121 address.
no-outgoing	Accepts an incoming call from the specified X.121 address, but does not attempt to place a call when data is received from the permanent virtual circuit. If data is received from the permanent virtual circuit while no call is connected, the PVC will be reset.
accept-reverse	Causes the Cisco IOS software to accept incoming reverse-charged calls. If this option is not present, the Cisco IOS software clears reverse-charged calls unless the interface accepts all reverse-charged calls.

Example

The following example configures PVC to SVC switching between two serial interfaces:

```
x25 routing
interface serial0
 encapsulation x25
 x25 address 201700
 x25 ltc 128
 x25 idle 2
interface serial2
 encapsulation x25 dce
 x25 address 101702

x25 route ^20 interface serial0
x25 route ^10 interface serial2
interface serial0

 x25 pvc 5 svc 101601 packetsize 128 128 windowsize 2 2 no-incoming
 x25 pvc 6 svc 101602 packetsize 128 128 windowsize 2 2 no-outgoing idle 0
 x25 pvc 7 svc 101603 packetsize 128 128 windowsize 2 2
```

Any call with a destination address beginning with 20 will be routed to serial interface 0. Any call with a destination address beginning with 10 will be routed to serial interface 2. (Note that incoming calls will not be routed back to the same interface from which they arrived.)

Traffic received on PVC 5 on serial interface 0 will cause a call to be placed from address 201700 to the X.121 address 101601. The routing table will then forward the call to serial interface 2. If no data is sent or received on the circuit for two minutes, the call will be cleared, as defined by the **x25 idle** command. All incoming calls from 101601 to 201700 will be refused, as defined by the *no-incoming* attribute.

The second **x25 pvc** command configures the circuit to allow incoming calls from 101602 to 201700 to be connected to PVC 6 on serial interface 1. Because idle is set to 0, the call will remain connected until cleared by the remote host or an X.25 restart. Because outgoing calls are not permitted for this connection, if traffic is received on PVC 6 on serial interface 0 before the call is established, the traffic will be discarded and the PVC will be reset.

The last **x25 pvc** command configures the circuit to accept an incoming call from 101603 to 201700 and connects the call to PVC 7 on serial interface 0. If no data is sent or received on the circuit for two minutes, the call will be cleared. If traffic is received on PVC 7 on serial interface 0 before the call is established, a call will be placed to 101503 to 201700.

x25 pvc (XOT)

To connect two permanent virtual circuits (PVCs) across a TCP/IP LAN, use the XOT service form of the **x25 pvc** interface configuration command.

> **x25 pvc** *number1* xot *address* **interface serial** *string* pvc *number2* [*option*]

Syntax	Description
number1	PVC number of the connecting device.
xot	Indicates two PVCs will be connected across a TCP/IP LAN using XOT.
address	IP address of the device to which you are connecting.
interface serial	Indicates that the interface is serial.
string	Serial interface specification that accepts either a number or a string in model 7000 format (*number/number*) to denote the serial interface.
pvc	Indicates a PVC.
number2	Remote PVC number on the target interface.
option	(Optional.) Adds certain features for the connection; can be either option listed in Table 12–22.

Default

No PVCs are connected across a TCP/IP LAN. The PVC window and packet sizes default to the interface default values.

Command Mode

Interface configuration

Usage Guidelines

This command first appeared in Cisco IOS Release 10.3.

Use the PVC tunnel commands to tell the Cisco IOS software what the far end of the PVC is connected to. The incoming and outgoing packet sizes and window sizes must match the remote PVC outgoing and incoming sizes.

Each X.25-over-TCP (XOT) connection relies on a TCP session to carry traffic. To ensure that these TCP sessions remain connected in the absence of XOT traffic, use the **service tcp-keepalives-in** and **service tcp-keepalives-out** global configuration commands. If TCP keepalives are not enabled, XOT permanent virtual circuits might encounter problems if one end of the connection is reloaded. When the reloaded host attempts to establish a new connection, the other host refuses the new connection because it has not been informed that the old session is no longer active. Recovery from this state requires the other host to be informed that its TCP session is no longer viable so that it attempts to reconnect the PVC.

Also, TCP keepalives inform a router when an XOT SVC session is not active, thus freeing the router's resources.

Table 12–22 lists the PVC tunnel options supported by X.25.

Table 12–22   *X.25 PVC Tunnel Options*

Option	Description
packetsize *in-size out-size*	Maximum input packet size (*in-size*) and output packet size (*out-size*) for the PVC. Both sizes must be one of the following values: 16, 32, 64, 128, 256, 512, 1024, 2048, or 4096.
windowsize *in-size out-size*	Packet count for input window (*in-size*) and output window (*out-size*) for the PVC. Both values should be the same, must be in the range 1 to 127, and must not be greater than or equal to the value set for the **x25 modulo** command.

Examples

The following example enters the parameters for one side of a connection destined for a platform other than the Cisco 7000 series with RSP7000:

```
service tcp-keepalives-in
service tcp-keepalives-out
interface serial 0
 x25 pvc 1 xot 172.20.1.2 interface serial 1 pvc 2
```

The following example enters the parameters for one side of a connection destined for the Cisco 7000 series with RSP7000:

```
service tcp-keepalives-in
service tcp-keepalives-out
```

```
interface serial 0
  x25 pvc 1 xot 172.20.1.2 interface serial 1/1 pvc 2
```

Related Commands

service tcp-keepalives-in
service tcp-keepalives-out

X25 REMOTE-RED

To set up the table that lists the Blacker Front End nodes (host or gateways) to which the router will send packets, use the **x25 remote-red** interface configuration command.

    x25 remote-red *host-ip-address* **remote-black** *blacker-ip-address*

Syntax	Description
host-ip-address	IP address of the host or router that the packets are being sent to.
remote-black	Delimits the addresses for the table being built.
blacker-ip-address	IP address of the remote BFE device in front of the host to which the packet is being sent.

Default

No table is set up.

Command Mode

Interface configuration

Usage Guidelines

This command first appeared in Cisco IOS Release 10.0.

The table that results from this command provides the address translation information that the router sends to the BFE when it is in emergency mode.

Example

The following example sets up a short table of BFE nodes for serial interface 0:

```
interface serial 0
  x25 remote-red 172.20.9.3 remote-black 172.20.9.13
  x25 remote-red 192.108.15.1 remote-black 192.108.15.26
```

Related Commands

show x25 remote-red
x25 bfe-decision

X25 ROUTE

To create an entry in the X.25 routing table (to be consulted for forwarding incoming calls and for placing outgoing PAD or protocol translation calls), use an appropriate form of the **x25 route** global configuration command. To remove an entry from the table, use the **no** form of the command.

> **x25 route** [*#position*] {[*selection*] [*modification*]} *disposition* [*xot-keepalive*]
> **no x25 route** [*#position*] {[*selection*] [*modification*]} *disposition*

Syntax	Description
#position	(Optional) A pound sign (#) followed by a number designates the position in the routing table at which to insert the new entry. If no *position* value is given, the entry is appended to the end of the routing table.
selection	(Optional) The *selection* options identify when the subsequent *modification* and *disposition* elements apply to an X.25 call; any or all variables may be specified for a route.
	Although each individual selection criterion is optional, at least one *selection* or *modification* element must be specified in the **x25 route** command.
modification	(Optional) Modifies the source or destination addresses of the selected calls. The standard regular expression substitution rules are used, where a match pattern and rewrite string direct the construction of a new string.
	Although each individual modification is optional, at least one *selection* or *modification* element must be specified in the **x25 route** command.
disposition	Specifies the disposition of a call matching the specified selection pattern.
xot-keepalive	(Optional) Specifies an XOT keepalive period and number of XOT keepalive retries. XOT relies on TCP to detect when the underlying connection is dead. TCP detects a dead connection when transmitted data goes unacknowledged for a given number of attempts over a period of time.

Default

No entry is created in the X.25 routing table.

Command Mode

Global configuration

Usage Guidelines

The enhanced **x25 route** command replaces the **x25 map cmns** command. The **x25 route alias** form of this command (supported in earlier releases) has been replaced by the **x25 alias** command.

The *selection* criteria **source** and **dest-ext** first appeared in Cisco IOS Release 11.2 F. The interface *disposition* to a CMNS destination first appeared in Cisco IOS Release 11.2 F; in prior releases,

CMNS routing information was implied by maps defining an NSAP prefix for a CMNS host's MAC address. The **clear** interface *disposition* first appeared in Cisco IOS Release 11.2 F; in prior releases, the disposition was implicit in a route to the Null 0 interface. The *modification* elements are long-standing, but they are newly applicable to all dispositions in Cisco IOS Release 11.2 F.

NOTES

The entire command must be entered on one line.

Selection Options

Selection options specify match criteria. When a call matches all selection criteria in an X.25 route, then the specified modification and disposition are used for the call.

As many as four selection options can be used to determine the route:

- Called X.121 network interface address (destination host address)
- Calling X.121 network interface address (source host address)
- Called address extension (destination NSAP address)
- X.25 packet's call user data field

Table 12–23 lists the *selection* options for the **x25 route** command. At least one *selection* or *modification* element must be specified in the **x25 route** command.

Table 12–23 *X25 Route Command Selection Options*

Selection Options	Description
destination-pattern	(Optional) Destination address pattern, which is a regular expression that can represent either one X.121 address (such as ^1111000$) or any address in a group of X.121 addresses (such as ^1111.*).
source *source-pattern*	(Optional) Source address pattern, which is a regular expression that can represent either one X.121 source address (such as ^2222000$) or any address in a group of X.121 addresses (such as ^2222.*).
dest-ext *nsap-destination-pattern*	(Optional) NSAP destination address pattern, which is a regular expression that can represent either an NSAP destination address (such as ^11.1111.0000$) or an NSAP prefix (such as ^11.1111.*). Note: A period (.) in the pattern is interpreted as a character wildcard, which will not interfere with a match to the actual period in the NSAP; if desired, an explicit character match may be used (such as ^11\.1111\..*).

Table 12–23 *X25 Route Command Selection Options, Continued*

Selection Options	Description
cud *user-data-pattern*	(Optional) Call user data pattern, which is specified as a regular expression of printable ASCII text. The CUD field may be present in a call packet. The first few bytes (commonly 4 bytes long) identify a protocol; the specified pattern is applied to any user data after the protocol identification.

NOTES

The X.121 and NSAP addresses are specified as regular expressions. A common error is to specify the address digits without anchoring them to the beginning and end of the address. For example, the regular expression 1111 will match an X.121 address that has four successive "1" digits somewhere in the address; to specify the single X.121 address, the form ^1111$ must be used.

Regular expressions are used to allow pattern-matching operations on the addresses and user data. A common operation is to do prefix matching on the X.121 DNIC field and route accordingly. The caret (^) is a special regular expression character that anchors the match at the beginning of the pattern. For example, the pattern ^3306 will match all X.121 addresses with a DNIC of 3306.

Modification Options

Addresses typically need to be modified when traffic from a private network that uses arbitrary X.121 addresses must transit a public data network, which must use its own X.121 addresses. The easiest way to meet this requirement is to specify in the **x25 route** command a way to modify the private address into a network X.121 address or to modify a network X.121 address into a private address. The addresses are modified so that no change to the private addressing scheme is required.

The *modification* options use the standard UNIX regular expression substitution operations to change an X.25 field. A pattern match is applied to an address field, which is rewritten as directed by a rewrite pattern.

Table 12–24 lists the *modification* options for the **x25 route** command. At least one *selection* or *modification* element must be specified in the **x25 route** command.

Table 12–24 *X25 Route Command Modification Options*

Modification Option	Description
substitute-source *rewrite-source*	(Optional) Calling X.121 address rewrite pattern. The source address, *source-pattern*, and this *rewrite-source* pattern are used to form a new source address. If no *source-pattern* is specified, any *destination-pattern* match pattern is used. If neither match pattern is specified, a default match pattern of .* is used. See Table 12–25 and Table 12–26 for summaries of pattern and character matching, respectively. See Table 12–27 for a summary of pattern rewrite elements.
substitute-dest *rewrite-dest*	(Optional) Called X.121 address rewrite pattern. The destination address, *destination-pattern*, and this *rewrite-dest* pattern are used to form a new destination address. If no *destination-pattern* is specified, a default match pattern of .* is used. See Table 12–25 and Table 12–26 for summaries of pattern and character matching, respectively. See Table 12–27 for a summary of pattern rewrite elements.

NOTES

As of Cisco IOS Release 11.3, the **substitute-source** and **substitute-dest** options also apply to PAD calls.

Source address. A modification of the source address is directed by the rewrite string using one of three possible match patterns. If the **source** *source-pattern* selection option is defined, it is used with the *source-rewrite* string to construct the new source address; otherwise, a *destination-pattern* regular expression is used (for backwards compatibility) or a wildcard regular expression (.*) is used. In the *rewrite-source* argument, the backslash character (\) indicates that the digit immediately following the argument selects a portion of the matched address to be inserted into the new called address.

Destination address. A modification of the destination address is directed by the rewrite string using one of two possible match patterns. If the *destination-pattern* selection option is defined, it is used with the *destination-rewrite* string to construct the new destination address; otherwise, a wildcard regular expression (.*) is used. In the *rewrite-dest* argument, the backslash character (\) indicates that the digit immediately following the argument selects a portion of the original called address to be inserted into the new called address.

Refer to Table 12–25, Table 12–26, and Table 12–27 for summaries of pattern matching, character matching, and pattern rewrite elements. Note that up to nine pairs of parentheses can be used to identify patterns to be included in the modified string.

Table 12–25   *Pattern Matching for X.25 Route Selection and Modification Options*

Pattern	Description
*	Matches 0 or more occurrences of the preceding character.
+	Matches 1 or more occurrences of the preceding character.
?	Matches 0 or 1 occurrences of the preceding character.*

* Precede the question mark with Ctrl-V to prevent the question mark from being interpreted as a help command.

Table 12–26   *Character Matching for X.25 Route Selection and Modification Options*

Character	Description
^	Matches the beginning of the input string.
$	Matches the end of the input string.
\char	Matches the single character *char* specified.
.	Matches any single character.

Table 12–27   *Pattern Replacements for X.25 Route Selection and Modification Options*

Pattern	Description
\0	The pattern is replaced by the entire original address.
\1...9	The pattern is replaced by strings that match the first through ninth parenthetical part of the X.121 address.

Disposition Option

The **xot-source** disposition option can improve the resilience of the TCP connection if, for instance, a loopback interface is specified. By default, a TCP connection's source IP address is that of the interface used to initiate the connection; a TCP connection will fail if either the source or destination IP address is no longer valid. Because a loopback interface never goes down, its IP address is always valid. Any TCP connections originated using a loopback interface can be maintained as long as a path exists to the destination IP address, which may also be the IP address of a loopback interface.

Table 12–28 lists the *disposition* choices for the **x25 route** command. You are required to select one of these choices.

Table 12–28 *X25 Route Command Dispositions*

Disposition	Description
interface *serial-interface*	Route the selected call to the specified X.25 serial interface.
interface *cmns-interface* mac *mac-address*	Route the selected call out the specified broadcast interface via CMNS to the LAN destination station. The broadcast interface type can be Ethernet, Token Ring, or FDDI. The interface numbering scheme depends on the router interface hardware.
xot *ip-address* [*ip2-address* [...[*ip6-address*]]] [xot-source *interface*]	Route the selected call to the XOT host at the specified IP address. Subsequent IP addresses are tried, in sequence, only if XOT is unable to establish a TCP connection with a prior address.
clear	Terminate the call.

XOT Keepalive Options

TCP maintains each connection using a keepalive mechanism that starts with a default time period and number of retry attempts. If a received XOT connection is dispatched using a route with explicit keepalive parameters, those values will be used for the TCP connection. If an XOT connection is sent using a route with explicit keepalive parameters, those values will be used for the TCP connection.

Table 12–29 lists and describes the *xot-keepalive* options for the **x25 route** command.

Table 12–29 *X25 Route Command XOT Keepalive Options*

XOT-Keepalive Option	Description
xot-keepalive-period *seconds*	Number of seconds between keepalives for XOT connections. The default is 60 seconds.
xot-keepalive-tries *count*	Number of times TCP keepalives should be sent before dropping the connection. The default value is 4 times.

X.25 Routing Action When a Match Is Found

If a matching route is found, the incoming call is forwarded to the next hop depending on the routing entry. If no match is found, the call is cleared. If the route specifies a serial interface running X.25 or a broadcast interface running CMNS, the router attempts to forward the call to that host. If the interface is not operational, the subsequent routes are checked for forwarding to an operational interface. If the interface is operational but out of available virtual circuits, the call is cleared. Otherwise, the expected Clear Request or Call Accepted message is forwarded back toward the originator. A call cannot be forwarded out the interface on which it arrived.

If the matching route specifies an XOT disposition, a TCP connection is established to port 1998 at the specified IP address, which must be an XOT host. The Call Request packet is forwarded to the remote host, which applies its own criteria to handle the call. If, upon receiving an XOT call, a routing table entry is not present, or the destination is unavailable, a Clear Request is sent back and the TCP connection is closed. Otherwise, the call is handled and the expected Clear Request or Call Accepted packet is returned. Incoming calls received via XOT connections that match a routing entry specifying an XOT destination are cleared. This restriction prevents Cisco routers from establishing an XOT connection to another router that would establish yet another XOT connection.

Examples

The following example uses regular expression pattern matching characters to match just the initial portion of the complete X.25 address. Any call with a destination address beginning with 3107 that is received on an interface other than serial 0 is forwarded to serial 0.

```
x25 route ^3107 interface serial 0
```

The following example prevents X.25 routing for calls that do not specify a source address:

```
x25 route source ^$ clear
```

The following example configures alternate XOT hosts for the routing entry. If the first address listed is not available, subsequent addresses are tried until a connection is made. If no connection can be formed, the call is cleared.

```
x25 route ^3106$ xot 172.20.2.5 172.20.7.10 172.10.7.9
```

The following example clears calls that contain a 3 in the source address. The disposition keyword **clear** is new:

```
x25 route source 3 clear
```

The following example clears calls that contain two consecutive 3s in the source address:

```
x25 route source 33 clear
```

The following example clears a call to the destination address, 9999:

```
x25 route ^9999$ clear
```

The following example specifies a route for specific source and destination addresses. (The ability to combine source and destination patterns is a new feature.)

```
x25 route ^9999$ source ^333$ interface serial 0
```

The following example routes the call to the XOT host at the specified IP address. The disposition keyword **xot** is new. In prior releases the keyword **ip** was used.

```
x25 route ^3333$ xot 172.21.53.61
```

The following example routes calls containing the destination extension address preamble 11.1234:

```
x25 route dest-ext ^11.1234.* interface serial 0
```

The following example rewrites the destination address as 9999. There must be a minimum of four 8s in the address. (More than four digits will be changed to four digits; for example, 8888888 will be changed to 9999.)

```
x25 route 8888 substitute-dest 9999 interface serial 0
```

The following example substitutes only part of the destination address. "^88" specifies that the original destination string must begin with 88. "(.*)" indicates that the string can end with any number, 0–9, and can be more than one digit. "99\1" changes the destination address to 99 plus whatever matches ".*" in the original destination address. For example, 8881 will be changed to 9981.

```
x25 route ^88(.*) substitute-dest 99\1 interface serial 0
```

The following example substitutes only part of the destination address and also removes a specified number of digits from the address. "^88" specifies the original destination string must begin with 88. "(..)" matches any two digits. "(.*)" specifies the string can end with any number, 0–9, and can occur zero or more times. Thus any address that starts with 88 and has four or more digits will be rewritten to start with 99 and omit the third and fourth digits. For example, 881234 will be changed to 9934.

```
x25 route ^88(..)(.*) substitute-dest 99\2 interface serial 0
```

The following example looks for a specified destination address and changes the source address. "9999" is the destination address. The original source address changes to "2222" because the call is made to the destination 9999.

```
x25 route ^9999$ substitute-source 2222 interface serial 0
```

The following example rewrites the source address based upon the source address. "9999" matches any destination address with four consecutive 9s. "^...(.*)" matches any source address with at least three digits; the command removes the first three digits and rewrites any digits after the first three as the new source address. For example, a call to 9999 from the source address 77721 will be forwarded using the calling address 21 and the called address 9999.

```
x25 route 9999 source ^...(.*) substitute-source \1 interface serial 0
```

The following example adds a digit to the patterns of the source and destination addresses. "09990" is the destination address pattern. The source can be any address. "9\0" specifies that a leading 9 be added to the destination address pattern. "3\0" specifies that a leading 3 be added to the source address pattern. For example, a call using source 03330 and destination 09990 will be changed to 303330 and 909990, respectively.

```
x25 route 09990 source .* substitute-dest 9\0 substitute-source 3\0 interface serial 0
```

Related Commands

show x25 route

X25 ROUTING

To enable X.25 switching or tunneling, use the **x25 routing** global configuration command. To disable the forwarding of X.25 calls, used the **no** form of this command.

x25 routing [use-tcp-if-defs]
no x25 routing

Syntax	Description
use-tcp-if-defs	(Optional) May be used to modify the acceptance of calls received over TCP.

Default

Disabled

Command Mode

Global configuration

Usage Guidelines

This command first appeared prior to Cisco IOS Release 10.0.

The **x25 routing** command enables X.25 switching between the X.25 services (X.25, CMNS, and XOT). X.25 calls will not be forwarded until this command is issued.

The **use-tcp-if-defs** keyword may be needed for receiving XOT calls from routers using older software versions. Normally, calls received over a TCP connection (remote routing reception) will have the flow control parameters (window sizes and maximum packet sizes) indicated because proper operation of routed X.25 requires that these values match at both ends of the connection.

Some previous versions of Cisco's software, however, do not ensure that these values are present in all calls. In this case, the Cisco IOS software normally forces universally acceptable flow control values (window sizes of 2 and maximum packet sizes of 128) on the connection. Because some equipment disallows modification of the flow control values in the call confirm, the **use-tcp-if-defs** keyword causes the router to use the default flow control values of the outgoing interface and indicates the resulting values in the call confirm. This modified behavior may allow easier migration to newer versions of the Cisco IOS software.

Example

The following example enables X.25 switching:
```
x25 routing
```

X25 ROA

To specify a sequence of packet network carriers, use the **x25 roa** global configuration command. To remove the specified name, use the **no** form of this command.

 x25 roa *name number*
 no x25 roa *name*

Syntax	Description
name	Recognized Operating Agency (ROA, formerly called a Recognized Private Operating Agency, or RPOA), which must be unique with respect to all other ROA names. It is used in the **x25 facility** and **x25 map** interface configuration commands.
number	A sequence of 1 or more numbers used to describe an ROA; up to 10 numbers are accepted.

Default

No packet network carriers are specified.

Command Mode

Global configuration

Usage Guidelines

This command first appeared prior to Cisco IOS Release 10.0.

This command specifies a list of transit ROAs to use, referenced by name.

Example

The following example sets an ROA name and then sends the list via the X.25 user facilities:

```
x25 roa green_list 23 35 36
interface serial 0
 x25 facility roa green_list
 x25 map ip 172.20.170.26 10 roa green_list
```

Related Commands

x25 facility
x25 map

X25 SUPPRESS-CALLED-ADDRESS

To omit the destination address in outgoing calls, use the **x25 suppress-called-address** interface configuration command. To reset this command to the default state, use the **no** form of this command.

    x25 suppress-called-address
    no x25 suppress-called-address

Syntax Description

This command has no arguments or keywords.

Default

The called address is sent.

Command Mode

Interface configuration

Usage Guidelines

This command first appeared prior to Cisco IOS Release 10.0.

This command omits the called (destination) X.121 address in Call Request packets and is required for networks that expect only subaddresses in the Called Address field.

As of Cisco IOS Release 11.3, this command also applies to PAD calls.

Example

The following example suppresses or omits the called address in Call Request packets:

```
interface serial 0
 x25 suppress-called-address
```

X25 SUPPRESS-CALLING-ADDRESS

To omit the source address in outgoing calls, use the **x25 suppress-calling-address** interface configuration command. To reset this command to the default state, use the **no** form of this command.

> **x25 suppress-calling-address**
> **no x25 suppress-calling-address**

Syntax Description

This command has no arguments or keywords.

Default

The calling address is sent.

Command Mode

Interface configuration

Usage Guidelines

This command first appeared prior to Cisco IOS Release 10.0.

This command omits the calling (source) X.121 address in Call Request packets and is required for networks that expect only subaddresses in the Calling Address field.

As of Cisco IOS Release 11.3, this command also applies to PAD calls.

Example

The following example suppresses or omits the calling address in Call Request packets:

```
interface serial 0
 x25 suppress-calling-address
```

X25 T10

Use the **x25 t10** interface configuration command to set the value of the Restart Indication retransmission timer (T10) on DCE devices.

> **x25 t10** *seconds*

Syntax	Description
seconds	Time in seconds.

Default

60 seconds

Command Mode

Interface configuration

Usage Guidelines

This command first appeared prior to Cisco IOS Release 10.0.

Example

The following example sets the T10 timer to 30 seconds:
```
interface serial 0
  x25 t10 30
```

X25 T11

To set the value of the Incoming Call timer (T11) on DCE devices, use the **x25 t11** interface configuration command.

    x25 t11 *seconds*

Syntax	Description
seconds	Time in seconds.

Default

180 seconds

Command Mode

Interface configuration

Usage Guidelines

This command first appeared prior to Cisco IOS Release 10.0.

Example

The following example sets the T11 timer to 90 seconds:
```
interface serial 0
  x25 t11 90
```

X25 T12

To set the value of the Reset Indication retransmission timer (T12) on DCE devices, use the **x25 t12** interface configuration command.

    x25 t12 *seconds*

Syntax	Description
seconds	Time in seconds.

Default

60 seconds

Command Mode

Interface configuration

Usage Guidelines

This command first appeared prior to Cisco IOS Release 10.0.

Example

The following example sets the T12 timer to 30 seconds:
```
interface serial 0
  x25 t12 30
```

x25 T13

To set the value of the Clear Indication retransmission timer (T13) on DCE devices, use the **x25 t13** interface configuration command.

   x25 t13 *seconds*

Syntax	Description
seconds	Time in seconds.

Default

60 seconds

Command Mode

Interface configuration

Usage Guidelines

This command first appeared prior to Cisco IOS Release 10.0.

Example

The following example sets the T13 timer to 30 seconds:
```
interface serial 0
  x25 t13 30
```

x25 t20

To set the value of the Restart Request retransmission timer (T20) on DTE devices, use the **x25 t20** interface configuration command.

    x25 t20 *seconds*

Syntax	Description
seconds	Time in seconds.

Default

180 seconds

Command Mode

Interface configuration

Usage Guidelines

This command first appeared prior to Cisco IOS Release 10.0.

Example

The following example sets the T20 timer to 90 seconds:

```
interface serial 0
  x25 t20 90
```

x25 t21

To set the value of the Call Request timer (T21) on DTE devices, use the **x25 t21** interface configuration command.

    x25 t21 *seconds*

Syntax	Description
seconds	Time in seconds.

Default

200 seconds

Command Mode

Interface configuration

Usage Guidelines

This command first appeared prior to Cisco IOS Release 10.0.

Command Reference

Example

The following example sets the T21 timer to 100 seconds:
```
interface serial 0
  x25 t21 100
```

X25 T22

To set the value of the Reset Request retransmission timer (T22) on DTE devices, use the **x25 t22** interface configuration command.

    x25 t22 *seconds*

Syntax	Description
seconds	Time in seconds.

Default

180 seconds

Command Mode

Interface configuration

Usage Guidelines

This command first appeared prior to Cisco IOS Release 10.0.

Example

The following example sets the T22 timer to 90 seconds:
```
interface serial 0
  x25 t22 90
```

X25 T23

To set the value of the Clear Request retransmission timer (T23) on DTE devices, use the **x25 t23** interface configuration command.

    x25 t23 *seconds*

Syntax	Description
seconds	Time in seconds.

Default

180 seconds

Command Mode

Interface configuration

Usage Guidelines

This command first appeared prior to Cisco IOS Release 10.0.

Example

The following example sets the T23 timer to 90 seconds:

```
interface serial 0
  x25 t23 90
```

X25 THRESHOLD

To set the data packet acknowledgment threshold, use the **x25 threshold** interface configuration command.

    x25 threshold *delay-count*

Syntax	Description
delay-count	Value between zero and the input window size. A value of 1 sends one Receiver Ready acknowledgment per packet.

Default

0 (which disables the acknowledgment threshold)

Command Mode

Interface configuration

Usage Guidelines

This command first appeared in Cisco IOS Release 11.2F; it replaces the long-standing form **x25 th.**

This command instructs the router to send acknowledgment packets when it is not busy sending other packets, even if the number of input packets has not reached the input window size count.

The router sends an acknowledgment packet when the number of input packets reaches the count you specify, providing that there are no other packets to send. For example, if you specify a count of 1, the router will send an acknowledgment per input packet if unable to "piggyback" the acknowledgment of an outgoing data packet. This command improves line responsiveness at the expense of bandwidth.

This command only applies to encapsulated traffic over X.25 (datagram transport), not to routed traffic.

Example

The following example sends an explicit Receiver Ready acknowledgment when it has received 5 data packets that it has not acknowledged:

```
interface serial 1
  x25 threshold 5
```

Related Commands

x25 win
x25 wout

X25 USE-SOURCE-ADDRESS

To override the X.121 addresses of outgoing calls forwarded over a specific interface, use the **x25 use-source-address** interface configuration command. Use the **no** form of this command to prevent updating the source addresses of outgoing calls.

> **x25 use-source-address**
> **no x25 use-source-address**

Syntax Description

This command has no arguments or keywords.

Default

Disabled

Command Mode

Interface configuration

Usage Guidelines

This command first appeared prior to Cisco IOS Release 10.0.

Some X.25 calls, when forwarded by the X.25 switching support, need the calling (source) X.121 address updated to that of the outgoing interface. This update is necessary when you are forwarding calls from private data networks to public data networks (PDNs).

Example

The following example shows how to prevent updating the source addresses of outgoing X.25 calls on serial interface 0 once calls have been forwarded:

```
interface serial 0
  no x25 use-source-address
```

X25 WIN

To change the default incoming window size to match that of the network, use the **x25 win** interface configuration command.

    x25 win *packets*

Syntax	Description
packets	Packet count that can range from 1 to one less than the window modulus.

Default

2 packets

Command Mode

Interface configuration

Usage Guidelines

This command first appeared prior to Cisco IOS Release 10.0.

This command determines the default number of packets that a virtual circuit can receive before sending an X.25 acknowledgment. To maintain high bandwidth utilization, assign this limit the largest number that the network allows.

___

NOTES

Set **x25 win** and **x25 wout** to the same value unless your network supports asymmetric input and output window sizes.

___

Example

The following example specifies that 5 packets may be received before an X.25 acknowledgment is sent:

```
interface serial 1
  x25 win 5
```

Related Commands

x25 modulo
x25 threshold
x25 wout

X25 WOUT

To change the default outgoing window size to match that of the network, use the **x25 wout** interface configuration command.

    x25 wout *packets*

Syntax	Description
packets	Packet count that can range from 1 to one less than the window modulus.

Default

2 packets

Command Mode

Interface configuration

Usage Guidelines

This command first appeared prior to Cisco IOS Release 10.0.

This command determines the default number of packets that a virtual circuit can send before waiting for an X.25 acknowledgment. To maintain high bandwidth utilization, assign this limit the largest number that the network allows.

NOTES

Set **x25 win** and **x25 wout** to the same value unless your network supports asymmetric input and output window sizes.

Example

The following example specifies a default limit of 5 for the number of outstanding unacknowledged packets for virtual circuits:

```
interface serial 1
  x25 wout 5
```

Related Commands

x25 modulo
x25 threshold
x25 win

X29 ACCESS-LIST

To limit access to the access server from certain X.25 hosts, use the **x29 access-list** global configuration command. To delete an entire access list, use the **no** form of this command.

>   **x29 access-list** *access-list-number* {deny | permit} *x121-address*
>   **no x29 access-list** *access-list-number*

Syntax	Description
access-list-number	Number of the access list. It can be any value between 1 and 199.
deny	Denies access and clears call requests immediately.
permit	Permits access to the protocol translator.
x121-address	If applied as an inbound access class, specifies the X.121 address that can or cannot have access (with or without regular expression pattern-matching characters). The X.121 address is the source address of the incoming packet.
	If applied as an outbound access class, then the address specifies a destination to which connections are allowed.

Default

No access lists are defined.

Command Mode

Global configuration

Usage Guidelines

This command first appeared in Cisco IOS Release 10.0.

An access list can contain any number of access list items. The list items are processed in the order in which you entered them, with the first match causing the permit or deny condition. If an X.121 address does not match any of the regular expressions in the access list, access is denied.

Access lists take advantage of the message field defined by Recommendation X.29, which describes procedures for exchanging data between two PADs, or between a PAD and a DTE device.

The UNIX-style regular expression characters allow for pattern matching of characters and character strings in the address. Various pattern-matching constructions are available that allow many addresses to be matched by a single regular expressions.

The access lists must be applied to a vty with the **access-class** command.

Example

The following example permits connections to hosts with addresses beginning with the string 31370:

```
x29 access-list 2 permit ^31370
```

X29 PROFILE

To create a PAD profile script for use by the **translate** command, use the **x29 profile** global configuration command.

 x29 profile {**default** | *name*} *parameter:value* [*parameter:value*]

Syntax	Description
default	Specifies default profile script.
name	Name of the PAD profile script.
parameter:value	X.3 PAD parameter number and value separated by a colon. You can specify multiple parameter-value pairs.

Default

The default PAD profile script is used. The default for inbound connections is:

```
2:0, 4:1, 15:0, 7:21
```

Command Mode

Global configuration

Usage Guidelines

This command first appeared in Cisco IOS Release 10.0.

When an X.25 connection is established, the access server acts as if an X.29 Set Parameter packet had been sent containing the parameters and values set by the **x29 profile** command. It then sets the access server accordingly.

For incoming PAD connections, the Protocol Translator uses a default PAD profile to set the remote X.3 PAD parameters unless a profile script is defined with the **translate** command.

Examples

The following profile script turns local edit mode on when the connection is made and establishes local echo and line termination upon receipt of a Return packet. The name *linemode* is used with the **translate** command to effect use of this script.

```
x29 profile linemode 2:1 3:2 15:1
```

To override the default PAD profile, create a PAD profile script named "default" by using the following command:

```
x29 profile default 2:1 4:1, 15:0, 4:0
```

Related Commands

translate

APPENDIX A

Understanding X.25 Facility Handling

This appendix provides reference material describing how X.25 facilities are handled by the Cisco IOS software.

FACILITY HANDLING IN ENCAPSULATED X.25 VIRTUAL CIRCUITS

A router either originates or accepts encapsulation switched virtual circuits (SVCs) to transport LAN traffic through an X.25 network.

When the router originates a call for LAN traffic encapsulation, the facilities in the call are controlled by the facilities configured for the interface and the map statement that specifies the LAN and X.25 encapsulation. Because a router can be attached to a public data network (PDN), the interface and map configurations allow a number of facilities to be specified in outgoing calls. These facilities are specified in all originated calls relating to the given interface and map with one exception—the incoming and outgoing maximum packet sizes proposed are lowered if the lower layer (LAPB) cannot support the specified data packet size.

When the router accepts an encapsulation call, many facilities are simply ignored. The maximum packet sizes are lowered if the lower layer (LAPB) cannot support the sizes proposed. A reverse-charge call is cleared if neither the interface nor the map allows it. A call that specifies a network user identification (NUID) is cleared if the user authentication fails.

FACILITY HANDLING IN ROUTED X.25 VIRTUAL CIRCUITS

Routed X.25 traffic might have facilities added, deleted, or modified.

Standard (1984 X.25) Facilities

Table A–1 describes how standard (1984 X.25) facilities are treated when routing a SVC. To configure these facilities, refer to the "Configuring X.25 User Facilities" section in Chapter 11, "Configuring X.25 and LAPB."

523

Table A–1 *Treatment of Standard X.25 Facilities*

Facility	Treatment
Flow Control Negotiation (negotiation of window size and maximum packet size) • Requested flow control values do not match the outgoing interface's defaults. • Requested values match the outgoing interface's defaults. • Requested maximum packet size exceeds the capability of either interface. • Call is routed from a modulo 128 interface to a modulo 8 interface. • Call is remotely routed over a TCP connection. • Call is received from an X.25 over a TCP connection without one or more flow control parameter values. • Accepted flow control parameter values are different, for any reason, from the values proposed for the incoming call.	The Cisco IOS software adds, removes, or changes flow control parameter values to match the values on both interfaces, as described in the following cases: • Inserts flow control parameters into the outgoing switched call. • Strips parameter values from the outgoing switched call. • Lowers the packet size to the largest value that can be supported by the two interfaces. • Lowers the larger requested window size to 7. • Ensures that both proposed maximum packet sizes and proposed window sizes for a call are present. • By default, forces the call to use the maximum packet sizes (128/128) and window sizes (2/2). If the **x25 routing use-tcp-if-defs** command and keyword are specified, the router supplies the call with the default values of the outgoing serial interface. In either case, the Call Confirm packet sent back over the X.25-over-TCP (XOT) connection indicates the final flow control values negotiated for the connection. • Sends an outgoing Call Accepted packet that indicates the accepted flow control values.
Throughput Negotiation	Forwards the incoming Throughput facility.
Closed User Group Selection	Forwards a basic format Closed User Group (CUG) selection facility; any other format of CUG selection (extended format, CUG with outgoing access or Bilateral CUG) will be stripped.
Reverse Charging	Forwards an incoming Reverse Charging facility.
Fast Select	Forwards an incoming Fast Select facility.

Table A–1 *Treatment of Standard X.25 Facilities, Continued*

Facility	Treatment
Network User Identification	Forwards an incoming NUID facility on a Call packet; an NUID facility on a Call Accepted packet is stripped.
Charging Information	Strips any Charging Information or Request.
RPOA Selection	Strips any RPOA Selection.
Called Line Address Modified Notification	Forwards a Called Line Address Modified Notification.
Call Redirection Notification	Strips a Call Redirection Notification.
Transit Delay Selection	Forwards an incoming Transit Delay facility.

The implementation of X.25 prior to Release 9.1(4.1) software did not insert flow control parameter values into Call packets sent over X.25-over-TCP (XOT) connections. When such an XOT call is received by Release 9.1(4.1) or later, the call is forced to use the standard flow control values. This use may cause migration problems when the router is connecting X.25 equipment that is not capable of negotiating flow control parameters; you can use the optional **use-tcp-if-defs** keyword of the **x25 routing** command if you encounter this problem.

ITU-T-Specified Marker Facilities

Table A–2 describes how CCITT/ITU-T-specified marker facilities are treated when routing an SVC.

Table A–2 *Default Treatment of ITU-T-Specified Marker Facilities*

Facility	Treatment
Calling Address Extension	Forwards an incoming Calling Address Extension facility.
Called Address Extension	Forwards an incoming Called Address Extension facility.
Quality of Service Negotiation	Strips any of the Quality of Service facilities.
Expedited Data Negotiation	Strips an Expedited Data Negotiation facility.

The router requires the Calling Address Extension facility to route to a CMNS host.

The encoding of any CCITT/ITU-T facilities is preceded by a marker, as displayed in the output of the **debug x25** command.

Local Marker Facilities Specified for DDN or BFE X.25

Table A–3 describes how local marker facilities are treated when routing an SVC.

Table A–3   *Default Treatment of Local Marker Facilities Specified for DDN or BFE X.25*

Facility	Treatment
DDN Service Type	Strips an incoming DDN Service Type facility from a call, but inserts DDN Service Type if a forwarded Call Accepted packet specifies a DDN precedence facility.
DDN Precedence	Forwards an incoming DDN Precedence facility. However, both the input and output interfaces need to be configured for DDN X.25 encapsulation. To configure treatment of this facility, see the "Defining IP Precedence Handling" section in Chapter 11.
BFE Emergency Mode Addressing	Strips an incoming BFE Emergency Mode Addressing facility. To configure treatment of this facility, see the "Configuring Blacker Front End (BFE) X.25" section in Chapter 11.

The Cisco IOS software supports DDN Standard service but not DDN Basic service. Consequently, the DDN Service Type facility does not have to be configured.

Index